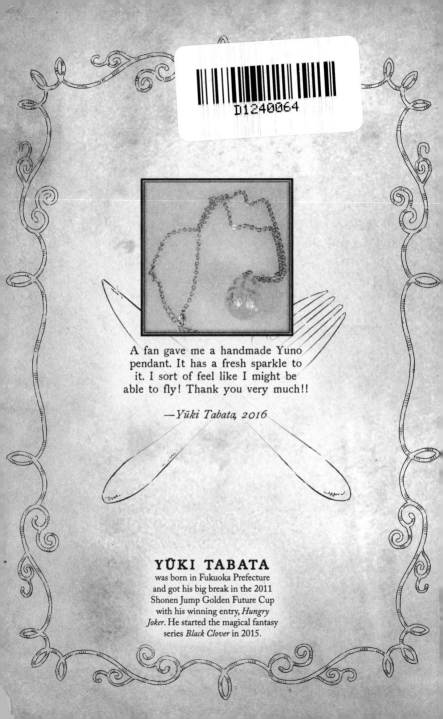

A fan gave me a handmade Yuno pendant. It has a fresh sparkle to it. I sort of feel like I might be able to fly! Thank you very much!!

—*Yūki Tabata, 2016*

YŪKI TABATA

was born in Fukuoka Prefecture and got his big break in the 2011 Shonen Jump Golden Future Cup with his winning entry, *Hungry Joker*. He started the magical fantasy series *Black Clover* in 2015.

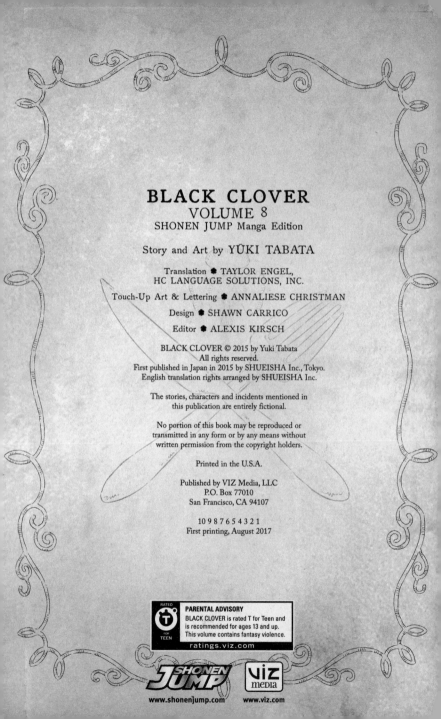

BLACK CLOVER
VOLUME 8
SHONEN JUMP Manga Edition

Story and Art by YŪKI TABATA

Translation ❀ TAYLOR ENGEL,
HC LANGUAGE SOLUTIONS, INC.

Touch-Up Art & Lettering ❀ ANNALIESE CHRISTMAN

Design ❀ SHAWN CARRICO

Editor ❀ ALEXIS KIRSCH

BLACK CLOVER © 2015 by Yuki Tabata
All rights reserved.
First published in Japan in 2015 by SHUEISHA Inc., Tokyo.
English translation rights arranged by SHUEISHA Inc.

The stories, characters and incidents mentioned in
this publication are entirely fictional.

No portion of this book may be reproduced or
transmitted in any form or by any means without
written permission from the copyright holders.

Printed in the U.S.A.

Published by VIZ Media, LLC
P.O. Box 77010
San Francisco, CA 94107

10 9 8 7 6 5 4 3 2 1
First printing, August 2017

RATED
T
FOR
TEEN

PARENTAL ADVISORY
BLACK CLOVER is rated T for Teen and
is recommended for ages 13 and up.
This volume contains fantasy violence.
ratings.viz.com

RO4500ZI440

SHONEN JUMP MANGA

Asta

Luck

Magna

Vetto

Noelle

Finral

Vanessa

Black ✦ Clover

YŪKI TABATA

8

DESPAIR VS. HOPE

Characters

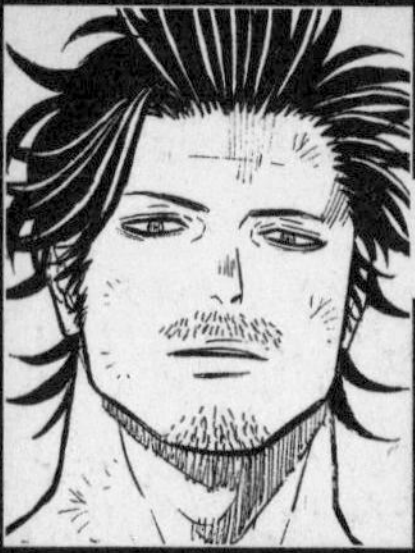

Yami Sukehiro

Member of:
The Black Bulls
Magic: Dark

A captain who looks fierce and has a hot temper, but is very popular with his brigade.

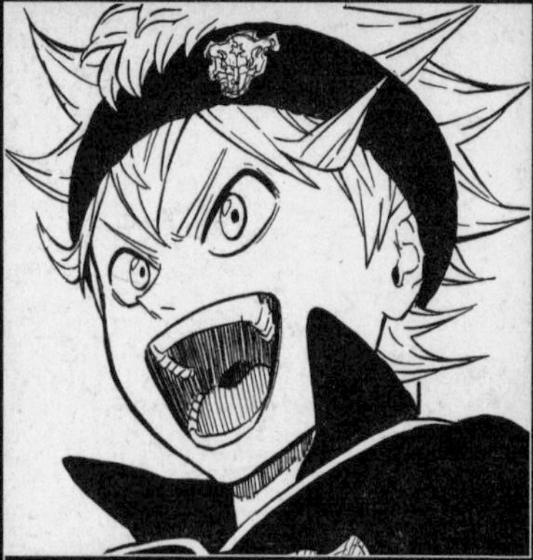

Asta

Squad: The Black Bulls
Magic: None (Anti-Magic)

He has no magic, but he's working to become the Wizard King through sheer guts and his well-trained body.

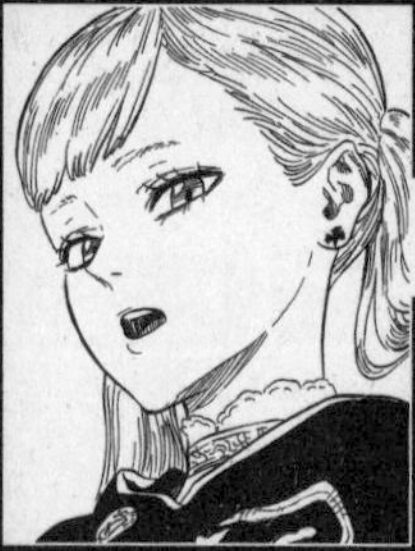

Noelle Silva

Member of:
The Black Bulls
Magic: Water

A royal. She's really impudent, but can be kind too.

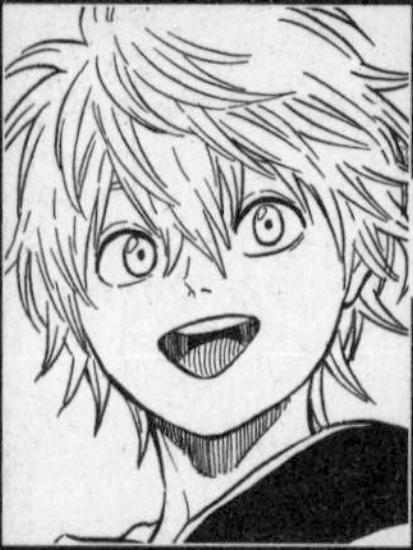

Luck Voltia

Member of:
The Black Bulls
Magic: Lightning

A battle maniac who smiles constantly and has a problematic personality.

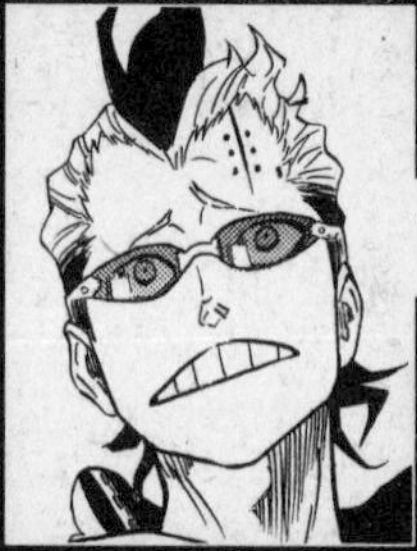

Magna Swing

Member of:
The Black Bulls
Magic: Flame

He has the temperament of a delinquent, but he's quite manly and good at taking care of others.

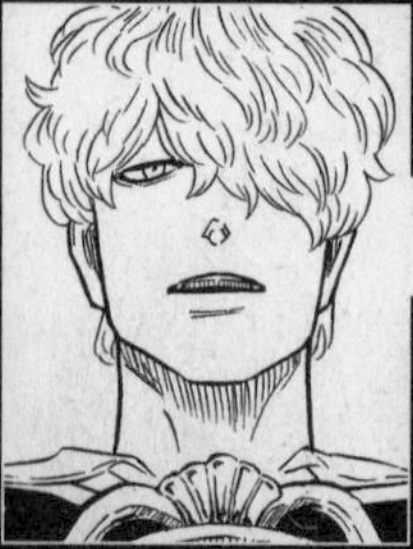

Gauche Adlai

Member of:
The Black Bulls
Magic: Mirror

A former convict with a blind, pathological love for his little sister.

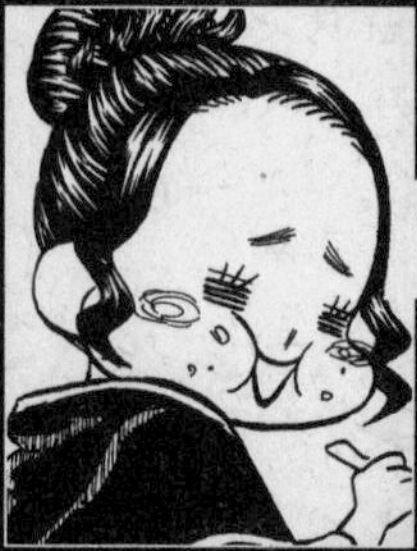

Charmy Pappitson

Member of:
The Black Bulls
Magic: Cotton

She's small, but she eats like a maniac.

Vanessa Enoteca

Member of:
The Black Bulls
Magic: Thread

A witch with an unparalleled love of liquor who was exiled from a distinguished family.

Finral Roulacase

Member of:
The Black Bulls
Magic: Spatial

A flirt who likes girls so much it gets in the way of his missions.

Kiato

Magic: Dance

A priest mage at the Underwater Temple. He wants to become a dancer.

Kahono

Magic: Song

A priest mage at the Underwater Temple. She dreams of becoming an idol singer.

Vetto

Member of: The Eye of the Midnight Sun
Magic: Beast

One of the three group executives, The Third Eye. Boasts overwhelming combat power.

High Priest

Magic: Game

The head of the Underwater Temple. A very hyper old guy.

❋ ❋ ❋

STORY

In a world where magic is everything, Asta and Yuno are both found abandoned on the same day at a church in the remote village of Hage. Both dream of becoming the Wizard King, the highest of all mages, and they spend their days working toward that dream.

The year they turn 15, both receive grimoires, magic books that amplify their bearer's magic. They take the entrance exam for the Magic Knights, nine groups of mages under the direct control of the Wizard King. Yuno, whose magic is strong, joins the Golden Dawn, an elite group, while Asta, who has no magic at all, joins the Black Bulls, a group of misfits. With this, the two finally take their first step toward becoming the Wizard King…

In order to get the magic stone sought by the Eye of the Midnight Sun, Asta and company head to the Underwater Temple, a very dangerous region filled with strong magic. With the magic stone as the prize, they begin a battle royale with the temple's mage priests, but suddenly, right in the middle of the fight, Vetto of the Third Eye appears!

CONTENTS

BLACK ❖ CLOVER

8

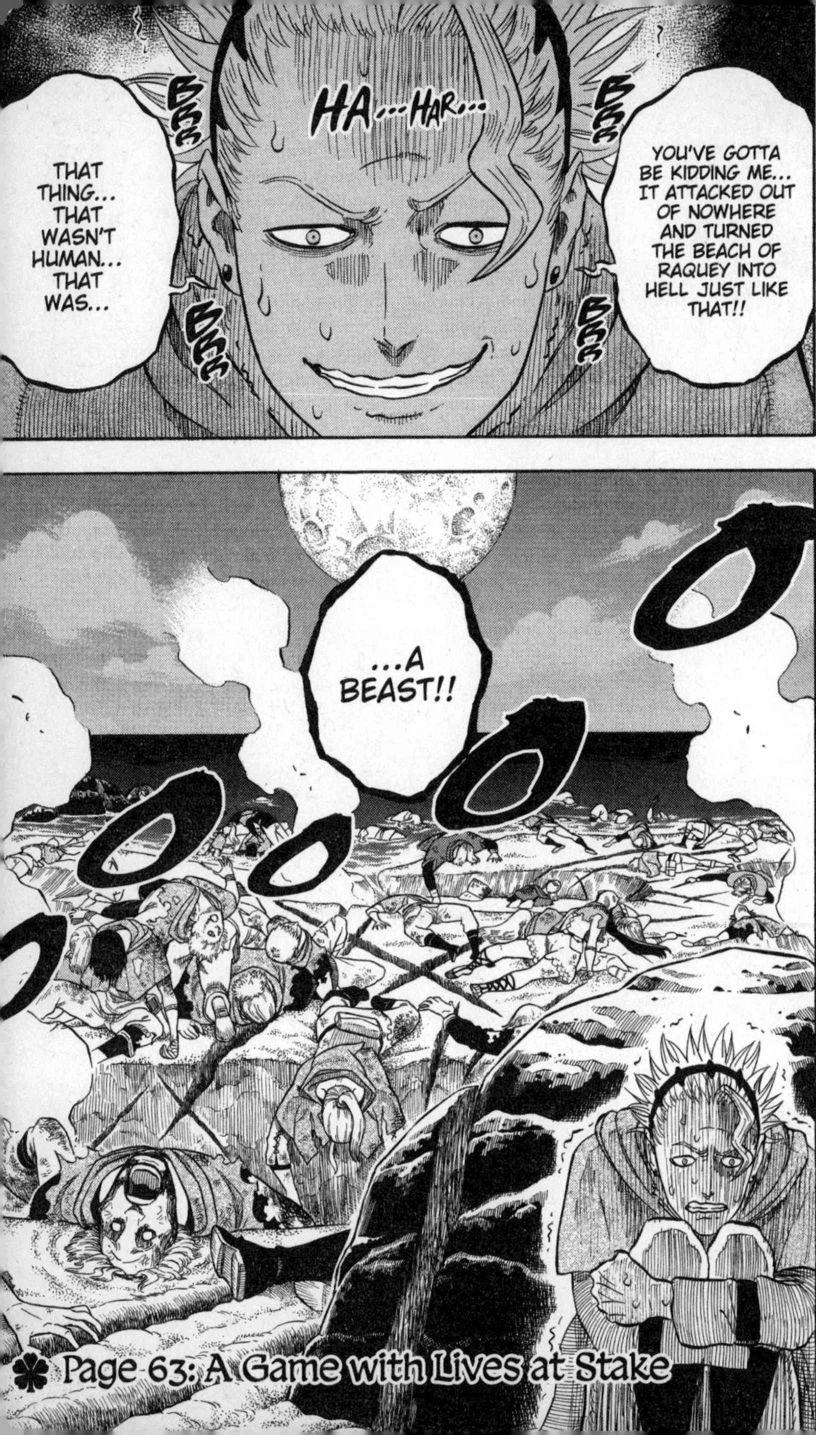
BRR
HA...HAR...
YOU'VE GOTTA BE KIDDING ME... IT ATTACKED OUT OF NOWHERE AND TURNED THE BEACH OF RAQUEY INTO HELL JUST LIKE THAT!!
BRR
BRR
THAT THING... THAT WASN'T HUMAN... THAT WAS...
BRR
...A BEAST!!
Page 63: A Game with Lives at Stake

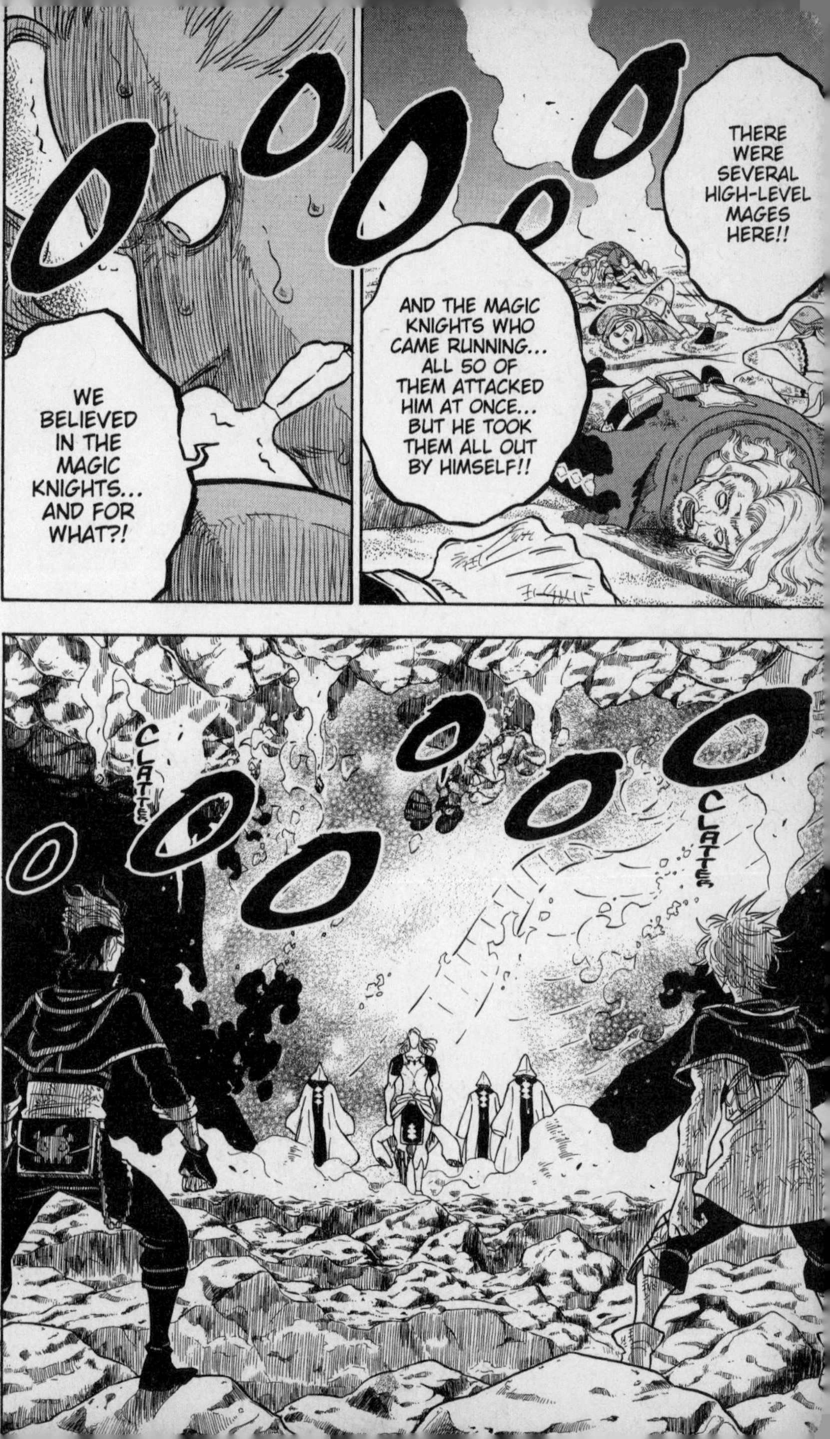
THERE WERE SEVERAL HIGH-LEVEL MAGES HERE!!
AND THE MAGIC KNIGHTS WHO CAME RUNNING... ALL 50 OF THEM ATTACKED HIM AT ONCE... BUT HE TOOK THEM ALL OUT BY HIMSELF!!
WE BELIEVED IN THE MAGIC KNIGHTS... AND FOR WHAT?!
CLATTER
CLATTER

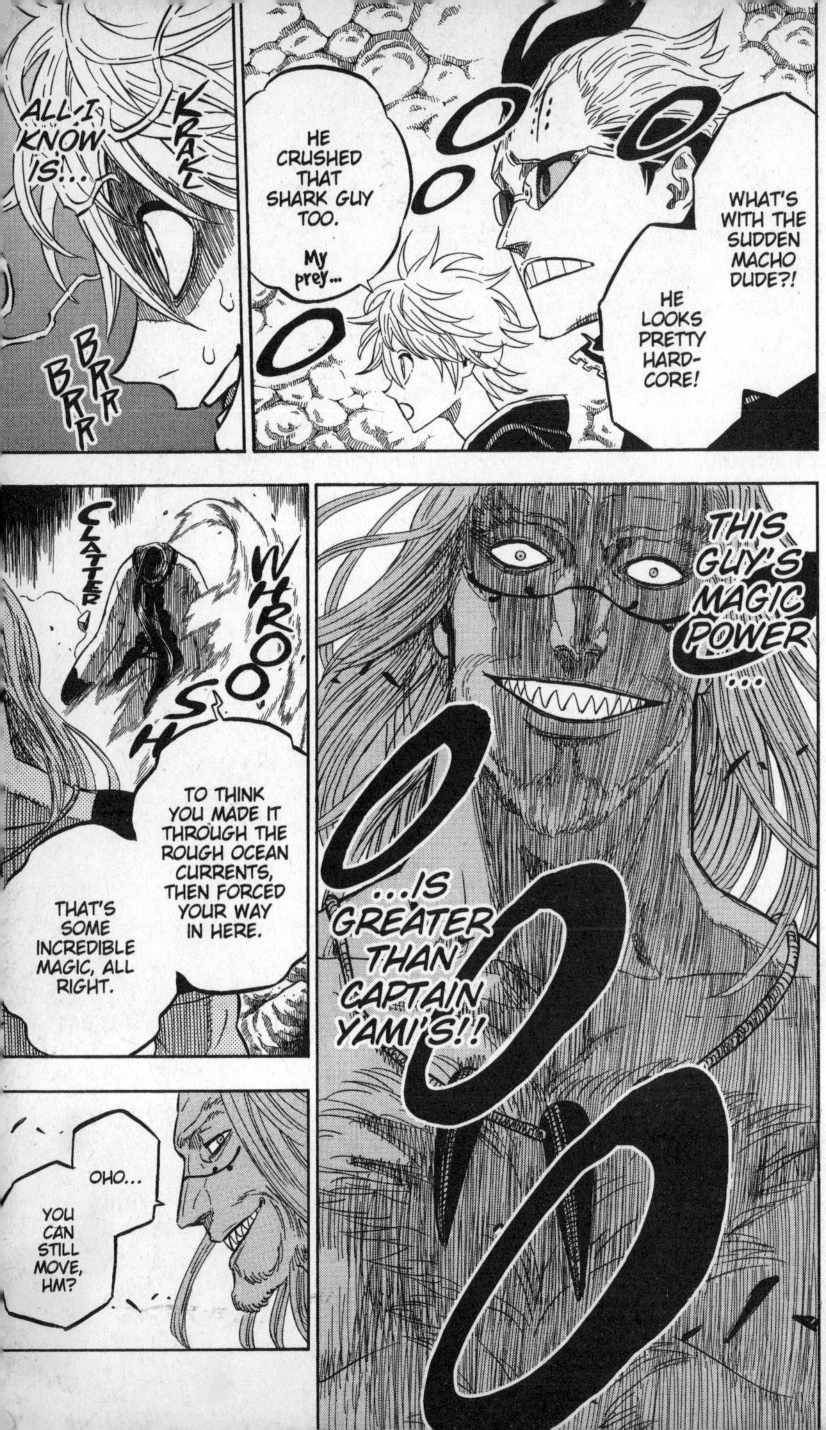
WHAT'S WITH THE SUDDEN MACHO DUDE?!
HE LOOKS PRETTY HARD-CORE!
HE CRUSHED THAT SHARK GUY TOO.
My prey...
KRAKL
ALL I KNOW IS...
BRRR BRRR
THIS GUY'S MAGIC POWER...
...IS GREATER THAN CAPTAIN YAMI'S!!
CLATTER
WHROOOSH
TO THINK YOU MADE IT THROUGH THE ROUGH OCEAN CURRENTS, THEN FORCED YOUR WAY IN HERE.
THAT'S SOME INCREDIBLE MAGIC, ALL RIGHT.
OHO...
YOU CAN STILL MOVE, HM?

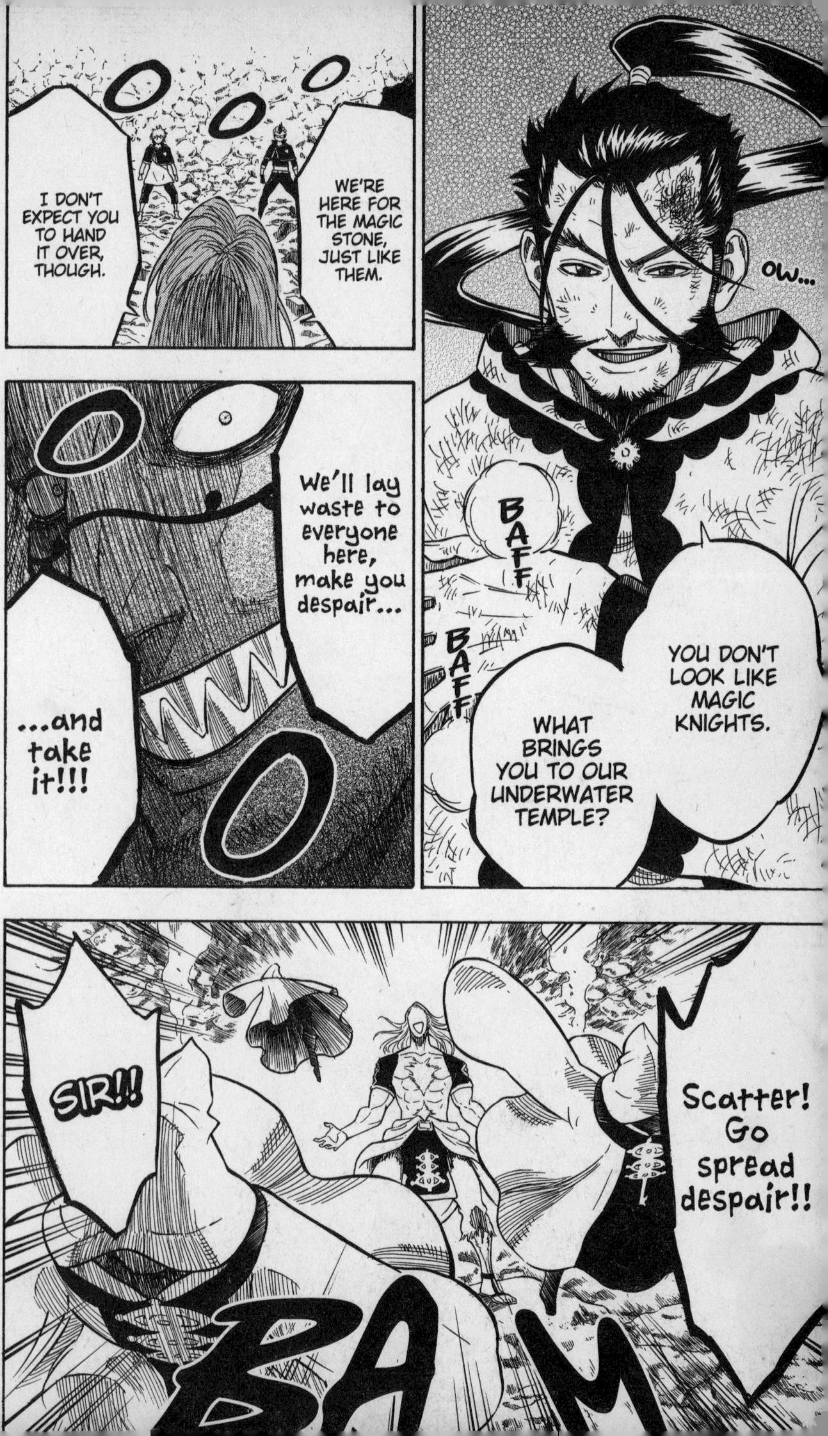
OW...
BAFF
BAFF
YOU DON'T LOOK LIKE MAGIC KNIGHTS.
WHAT BRINGS YOU TO OUR UNDERWATER TEMPLE?
WE'RE HERE FOR THE MAGIC STONE, JUST LIKE THEM.
I DON'T EXPECT YOU TO HAND IT OVER, THOUGH.
We'll lay waste to everyone here, make you despair...
...and take it!!!
Scatter! Go spread despair!!
SIR!!
BAM

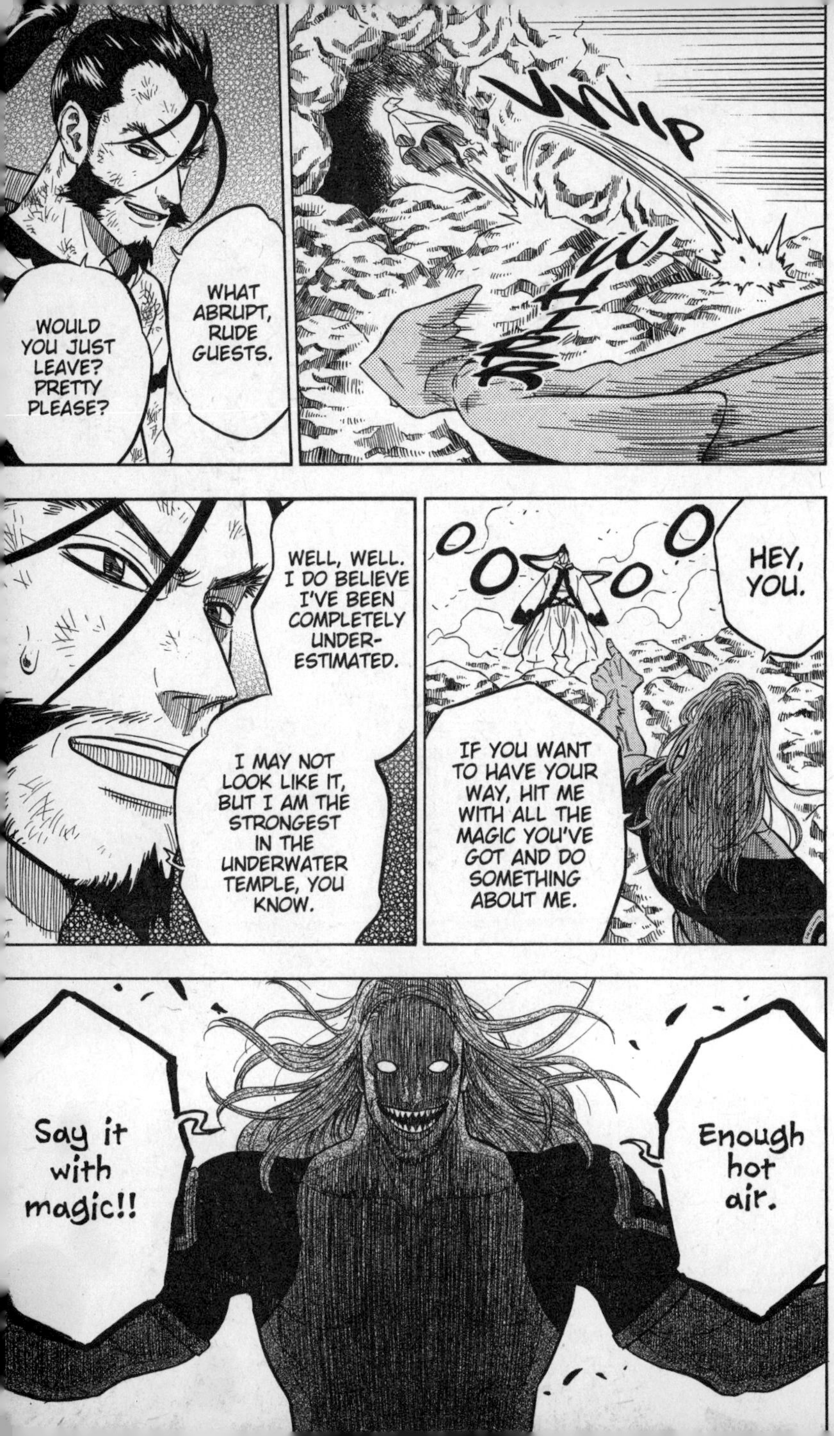
VVVIP
WHIRR
WHAT ABRUPT, RUDE GUESTS.
WOULD YOU JUST LEAVE? PRETTY PLEASE?
OOOOO
HEY, YOU.
IF YOU WANT TO HAVE YOUR WAY, HIT ME WITH ALL THE MAGIC YOU'VE GOT AND DO SOMETHING ABOUT ME.
WELL, WELL. I DO BELIEVE I'VE BEEN COMPLETELY UNDER-ESTIMATED.
I MAY NOT LOOK LIKE IT, BUT I AM THE STRONGEST IN THE UNDERWATER TEMPLE, YOU KNOW.
Enough hot air.
Say it with magic!!

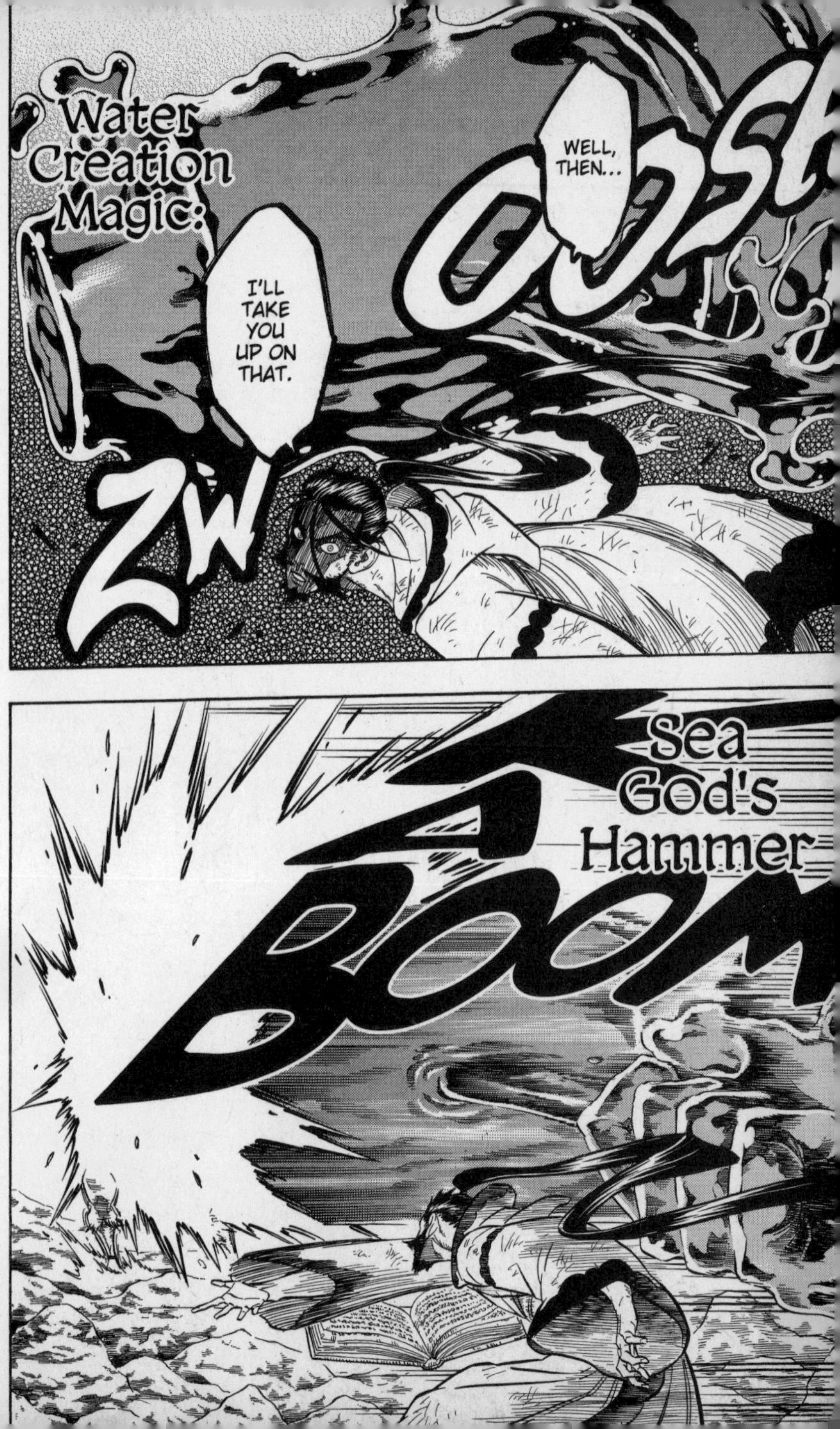
WELL, THEN...
Water Creation Magic:
I'LL TAKE YOU UP ON THAT.
ZW
Sea God's Hammer

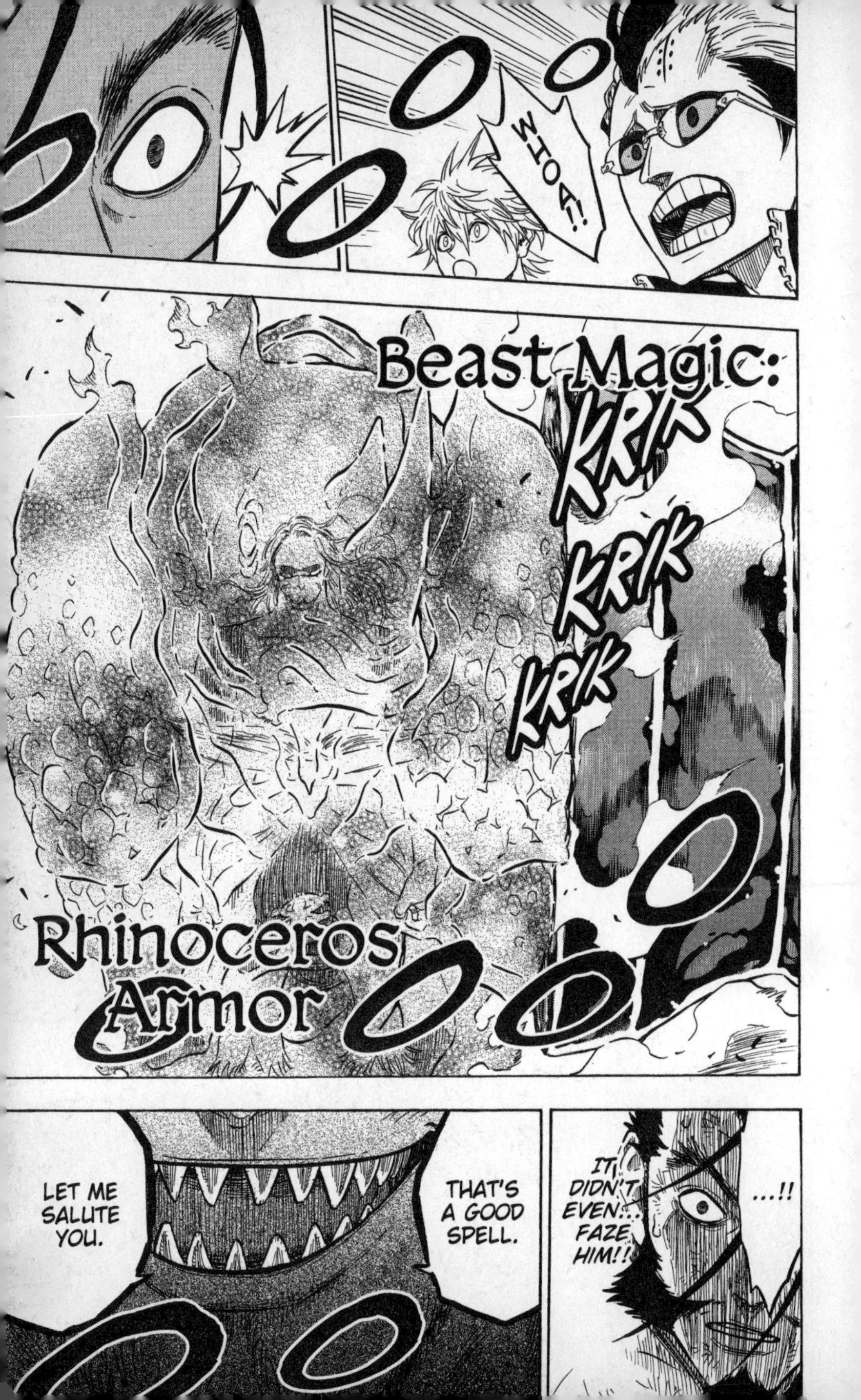
WHOA!!
Beast Magic: Rhinoceros Armor
KRIK
KRIK
KRIK
...!!
IT DIDN'T EVEN... FAZE HIM!!
THAT'S A GOOD SPELL.
LET ME SALUTE YOU.

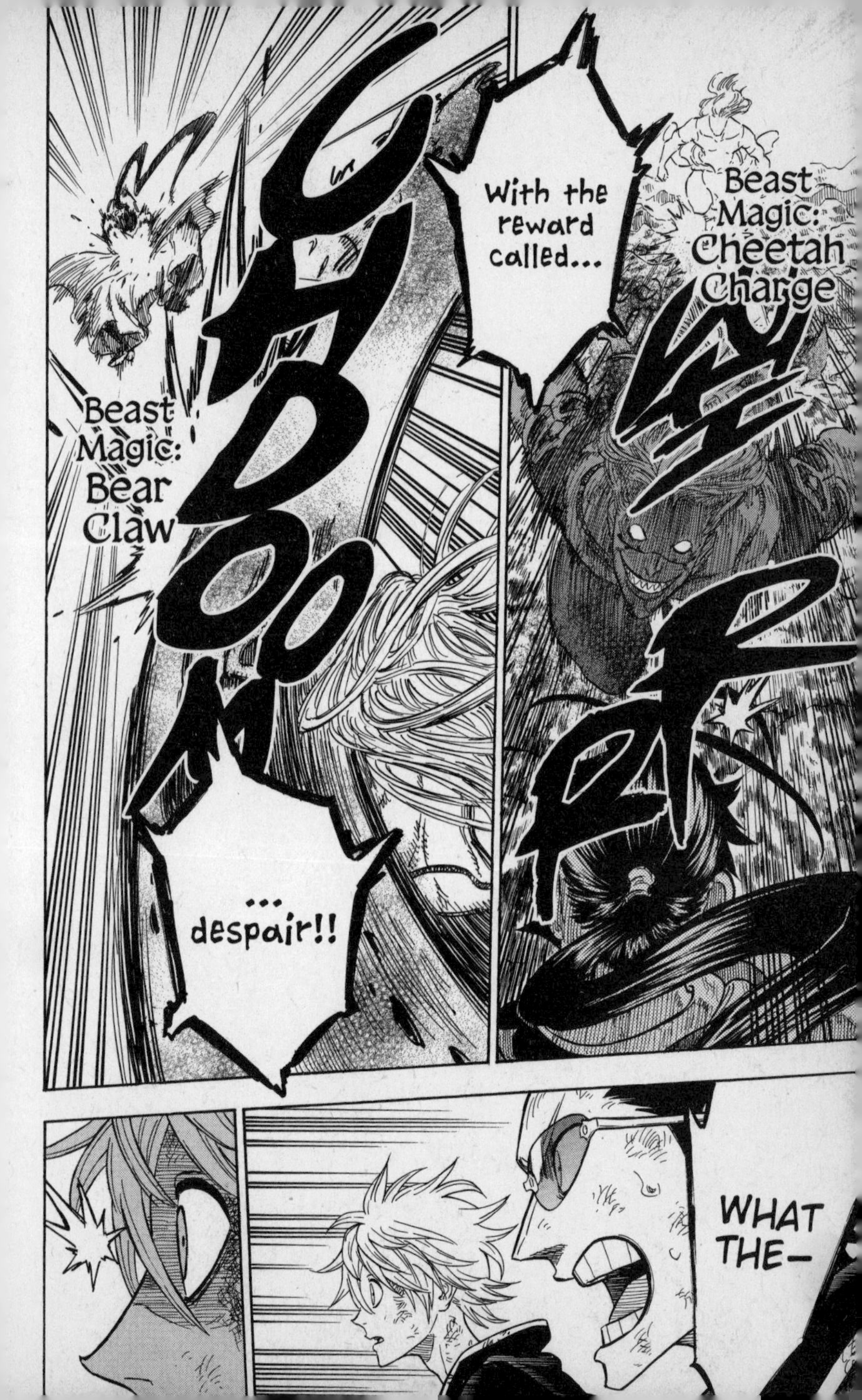
With the reward called...
Beast Magic: Cheetah Charge
Beast Magic: Bear Claw
...despair!!
WHAT THE—

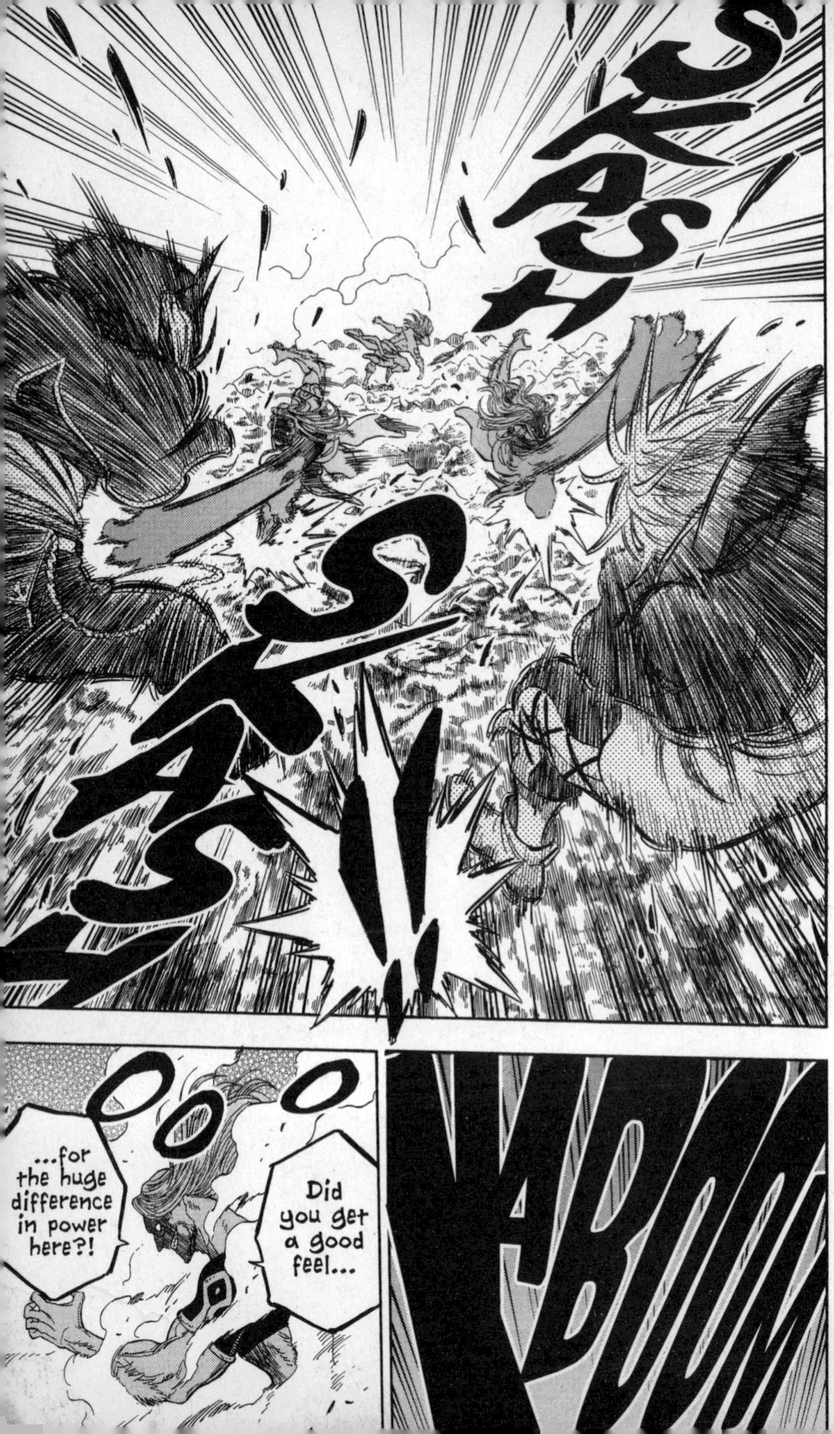
SKASH
SKASH
VABOOM
Did you get a good feel...
...for the huge difference in power here?!

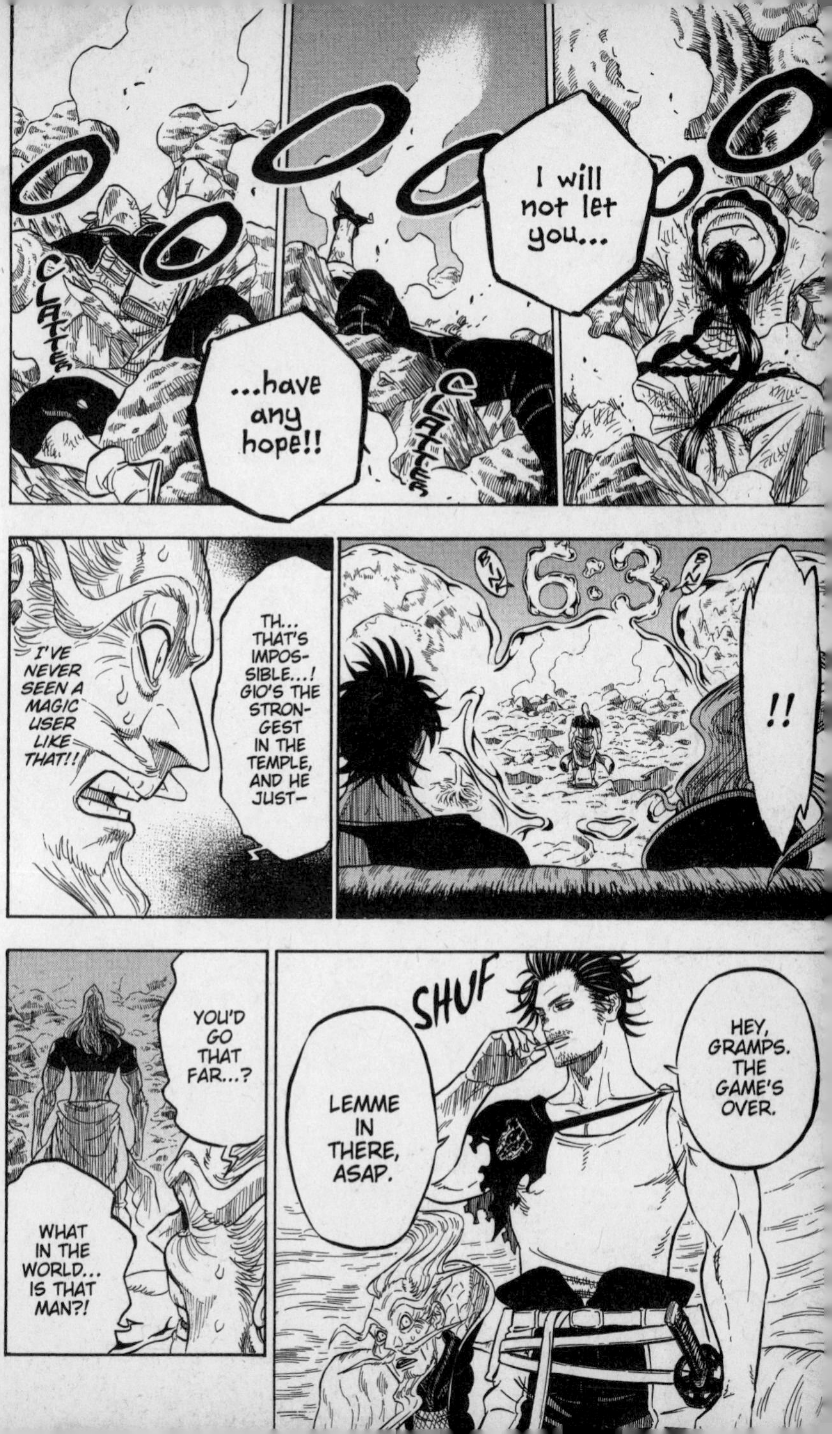
I will not let you...
CLATTER
...have any hope!!
CLATTER
6:3
!!
TH... THAT'S IMPOSSIBLE...! GIO'S THE STRONGEST IN THE TEMPLE, AND HE JUST—
I'VE NEVER SEEN A MAGIC USER LIKE THAT!!
HEY, GRAMPS. THE GAME'S OVER.
SHUF
LEMME IN THERE, ASAP.
YOU'D GO THAT FAR...?
WHAT IN THE WORLD... IS THAT MAN?!

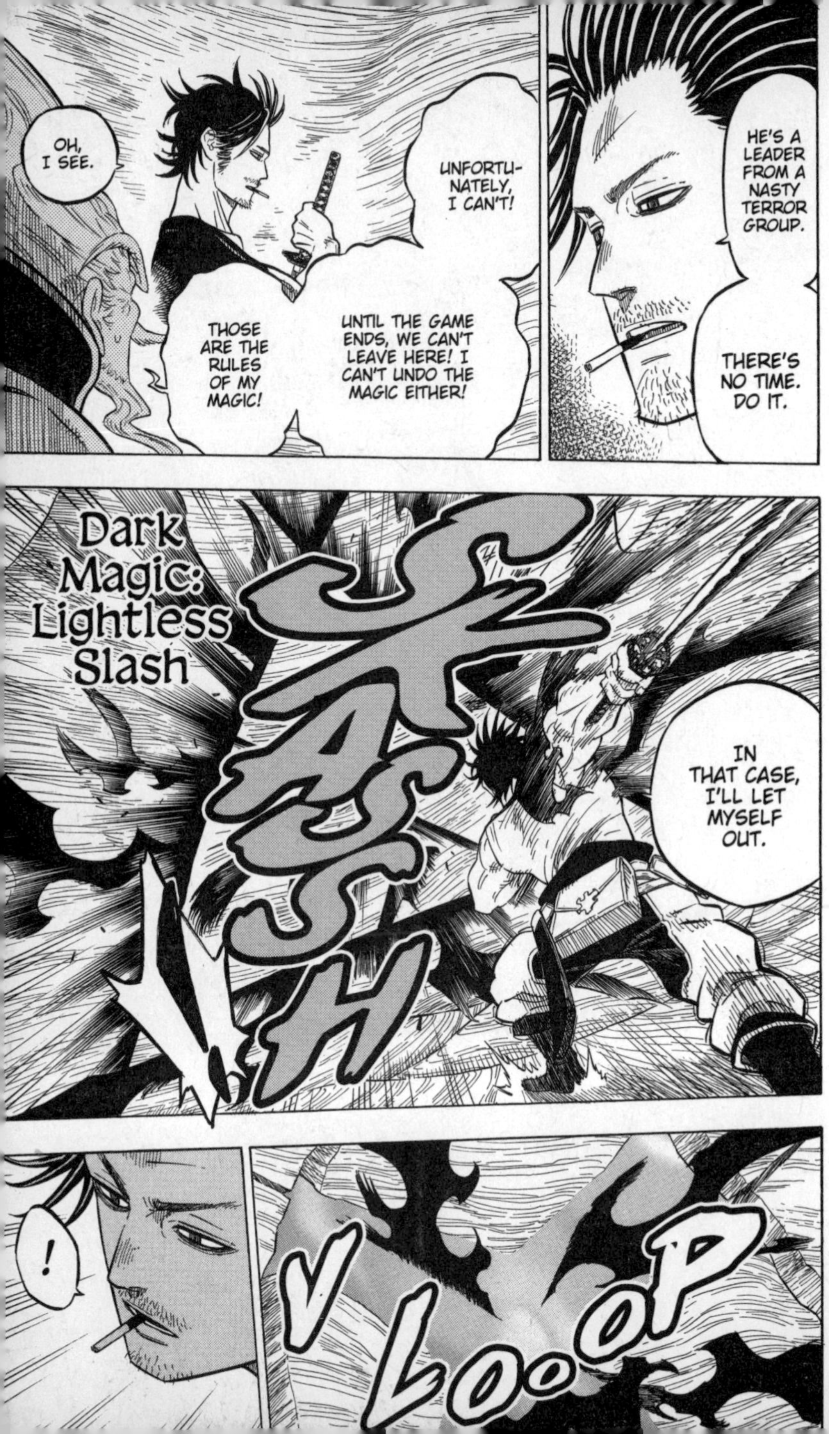
HE'S A LEADER FROM A NASTY TERROR GROUP.
THERE'S NO TIME. DO IT.
UNFORTUNATELY, I CAN'T!
UNTIL THE GAME ENDS, WE CAN'T LEAVE HERE! I CAN'T UNDO THE MAGIC EITHER!
THOSE ARE THE RULES OF MY MAGIC!
OH, I SEE.
IN THAT CASE, I'LL LET MYSELF OUT.
Dark Magic: Lightless Slash
SLASH
VLOOOP
!

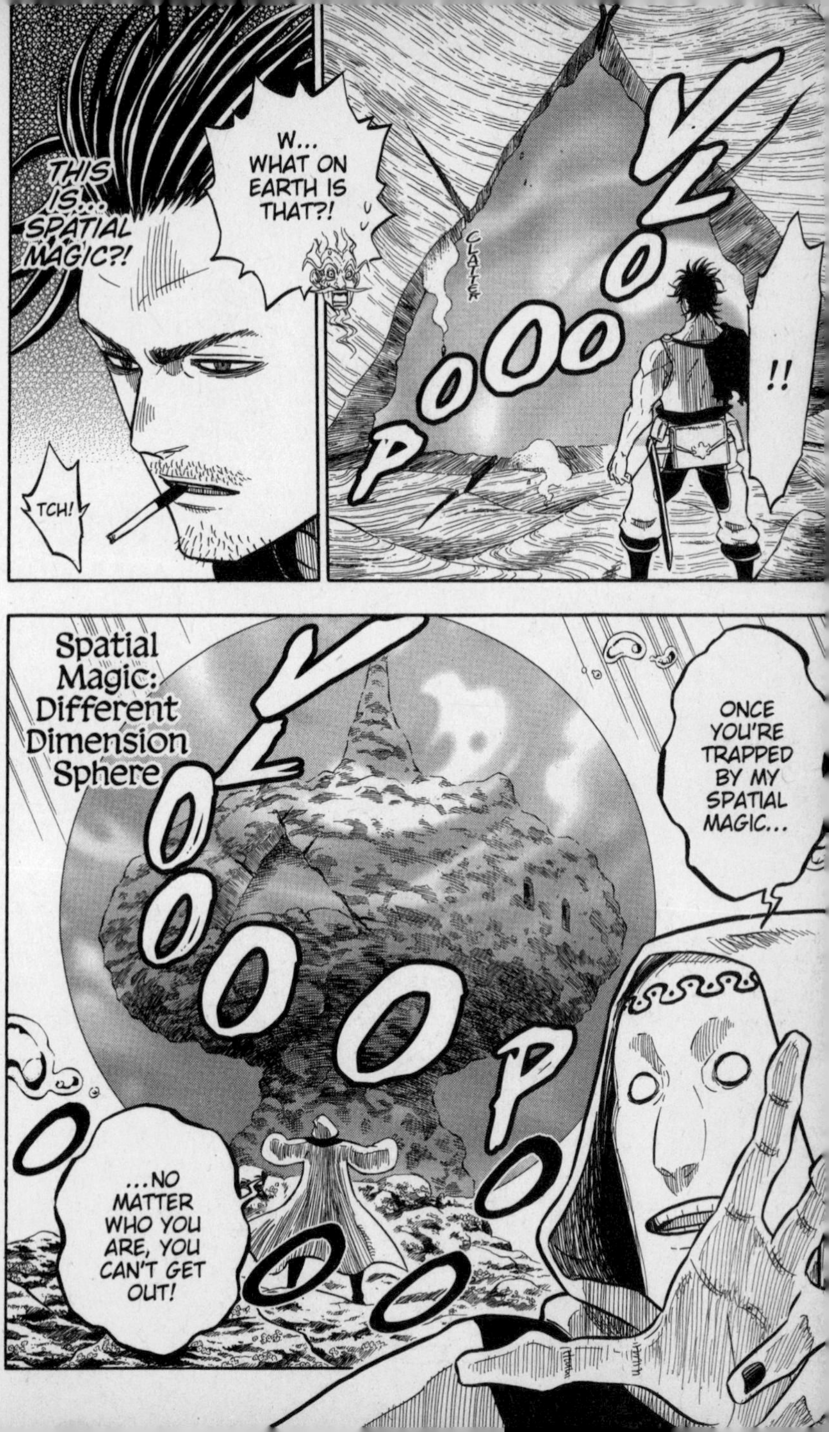
VOOOOOP
!!
W... WHAT ON EARTH IS THAT?!
CLATTER
THIS IS... SPATIAL MAGIC?!
TCH!
ONCE YOU'RE TRAPPED BY MY SPATIAL MAGIC...
VOOOOOOP
Spatial Magic: Different Dimension Sphere
...NO MATTER WHO YOU ARE, YOU CAN'T GET OUT!
OOO

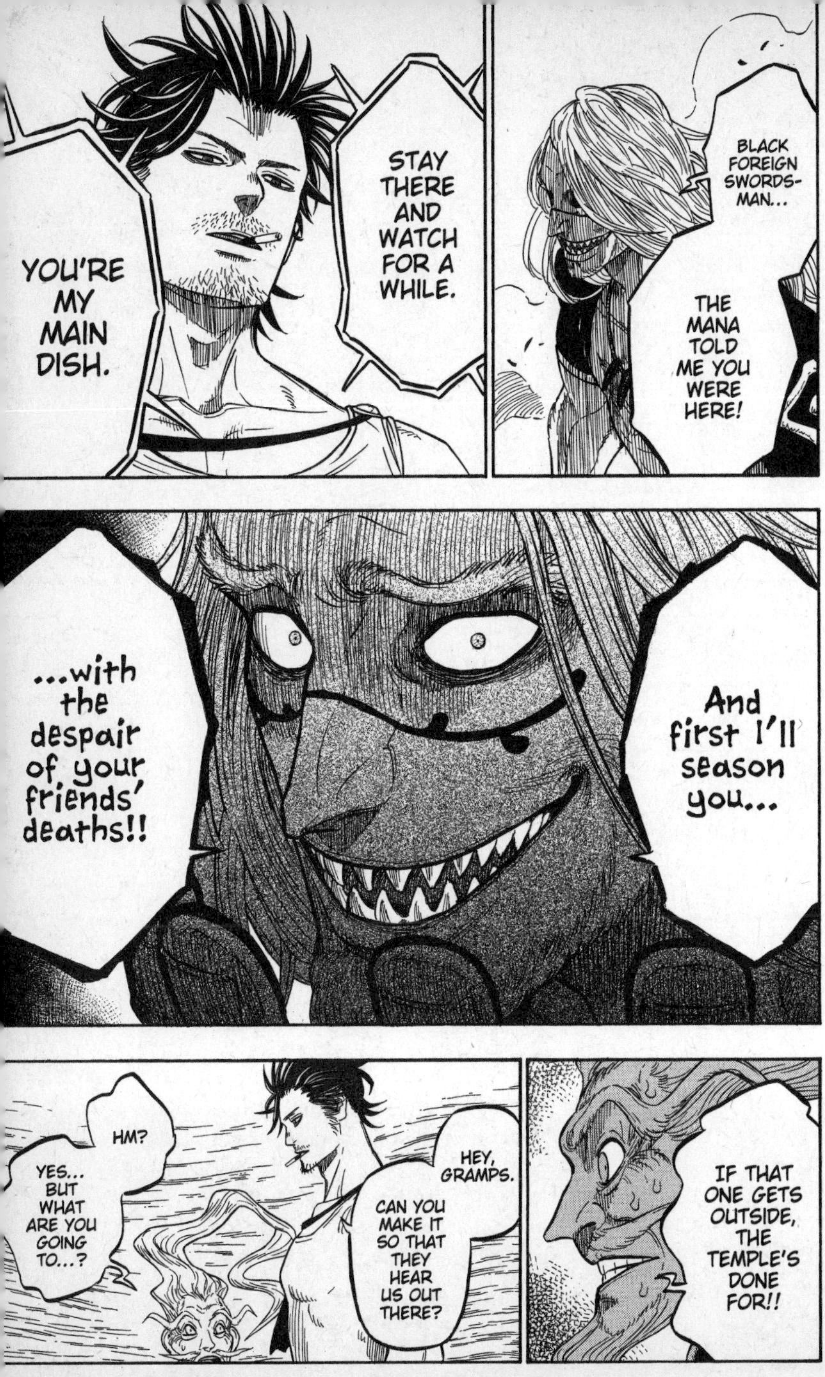
BLACK FOREIGN SWORDSMAN...
THE MANA TOLD ME YOU WERE HERE!
STAY THERE AND WATCH FOR A WHILE.
YOU'RE MY MAIN DISH.
And first I'll season you...
...with the despair of your friends' deaths!!
IF THAT ONE GETS OUTSIDE, THE TEMPLE'S DONE FOR!!
HEY, GRAMPS.
HM?
CAN YOU MAKE IT SO THAT THEY HEAR US OUT THERE?
YES... BUT WHAT ARE YOU GOING TO...?

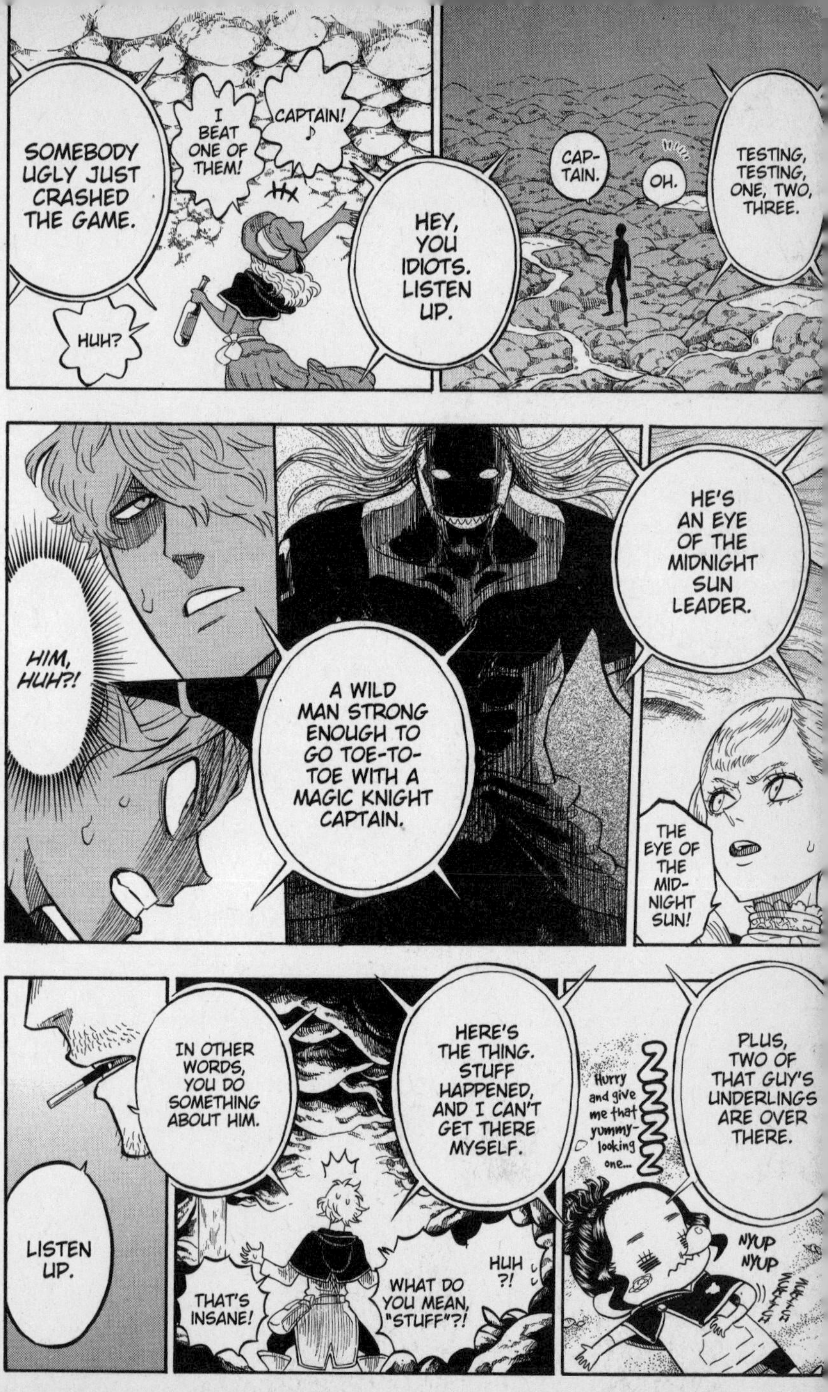
TESTING, TESTING, ONE, TWO, THREE.
OH.
CAP-TAIN.
HEY, YOU IDIOTS. LISTEN UP.
CAPTAIN! ♪
I BEAT ONE OF THEM!
SOMEBODY UGLY JUST CRASHED THE GAME.
HUH?
HE'S AN EYE OF THE MIDNIGHT SUN LEADER.
THE EYE OF THE MID-NIGHT SUN!
A WILD MAN STRONG ENOUGH TO GO TOE-TO-TOE WITH A MAGIC KNIGHT CAPTAIN.
HIM, HUH?!
PLUS, TWO OF THAT GUY'S UNDERLINGS ARE OVER THERE.
Hurry and give me that yummy-looking one...
NYUP NYUP
HERE'S THE THING. STUFF HAPPENED, AND I CAN'T GET THERE MYSELF.
HUH ?!
WHAT DO YOU MEAN, "STUFF"?!
THAT'S INSANE!
IN OTHER WORDS, YOU DO SOMETHING ABOUT HIM.
LISTEN UP.

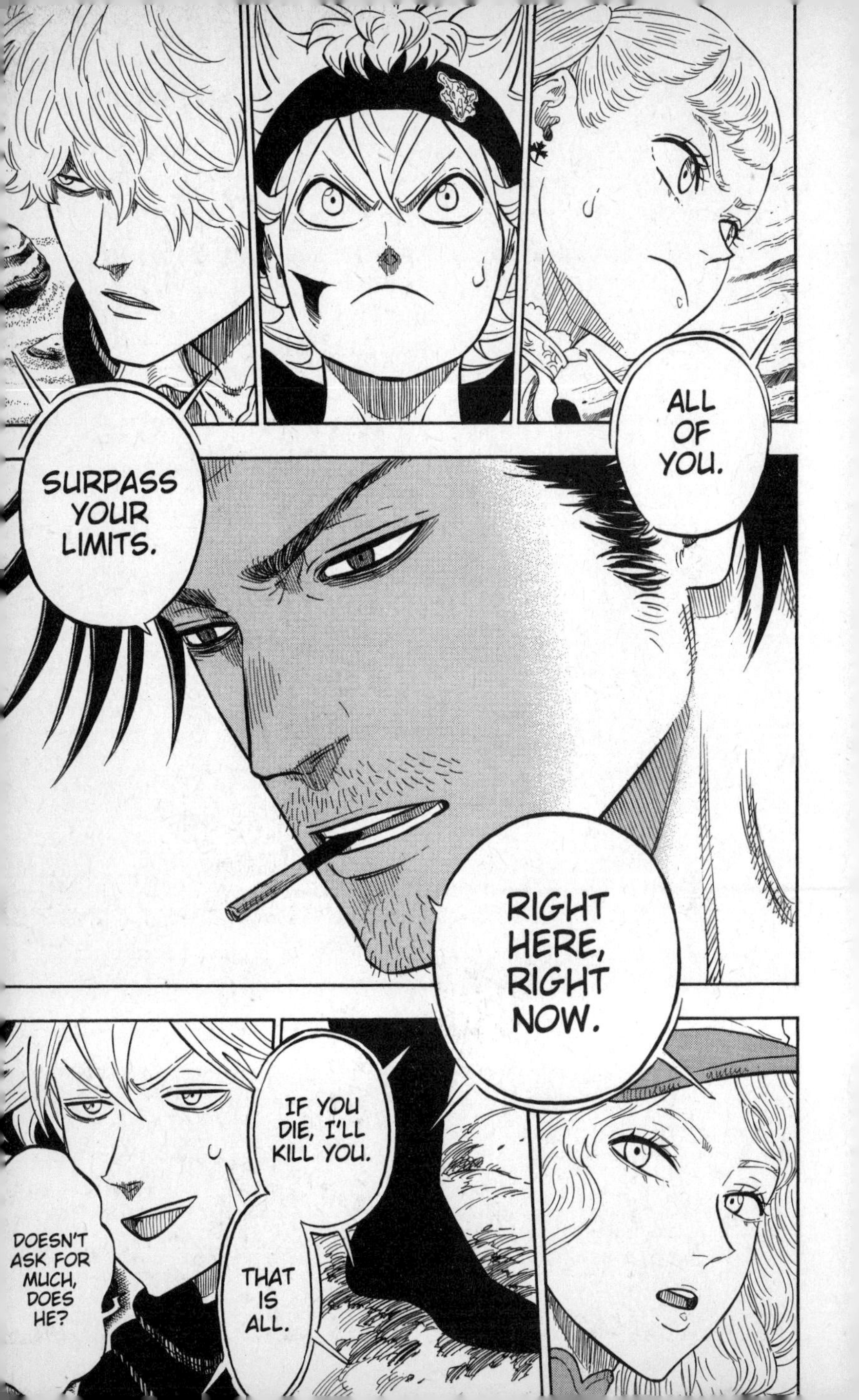
ALL OF YOU.
SURPASS YOUR LIMITS.
RIGHT HERE, RIGHT NOW.
IF YOU DIE, I'LL KILL YOU.
THAT IS ALL.
DOESN'T ASK FOR MUCH, DOES HE?

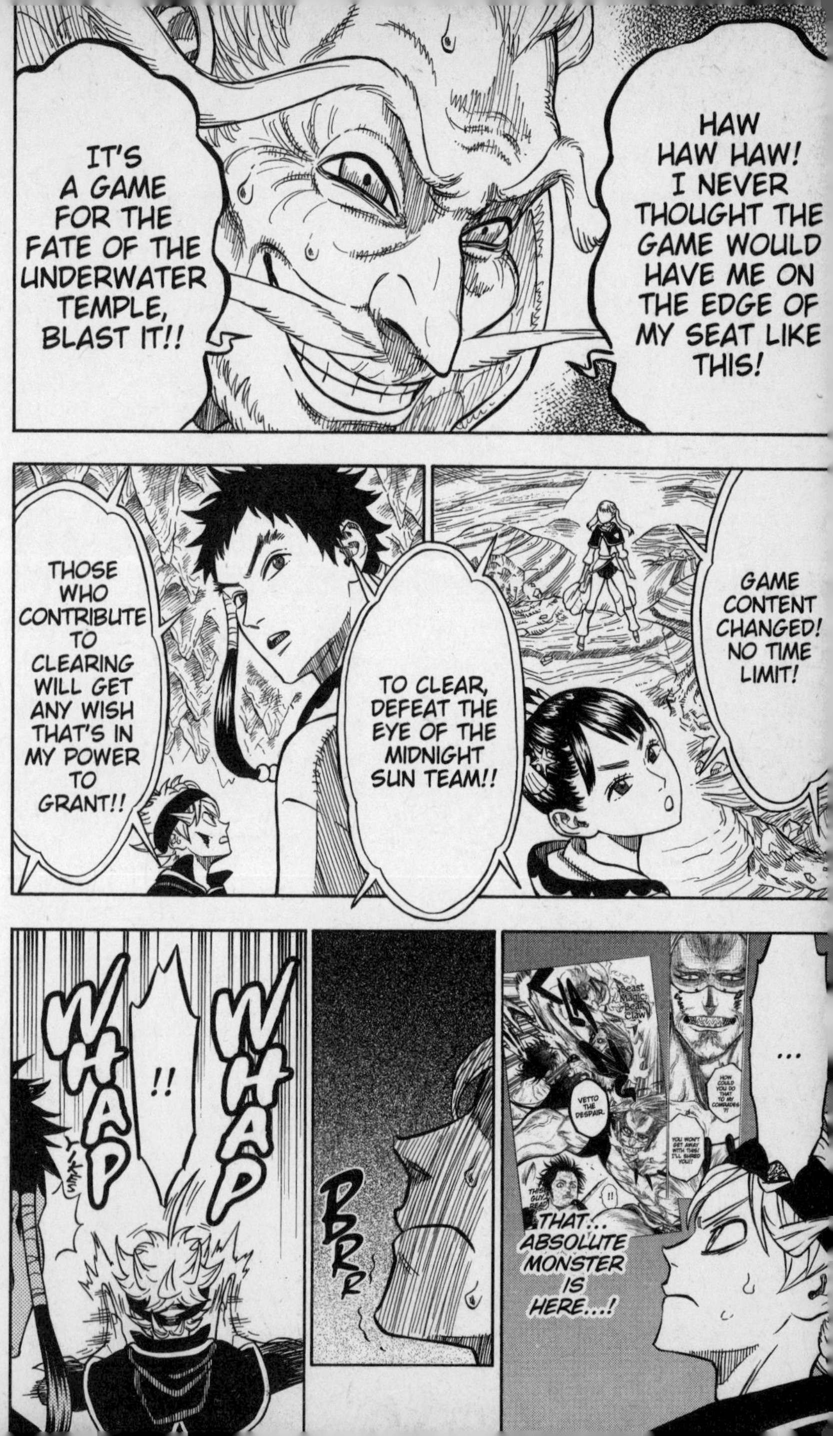
HAW HAW HAW! I NEVER THOUGHT THE GAME WOULD HAVE ME ON THE EDGE OF MY SEAT LIKE THIS!
IT'S A GAME FOR THE FATE OF THE UNDERWATER TEMPLE, BLAST IT!!
GAME CONTENT CHANGED! NO TIME LIMIT!
TO CLEAR, DEFEAT THE EYE OF THE MIDNIGHT SUN TEAM!!
THOSE WHO CONTRIBUTE TO CLEARING WILL GET ANY WISH THAT'S IN MY POWER TO GRANT!!
...
HOW COULD YOU DO THAT TO MY COMRADES?!
Beast Magic: Bear Claw
VETTO THE DESPAIR.
YOU WON'T GET AWAY WITH THIS! I'LL SHRED YOU!!
!!
THAT... ABSOLUTE MONSTER IS HERE...!
BRRR
!!
WHAP
WHAP
YIKES

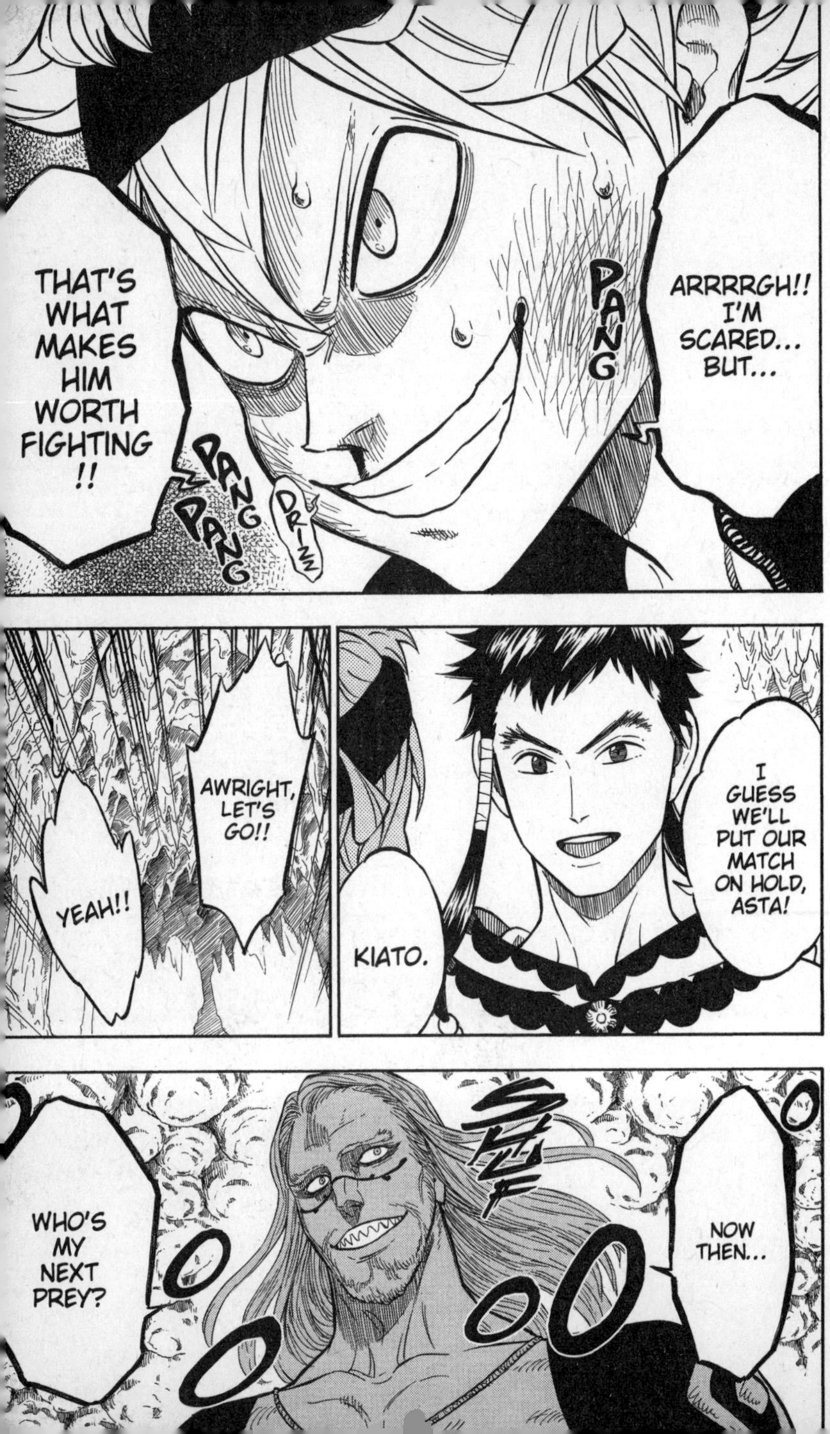
ARRRRGH!! I'M SCARED... BUT...
PANG
THAT'S WHAT MAKES HIM WORTH FIGHTING!!
PANG PANG
DRIZZ
I GUESS WE'LL PUT OUR MATCH ON HOLD, ASTA!
KIATO.
AWRIGHT, LET'S GO!!
YEAH!!
NOW THEN...
SHUF
WHO'S MY NEXT PREY?

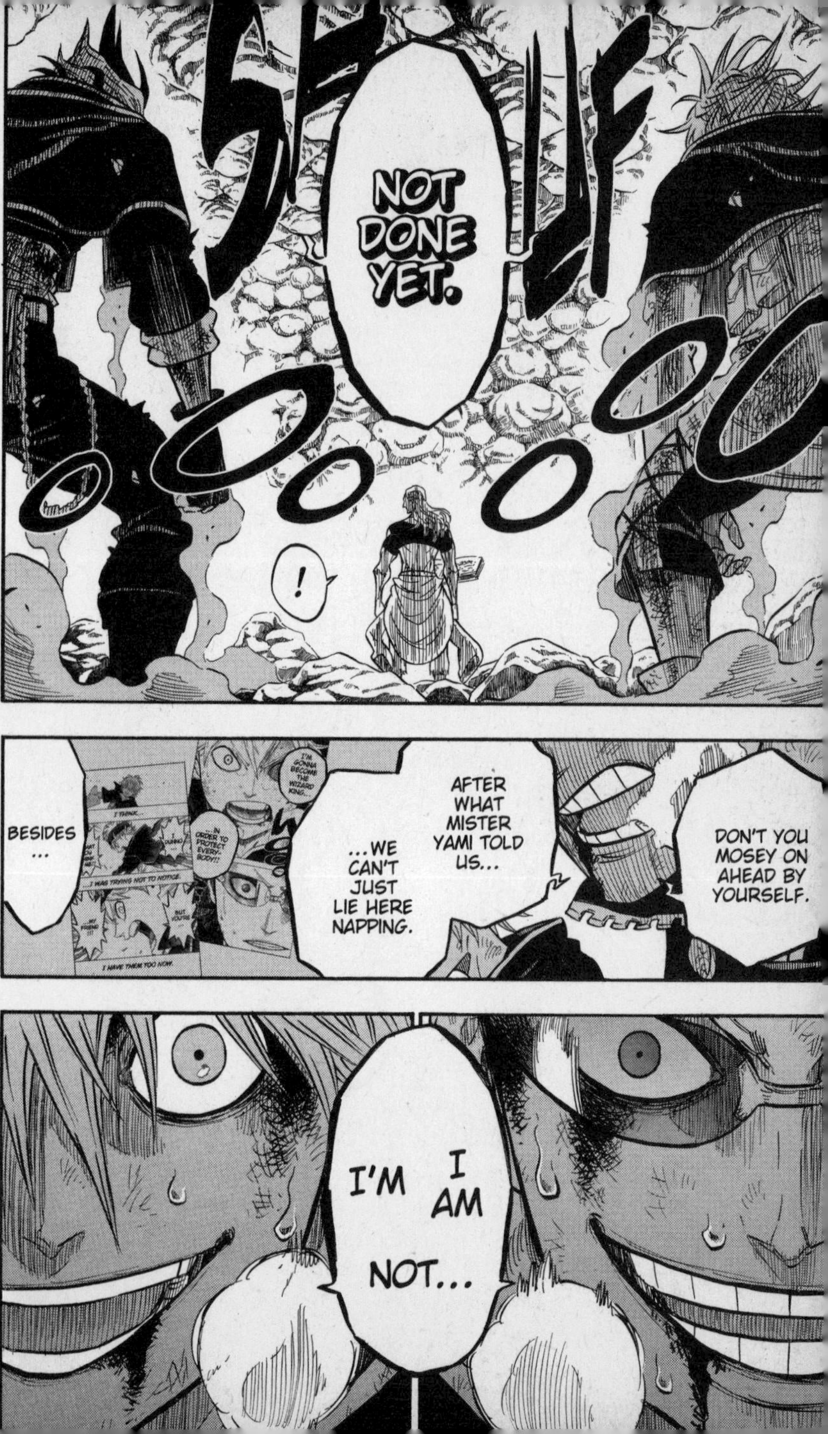
NOT DONE YET.
!
DON'T YOU MOSEY ON AHEAD BY YOURSELF.
AFTER WHAT MISTER YAMI TOLD US...
...WE CAN'T JUST LIE HERE NAPPING.
I'M GONNA BECOME THE WIZARD KING!
...IN ORDER TO PROTECT EVERY-BODY!!
...I WAS TRYING NOT TO NOTICE.
I HAVE THEM TOO NOW.
BESIDES...
I AM
I'M
NOT...

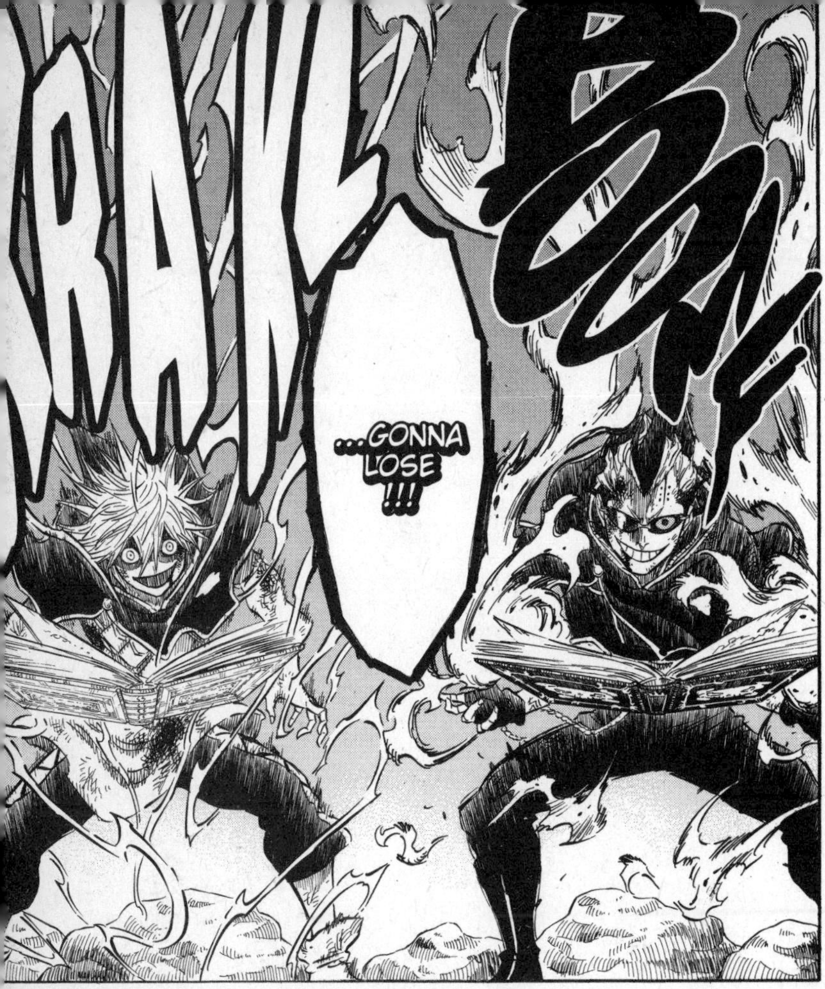
...GONNA LOSE !!!

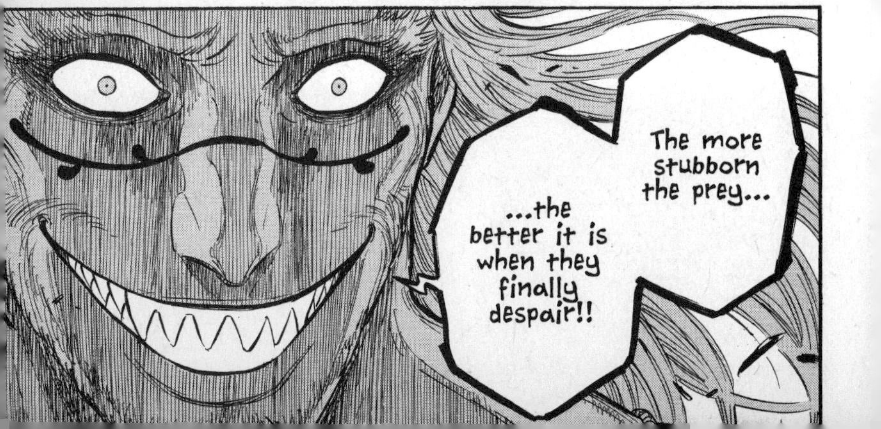
The more stubborn the prey...
...the better it is when they finally despair!!

The Assorted Questions Brigade

Good day! Good evening! Good morning! It's time for the letters corner. We got some pretty classy questions this time, so I'll answer them with everything I've got.

Q: There are a few things I'd like to know about Revchi!
   ❶ What brigade did he belong to?
   ❷ How many years ago did he leave it?
   ❸ When did he get the scar on his face, and did that scar have anything to do with him leaving the brigade?
   ❹ What happened to him after Asta defeated him? What is he doing now?

I...I had no idea anyone would care this much about Revchi!

A: ① The Purple Orcas.
   ② They made him leave two years ago.
   ③ He got that scar on his face right before leaving the brigade, on his last mission.
   ④ He's in a certain jail. At the moment, I hear he's waiting for a chance to break out of it...

❀   ❀   ❀

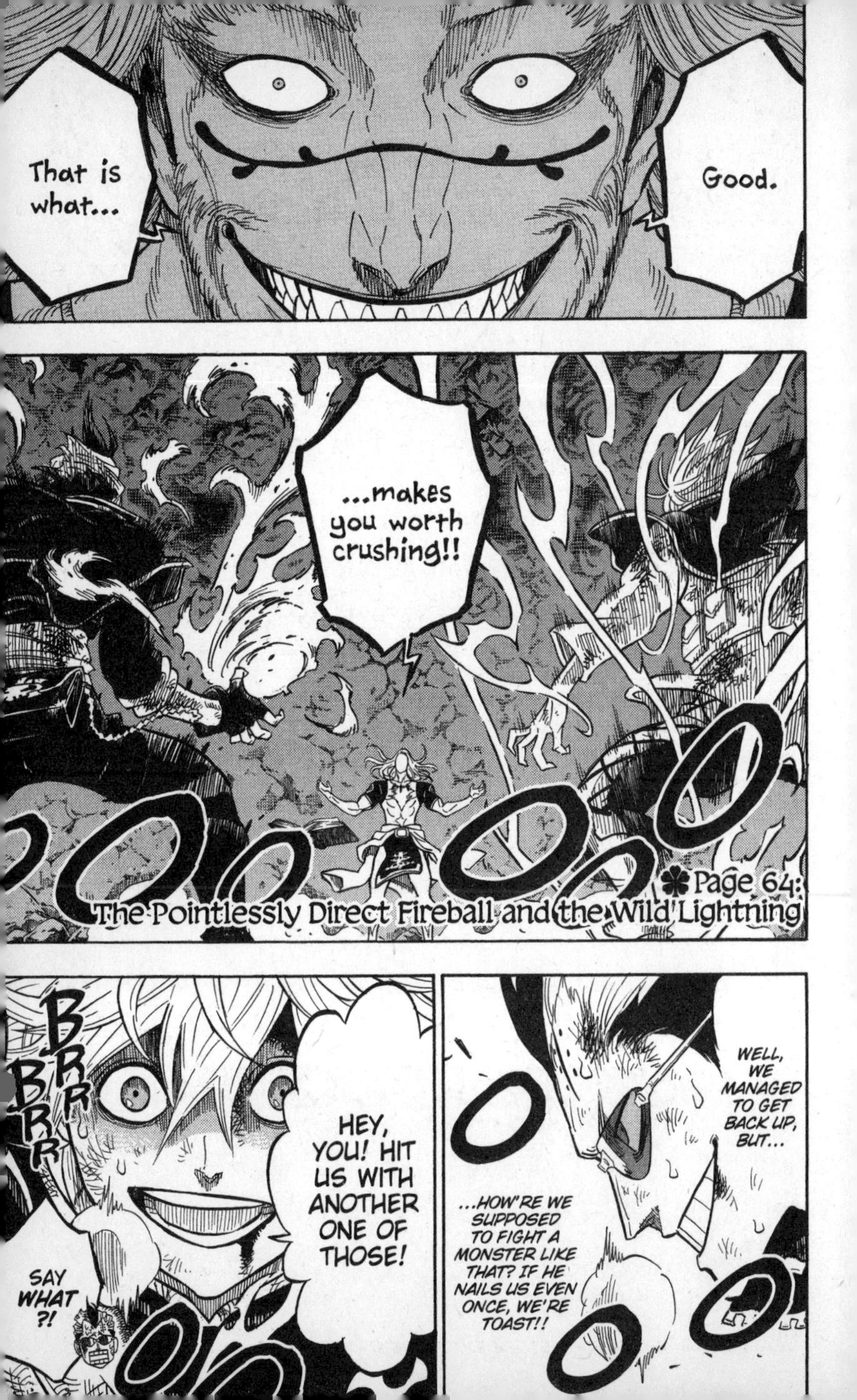
Good.
That is what...
...makes you worth crushing!!
Page 64: The Pointlessly Direct Fireball and the Wild Lightning
WELL, WE MANAGED TO GET BACK UP, BUT...
...HOW'RE WE SUPPOSED TO FIGHT A MONSTER LIKE THAT? IF HE NAILS US EVEN ONCE, WE'RE TOAST!!
HEY, YOU! HIT US WITH ANOTHER ONE OF THOSE!
BRRR BRRR
SAY WHAT?!

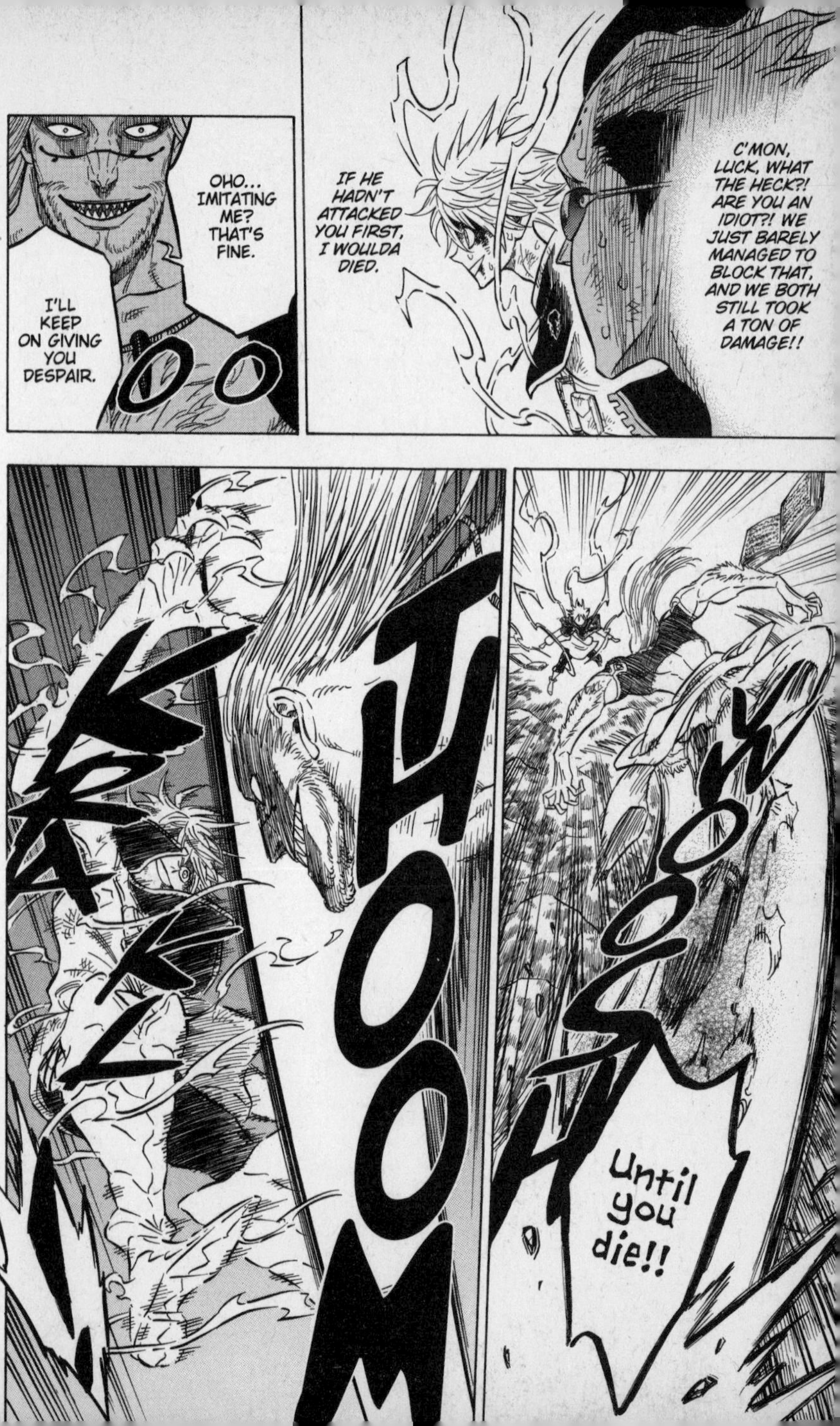
C'MON, LUCK, WHAT THE HECK?! ARE YOU AN IDIOT?! WE JUST BARELY MANAGED TO BLOCK THAT, AND WE BOTH STILL TOOK A TON OF DAMAGE!!
IF HE HADN'T ATTACKED YOU FIRST, I WOULDA DIED.
OHO... IMITATING ME? THAT'S FINE.
I'LL KEEP ON GIVING YOU DESPAIR.
Until you die!!

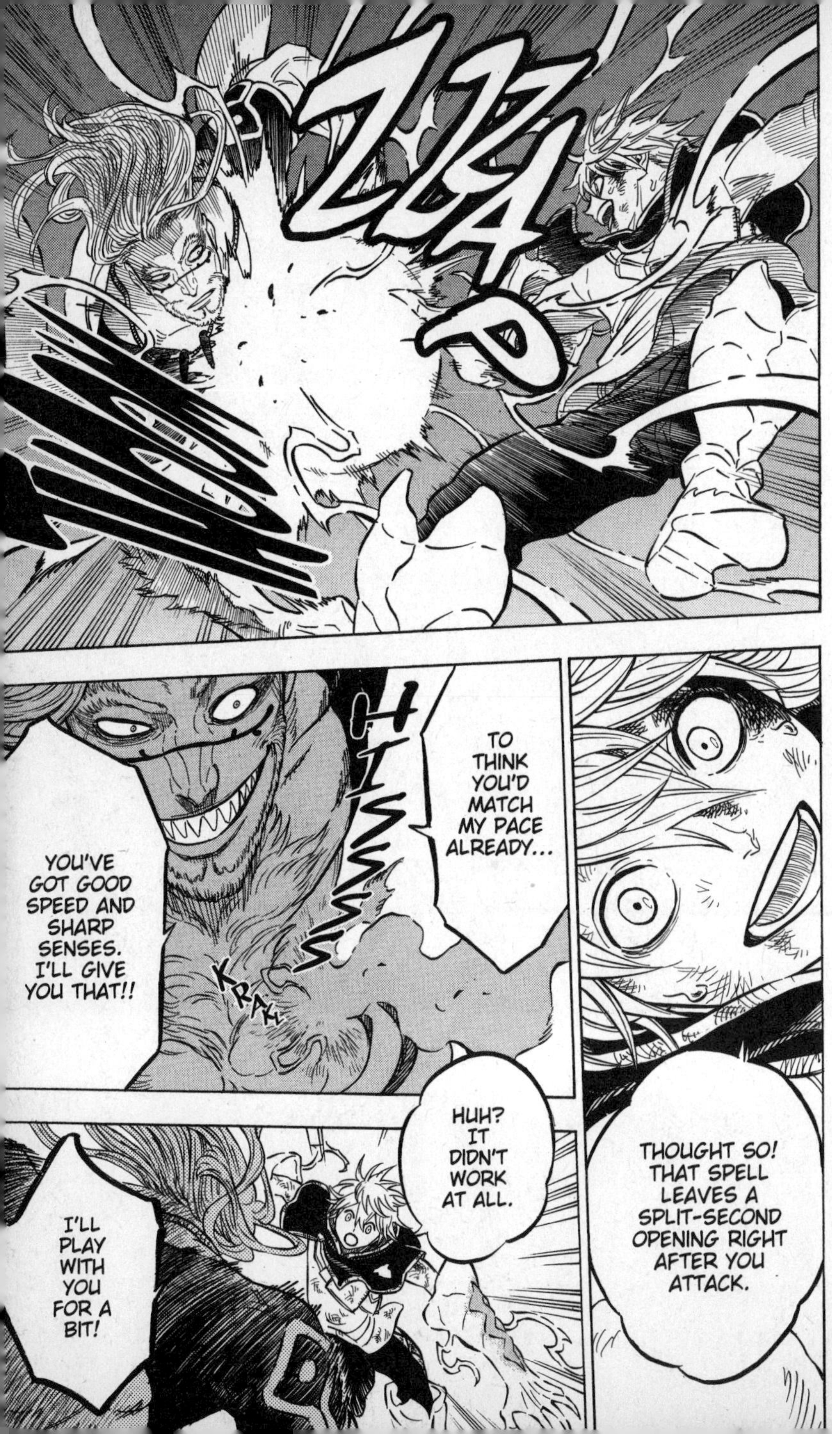
ZZZAP
HISSSSS
TO THINK YOU'D MATCH MY PACE ALREADY...
YOU'VE GOT GOOD SPEED AND SHARP SENSES. I'LL GIVE YOU THAT!!
KRAK
THOUGHT SO! THAT SPELL LEAVES A SPLIT-SECOND OPENING RIGHT AFTER YOU ATTACK.
HUH? IT DIDN'T WORK AT ALL.
I'LL PLAY WITH YOU FOR A BIT!

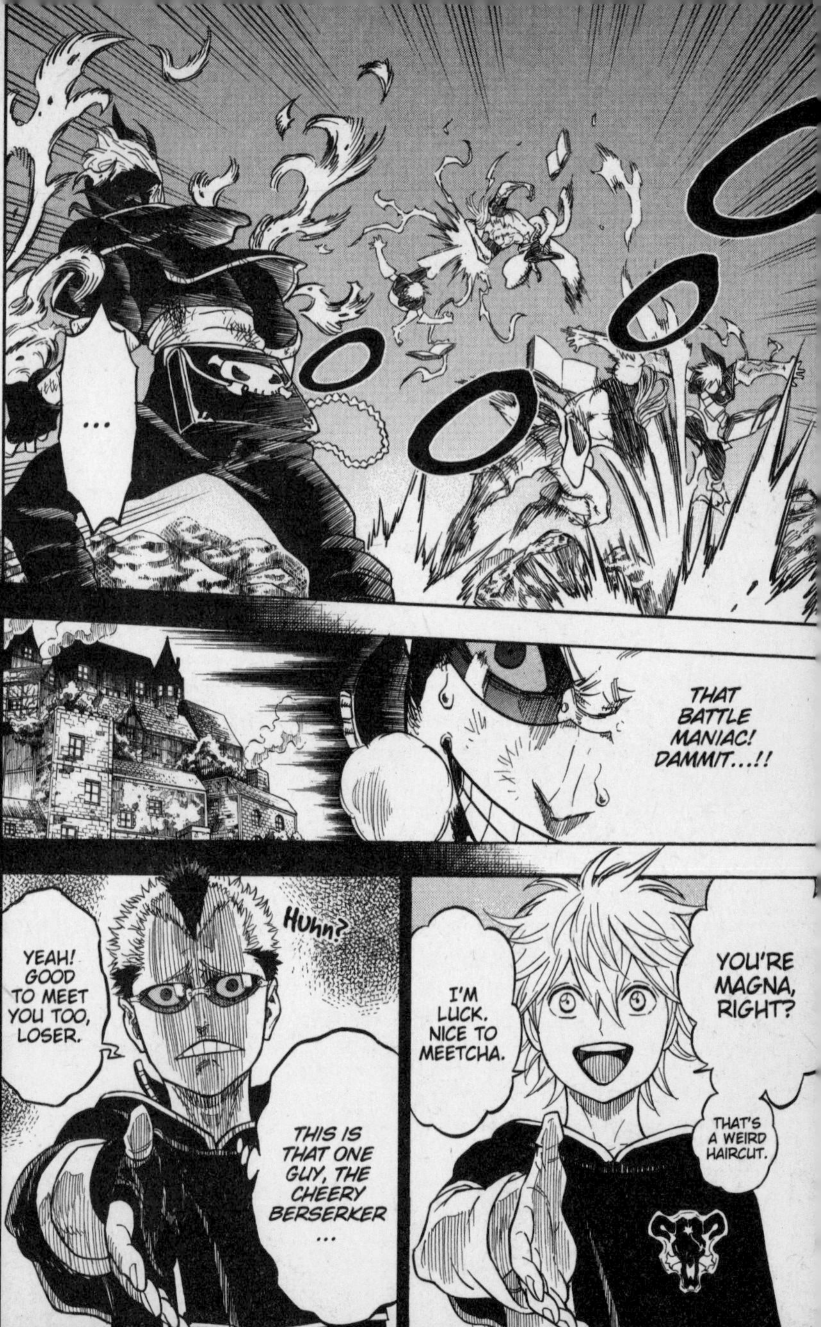
...
THAT BATTLE MANIAC! DAMMIT...!!
YOU'RE MAGNA, RIGHT?
I'M LUCK. NICE TO MEETCHA.
THAT'S A WEIRD HAIRCUT.
Huhn?
YEAH! GOOD TO MEET YOU TOO, LOSER.
THIS IS THAT ONE GUY, THE CHEERY BERSERKER ...

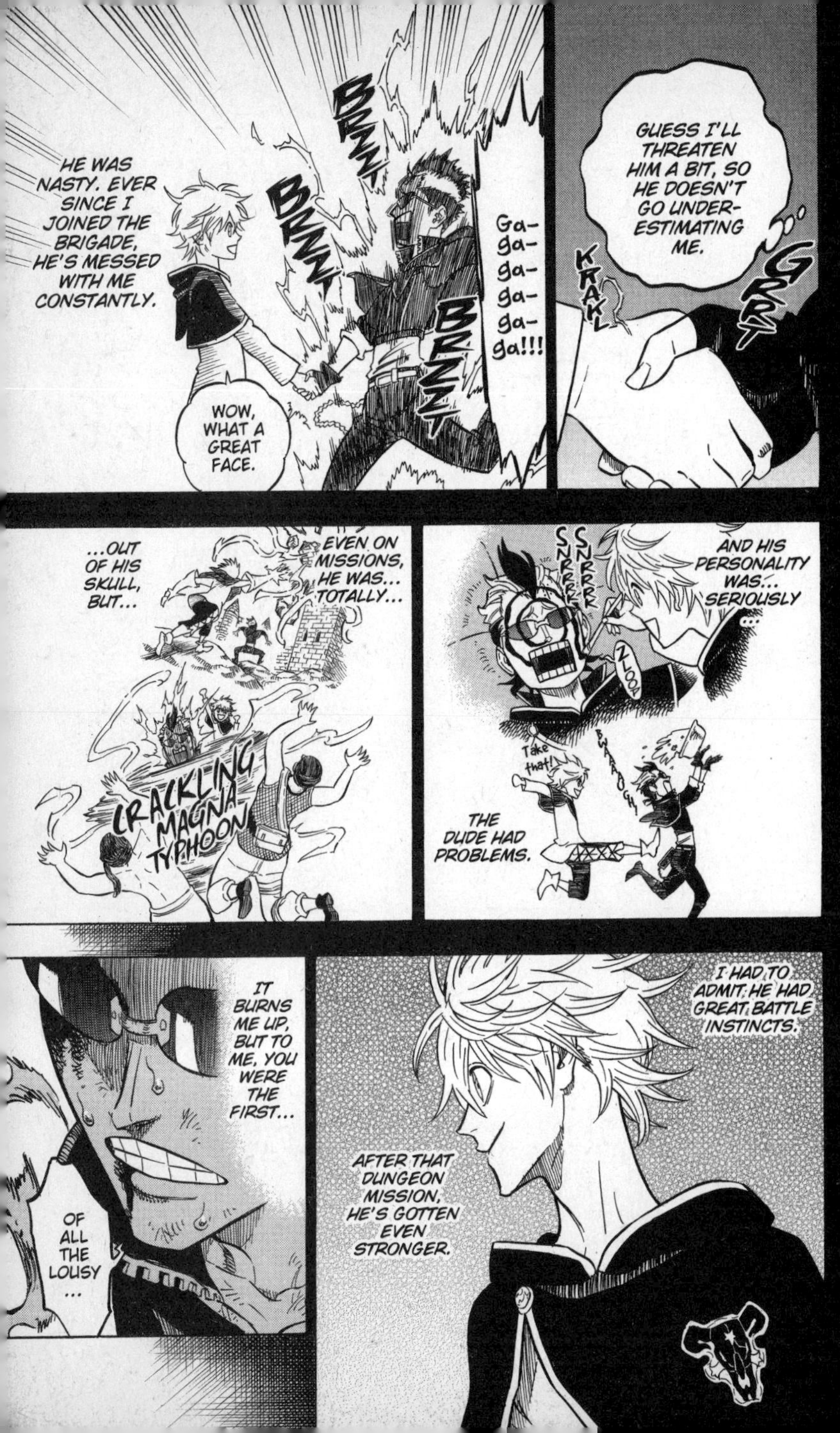
GUESS I'LL THREATEN HIM A BIT, SO HE DOESN'T GO UNDER-ESTIMATING ME.
KRAKL
GRRRT
HE WAS NASTY. EVER SINCE I JOINED THE BRIGADE, HE'S MESSED WITH ME CONSTANTLY.
BRZZZT
BRZZZT
Ga-ga-ga-ga-ga-ga!!!
BRZZZT
WOW, WHAT A GREAT FACE.
AND HIS PERSONALITY WAS... SERIOUSLY...
SNRRRK
SNRRRK
Take that!
THE DUDE HAD PROBLEMS.
EVEN ON MISSIONS, HE WAS... TOTALLY...
...OUT OF HIS SKULL, BUT...
CRACKLING MAGNA TYPHOON
I HAD TO ADMIT HE HAD GREAT BATTLE INSTINCTS.
AFTER THAT DUNGEON MISSION, HE'S GOTTEN EVEN STRONGER.
IT BURNS ME UP, BUT TO ME, YOU WERE THE FIRST...
OF ALL THE LOUSY...

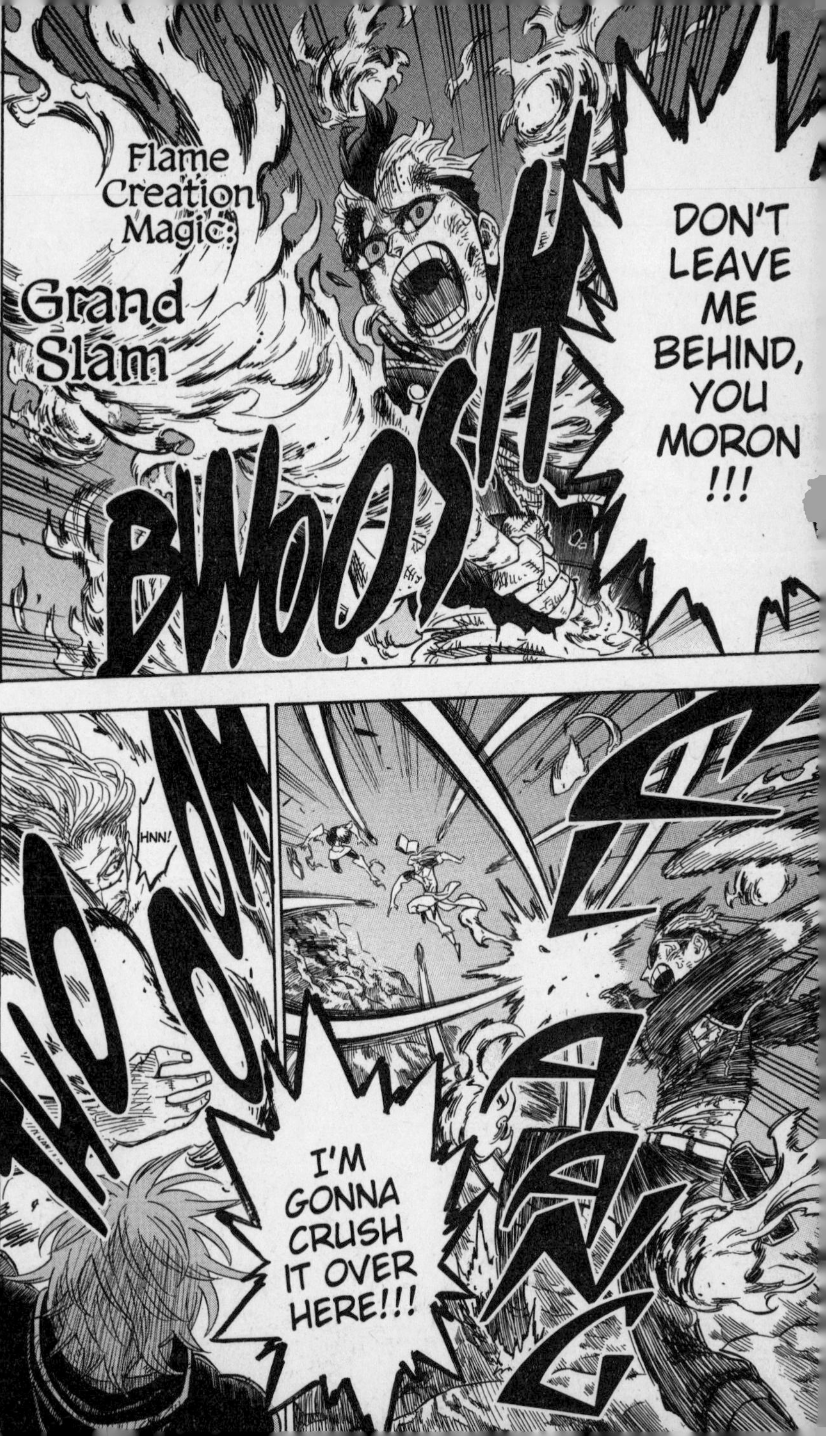
DON'T LEAVE ME BEHIND, YOU MORON!!!
Flame Creation Magic:
Grand Slam
BWOOSH
I'M GONNA CRUSH IT OVER HERE!!!
HNN!

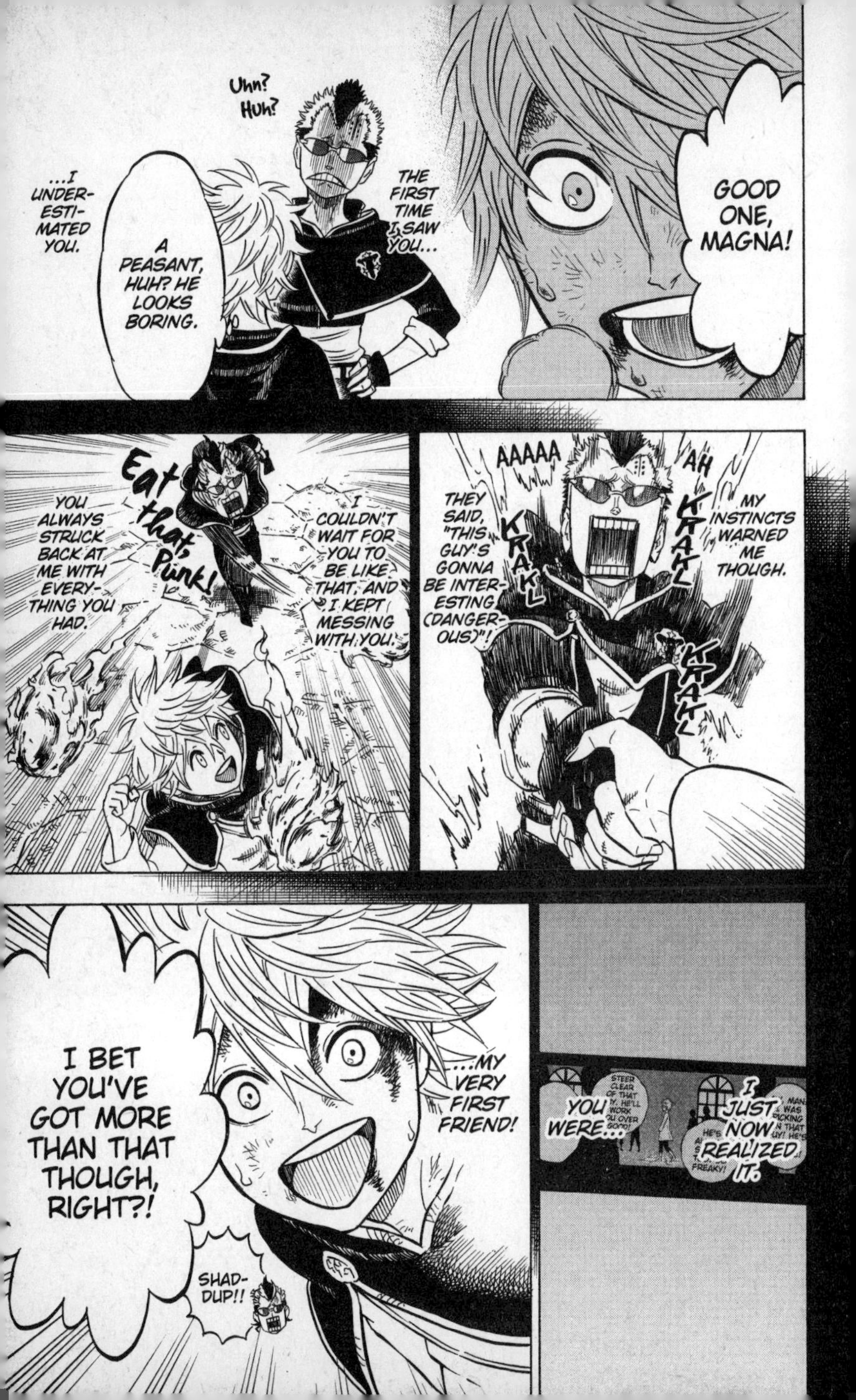
GOOD ONE, MAGNA!
Uhn? Huh?
THE FIRST TIME I SAW YOU...
A PEASANT, HUH? HE LOOKS BORING.
...I UNDERESTIMATED YOU.
AAAAA
AH
MY INSTINCTS WARNED ME THOUGH.
KRAKL
KRAKL
THEY SAID, "THIS GUY'S GONNA BE INTERESTING (DANGEROUS)"!
KRAKL
I COULDN'T WAIT FOR YOU TO BE LIKE THAT, AND I KEPT MESSING WITH YOU.
Eat that, Punk!
YOU ALWAYS STRUCK BACK AT ME WITH EVERYTHING YOU HAD.
I JUST NOW REALIZED IT.
YOU WERE...
...MY VERY FIRST FRIEND!
I BET YOU'VE GOT MORE THAN THAT THOUGH, RIGHT?!
SHADDUP!!

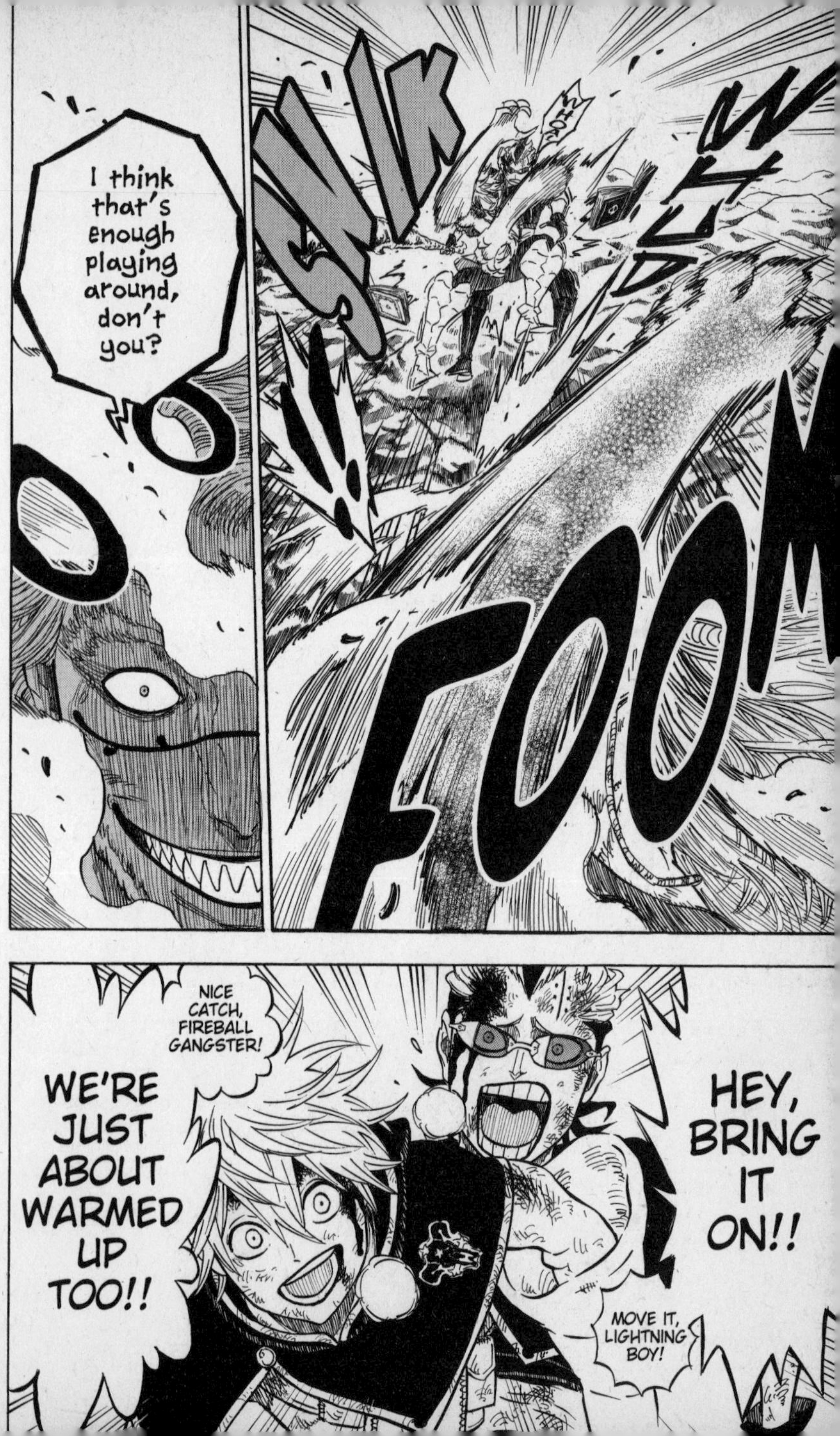
WHOA
FOOM
I think that's enough playing around, don't you?
HEY, BRING IT ON!!
MOVE IT, LIGHTNING BOY!
NICE CATCH, FIREBALL GANGSTER!
WE'RE JUST ABOUT WARMED UP TOO!!

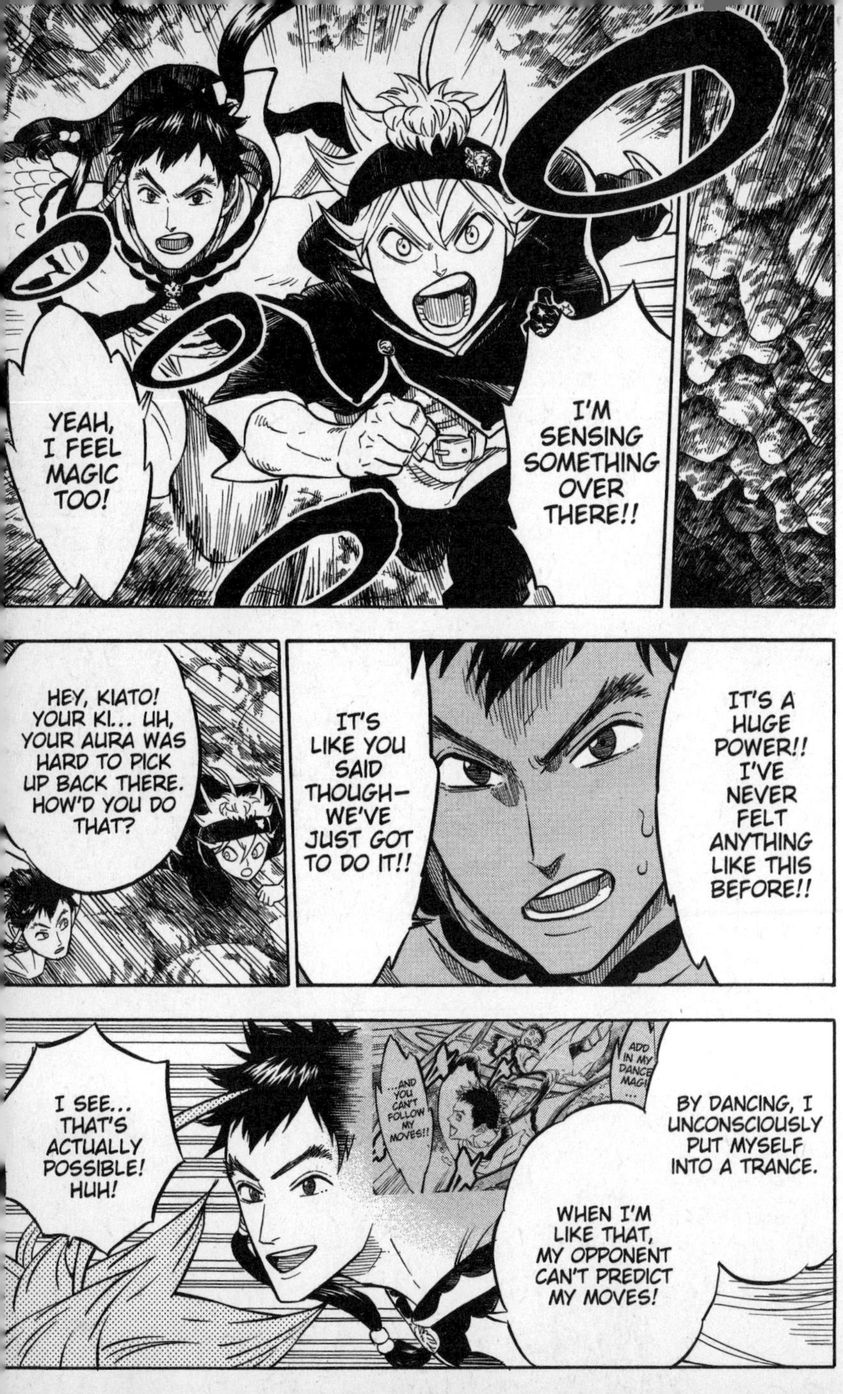
I'M SENSING SOMETHING OVER THERE!!
YEAH, I FEEL MAGIC TOO!
IT'S A HUGE POWER!! I'VE NEVER FELT ANYTHING LIKE THIS BEFORE!!
IT'S LIKE YOU SAID THOUGH— WE'VE JUST GOT TO DO IT!!
HEY, KIATO! YOUR KI... UH, YOUR AURA WAS HARD TO PICK UP BACK THERE. HOW'D YOU DO THAT?
BY DANCING, I UNCONSCIOUSLY PUT MYSELF INTO A TRANCE.
WHEN I'M LIKE THAT, MY OPPONENT CAN'T PREDICT MY MOVES!
...AND YOU CAN'T FOLLOW MY MOVES!!
I SEE... THAT'S ACTUALLY POSSIBLE! HUH!

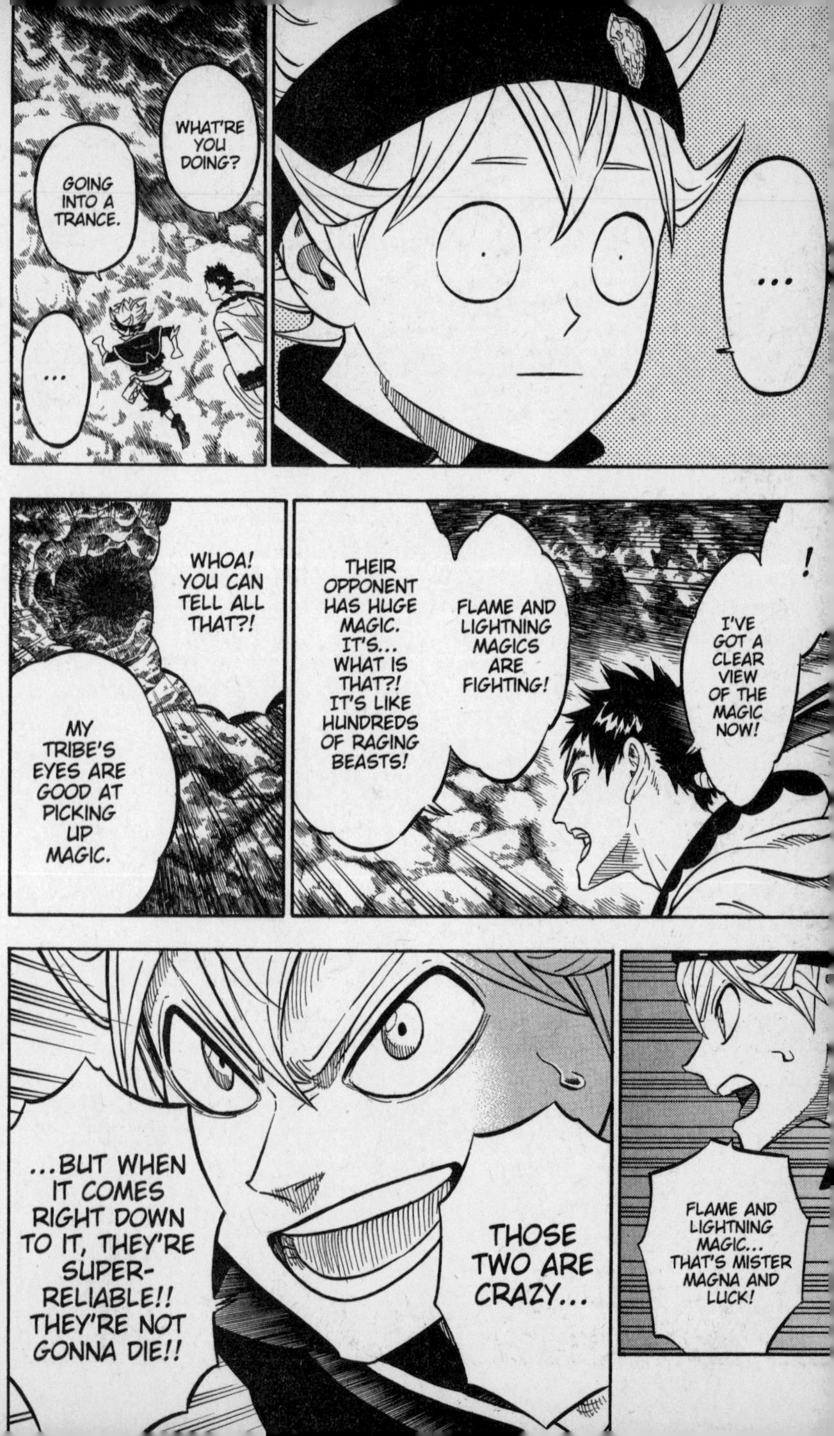
...
WHAT'RE YOU DOING?
GOING INTO A TRANCE.
...
!
I'VE GOT A CLEAR VIEW OF THE MAGIC NOW!
FLAME AND LIGHTNING MAGICS ARE FIGHTING!
THEIR OPPONENT HAS HUGE MAGIC. IT'S... WHAT IS THAT?! IT'S LIKE HUNDREDS OF RAGING BEASTS!
WHOA! YOU CAN TELL ALL THAT?!
MY TRIBE'S EYES ARE GOOD AT PICKING UP MAGIC.
FLAME AND LIGHTNING MAGIC... THAT'S MISTER MAGNA AND LUCK!
THOSE TWO ARE CRAZY...
...BUT WHEN IT COMES RIGHT DOWN TO IT, THEY'RE SUPER-RELIABLE!! THEY'RE NOT GONNA DIE!!

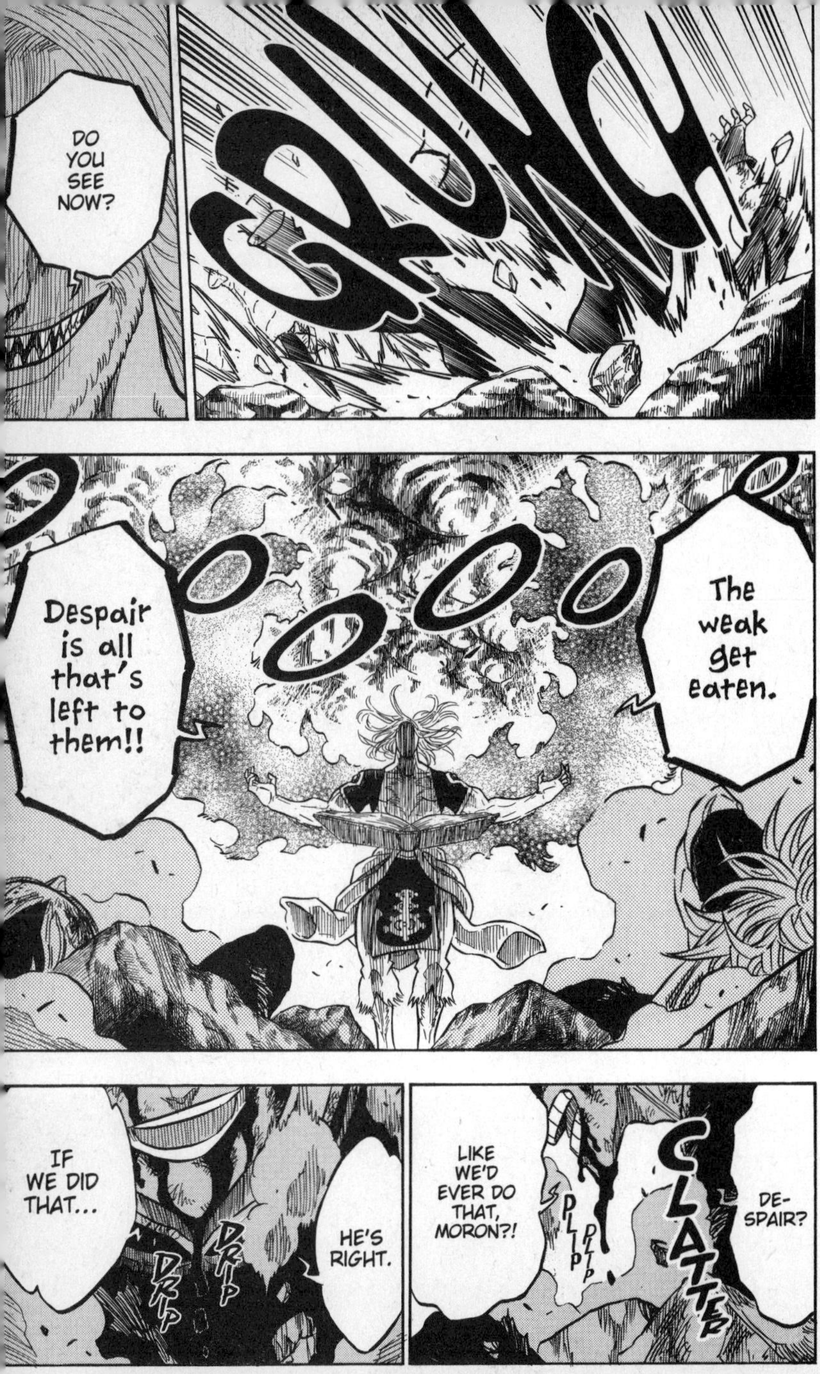
GUNCH!
DO YOU SEE NOW?
The weak get eaten.
Despair is all that's left to them!!
DE-SPAIR?
CLATTER
PLIP PLIP
LIKE WE'D EVER DO THAT, MORON?!
HE'S RIGHT.
DRIP DRIP
IF WE DID THAT...

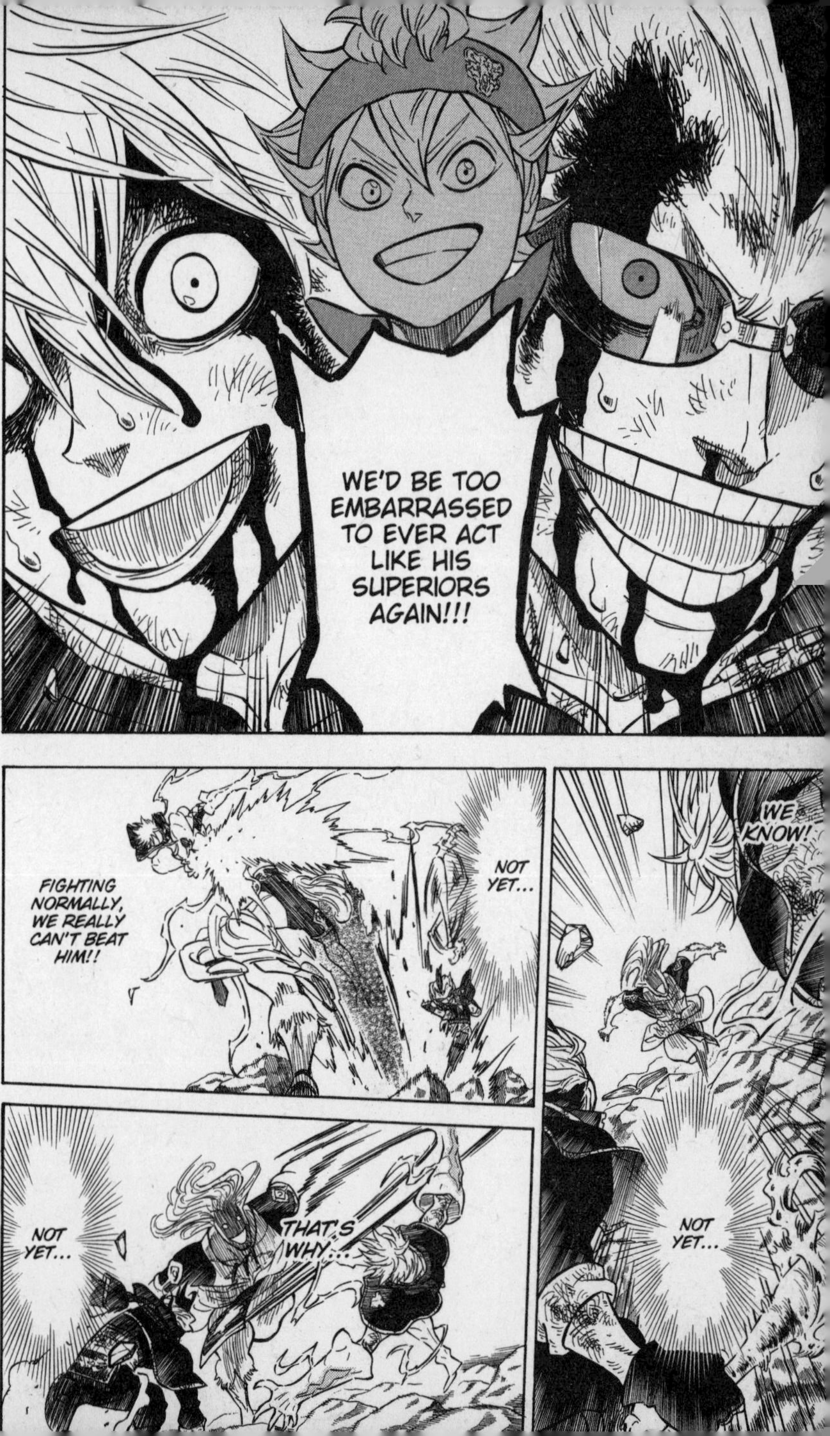
WE'D BE TOO EMBARRASSED TO EVER ACT LIKE HIS SUPERIORS AGAIN!!!
WE KNOW!
NOT YET...
NOT YET...
FIGHTING NORMALLY, WE REALLY CAN'T BEAT HIM!!
THAT'S WHY...
NOT YET...

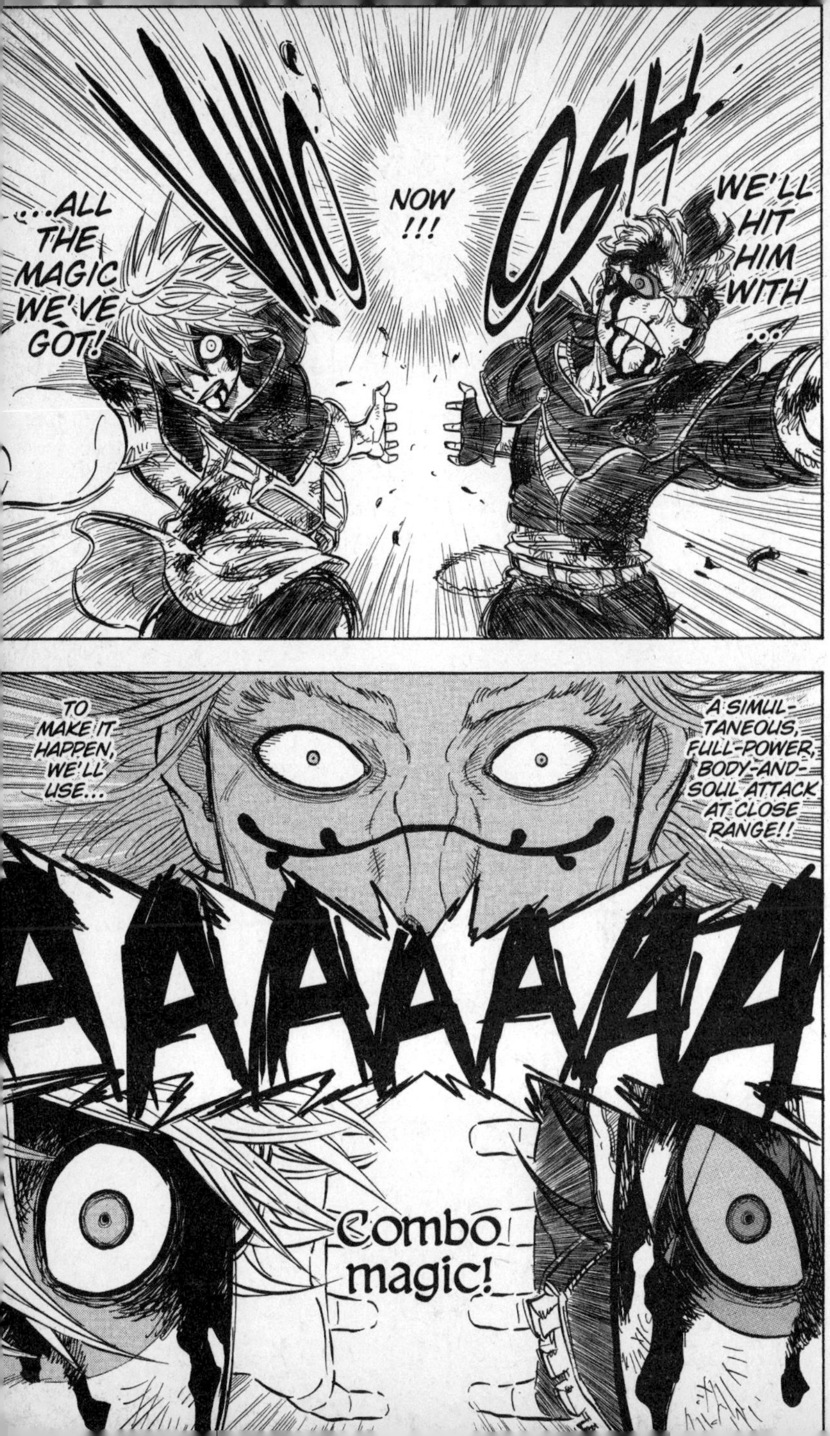
WHOOSH
WE'LL HIT HIM WITH...
NOW!!!
...ALL THE MAGIC WE'VE GOT!
A SIMUL-TANEOUS, FULL-POWER, BODY-AND-SOUL ATTACK AT CLOSE RANGE!!
TO MAKE IT HAPPEN, WE'LL USE...
AAAAAA
Combo magic!

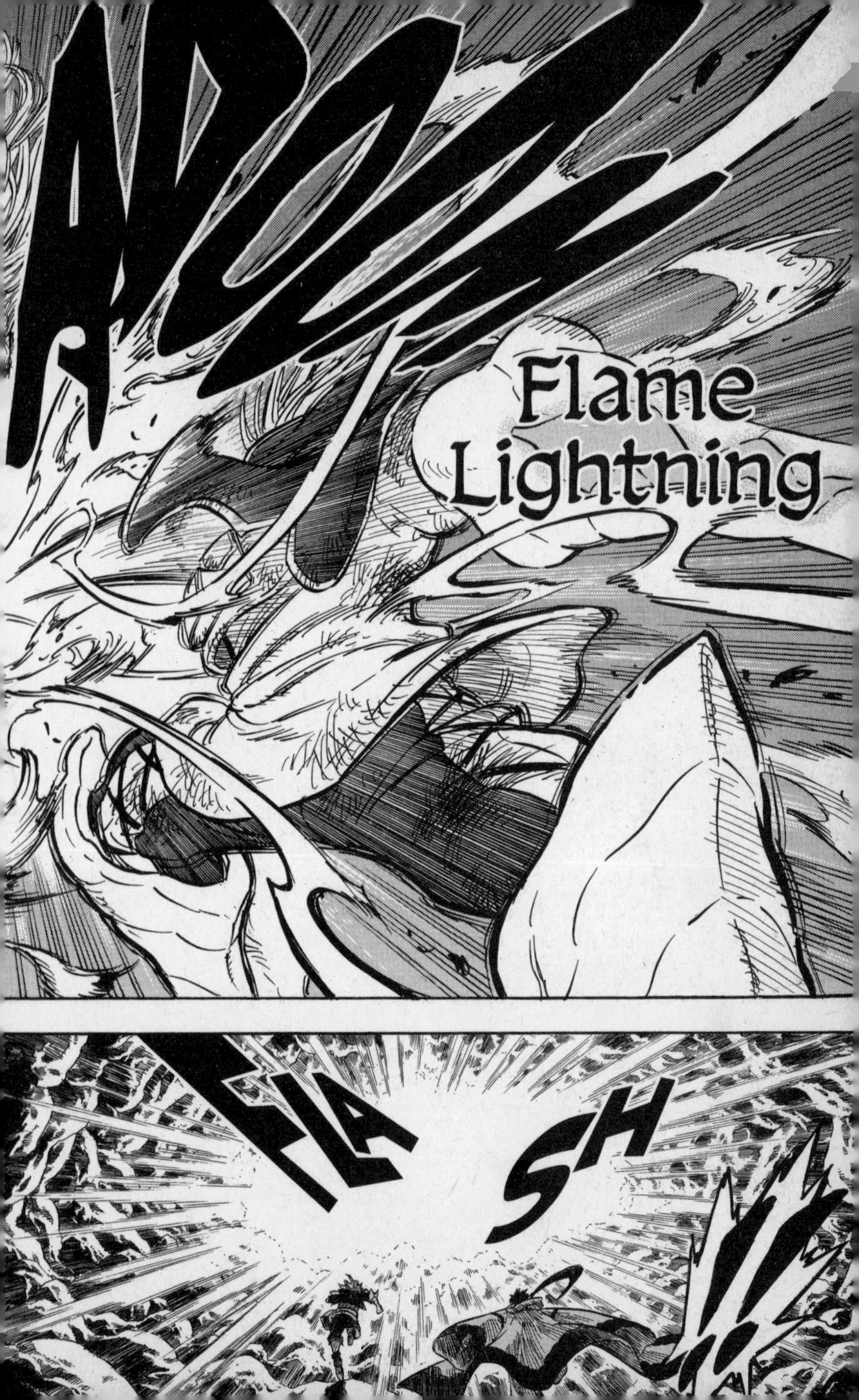
Flame Lightning
FLASH!!

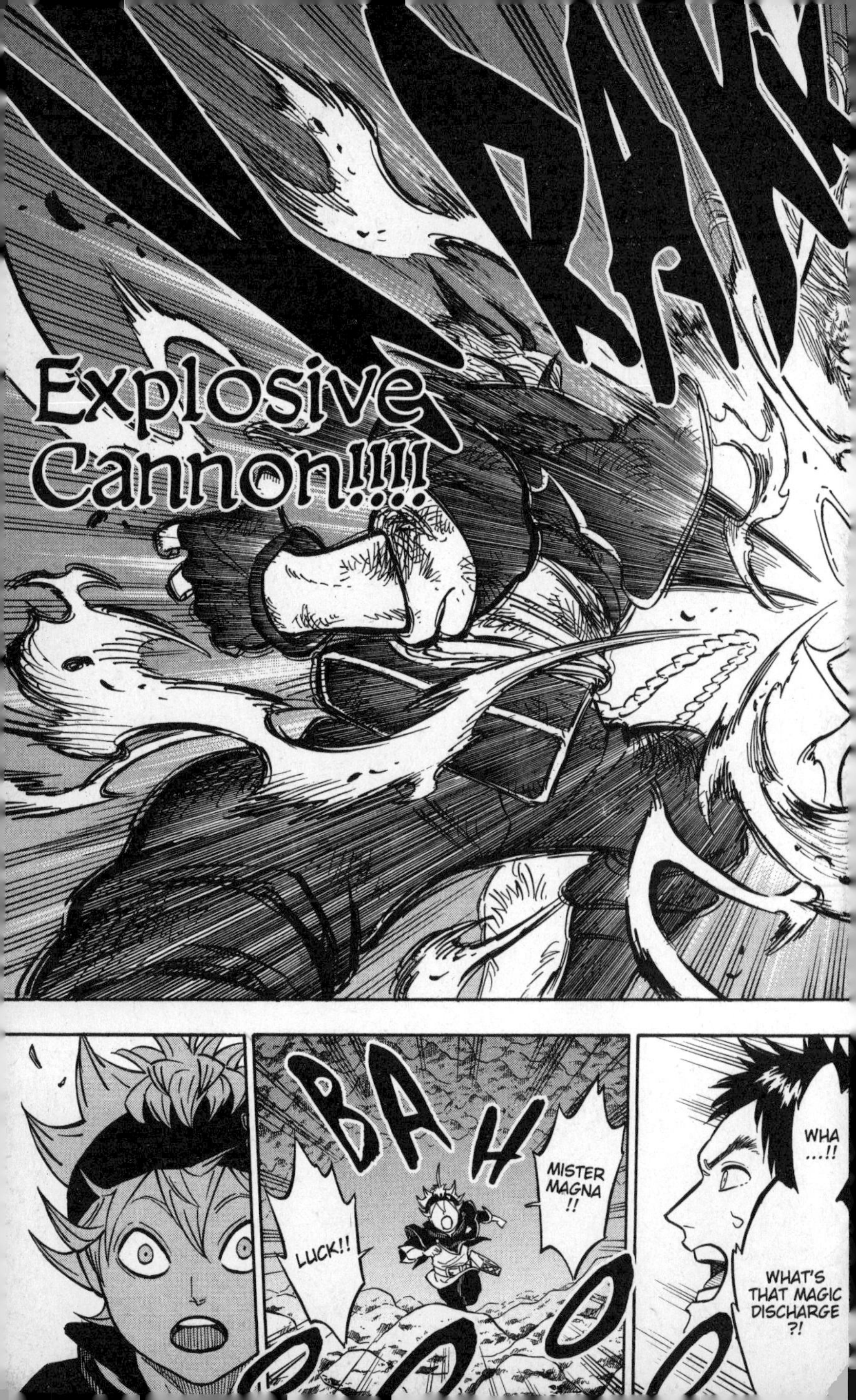

Explosive Cannon!!!!
WHA ...!!
WHAT'S THAT MAGIC DISCHARGE ?!
BAH
MISTER MAGNA !!
LUCK!!

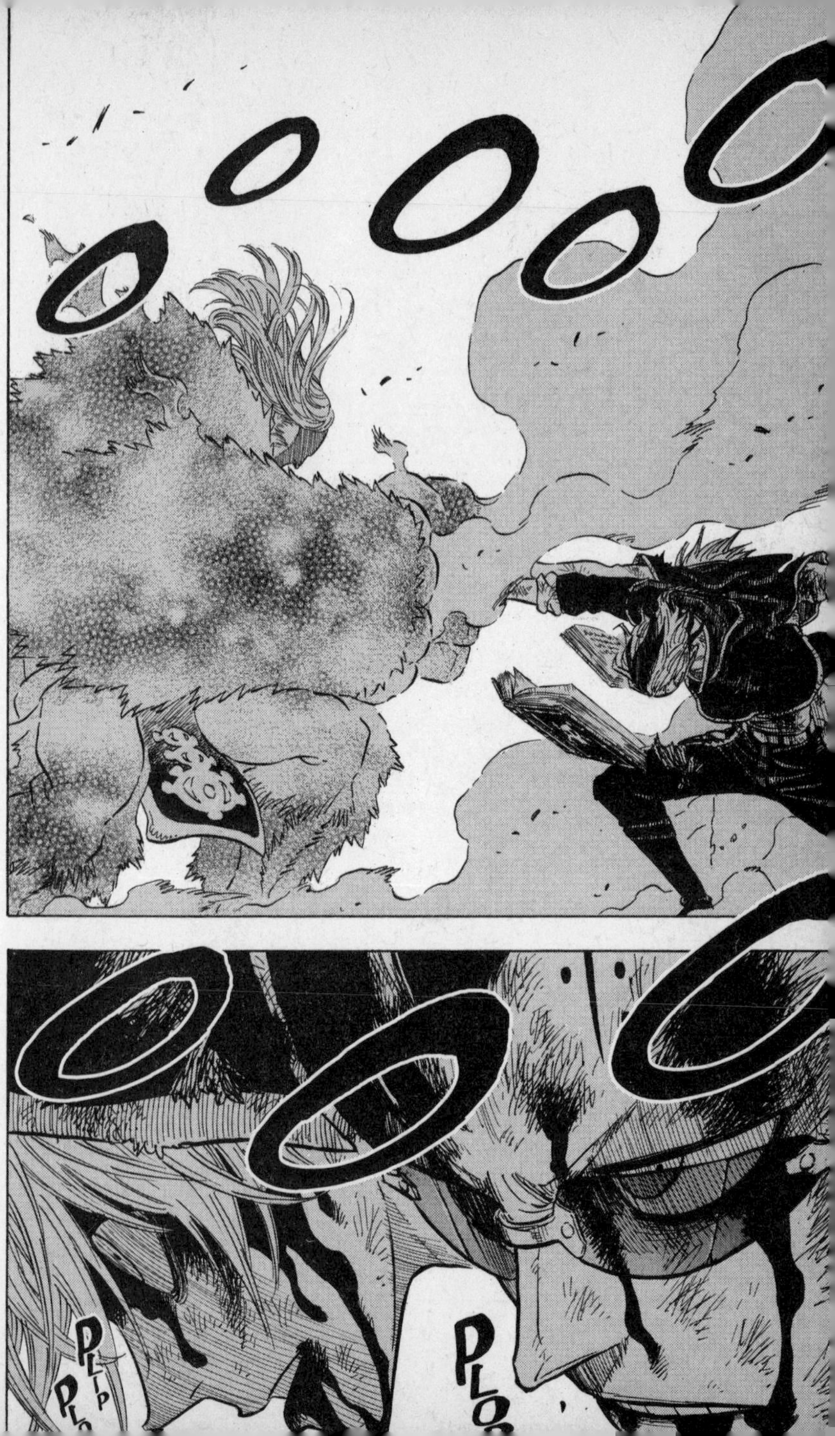
PLO
PLIP
PLO

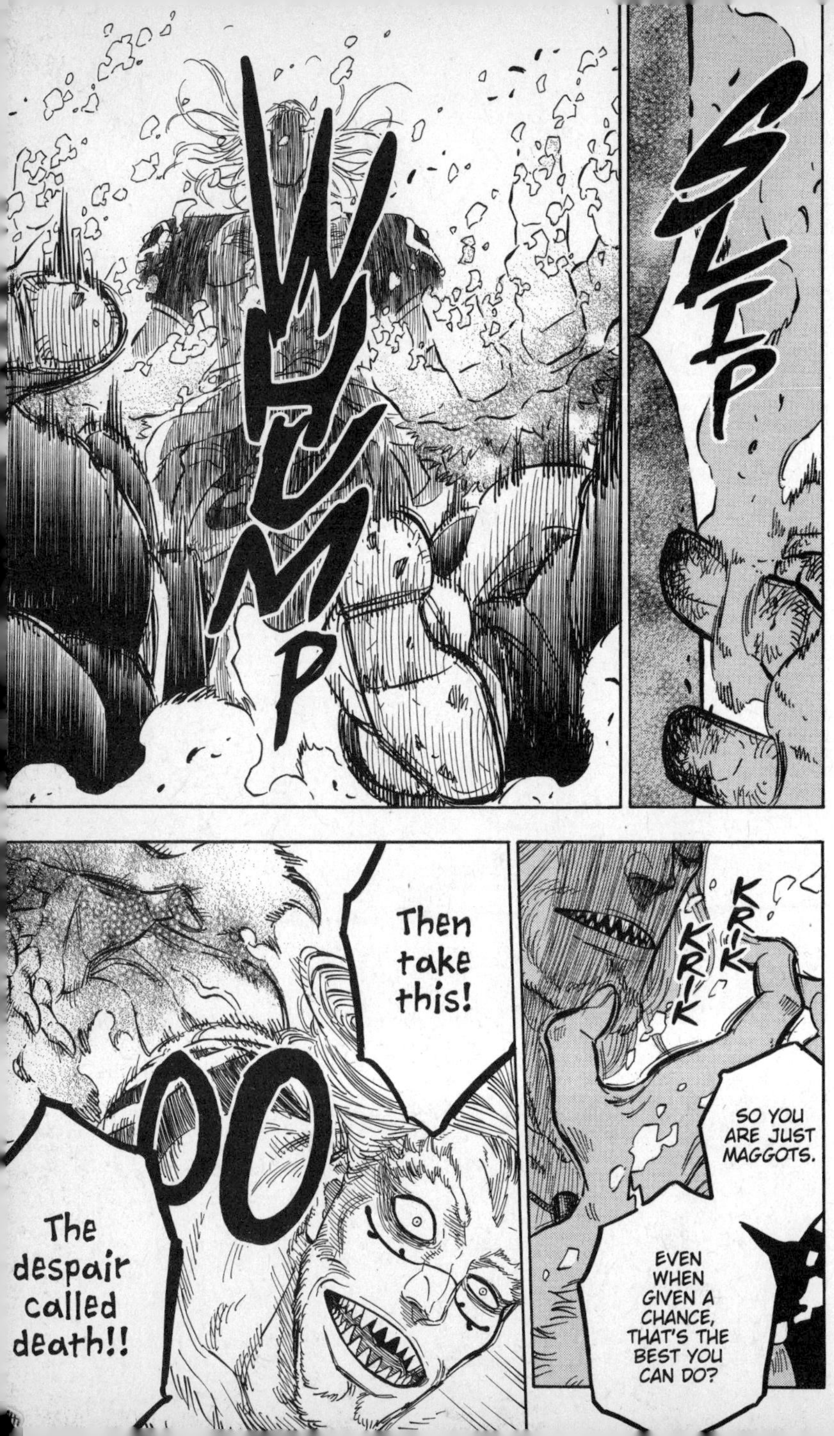
SLIP
WHUMP
KRIK KRIK
SO YOU ARE JUST MAGGOTS.
EVEN WHEN GIVEN A CHANCE, THAT'S THE BEST YOU CAN DO?
Then take this!
The despair called death!!

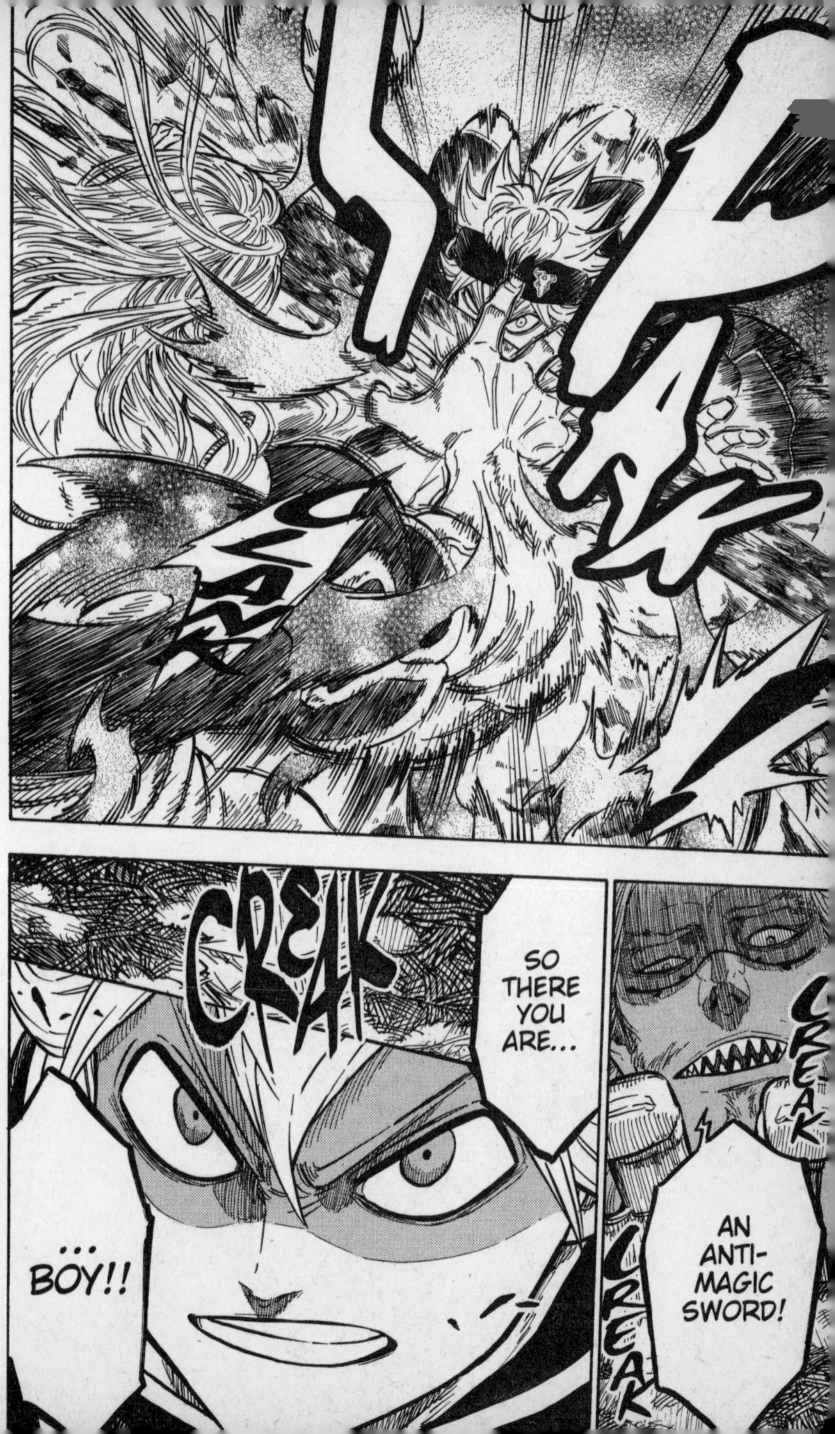
CLANK
CREAK
AN ANTI-MAGIC SWORD!
CREAK
CREAK
SO THERE YOU ARE...
...BOY!!

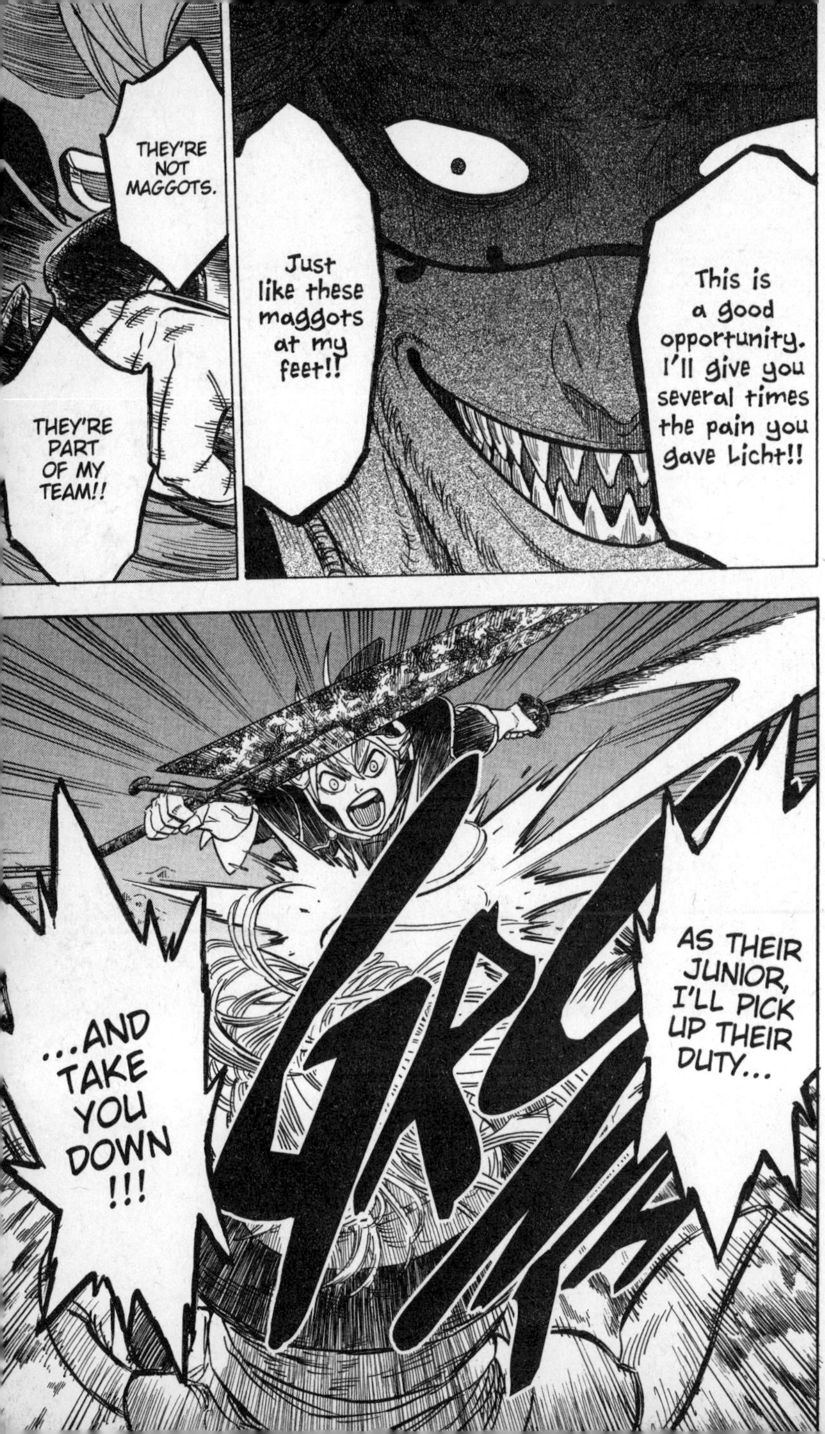
This is a good opportunity. I'll give you several times the pain you gave Licht!!
Just like these maggots at my feet!!
THEY'RE NOT MAGGOTS.
THEY'RE PART OF MY TEAM!!
AS THEIR JUNIOR, I'LL PICK UP THEIR DUTY...
...AND TAKE YOU DOWN!!!

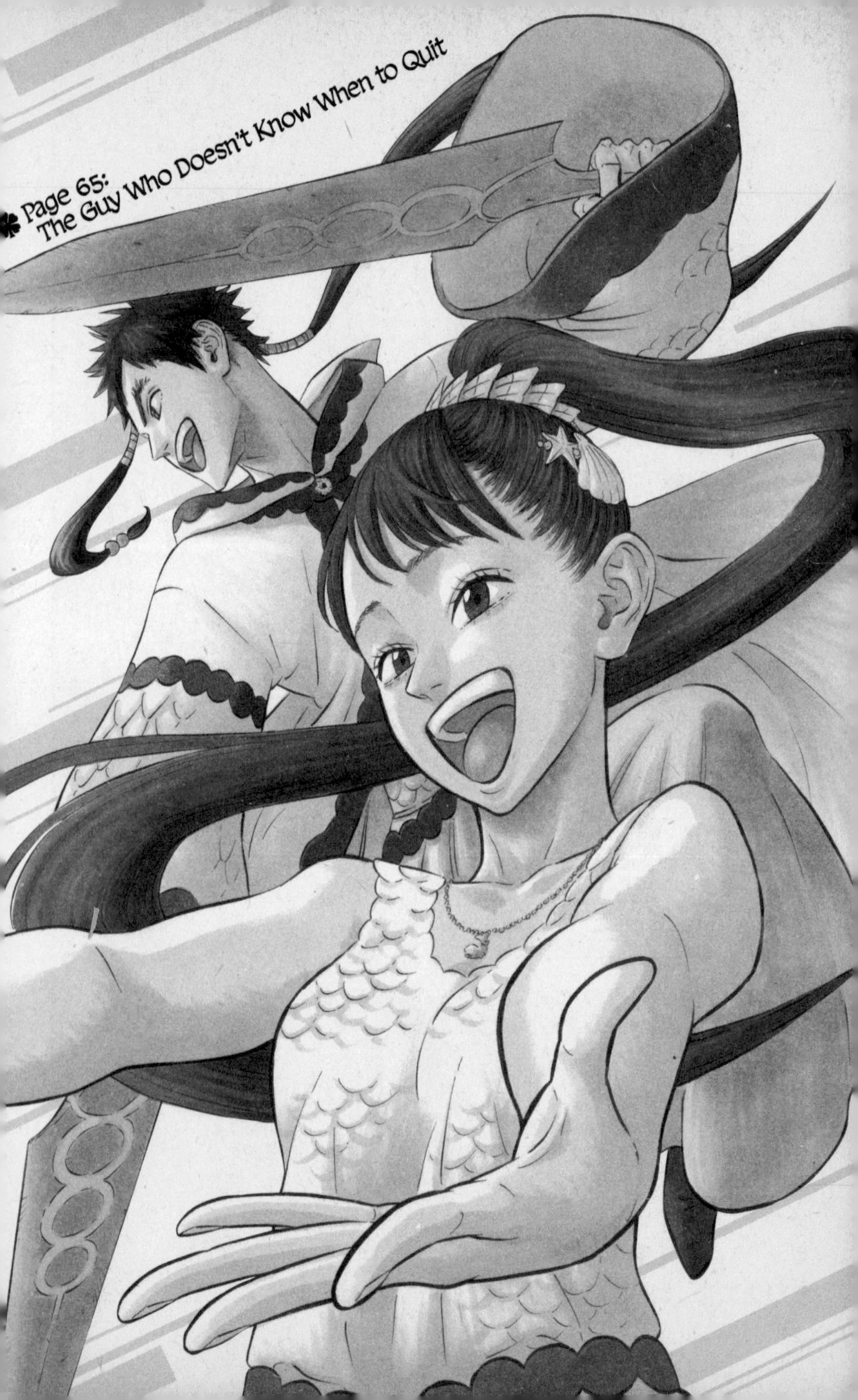
Page 65:
The Guy Who Doesn't Know When to Quit

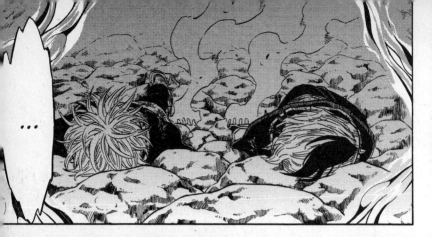

...

THAT COMBO MAGIC WAS INTENSELY POWERFUL, AND YET... THEY COULDN'T EVEN SCRATCH HIM?!

MAGNA. LUCK. YOU WERE REAL MEN!!

YOU BETTER STAND STRONG TOO...

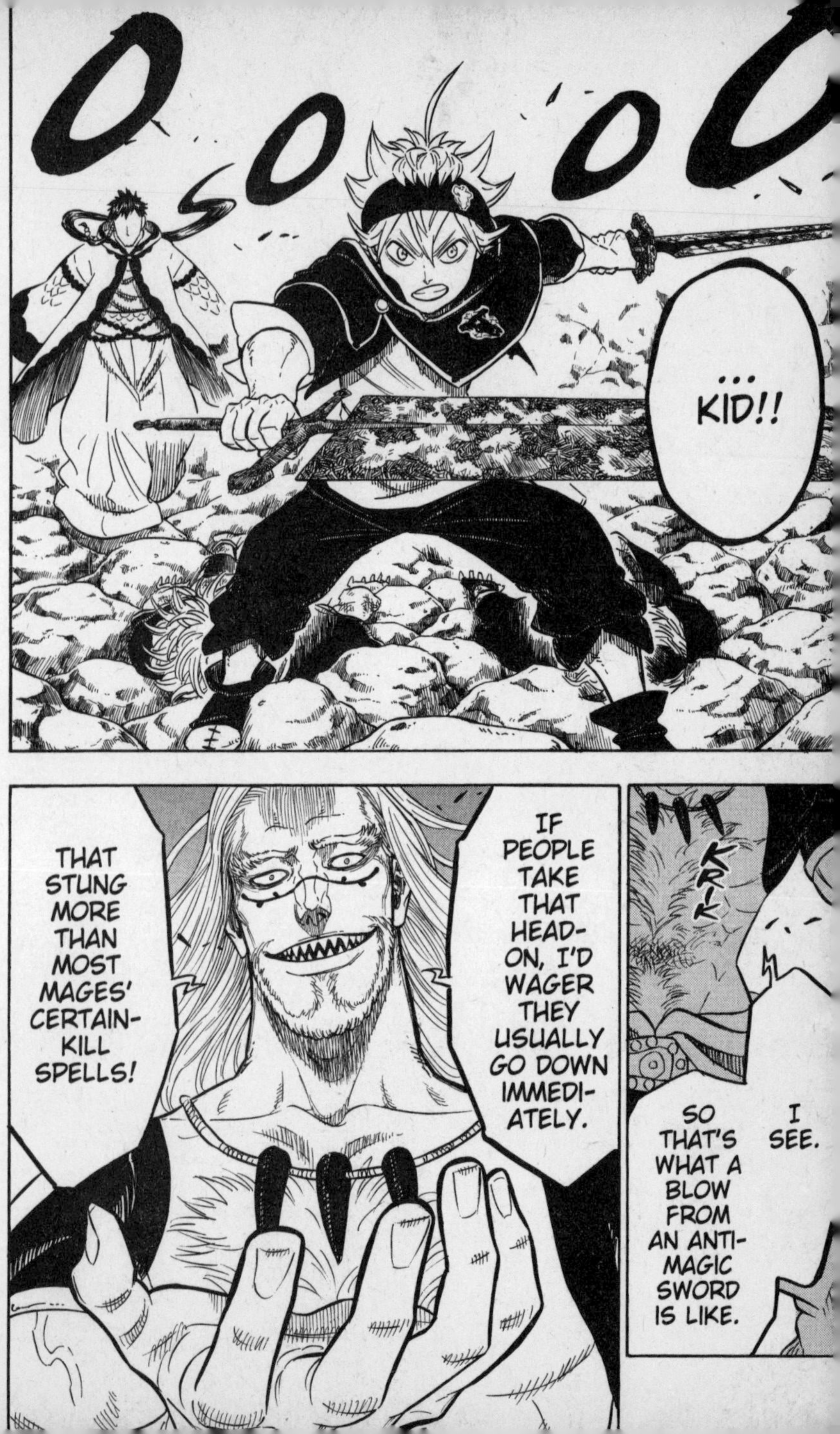
...KID!!
I SEE.
SO THAT'S WHAT A BLOW FROM AN ANTI-MAGIC SWORD IS LIKE.
KRIK
IF PEOPLE TAKE THAT HEAD-ON, I'D WAGER THEY USUALLY GO DOWN IMMEDIATELY.
THAT STUNG MORE THAN MOST MAGES' CERTAIN-KILL SPELLS!

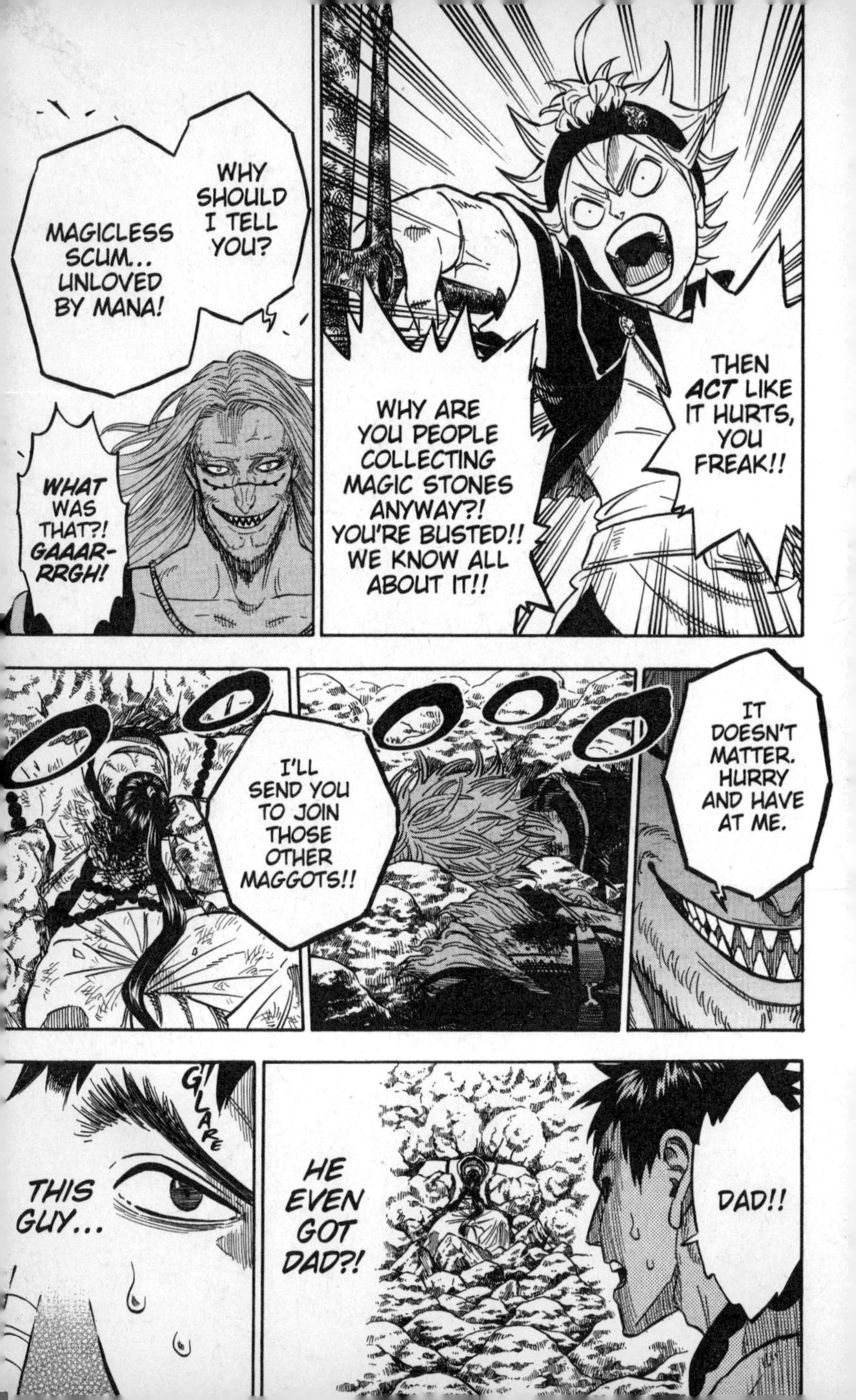
THEN ACT LIKE IT HURTS, YOU FREAK!!
WHY ARE YOU PEOPLE COLLECTING MAGIC STONES ANYWAY?! YOU'RE BUSTED!! WE KNOW ALL ABOUT IT!!
WHY SHOULD I TELL YOU?
MAGICLESS SCUM... UNLOVED BY MANA!
WHAT WAS THAT?! GAAAR-RRGH!
IT DOESN'T MATTER. HURRY AND HAVE AT ME.
I'LL SEND YOU TO JOIN THOSE OTHER MAGGOTS!!
DAD!!
HE EVEN GOT DAD?!
GLARE
THIS GUY...

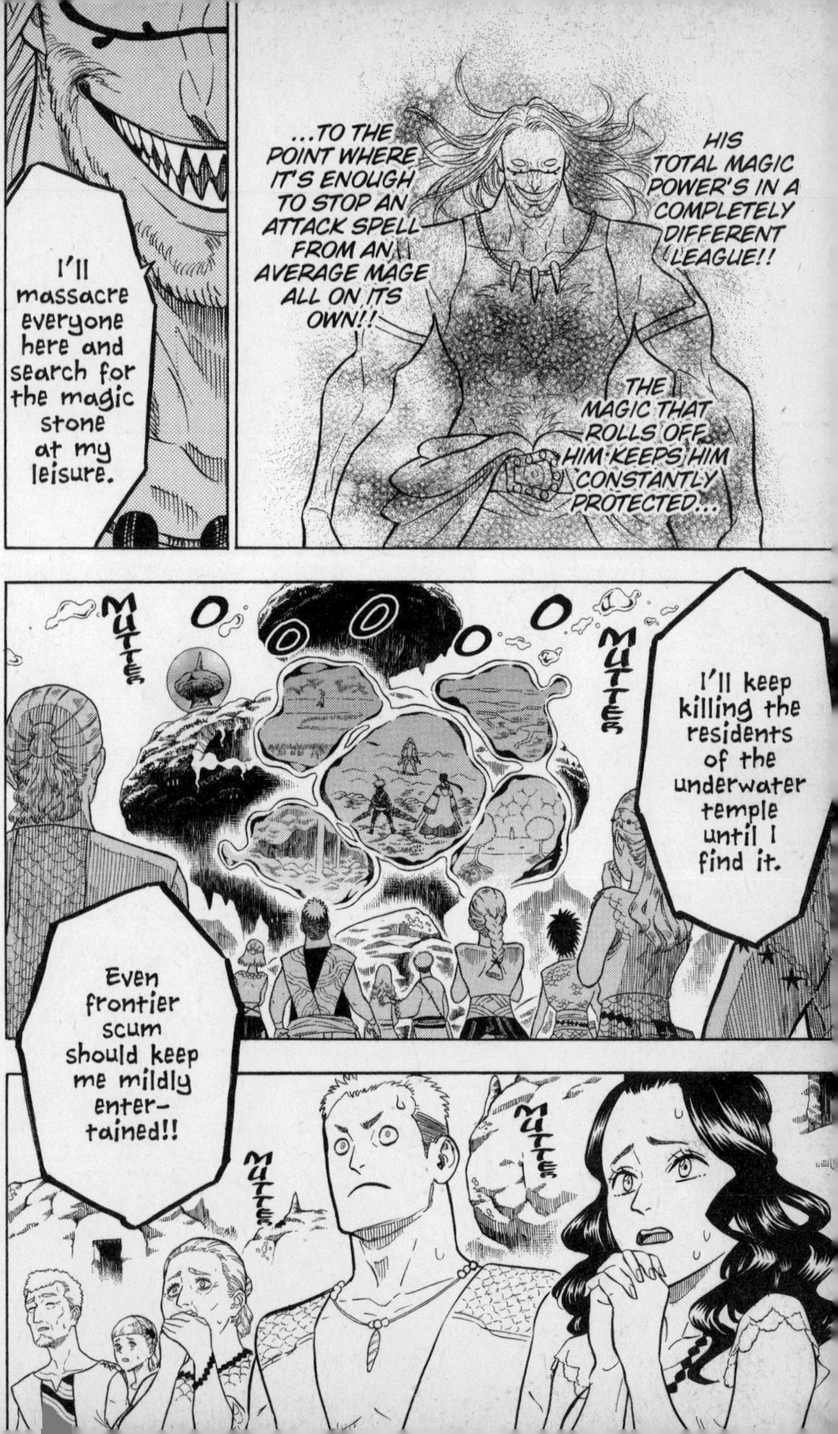
HIS TOTAL MAGIC POWER'S IN A COMPLETELY DIFFERENT LEAGUE!!
THE MAGIC THAT ROLLS OFF HIM KEEPS HIM CONSTANTLY PROTECTED...
...TO THE POINT WHERE IT'S ENOUGH TO STOP AN ATTACK SPELL FROM AN AVERAGE MAGE ALL ON ITS OWN!!
I'll massacre everyone here and search for the magic stone at my leisure.
MUTTER
I'll keep killing the residents of the underwater temple until I find it.
MUTTER
Even frontier scum should keep me mildly enter-tained!!
MUTTER
MUTTER

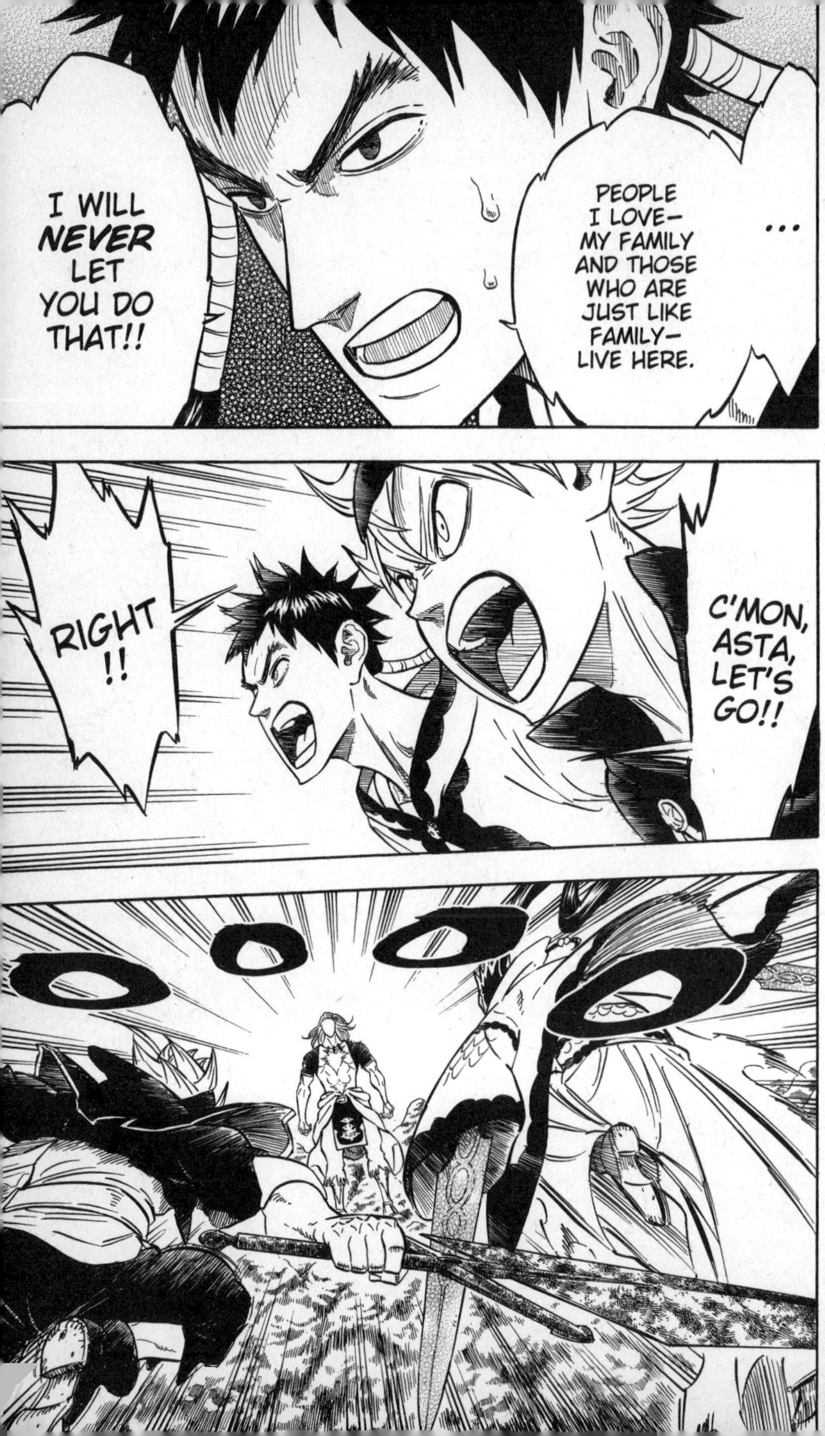
...
PEOPLE I LOVE—MY FAMILY AND THOSE WHO ARE JUST LIKE FAMILY—LIVE HERE.
I WILL NEVER LET YOU DO THAT!!
C'MON, ASTA, LET'S GO!!
RIGHT!!

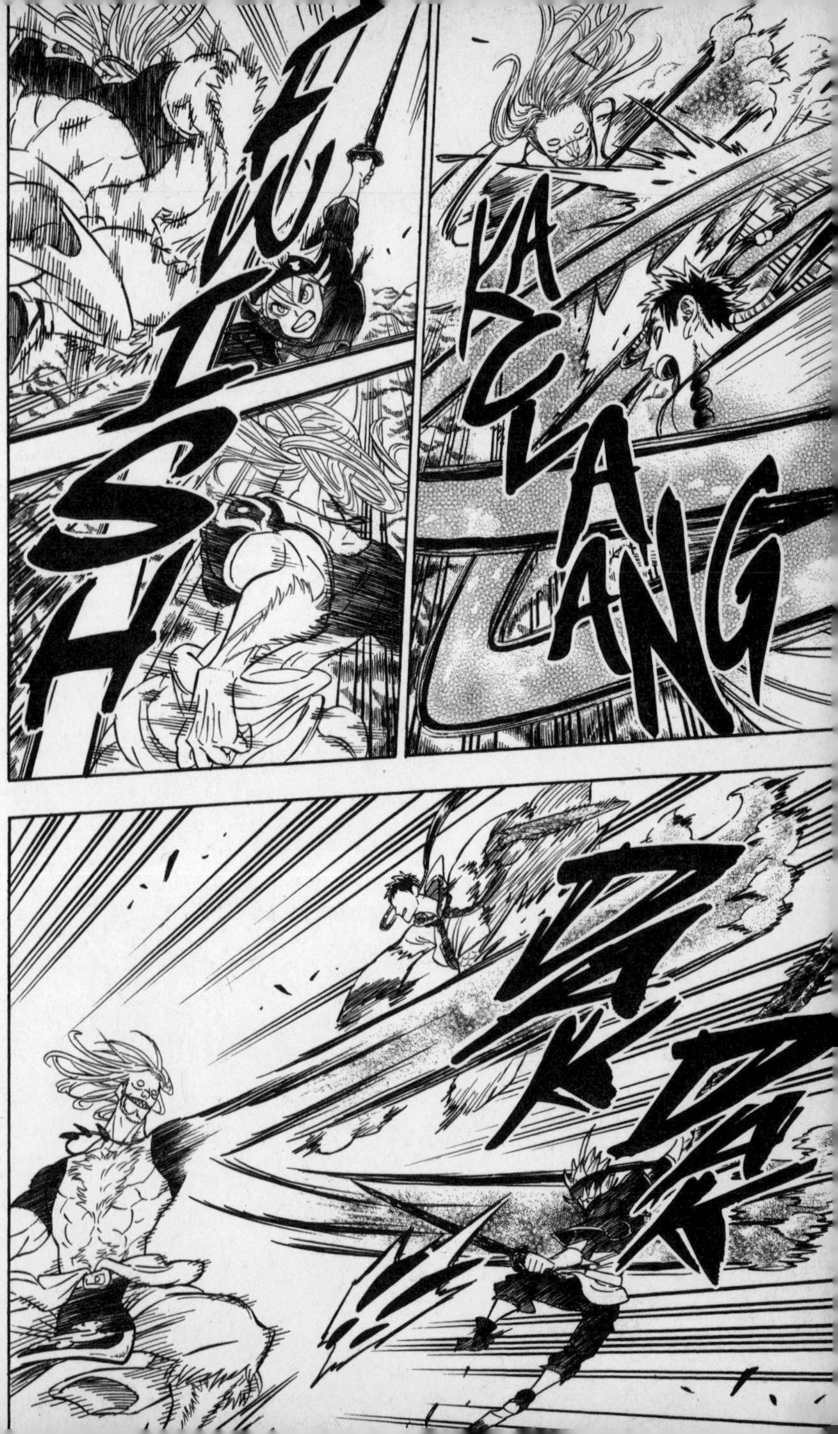
KA-CLANG
FWISH
ZAK
ZAK

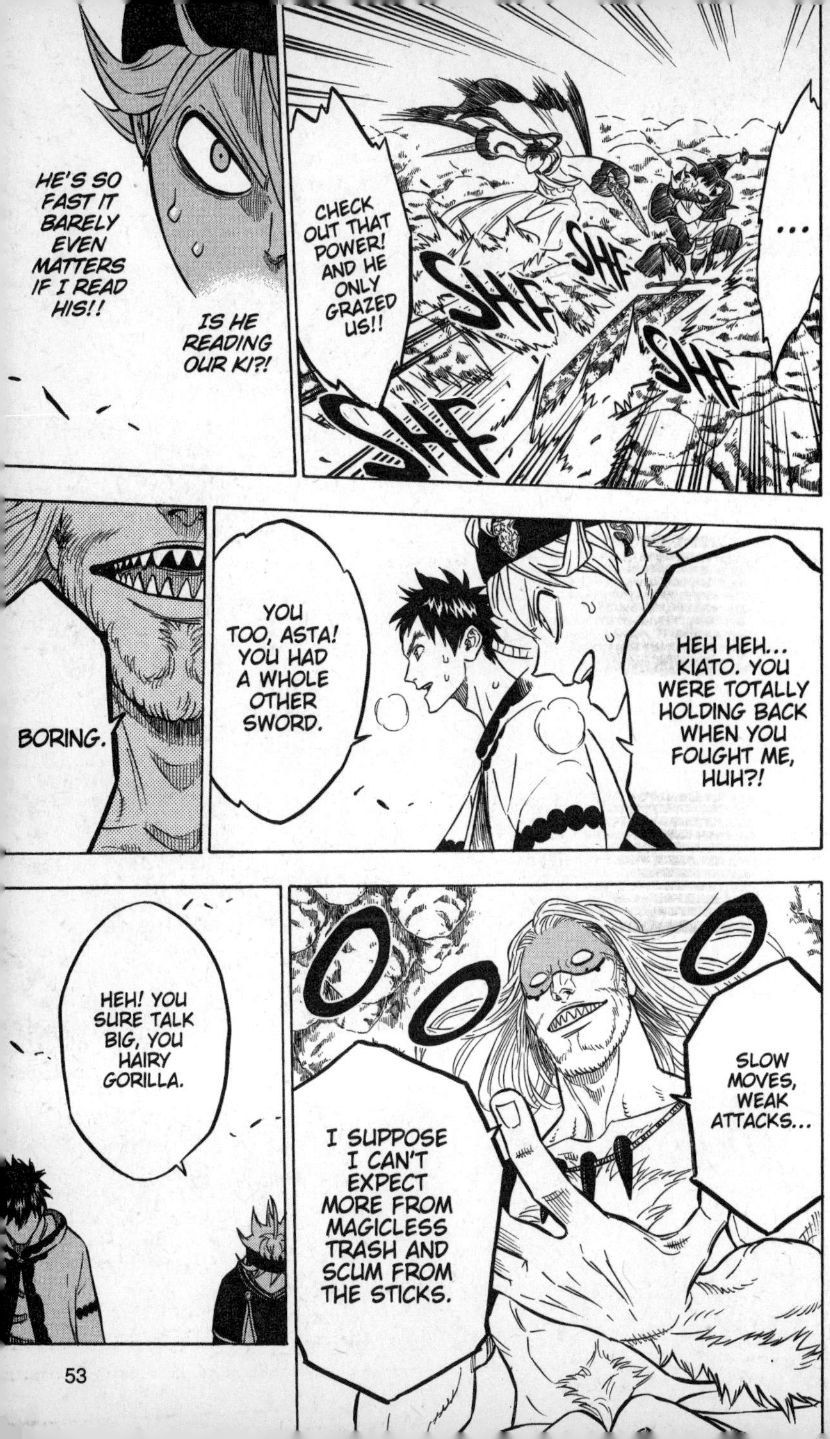
...
SHF SHF SHF SHF
CHECK OUT THAT POWER! AND HE ONLY GRAZED US!!
IS HE READING OUR KI?!
HE'S SO FAST IT BARELY EVEN MATTERS IF I READ HIS!!
HEH HEH... KIATO. YOU WERE TOTALLY HOLDING BACK WHEN YOU FOUGHT ME, HUH?!
YOU TOO, ASTA! YOU HAD A WHOLE OTHER SWORD.
BORING.
OOOO
SLOW MOVES, WEAK ATTACKS...
I SUPPOSE I CAN'T EXPECT MORE FROM MAGICLESS TRASH AND SCUM FROM THE STICKS.
HEH! YOU SURE TALK BIG, YOU HAIRY GORILLA.

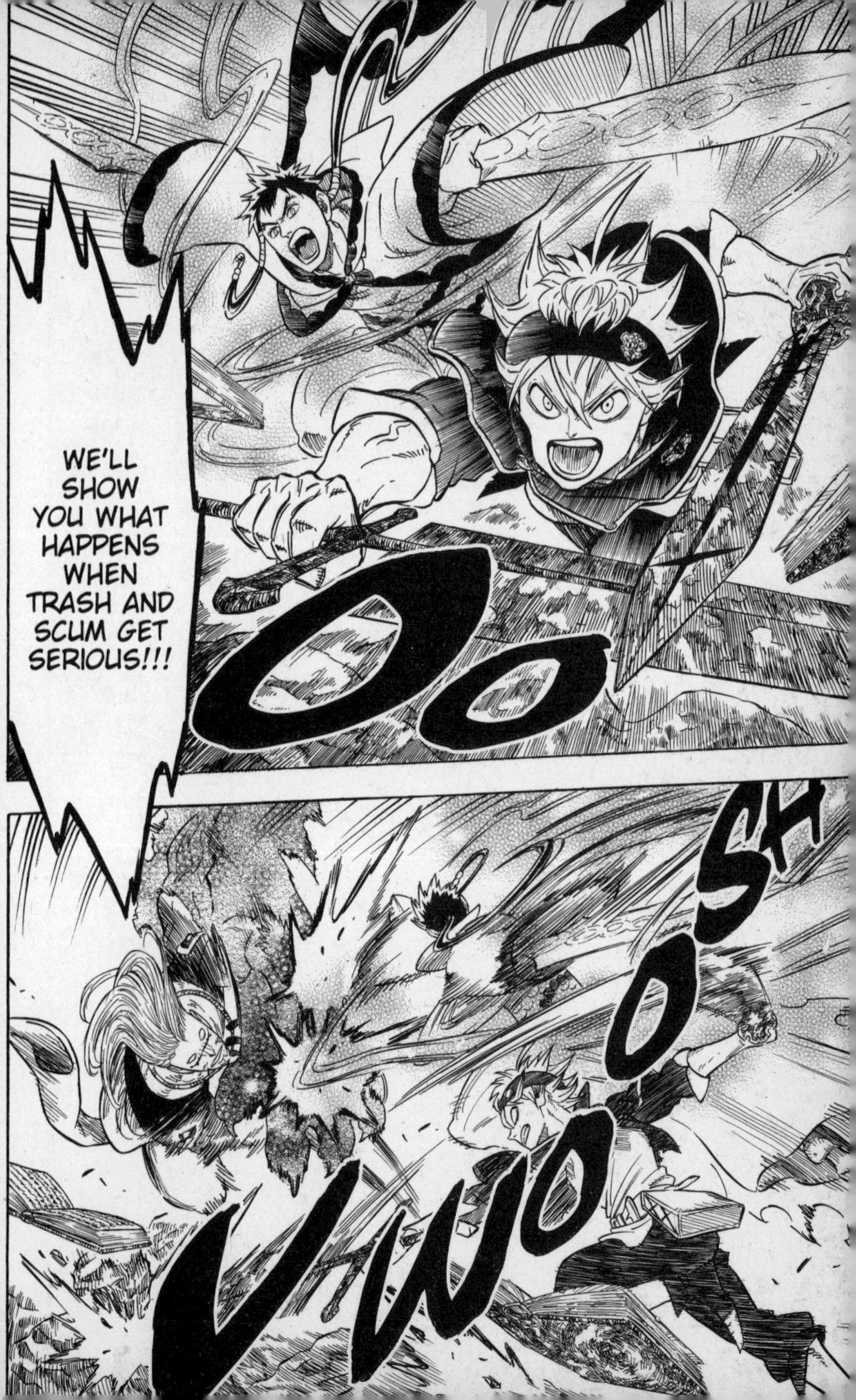
WE'LL SHOW YOU WHAT HAPPENS WHEN TRASH AND SCUM GET SERIOUS!!!
DO
VWOOOSH

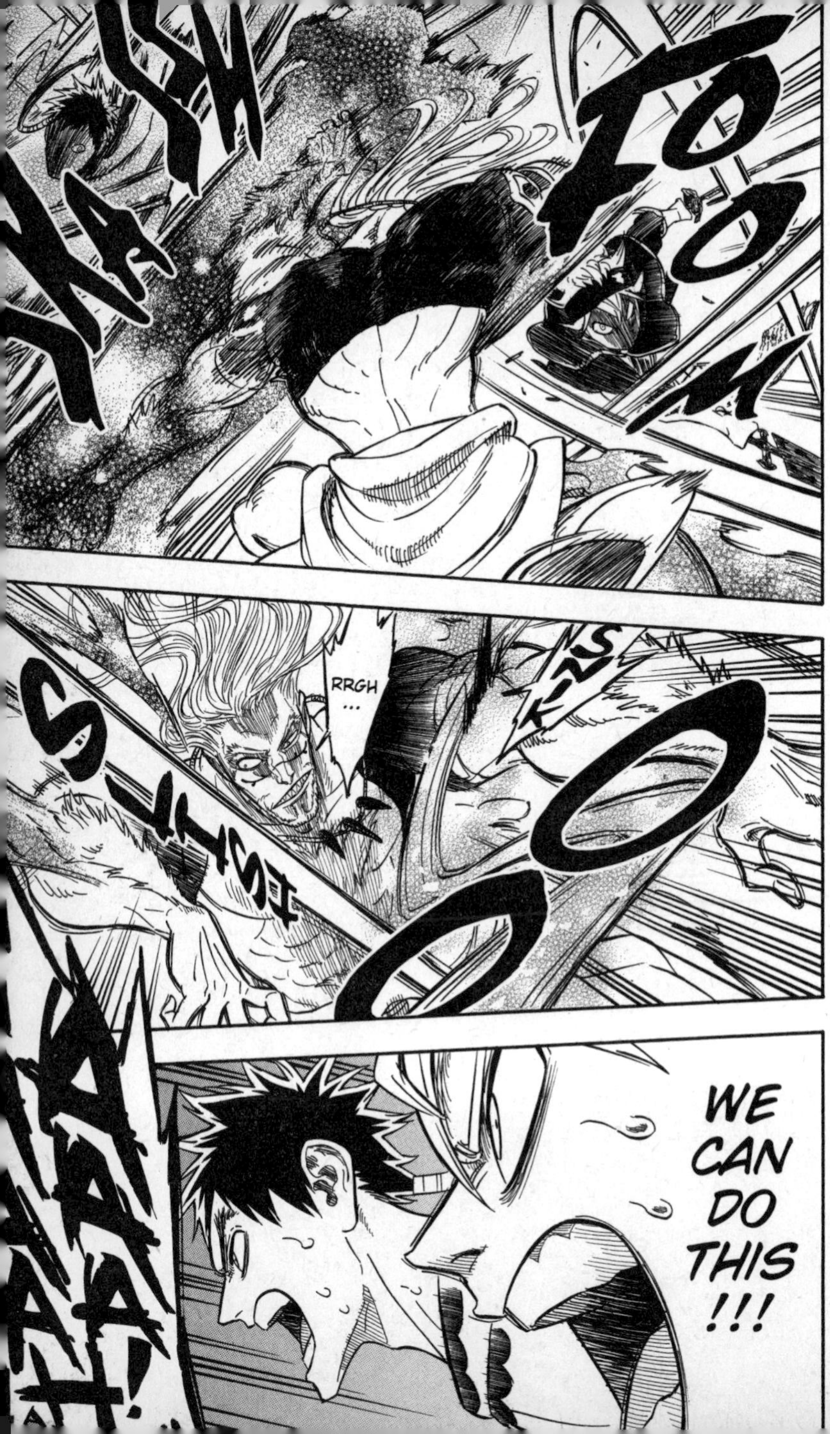
RRGH ...
WE CAN DO THIS!!!

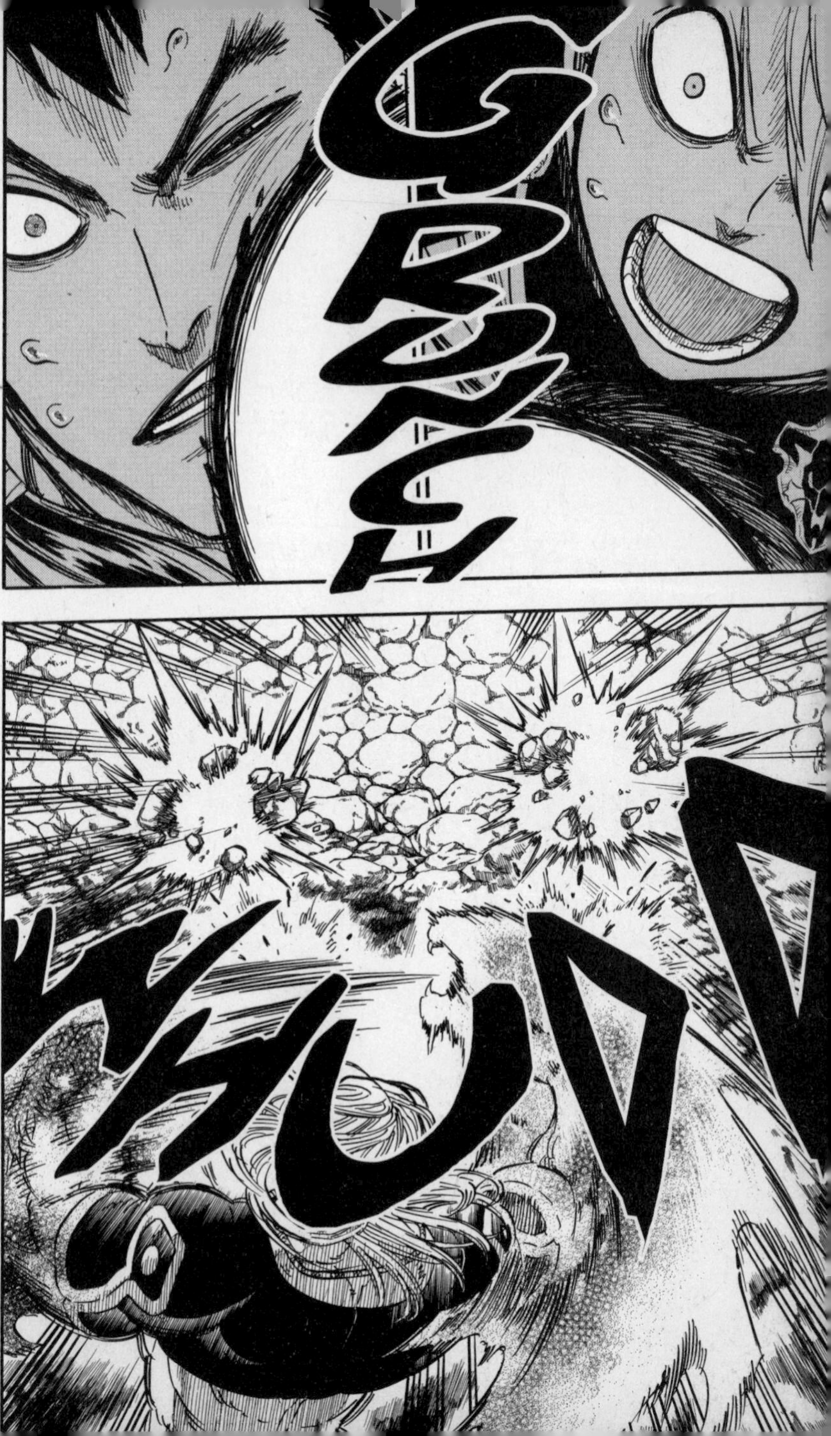

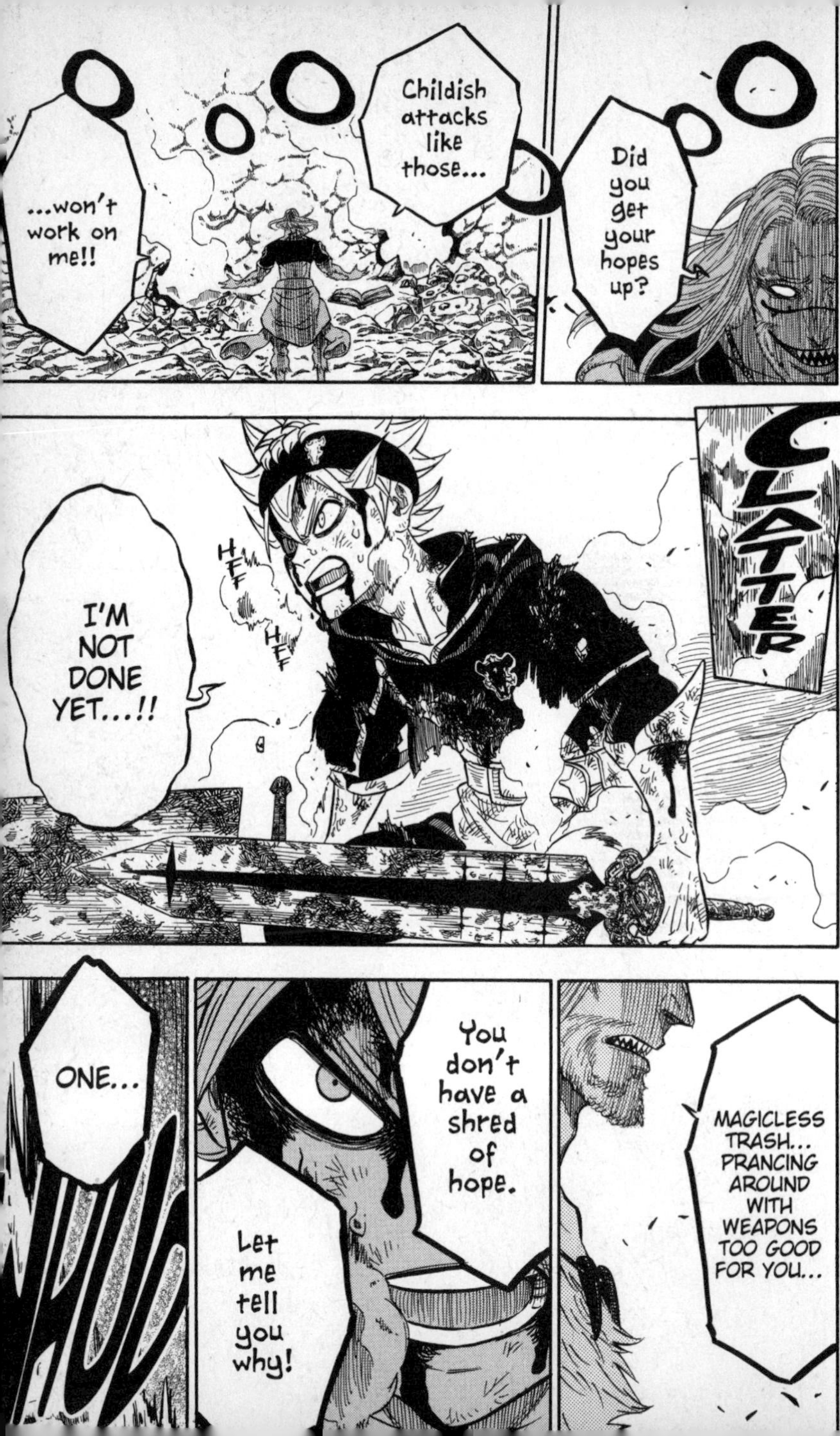
Did you get your hopes up?
Childish attacks like those...
...won't work on me!!
CLATTER
HFF
HFF
I'M NOT DONE YET...!!
MAGICLESS TRASH... PRANCING AROUND WITH WEAPONS TOO GOOD FOR YOU...
You don't have a shred of hope.
Let me tell you why!
ONE...

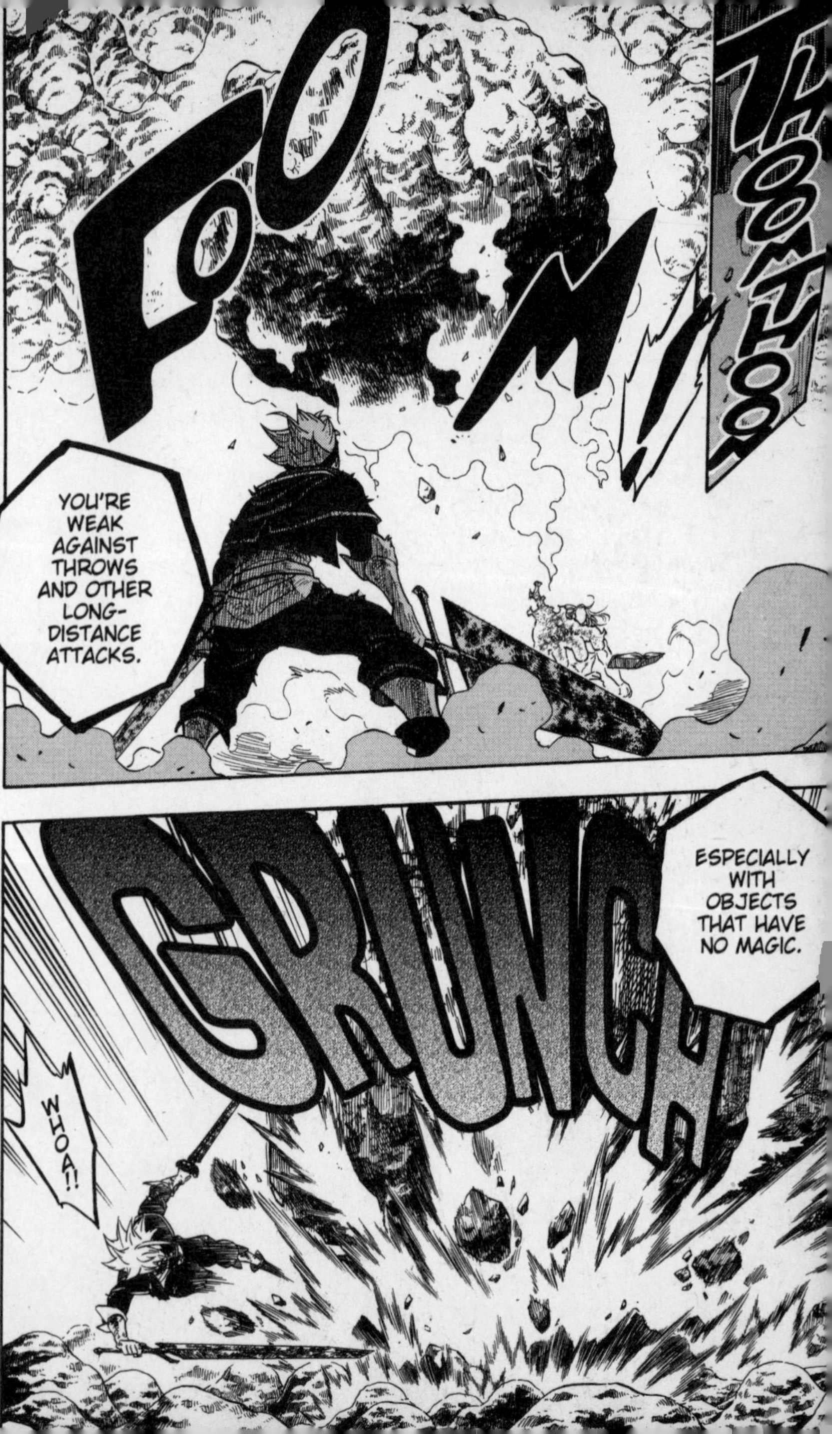
THOOOOM
FOOM!!
YOU'RE WEAK AGAINST THROWS AND OTHER LONG-DISTANCE ATTACKS.
ESPECIALLY WITH OBJECTS THAT HAVE NO MAGIC.
CRUNCH
WHOA!!

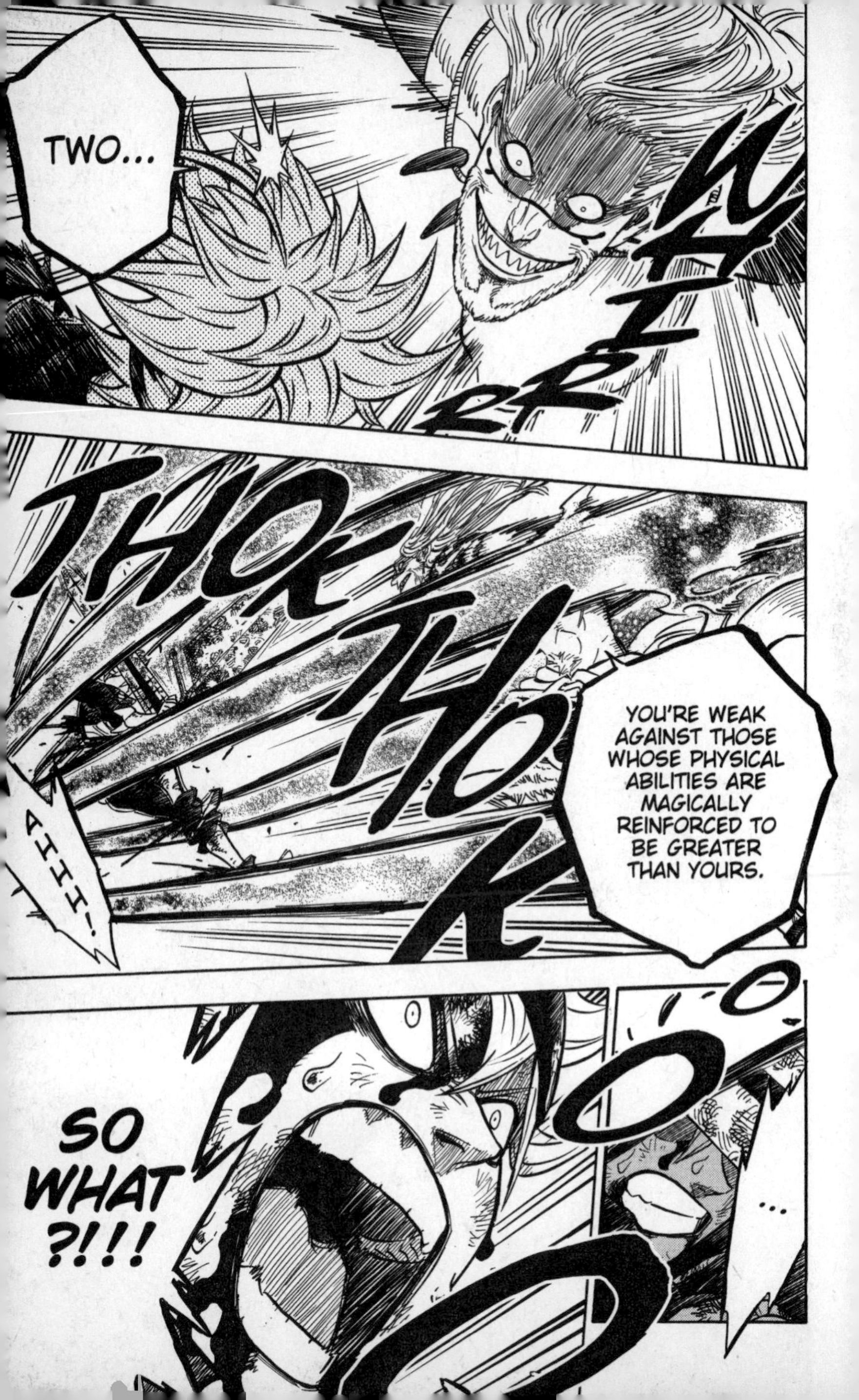
TWO...
WHIRR
YOU'RE WEAK AGAINST THOSE WHOSE PHYSICAL ABILITIES ARE MAGICALLY REINFORCED TO BE GREATER THAN YOURS.
THOK THOK
AHHH!
...
SO WHAT ?!!!

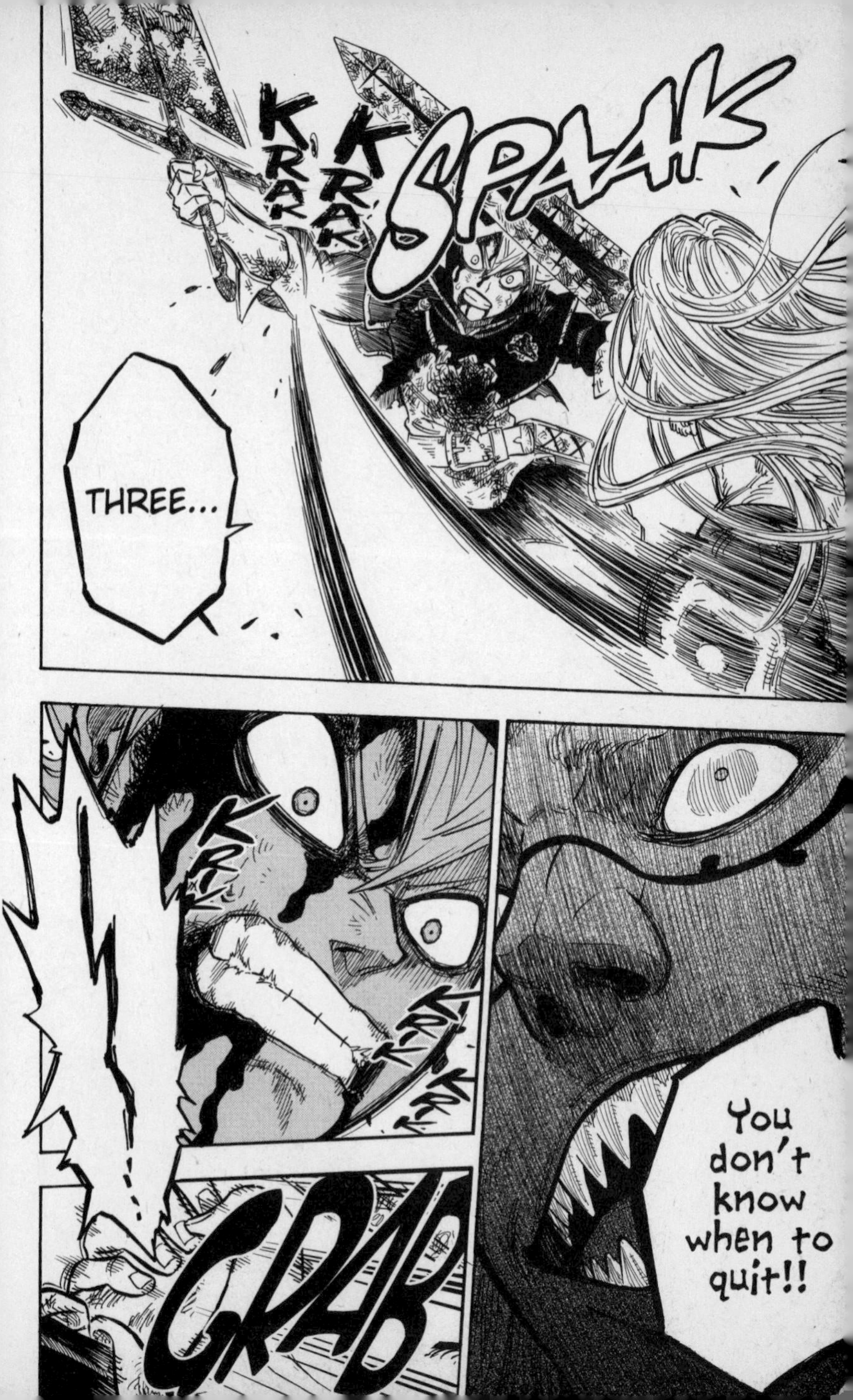
KRAK KRAK
SPAAK
THREE...
You don't know when to quit!!
KRIK KRIK
GRAB

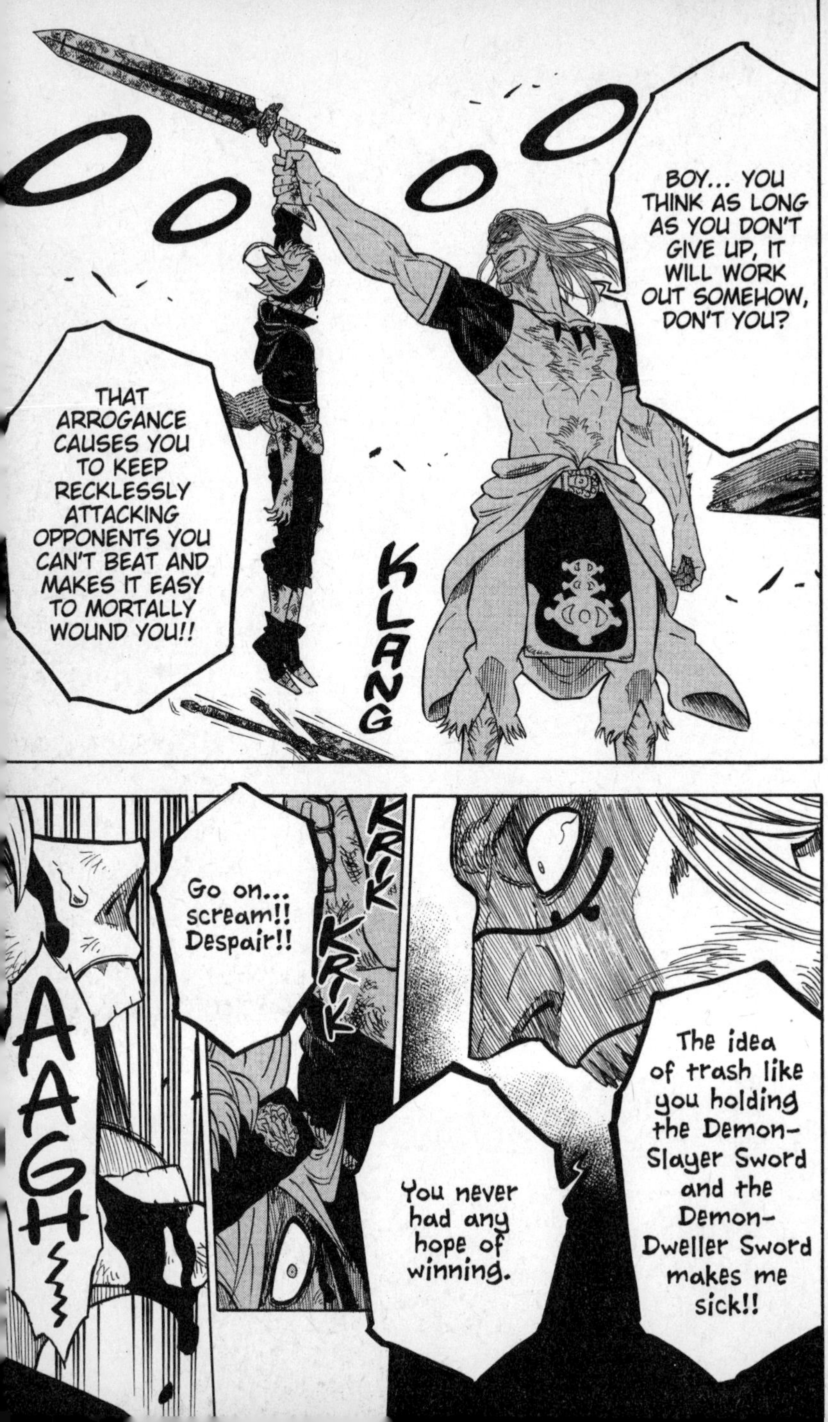
BOY... YOU THINK AS LONG AS YOU DON'T GIVE UP, IT WILL WORK OUT SOMEHOW, DON'T YOU?
THAT ARROGANCE CAUSES YOU TO KEEP RECKLESSLY ATTACKING OPPONENTS YOU CAN'T BEAT AND MAKES IT EASY TO MORTALLY WOUND YOU!!
KLANG
The idea of trash like you holding the Demon-Slayer Sword and the Demon-Dweller Sword makes me sick!!
You never had any hope of winning.
KRIK KRIK
Go on... scream!! Despair!!
AAAGH

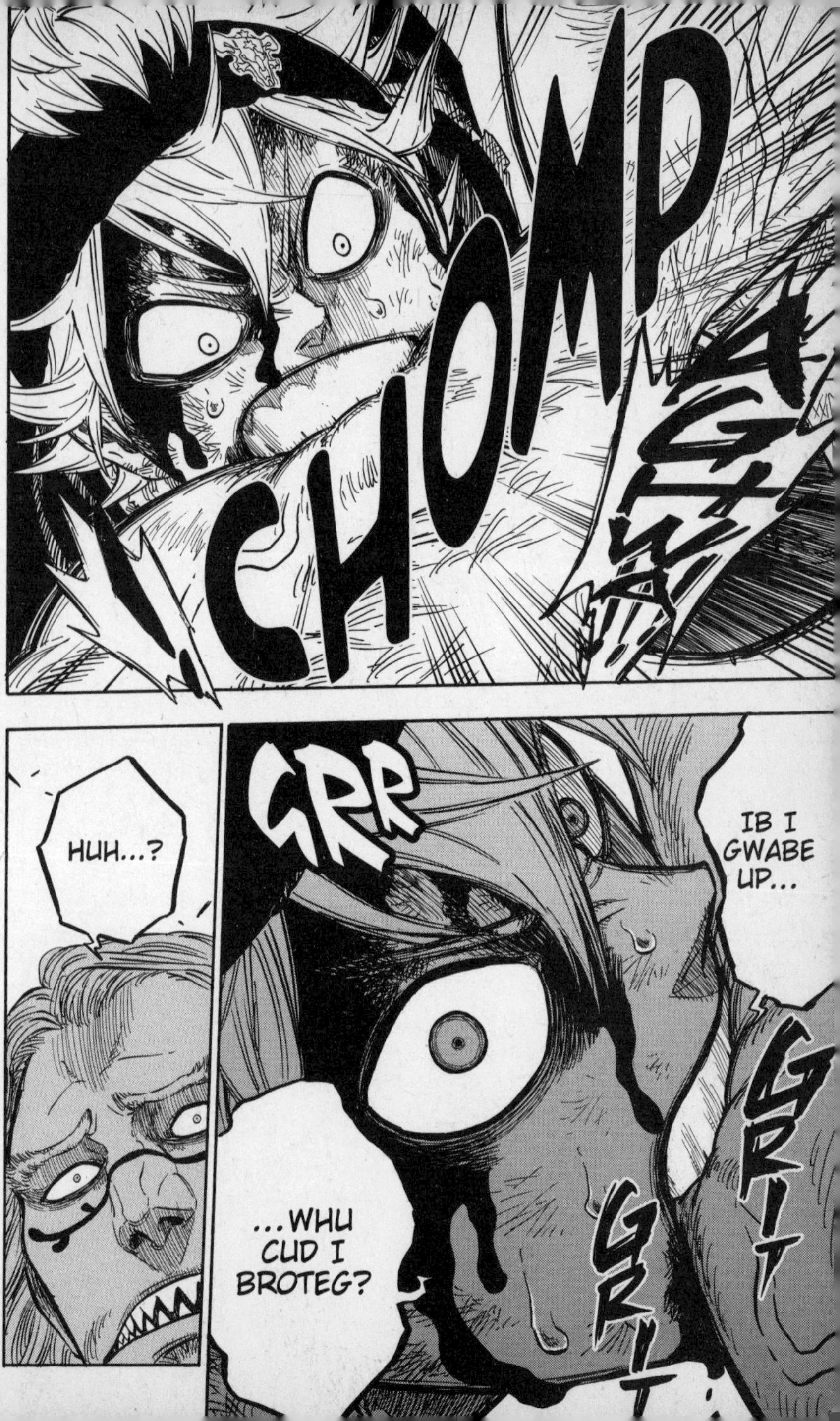
CHOMP
GRR
IB I GWABE UP...
...WHU CUD I BROTEG?
GRIT
GRIT
HUH...?

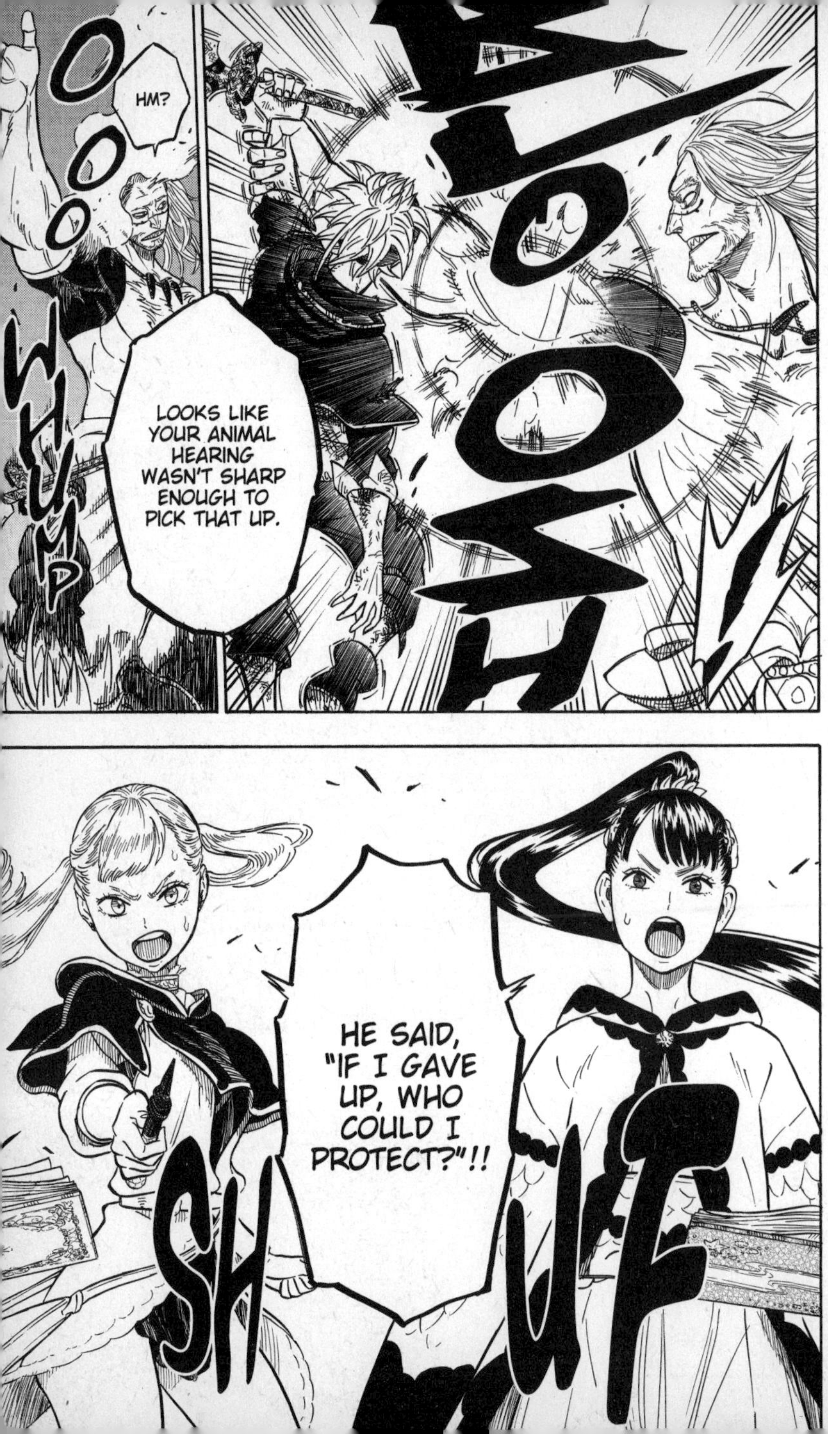

HM?
WHUMP
LOOKS LIKE YOUR ANIMAL HEARING WASN'T SHARP ENOUGH TO PICK THAT UP.
HE SAID, "IF I GAVE UP, WHO COULD I PROTECT?"!!

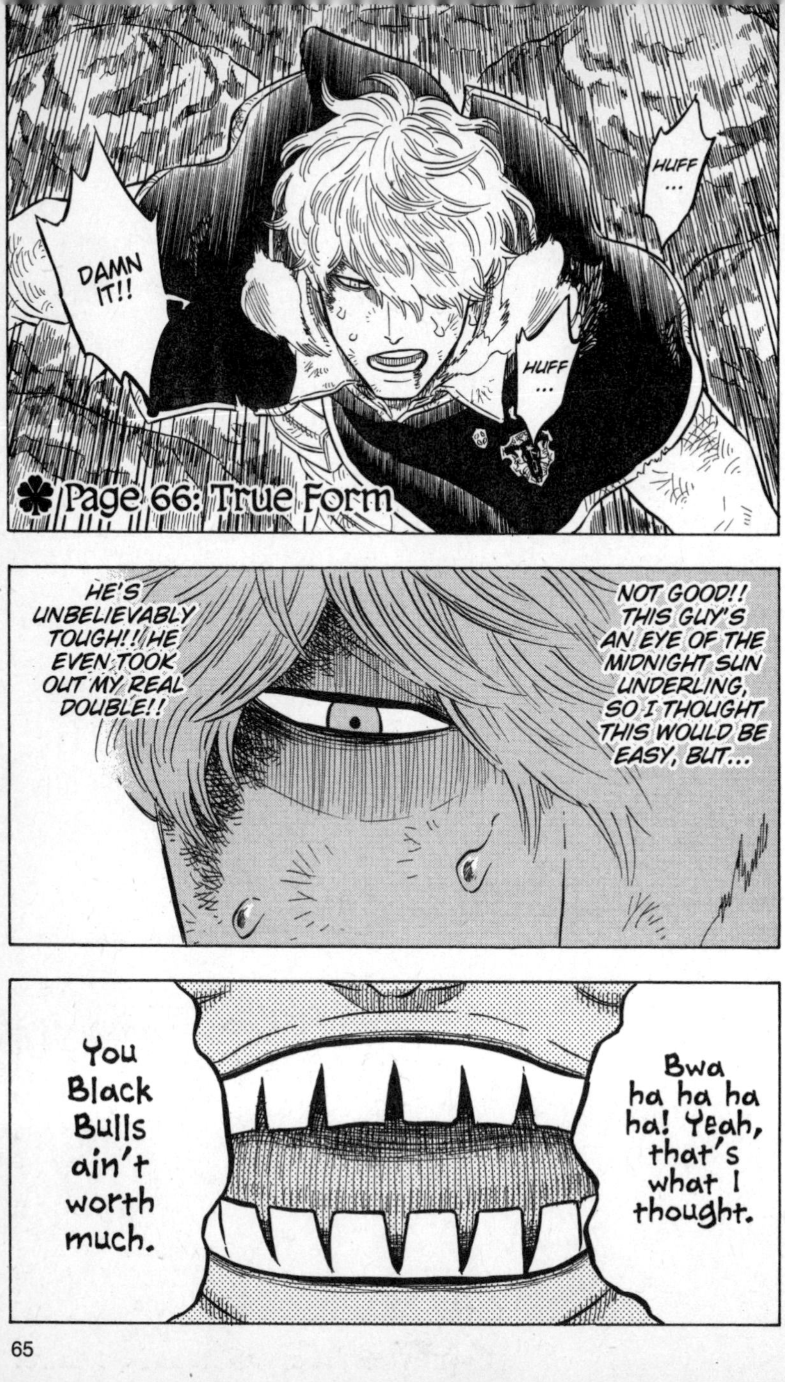
Page 66: True Form
HUFF ...
HUFF ...
DAMN IT!!
NOT GOOD!! THIS GUY'S AN EYE OF THE MIDNIGHT SUN UNDERLING, SO I THOUGHT THIS WOULD BE EASY, BUT...
HE'S UNBELIEVABLY TOUGH!! HE EVEN TOOK OUT MY REAL DOUBLE!!
Bwa ha ha ha ha! Yeah, that's what I thought.
You Black Bulls ain't worth much.

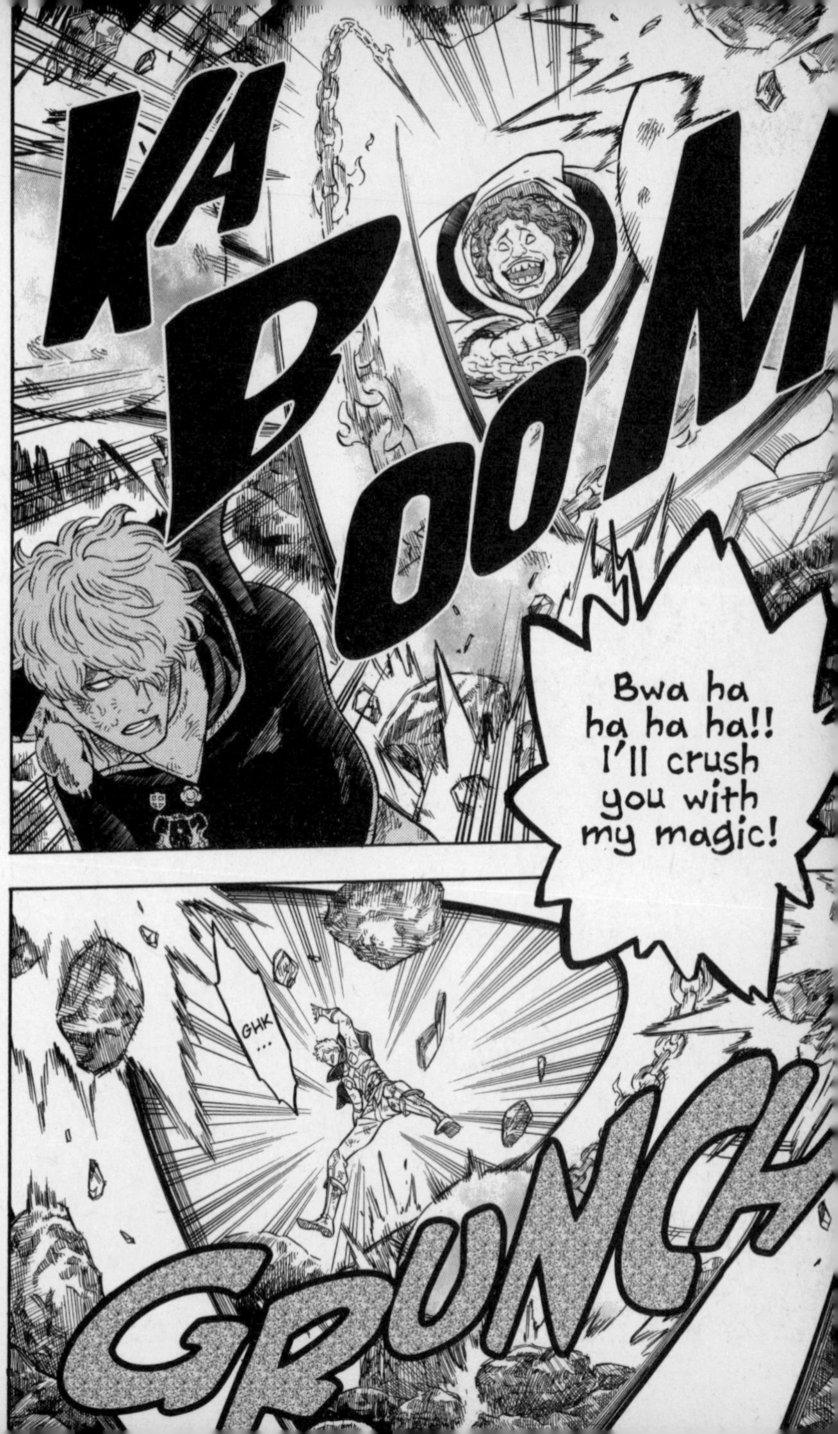
KA BOOM
Bwa ha ha ha ha!! I'll crush you with my magic!
CRUNCH
GHK...

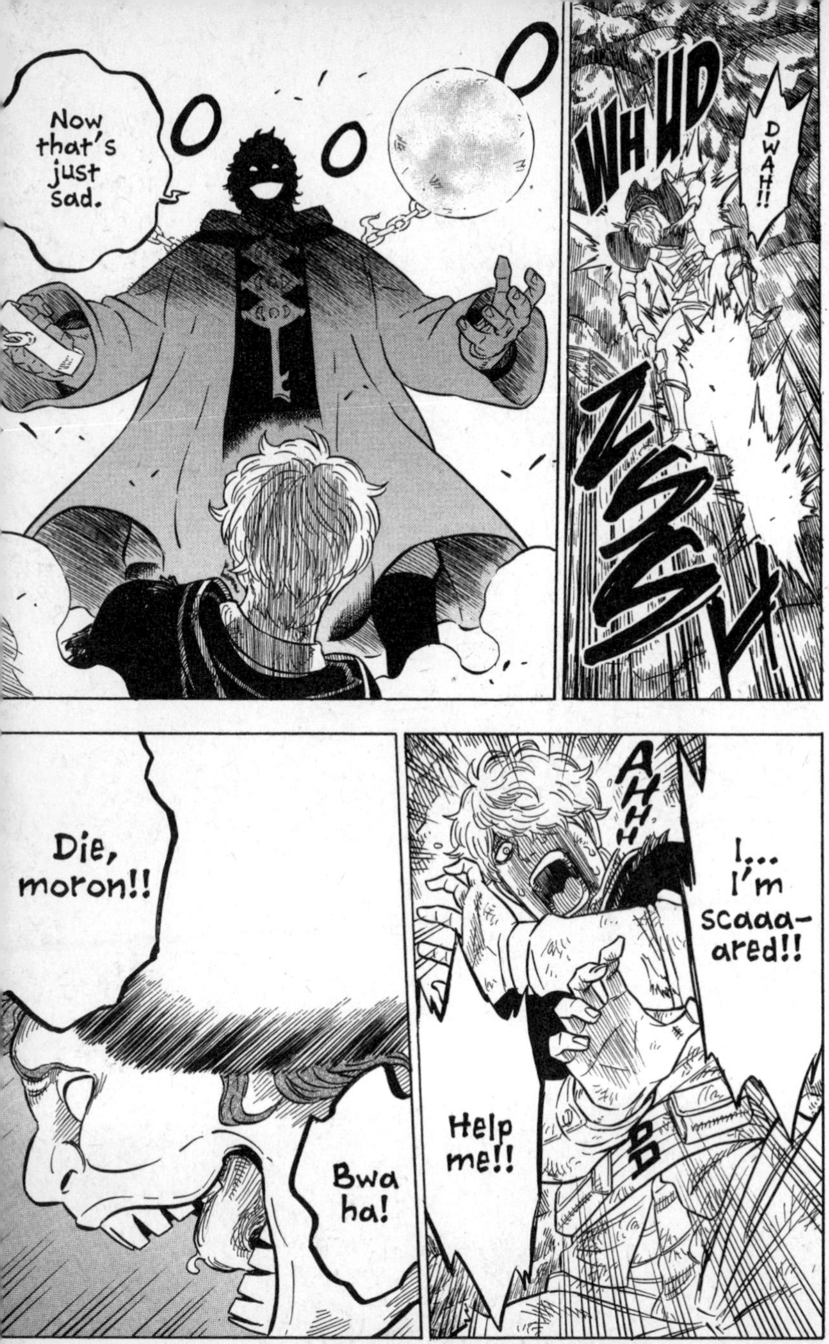
WHUD
DWAH!!
Now that's just sad.
AHHH
I... I'm scaaa-ared!!
Help me!!
Die, moron!!
Bwa ha!

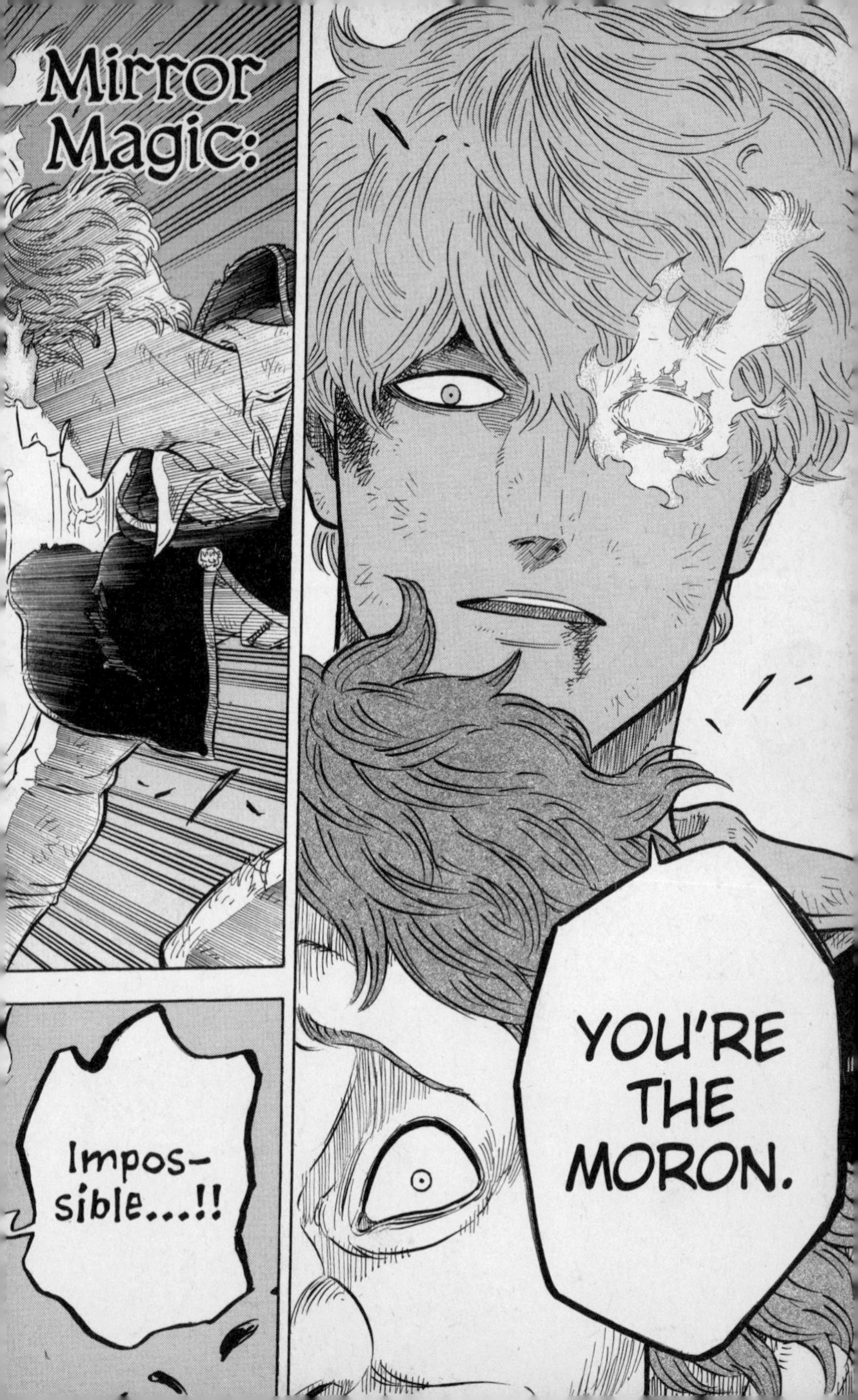
YOU'RE THE MORON.
Mirror Magic:
Impos-sible...!!

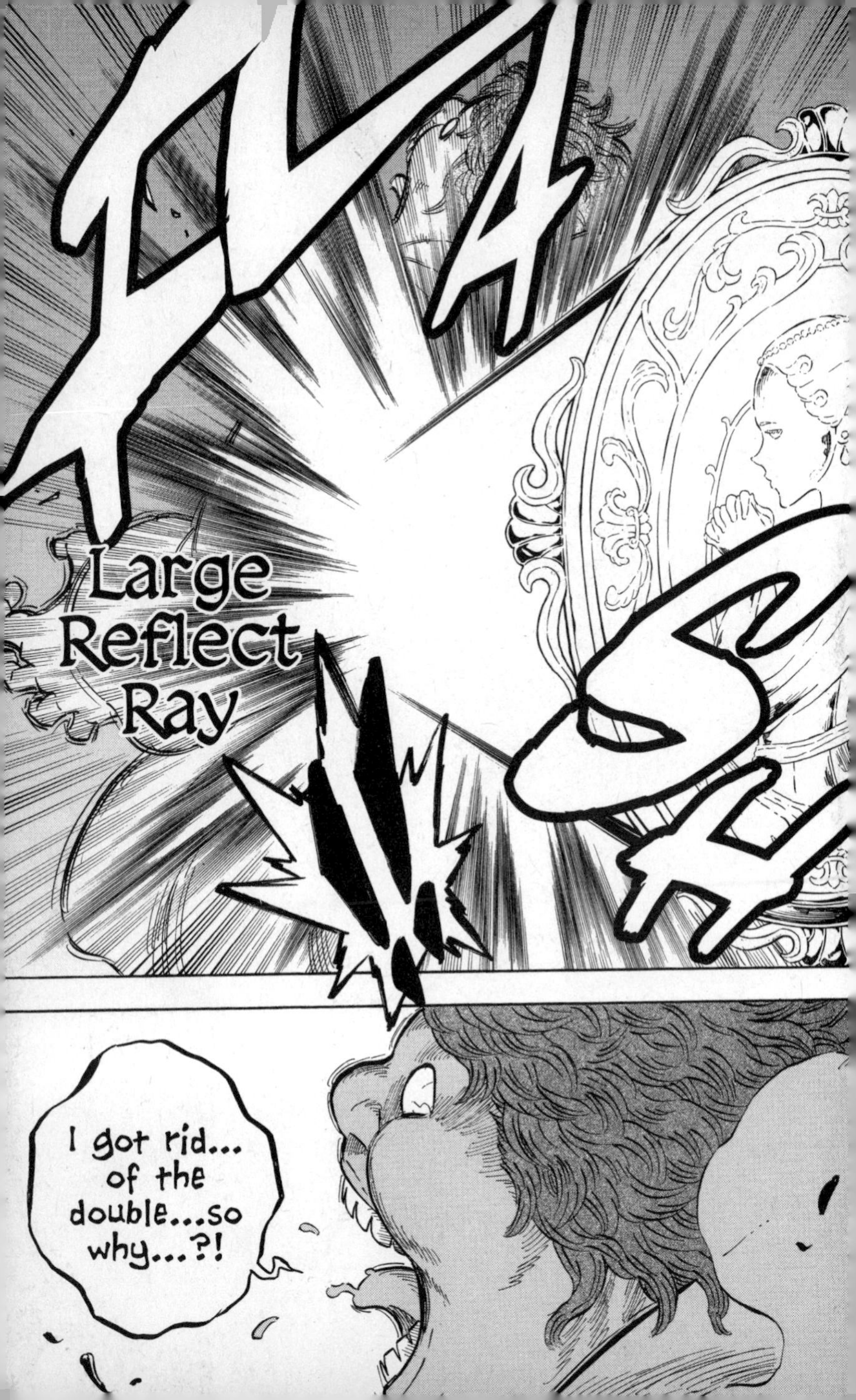
Large Reflect Ray
I got rid... of the double...so why...?!

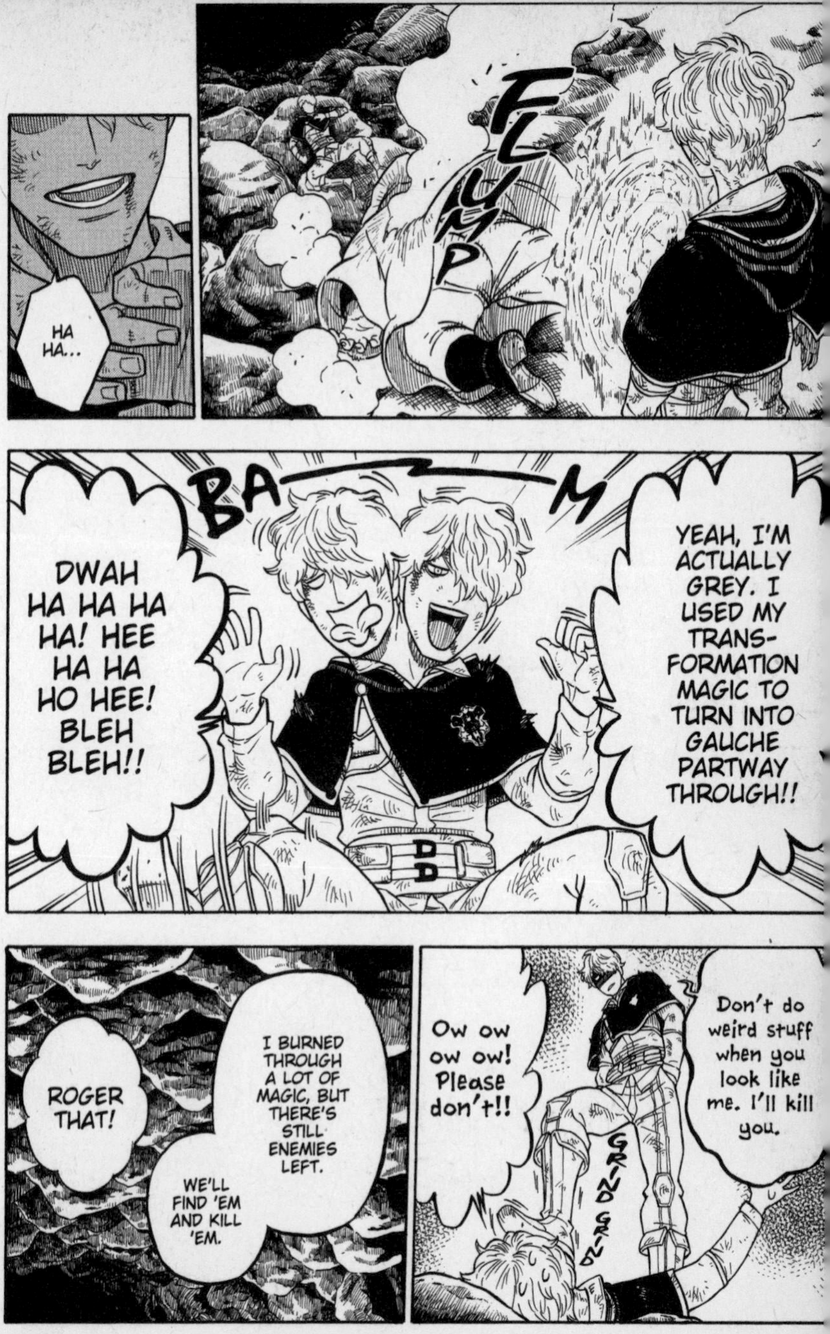
FLUMP
HA HA...
BAM
YEAH, I'M ACTUALLY GREY. I USED MY TRANS-FORMATION MAGIC TO TURN INTO GAUCHE PARTWAY THROUGH!!
DWAH HA HA HA HA! HEE HA HA HO HEE! BLEH BLEH!!
Don't do weird stuff when you look like me. I'll kill you.
Ow ow ow ow! Please don't!!
GRIND GRIND
I BURNED THROUGH A LOT OF MAGIC, BUT THERE'S STILL ENEMIES LEFT.
WE'LL FIND 'EM AND KILL 'EM.
ROGER THAT!

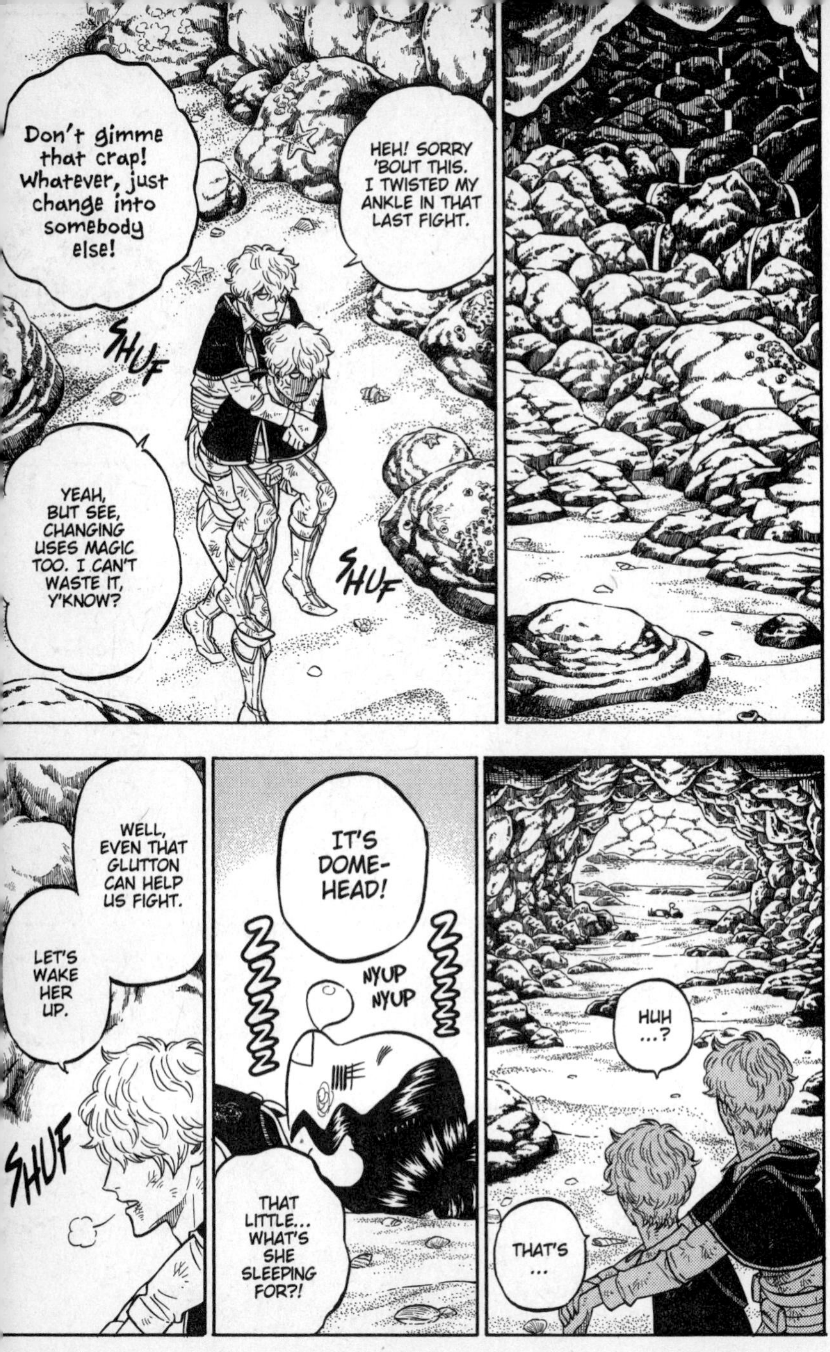
HEH! SORRY 'BOUT THIS. I TWISTED MY ANKLE IN THAT LAST FIGHT.
Don't gimme that crap! Whatever, just change into somebody else!
SHUF
YEAH, BUT SEE, CHANGING USES MAGIC TOO. I CAN'T WASTE IT, Y'KNOW?
SHUF
HUH ...?
THAT'S ...
IT'S DOME-HEAD!
ZZZZZ
NYUP NYUP
ZZZZZ
THAT LITTLE... WHAT'S SHE SLEEPING FOR?!
WELL, EVEN THAT GLUTTON CAN HELP US FIGHT.
LET'S WAKE HER UP.
SHUF

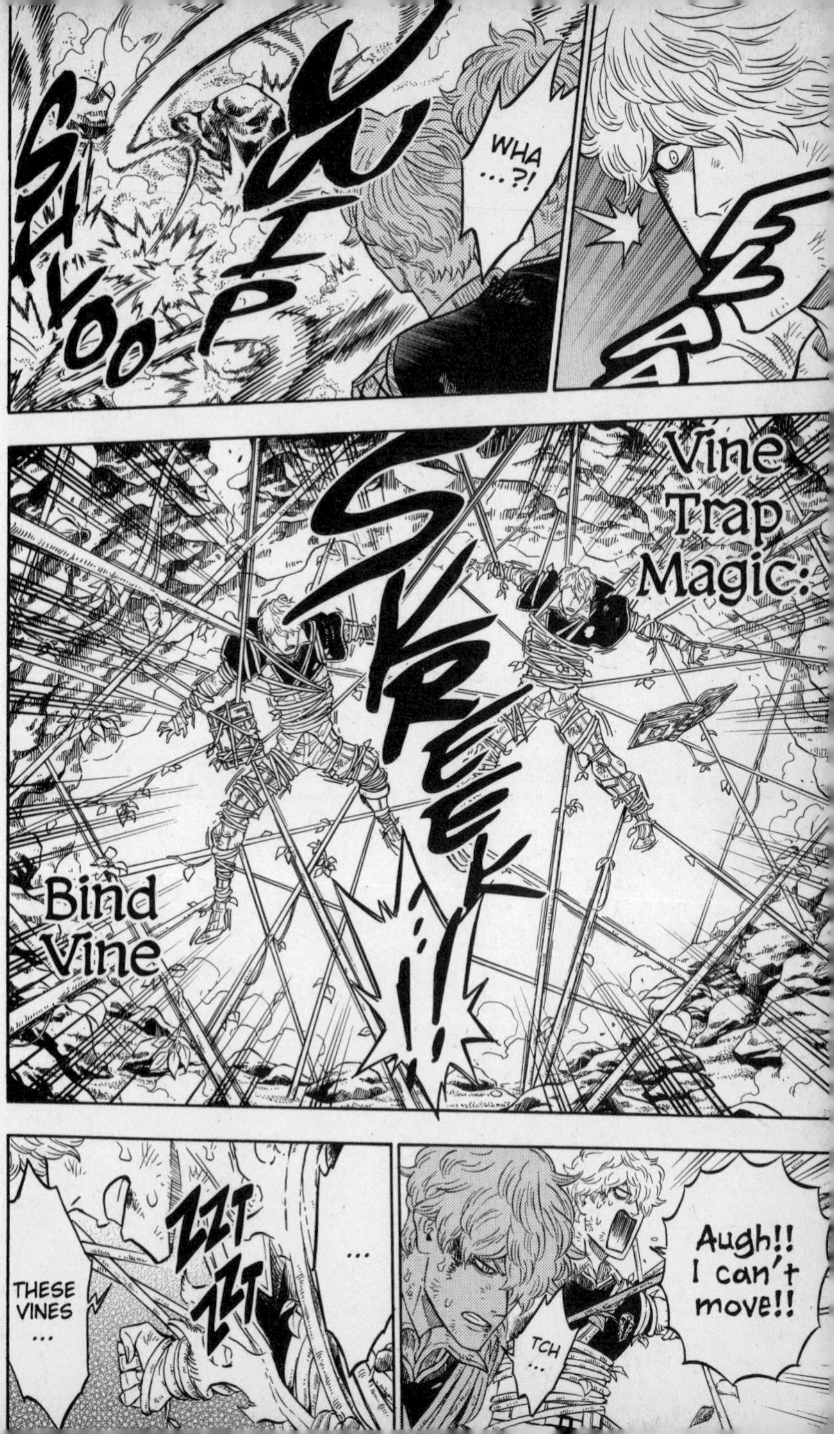
WHA ...?!
WHIP
SHVOOO
Vine Trap Magic:
SKREEK!!
Bind Vine
Augh!! I can't move!!
TCH ...
...
ZZT ZZT
THESE VINES ...

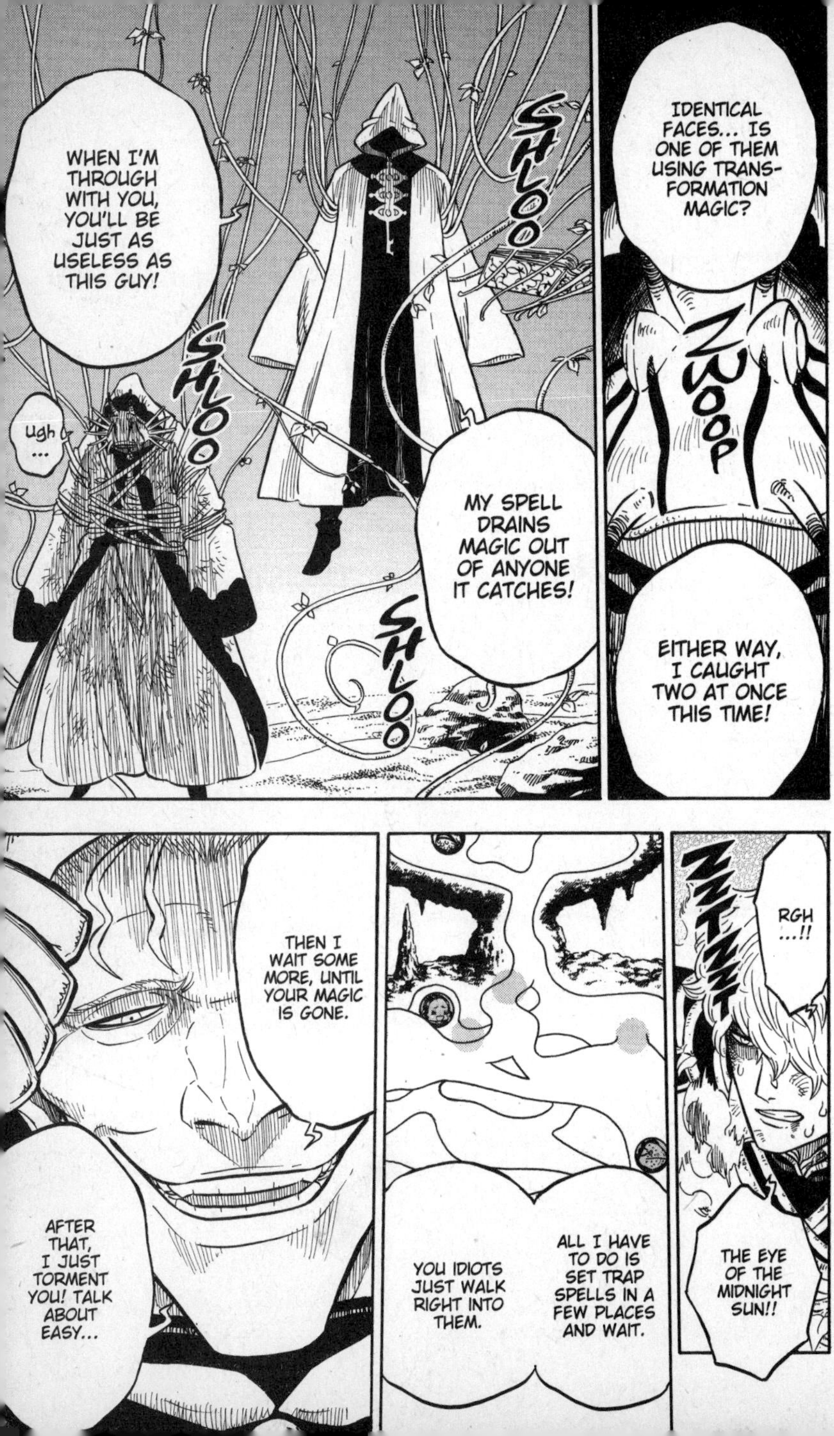
IDENTICAL FACES... IS ONE OF THEM USING TRANSFORMATION MAGIC?
ZWOOP
EITHER WAY, I CAUGHT TWO AT ONCE THIS TIME!
SHLOOO
WHEN I'M THROUGH WITH YOU, YOU'LL BE JUST AS USELESS AS THIS GUY!
SHLOOO
Ugh...
MY SPELL DRAINS MAGIC OUT OF ANYONE IT CATCHES!
SHLOOO
ZZZT
RGH...!!
THE EYE OF THE MIDNIGHT SUN!!
ALL I HAVE TO DO IS SET TRAP SPELLS IN A FEW PLACES AND WAIT.
YOU IDIOTS JUST WALK RIGHT INTO THEM.
THEN I WAIT SOME MORE, UNTIL YOUR MAGIC IS GONE.
AFTER THAT, I JUST TORMENT YOU! TALK ABOUT EASY...

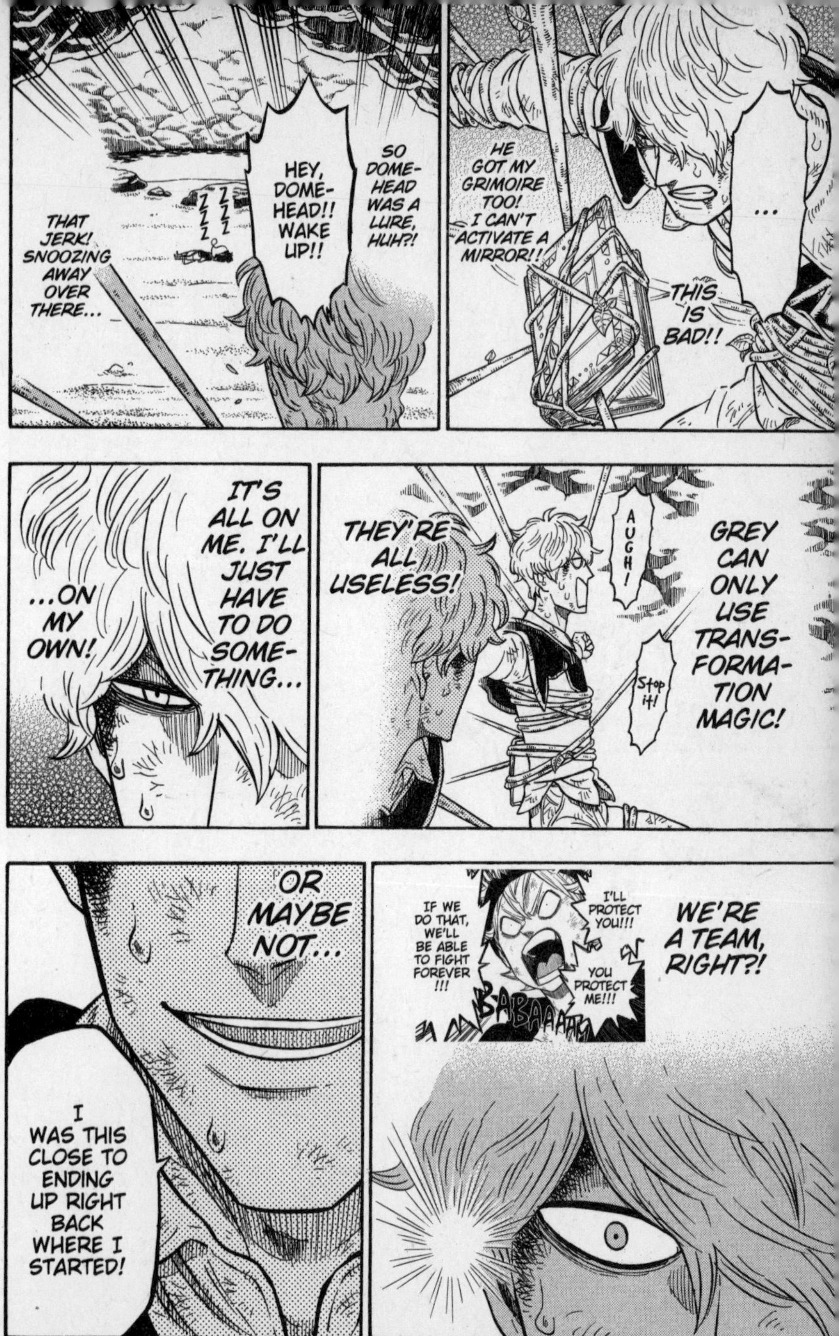
...
HE GOT MY GRIMOIRE TOO! I CAN'T ACTIVATE A MIRROR!!
THIS IS BAD!!
SO DOME-HEAD WAS A LURE, HUH?!
HEY, DOME-HEAD!! WAKE UP!!
Z Z Z Z Z Z Z
THAT JERK! SNOOZING AWAY OVER THERE...
GREY CAN ONLY USE TRANSFORMATION MAGIC!
AUGH!
Stop it!
THEY'RE ALL USELESS!
IT'S ALL ON ME. I'LL JUST HAVE TO DO SOMETHING...
...ON MY OWN!
WE'RE A TEAM, RIGHT?!
I'LL PROTECT YOU!!!
YOU PROTECT ME!!!
IF WE DO THAT, WE'LL BE ABLE TO FIGHT FOREVER!!!
BABAAAM
OR MAYBE NOT...
I WAS THIS CLOSE TO ENDING UP RIGHT BACK WHERE I STARTED!

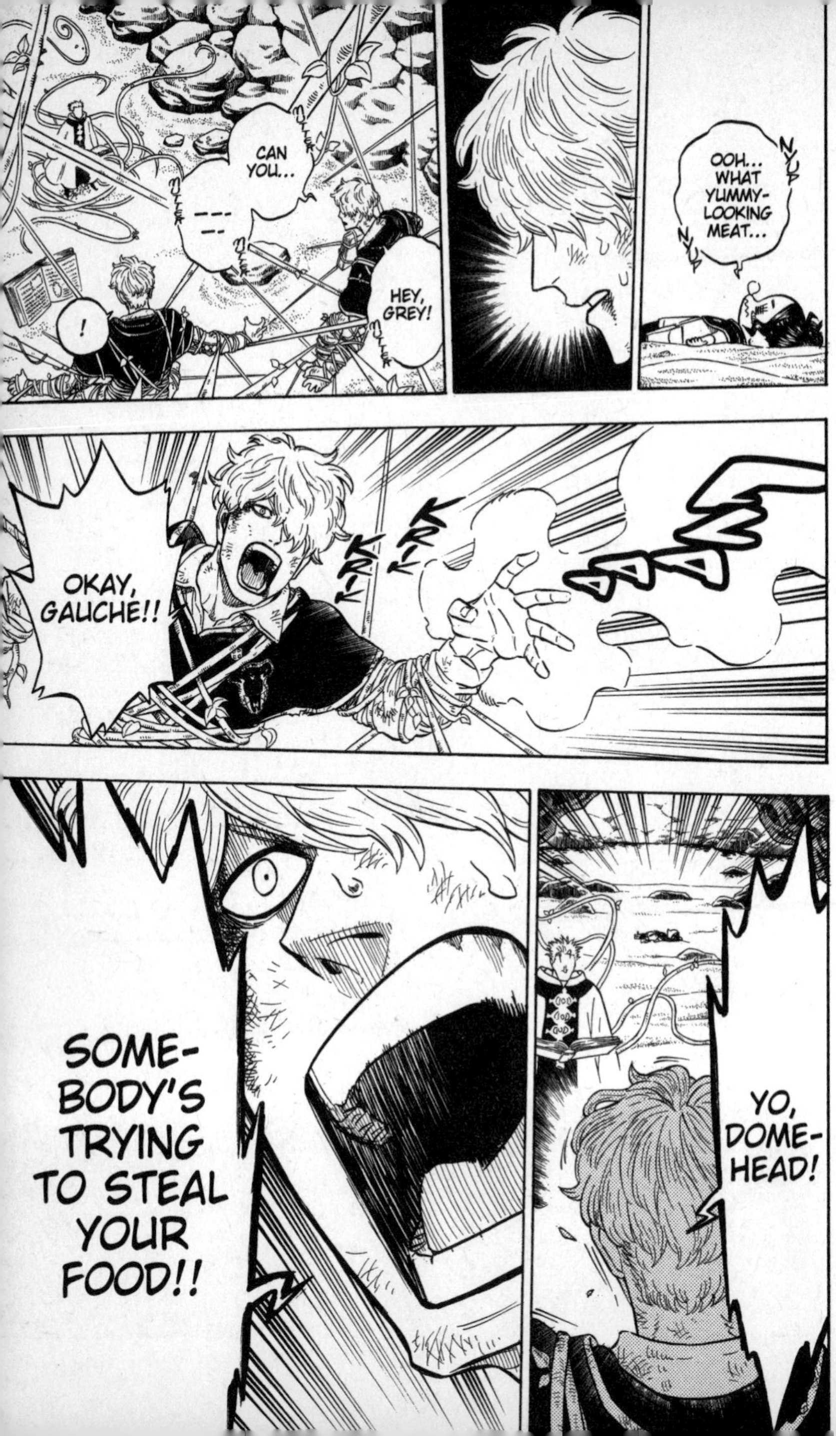
NYUP
OOH... WHAT YUMMY-LOOKING MEAT...
NYUP
HEY, GREY!
CAN YOU...
--- ---
!
OKAY, GAUCHE!!
YO, DOME-HEAD!
SOME-BODY'S TRYING TO STEAL YOUR FOOD!!

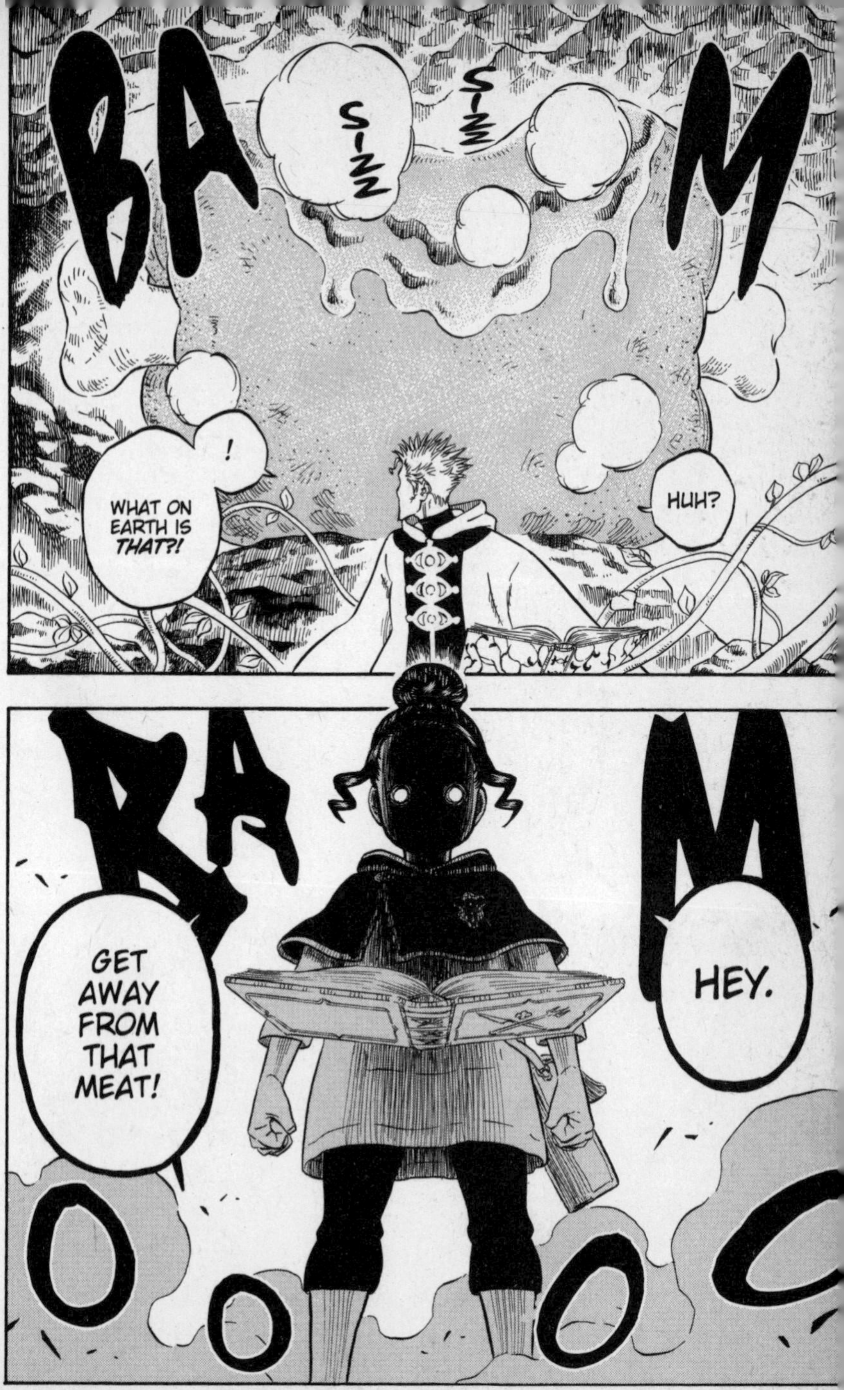
BAM
SIZZ
SIZZ
HUH?
!
WHAT ON EARTH IS *THAT?!*
BAM
HEY.
GET AWAY FROM THAT MEAT!

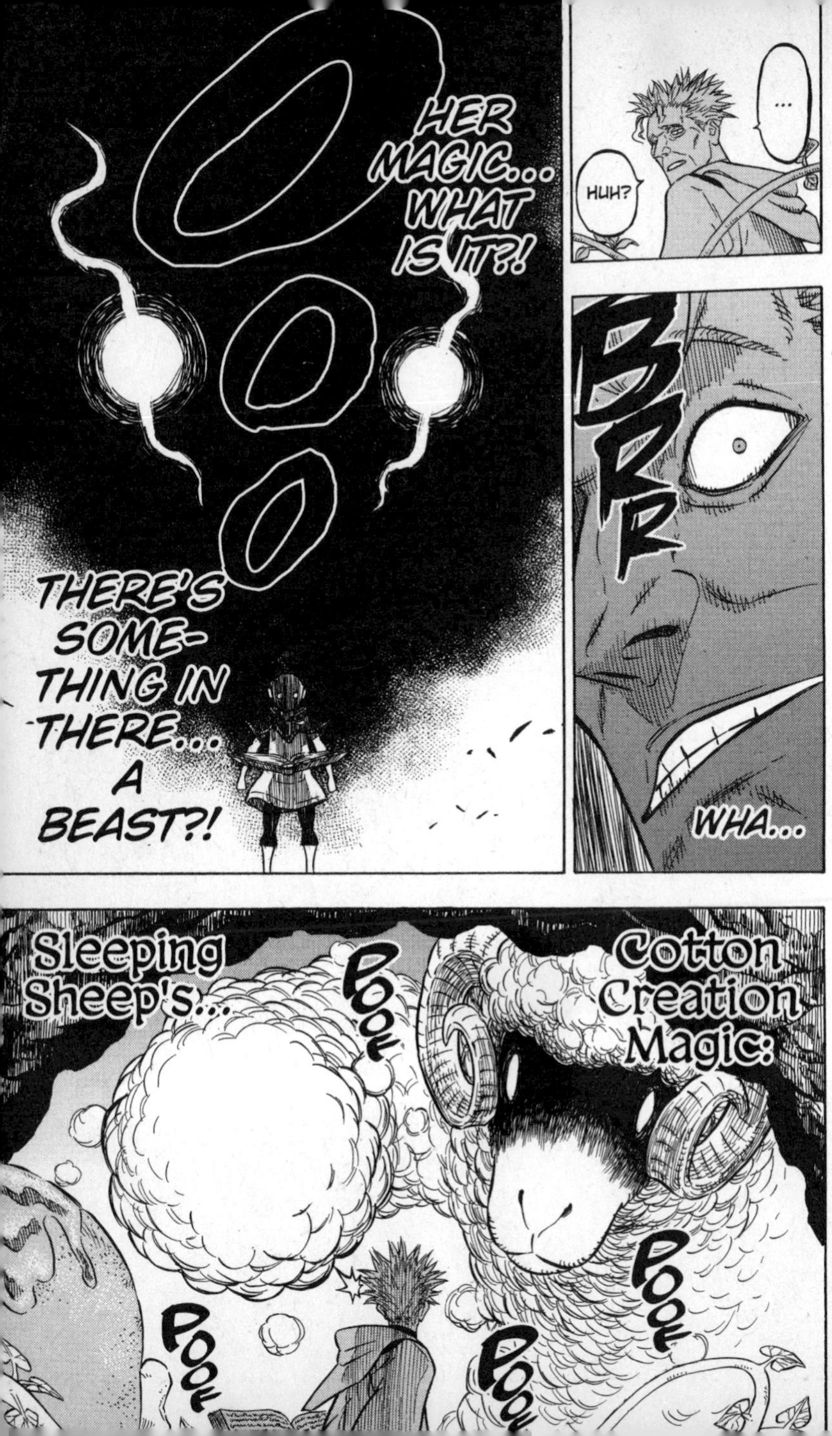
...
HUH?
BRR
WHA...
HER MAGIC... WHAT IS IT?!
THERE'S SOME-THING IN THERE... A BEAST?!
Cotton Creation Magic:
Sleeping Sheep's...
POOF
POOF
POOF
POOF

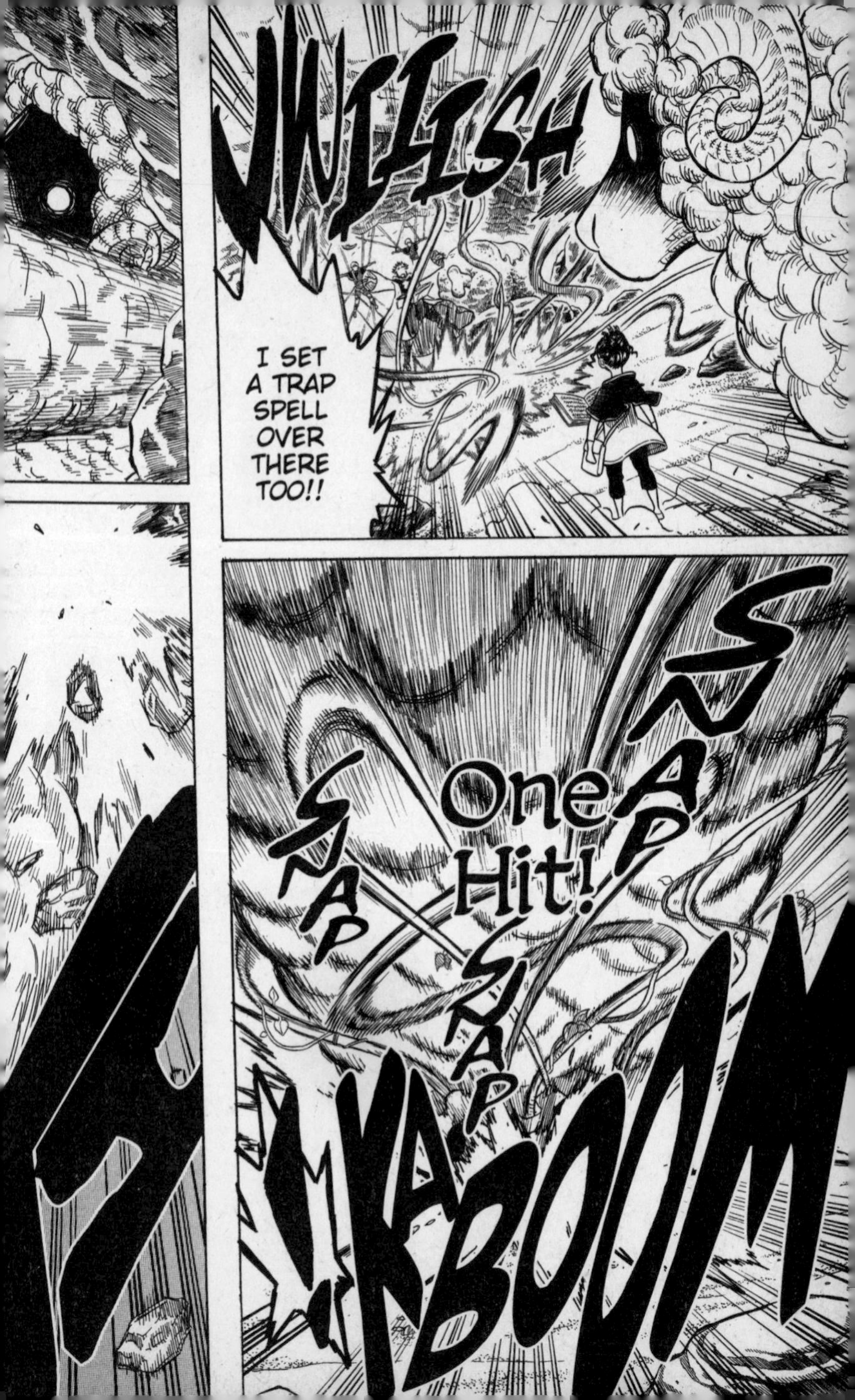
WHIISH
I SET A TRAP SPELL OVER THERE TOO!!
SNAP
One Hit!
SNAP
SNAP
KABOOM

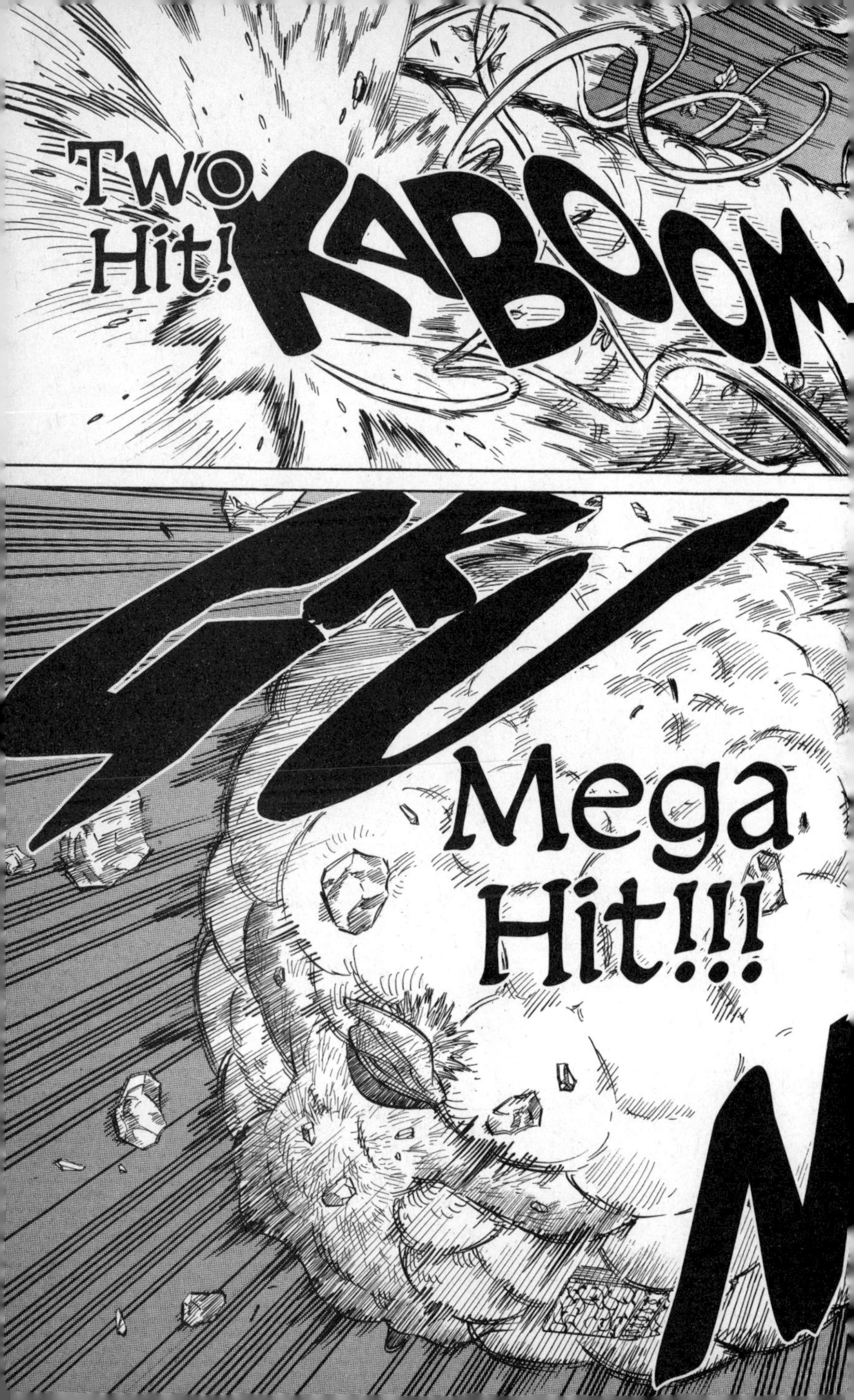
Two Hit!
KABOOM
Mega Hit!!!

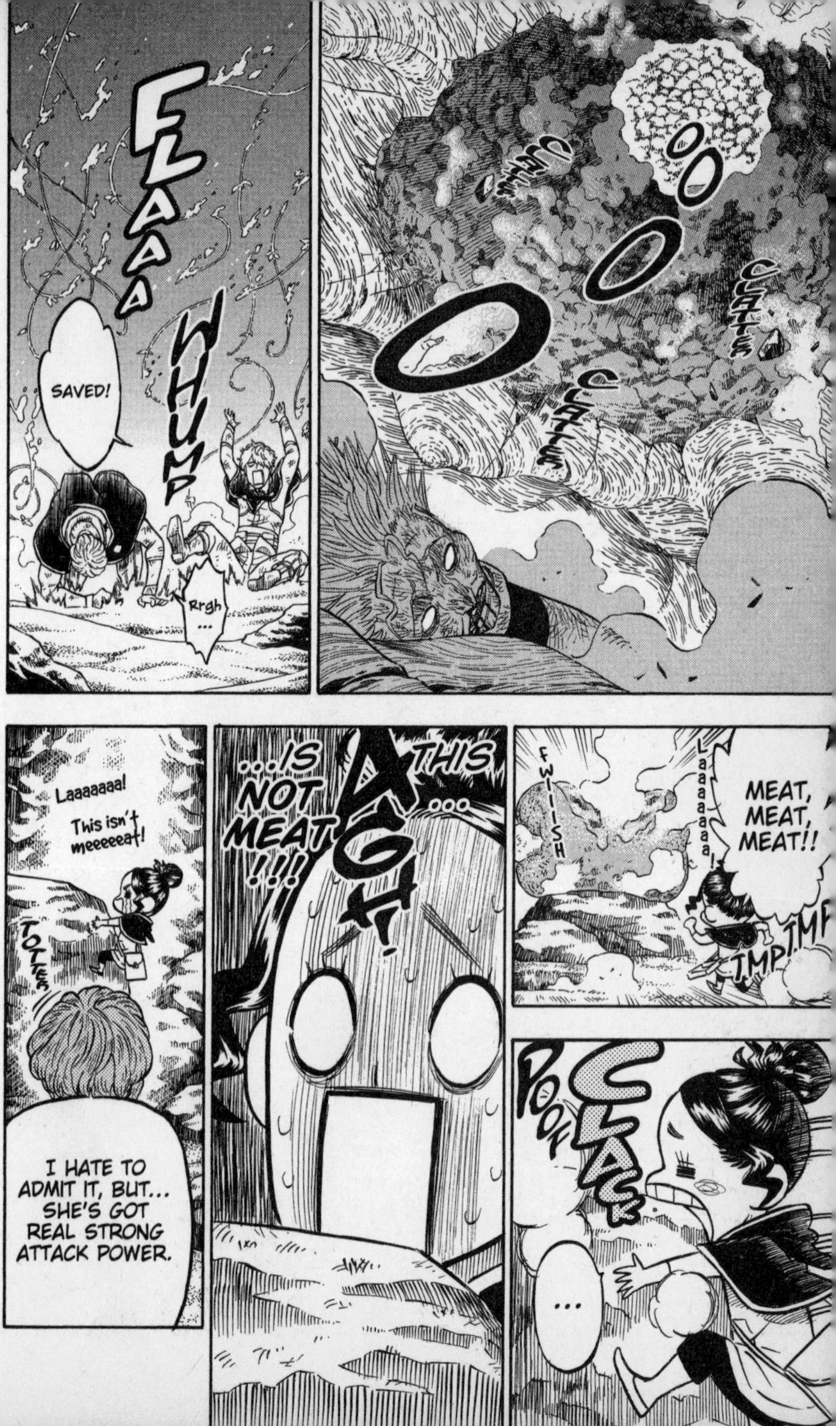
OOOO
CLATTER
CLATTER
CLATTER
FLAAAA
WHUMP
SAVED!
Rrgh...
MEAT, MEAT, MEAT!!
Laaaaaaa!
FWISH
TMP TMP
POON
CLACK
...
THIS...
...IS NOT MEAT!!!
AGH!
Laaaaaaa!
This isn't meeeeeat!
TOTTER
I HATE TO ADMIT IT, BUT... SHE'S GOT REAL STRONG ATTACK POWER.

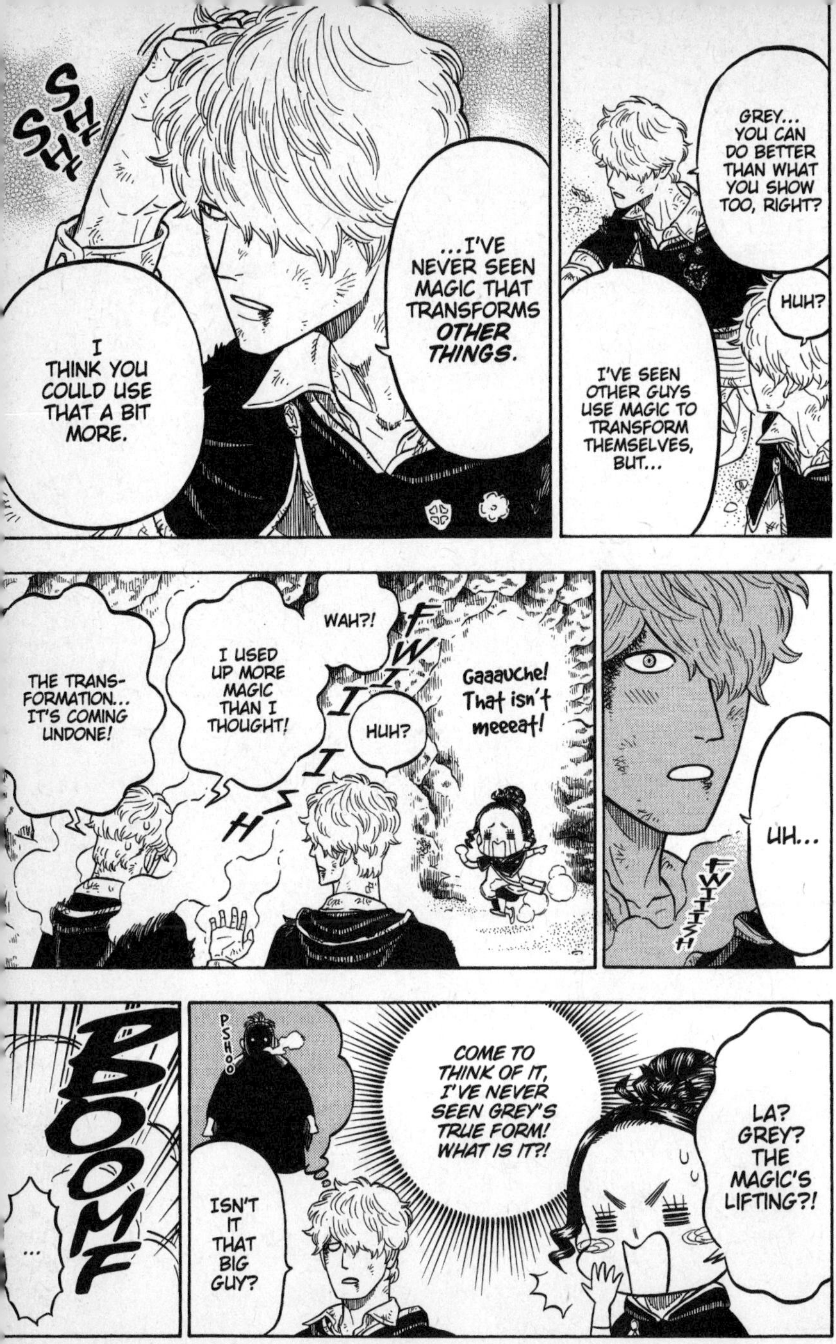
GREY... YOU CAN DO BETTER THAN WHAT YOU SHOW TOO, RIGHT?
HUH?
I'VE SEEN OTHER GUYS USE MAGIC TO TRANSFORM THEMSELVES, BUT...
...I'VE NEVER SEEN MAGIC THAT TRANSFORMS OTHER THINGS.
I THINK YOU COULD USE THAT A BIT MORE.
SHF SHF
UH...
FWIIISH
Gaaauche! That isn't meeeat!
HUH?
FWIIIISH
WAH?!
I USED UP MORE MAGIC THAN I THOUGHT!
THE TRANS-FORMATION... IT'S COMING UNDONE!
LA? GREY? THE MAGIC'S LIFTING?!
COME TO THINK OF IT, I'VE NEVER SEEN GREY'S TRUE FORM! WHAT IS IT?!
PSHOO
ISN'T IT THAT BIG GUY?
BOOMF
...

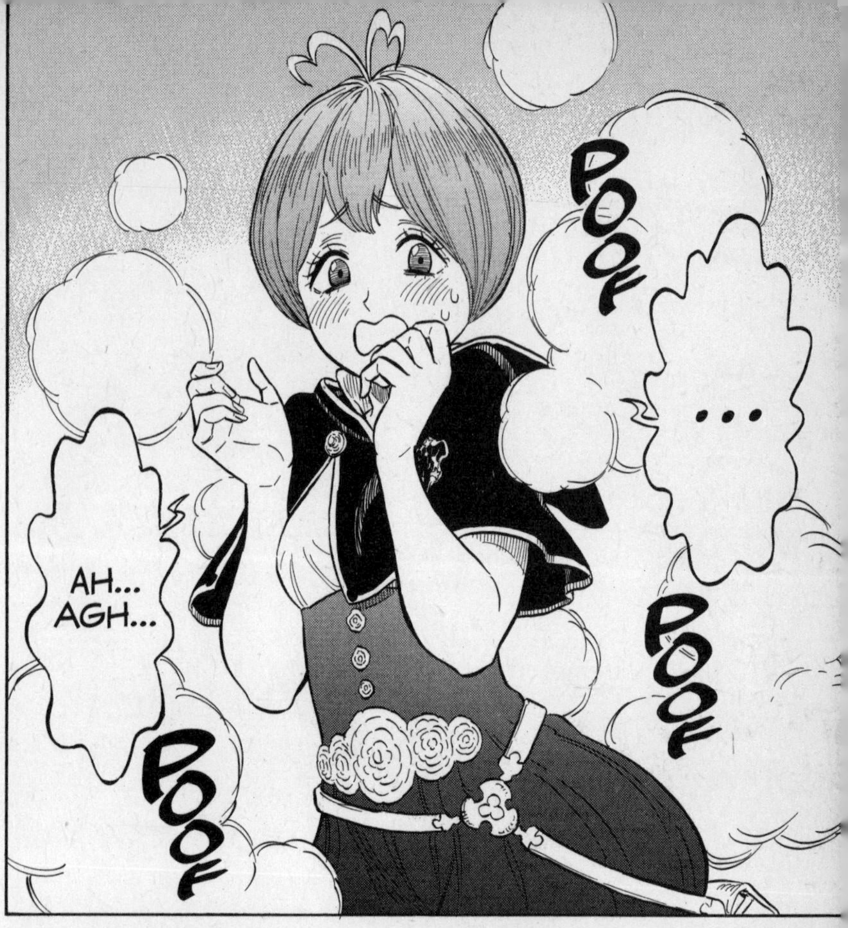
POOF
...
POOF
AH... AGH...
POOF

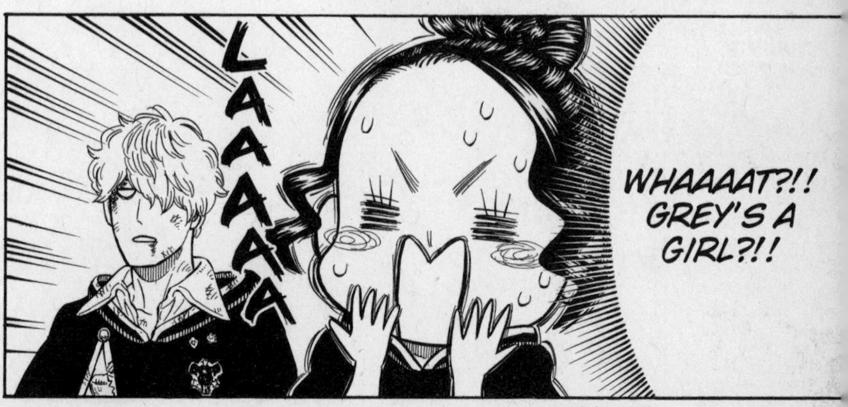
WHAAAAT?!! GREY'S A GIRL?!!
LAAAAAA

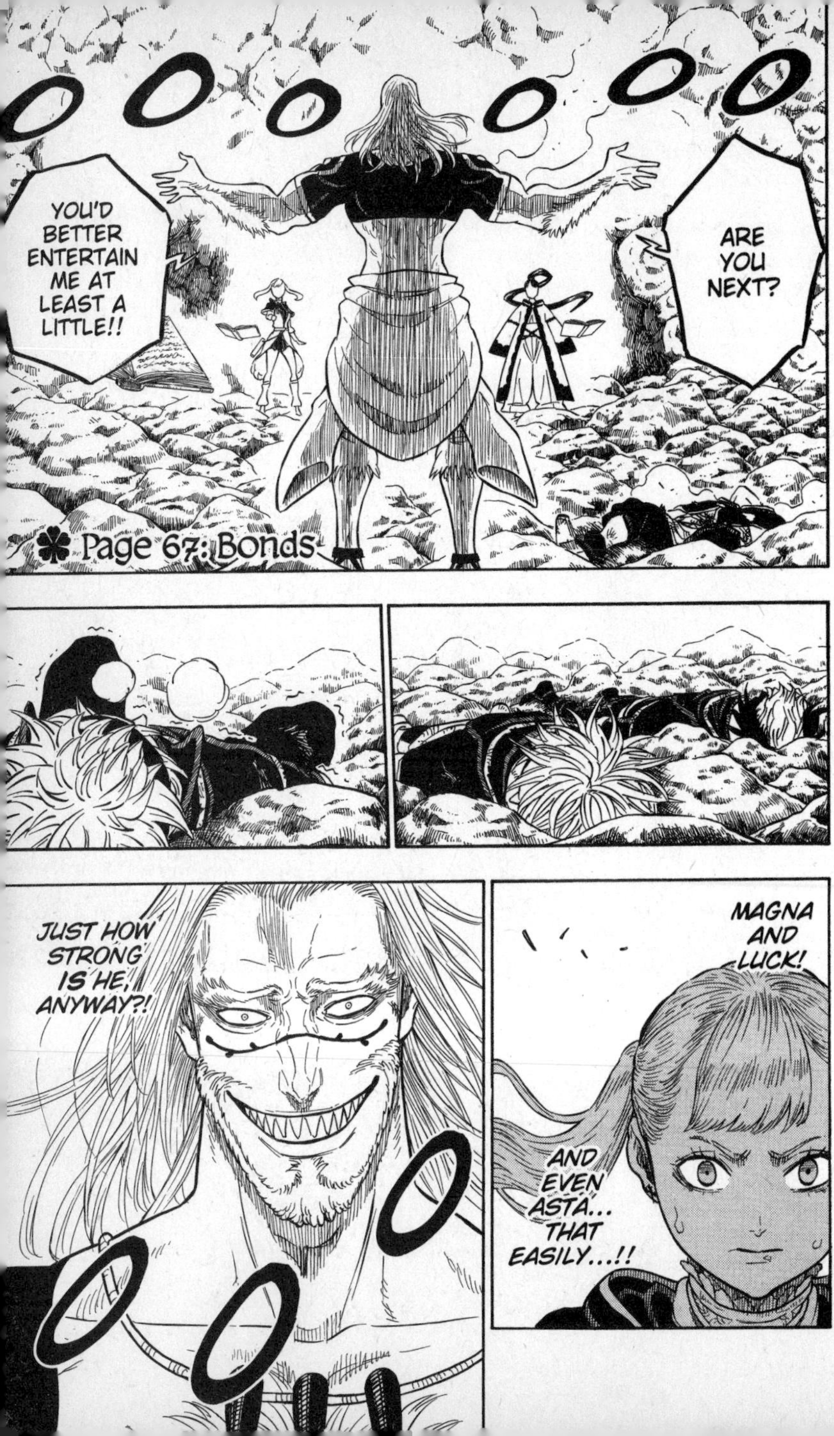
ARE YOU NEXT?
YOU'D BETTER ENTERTAIN ME AT LEAST A LITTLE!!
Page 67: Bonds
MAGNA AND LUCK!
AND EVEN ASTA... THAT EASILY...!!
JUST HOW STRONG IS HE, ANYWAY?!

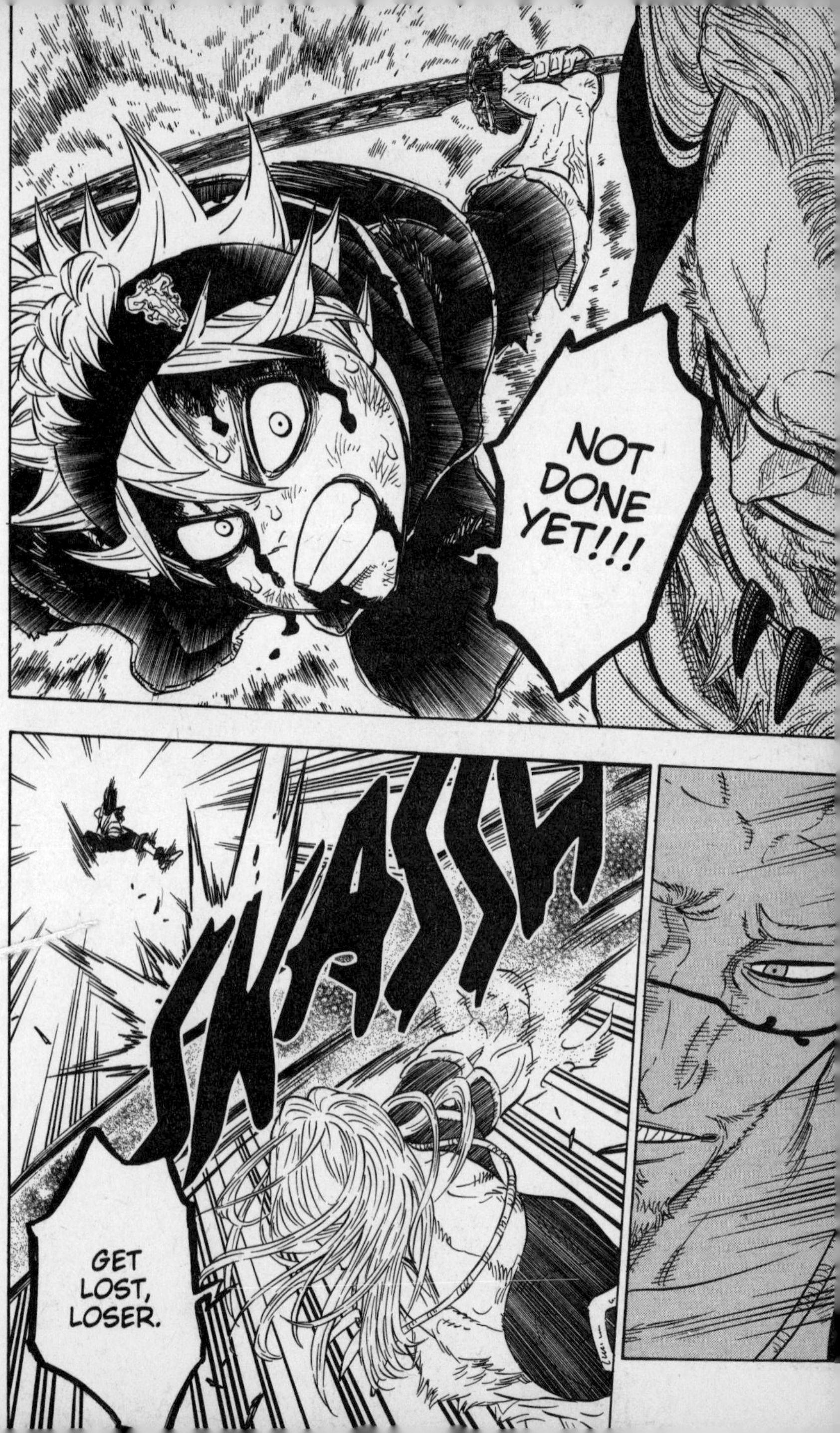
NOT DONE YET!!!
GET LOST, LOSER.

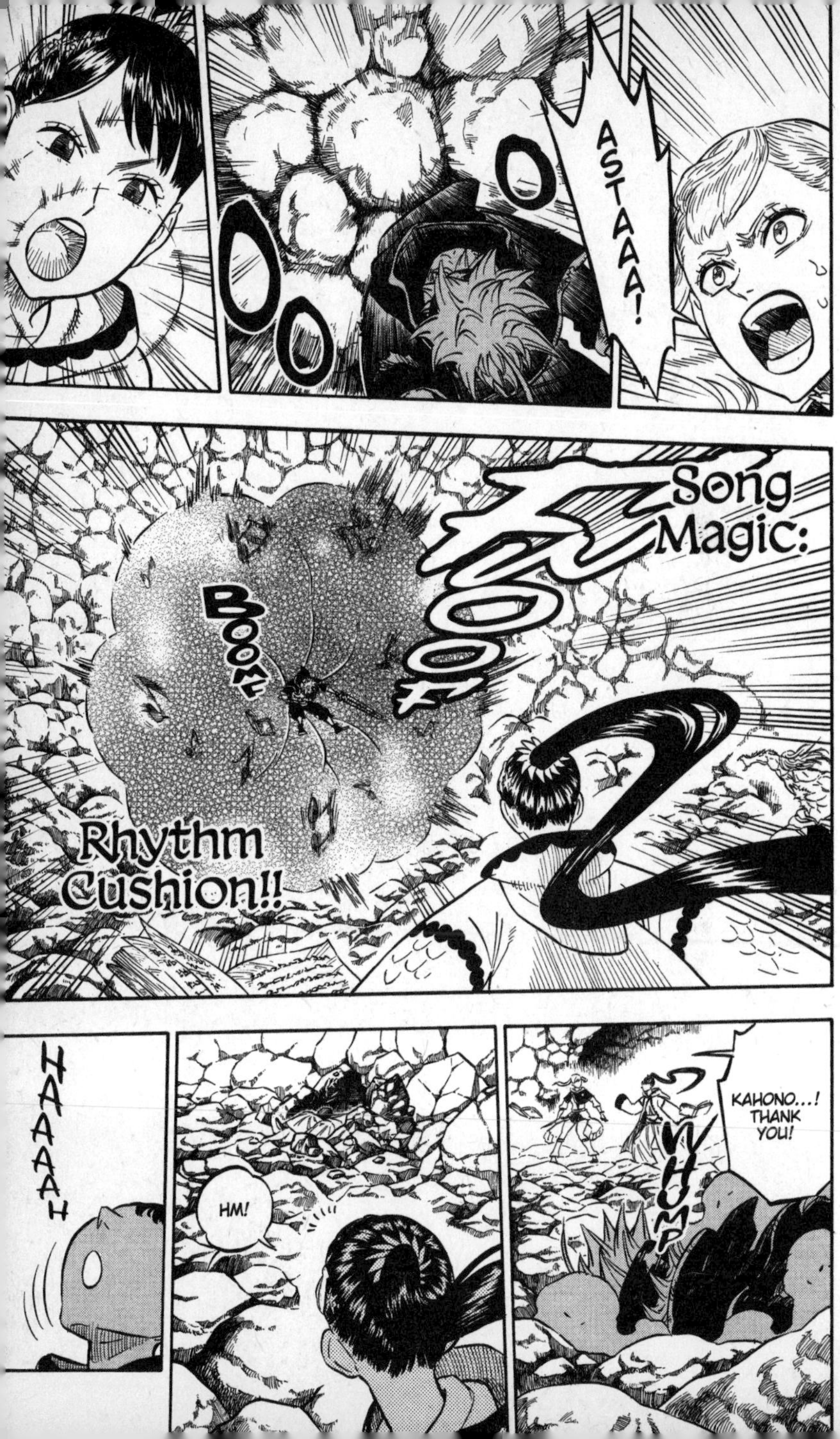
ASTAAAA!
OOOOO
FWOOOF
Song Magic:
BOOOM
Rhythm Cushion!!
KAHONO...! THANK YOU!
WHUMP
HM!
HAAAAAH

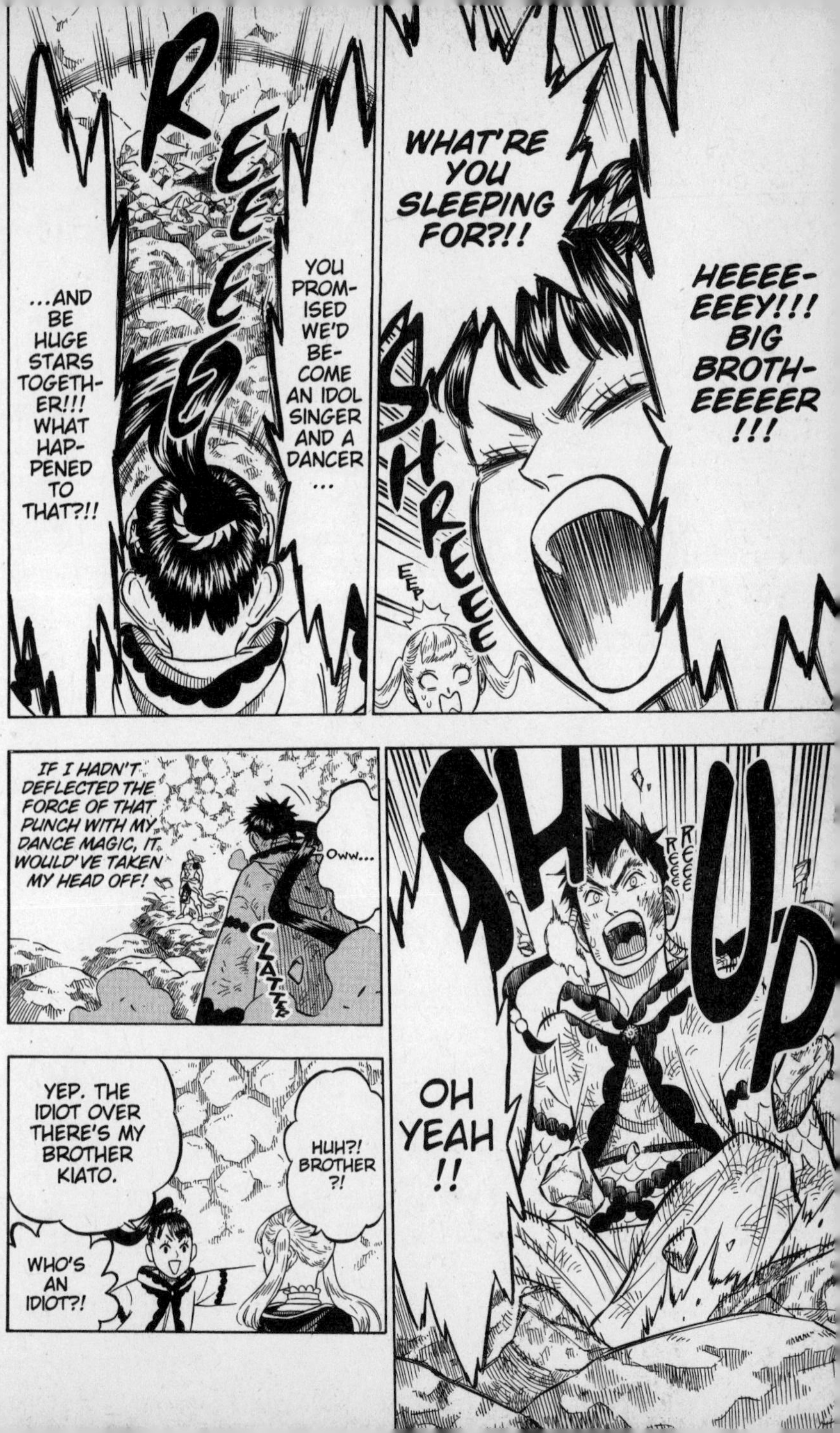
HEEEEEEEY!!! BIG BROTHEEEEEER!!!
WHAT'RE YOU SLEEPING FOR?!!
SHREEEE
EEP
REEEEE
YOU PROMISED WE'D BECOME AN IDOL SINGER AND A DANCER...
...AND BE HUGE STARS TOGETHER!!! WHAT HAPPENED TO THAT?!!
SHUP
REEE REEE
OH YEAH!!
IF I HADN'T DEFLECTED THE FORCE OF THAT PUNCH WITH MY DANCE MAGIC, IT WOULD'VE TAKEN MY HEAD OFF!
OWW...
CLATTER
HUH?! BROTHER?!
YEP. THE IDIOT OVER THERE'S MY BROTHER KIATO.
WHO'S AN IDIOT?!

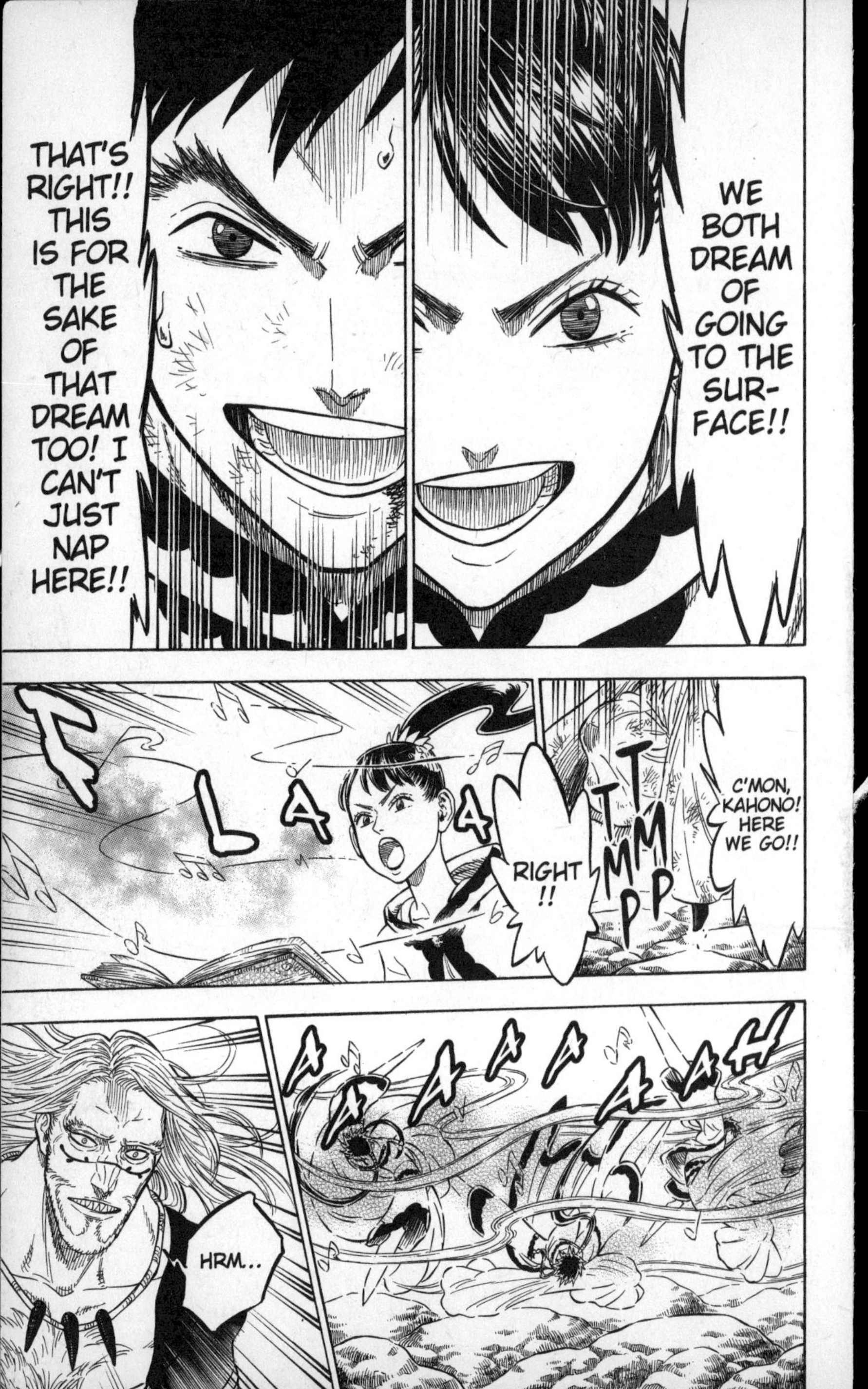
WE BOTH DREAM OF GOING TO THE SUR-FACE!!
THAT'S RIGHT!! THIS IS FOR THE SAKE OF THAT DREAM TOO! I CAN'T JUST NAP HERE!!
C'MON, KAHONO! HERE WE GO!!
TMP TMP
RIGHT!!
FLAA
AAAAAAAAH
HRM...

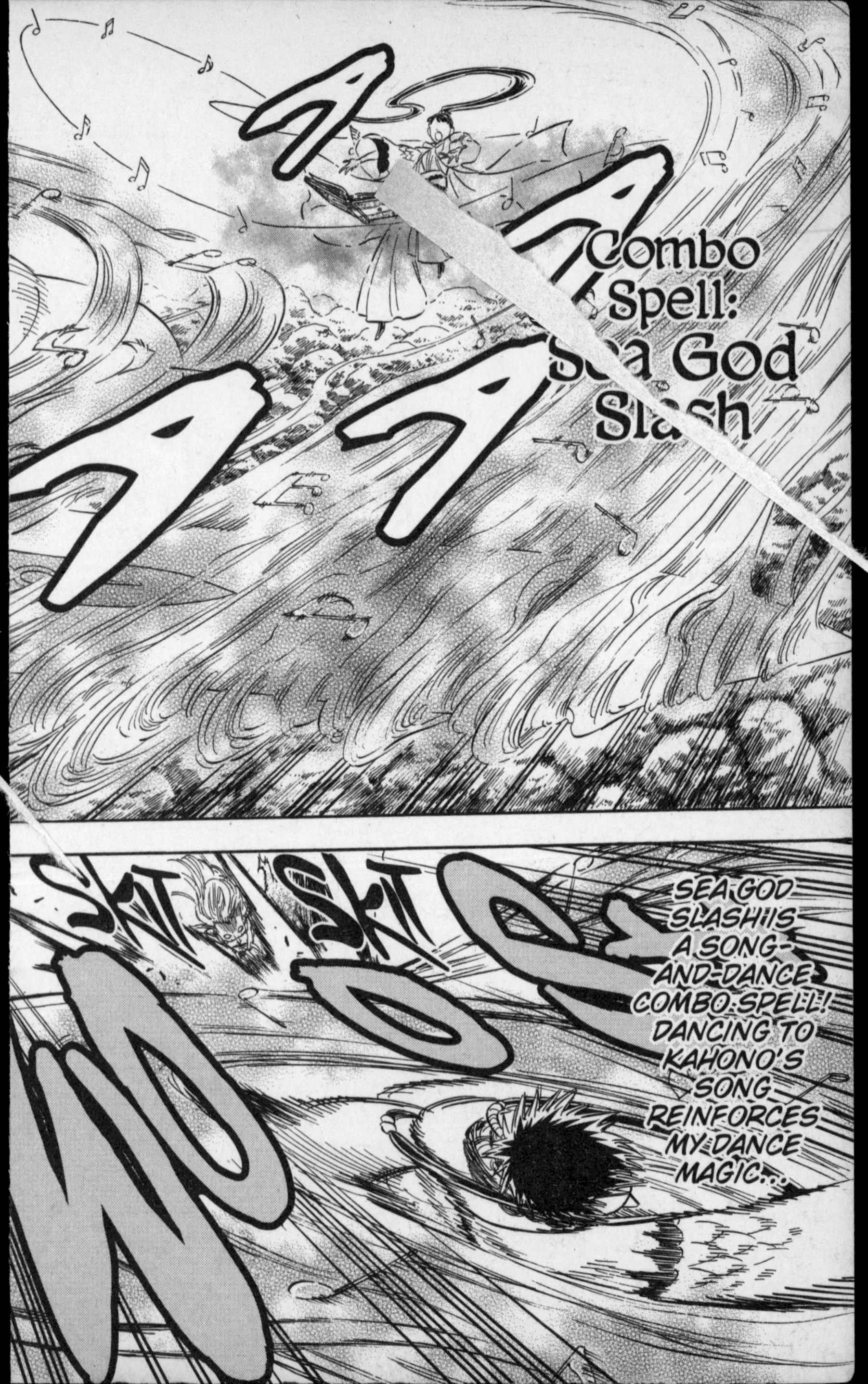
AAAA
Combo Spell: Sea God Slash
SKT SKT
SEA GOD SLASH IS A SONG-AND-DANCE COMBO SPELL! DANCING TO KAHONO'S SONG REINFORCES MY DANCE MAGIC...

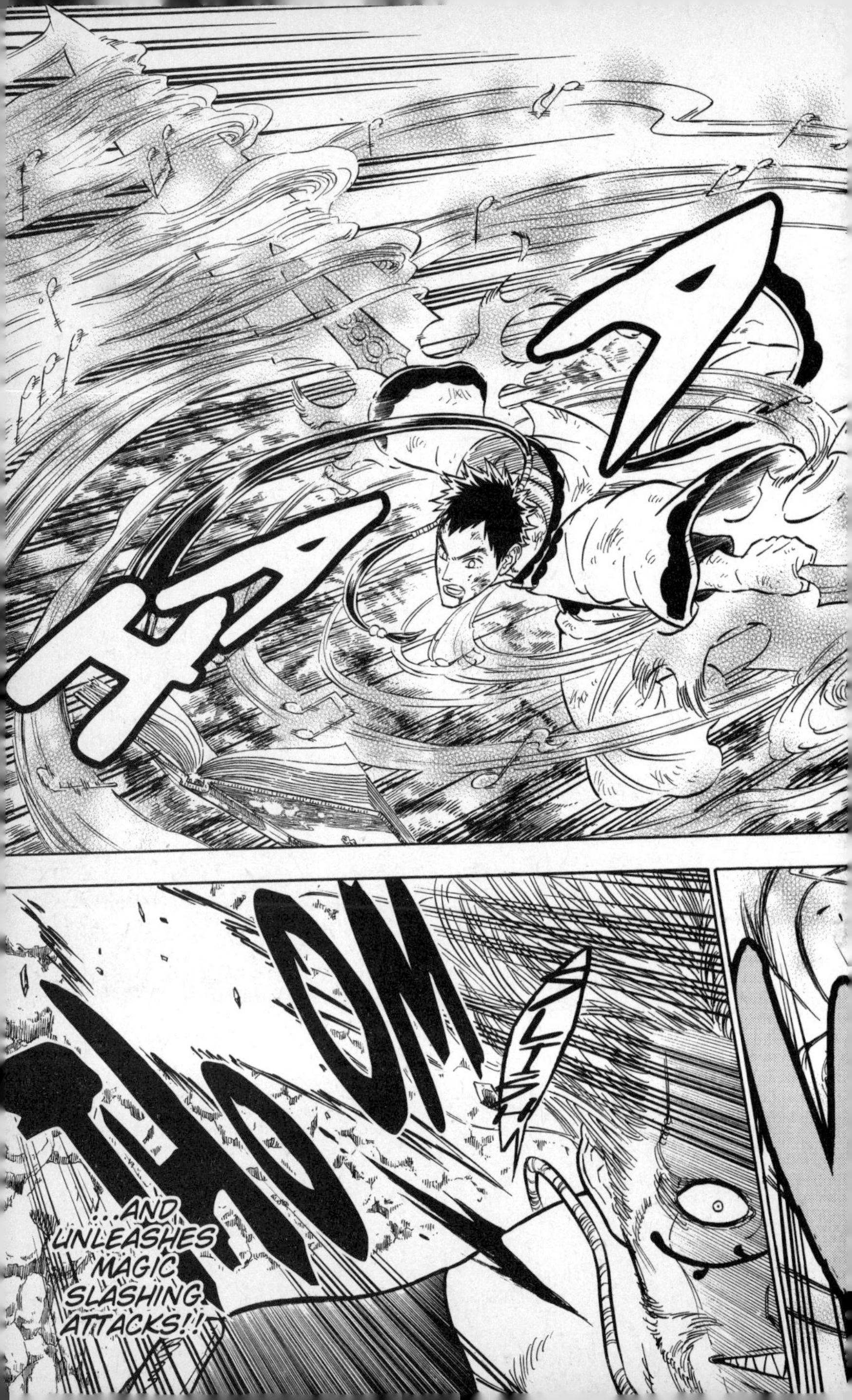
HAA
THOOM
...AND UNLEASHES MAGIC SLASHING ATTACKS!!

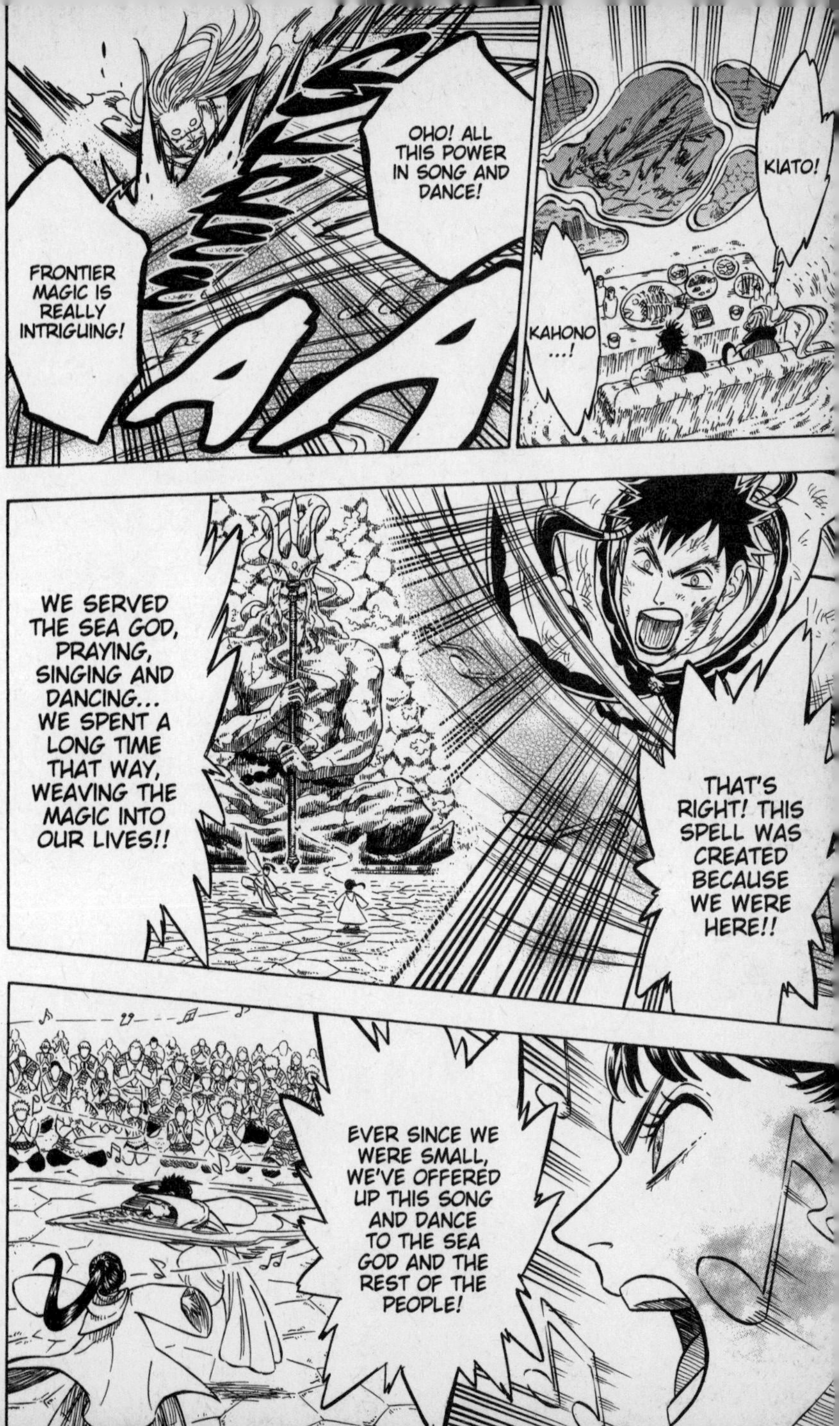
KIATO!
KAHONO ...!
OHO! ALL THIS POWER IN SONG AND DANCE!
FRONTIER MAGIC IS REALLY INTRIGUING!
THAT'S RIGHT! THIS SPELL WAS CREATED BECAUSE WE WERE HERE!!
WE SERVED THE SEA GOD, PRAYING, SINGING AND DANCING... WE SPENT A LONG TIME THAT WAY, WEAVING THE MAGIC INTO OUR LIVES!!
EVER SINCE WE WERE SMALL, WE'VE OFFERED UP THIS SONG AND DANCE TO THE SEA GOD AND THE REST OF THE PEOPLE!

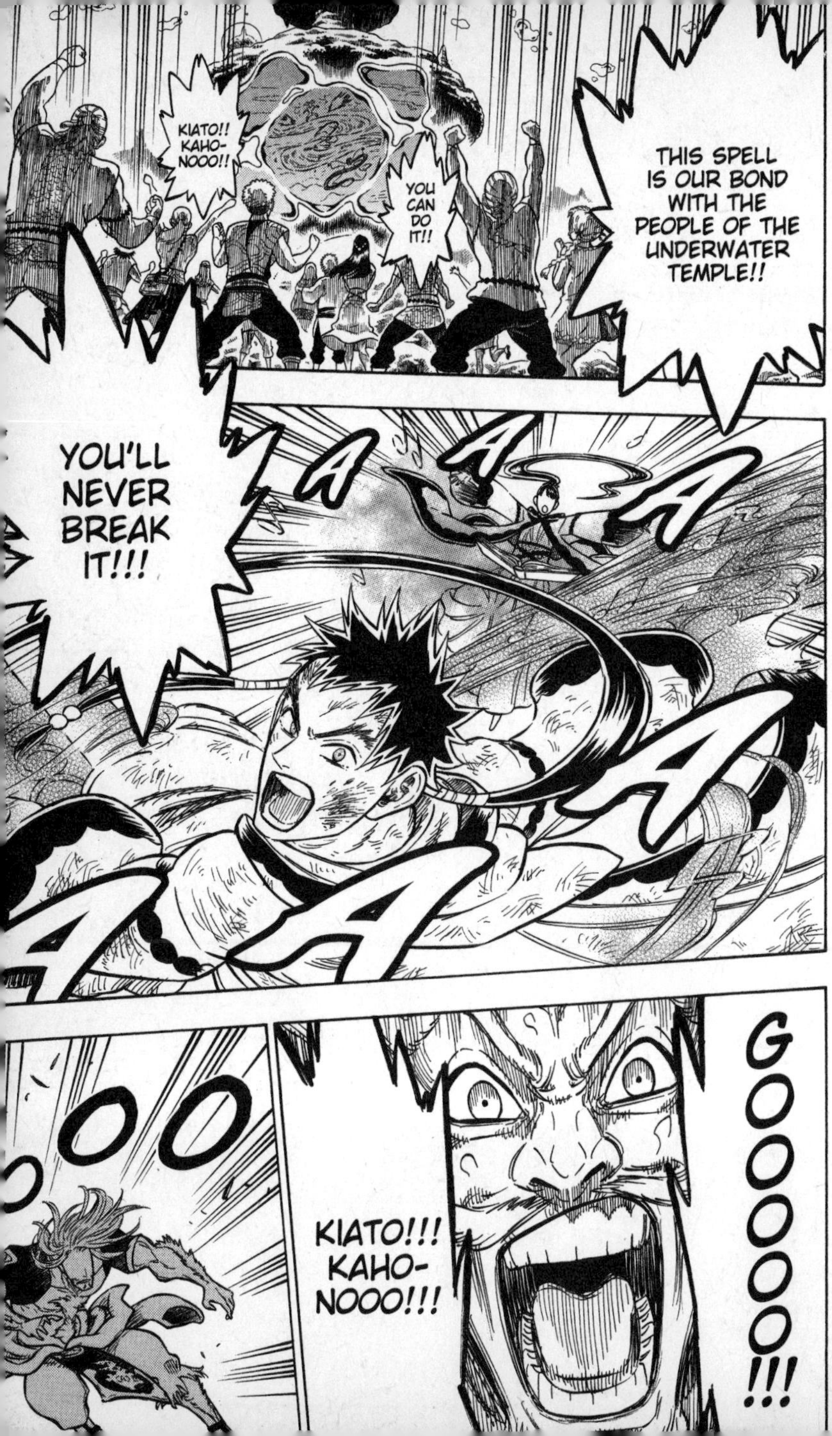
THIS SPELL IS OUR BOND WITH THE PEOPLE OF THE UNDERWATER TEMPLE!!
YOU CAN DO IT!!
KIATO!! KAHO-NOOO!!
YOU'LL NEVER BREAK IT!!!
AAAAAAA
GOOOOOO!!!
KIATO!!! KAHO-NOOO!!!
OOO

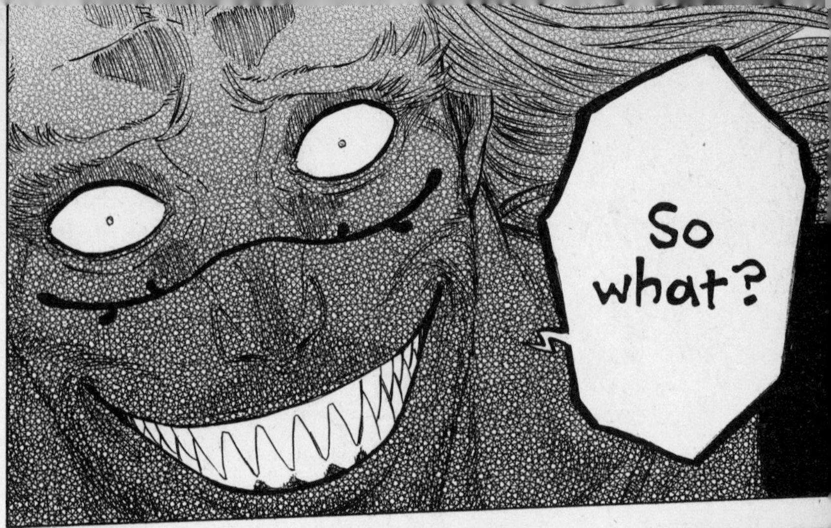
So what?
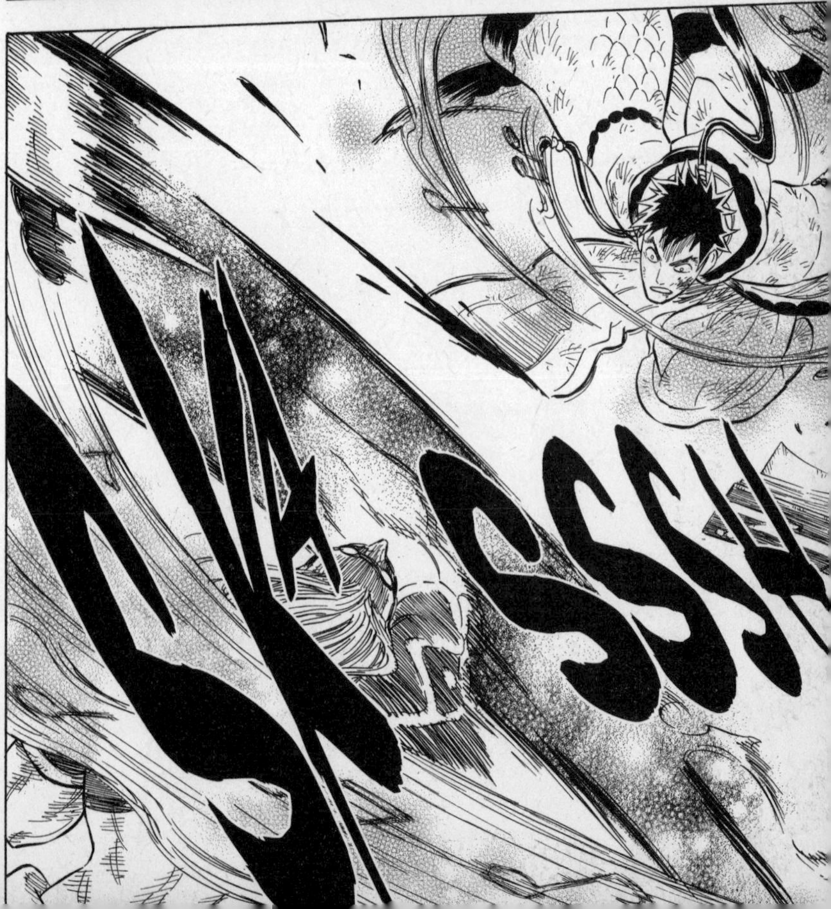
CHASSSH

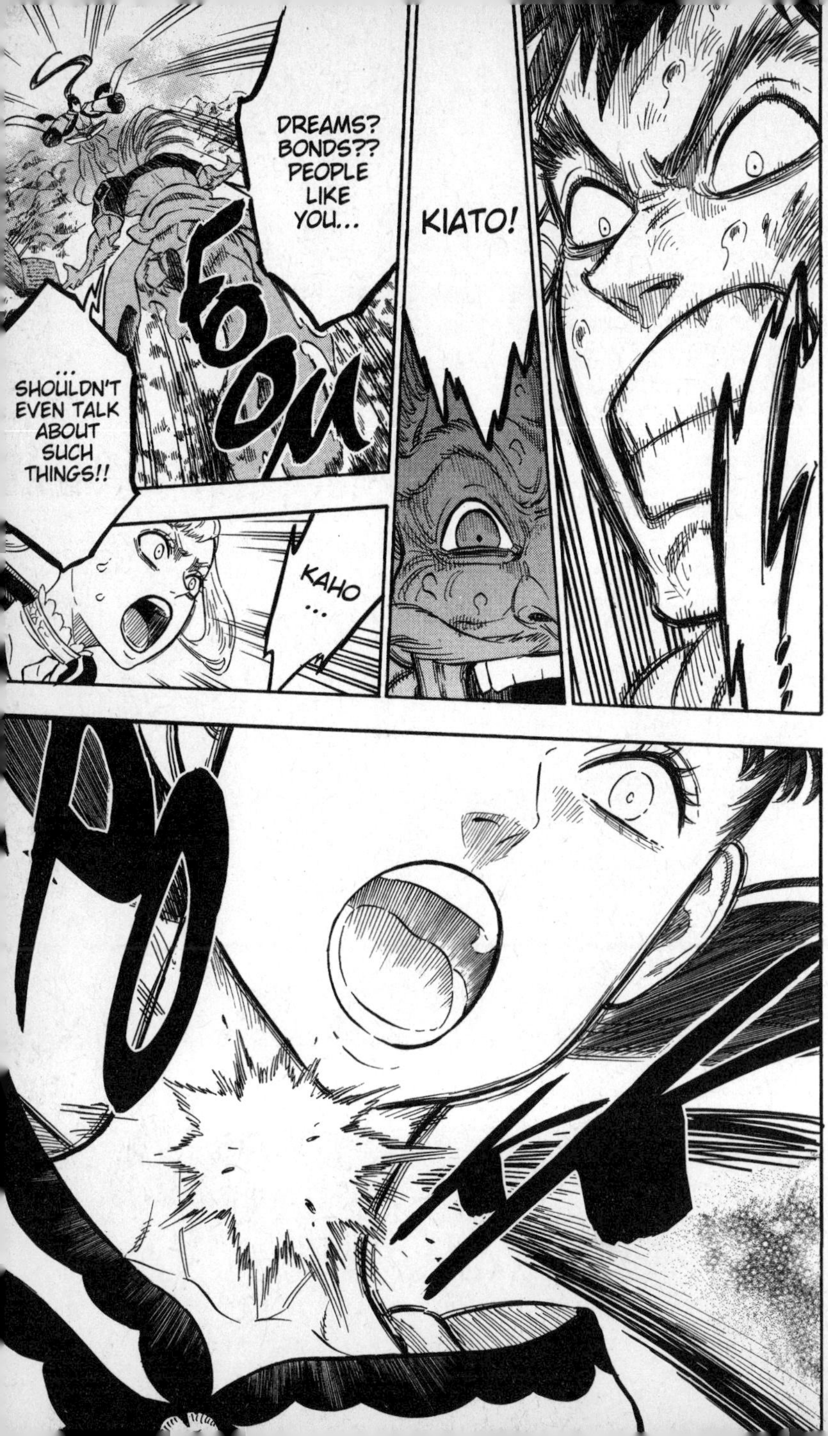
KIATO!
DREAMS? BONDS?? PEOPLE LIKE YOU...
...SHOULDN'T EVEN TALK ABOUT SUCH THINGS!!
KAHO ...

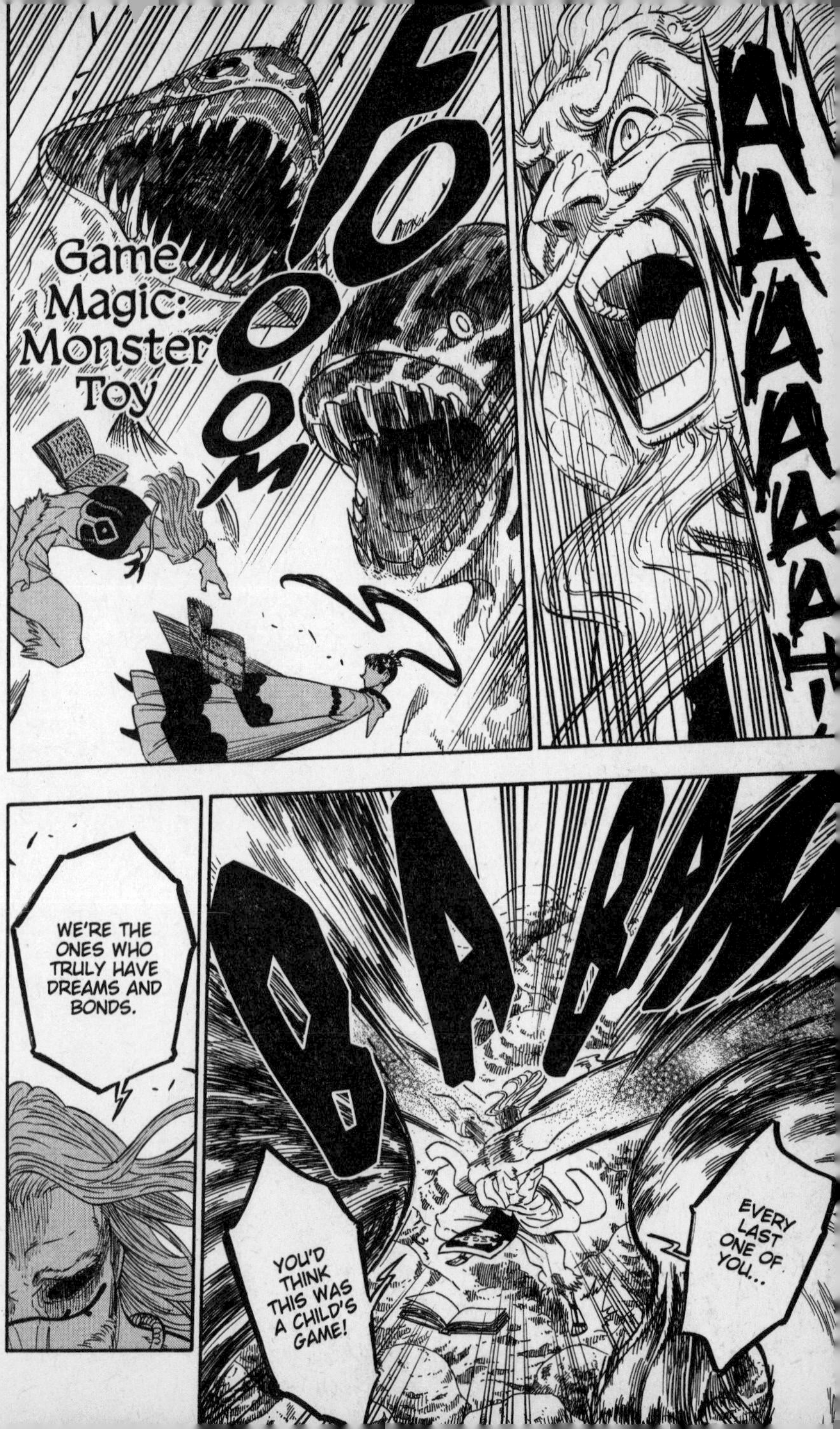
Game Magic: Monster Toy
EVERY LAST ONE OF YOU...
YOU'D THINK THIS WAS A CHILD'S GAME!
WE'RE THE ONES WHO TRULY HAVE DREAMS AND BONDS.

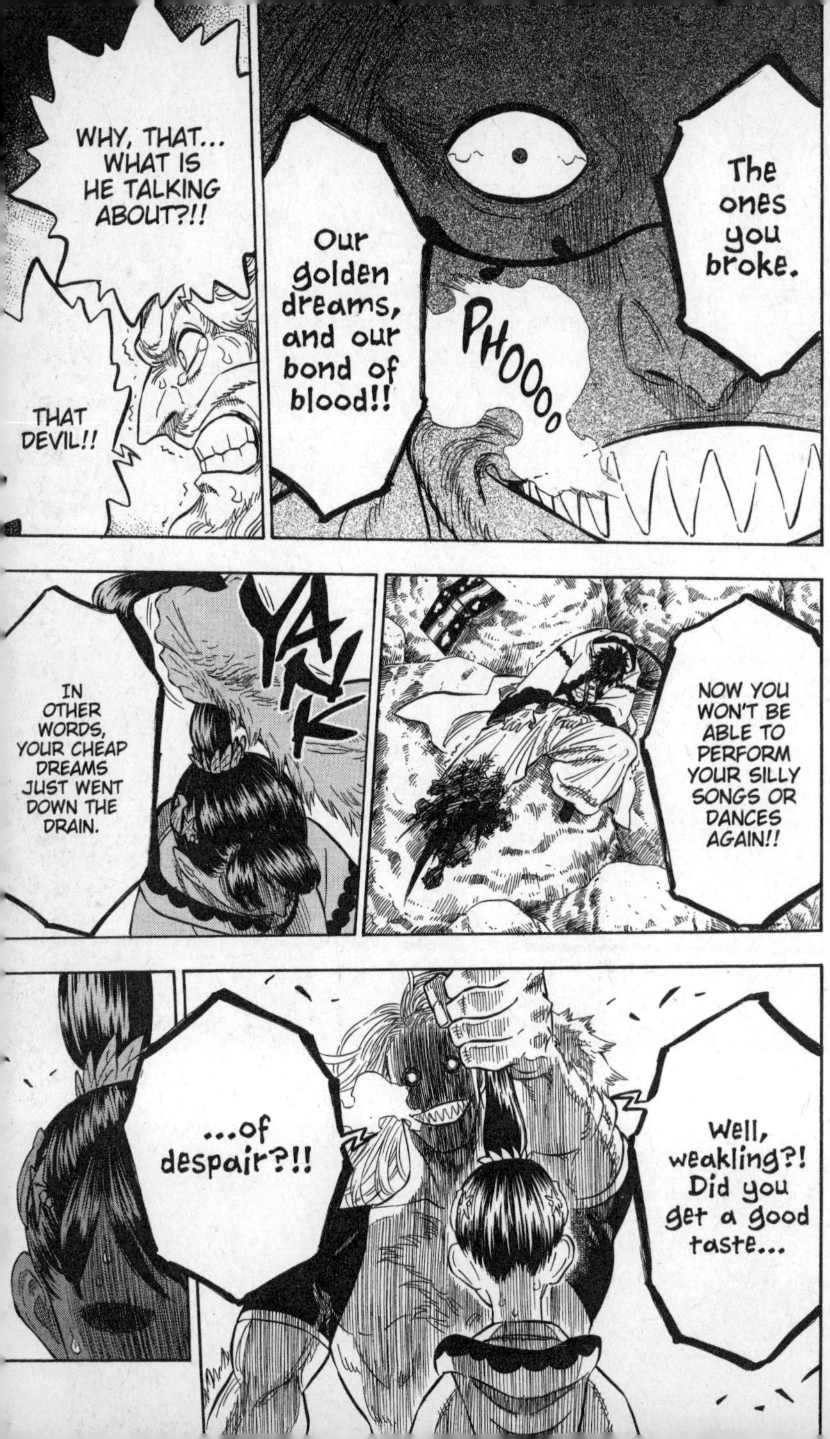
The ones you broke.
Our golden dreams, and our bond of blood!!
PHOOOOo
WHY, THAT... WHAT IS HE TALKING ABOUT?!!
THAT DEVIL!!
NOW YOU WON'T BE ABLE TO PERFORM YOUR SILLY SONGS OR DANCES AGAIN!!
YANK
IN OTHER WORDS, YOUR CHEAP DREAMS JUST WENT DOWN THE DRAIN.
Well, weakling?! Did you get a good taste...
...of despair?!!

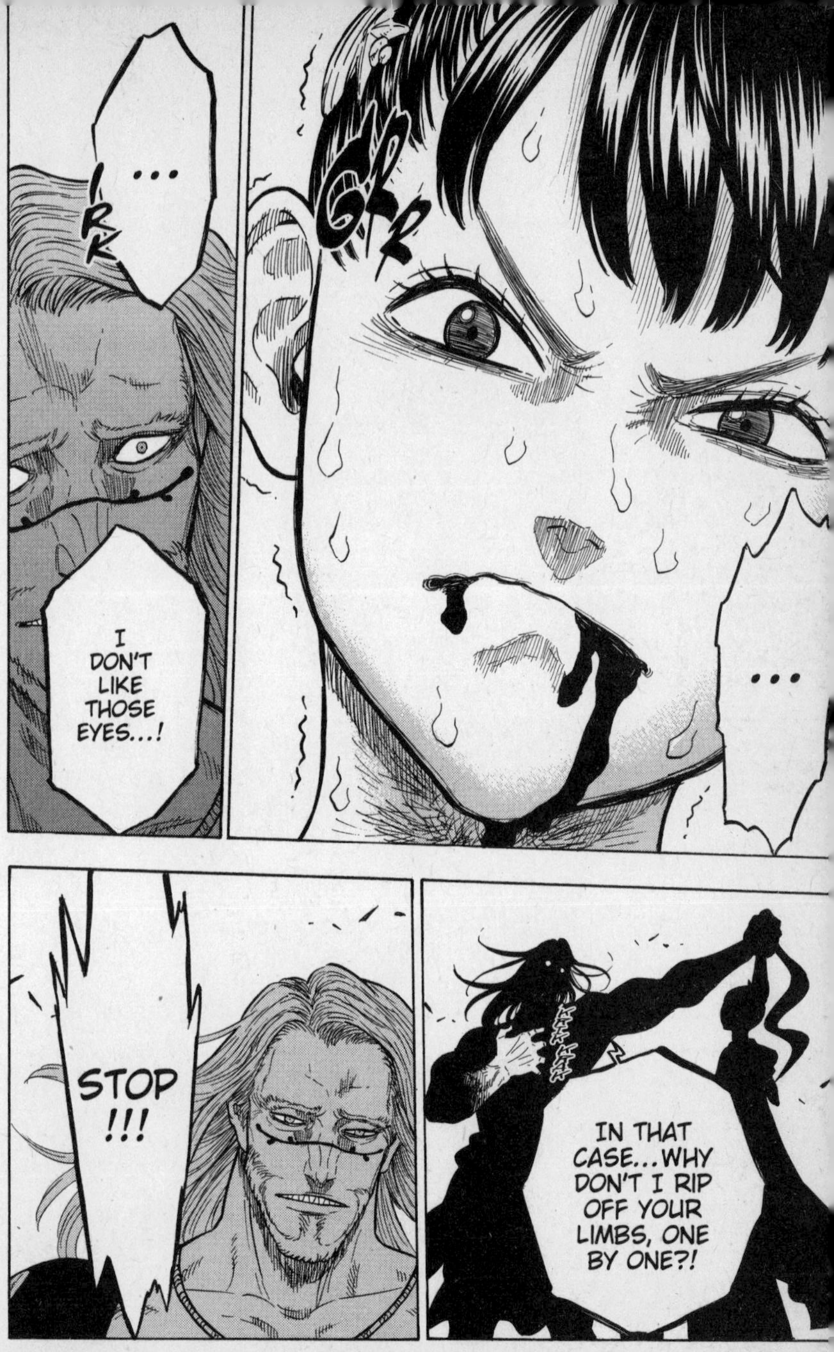
GRR
...
...
IRK
I DON'T LIKE THOSE EYES...!
IN THAT CASE...WHY DON'T I RIP OFF YOUR LIMBS, ONE BY ONE?!
STOP!!!

YOU THINK YOU CAN STOP ME WITH WORDS?

...GO!!

LET HER...

...ON SOMETHING LIKE HIM?!

IN ANY CASE... WOULD MY ATTACKS EVEN WORK...

WHEN HE HAD ASTA EARLIER... I COULDN'T ATTACK THEN EITHER!

IF I MISS... I MIGHT HIT KA-HONO!

BOY, YOU THINK AS LONG AS YOU DON'T GIVE UP, IT'LL WORK OUT SOMEHOW? DON'T YOU...

THAT STRANGE SEX YOU KEEP RECKLESSLY ATTACKING OPPONENTS YOU CAN'T BEAT AND MAKES IT EASY TO MORTALLY WOUND YOU!

KLANG

...

...

Are you finished? Then just watch from there, dog.

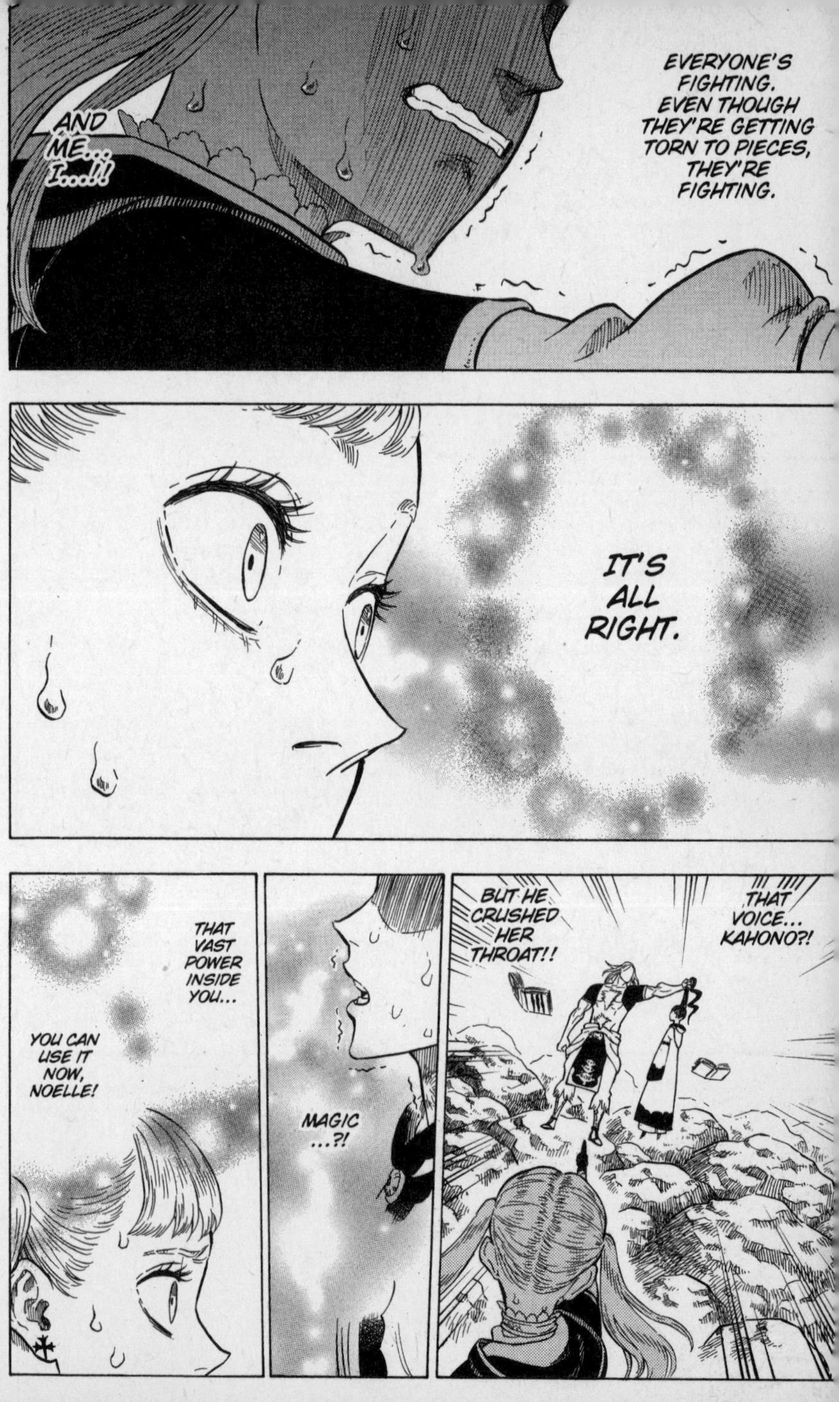
EVERYONE'S FIGHTING. EVEN THOUGH THEY'RE GETTING TORN TO PIECES, THEY'RE FIGHTING.
AND ME... I...!!
IT'S ALL RIGHT.
THAT VOICE... KAHONO?!
BUT HE CRUSHED HER THROAT!!
MAGIC ...?!
THAT VAST POWER INSIDE YOU...
YOU CAN USE IT NOW, NOELLE!

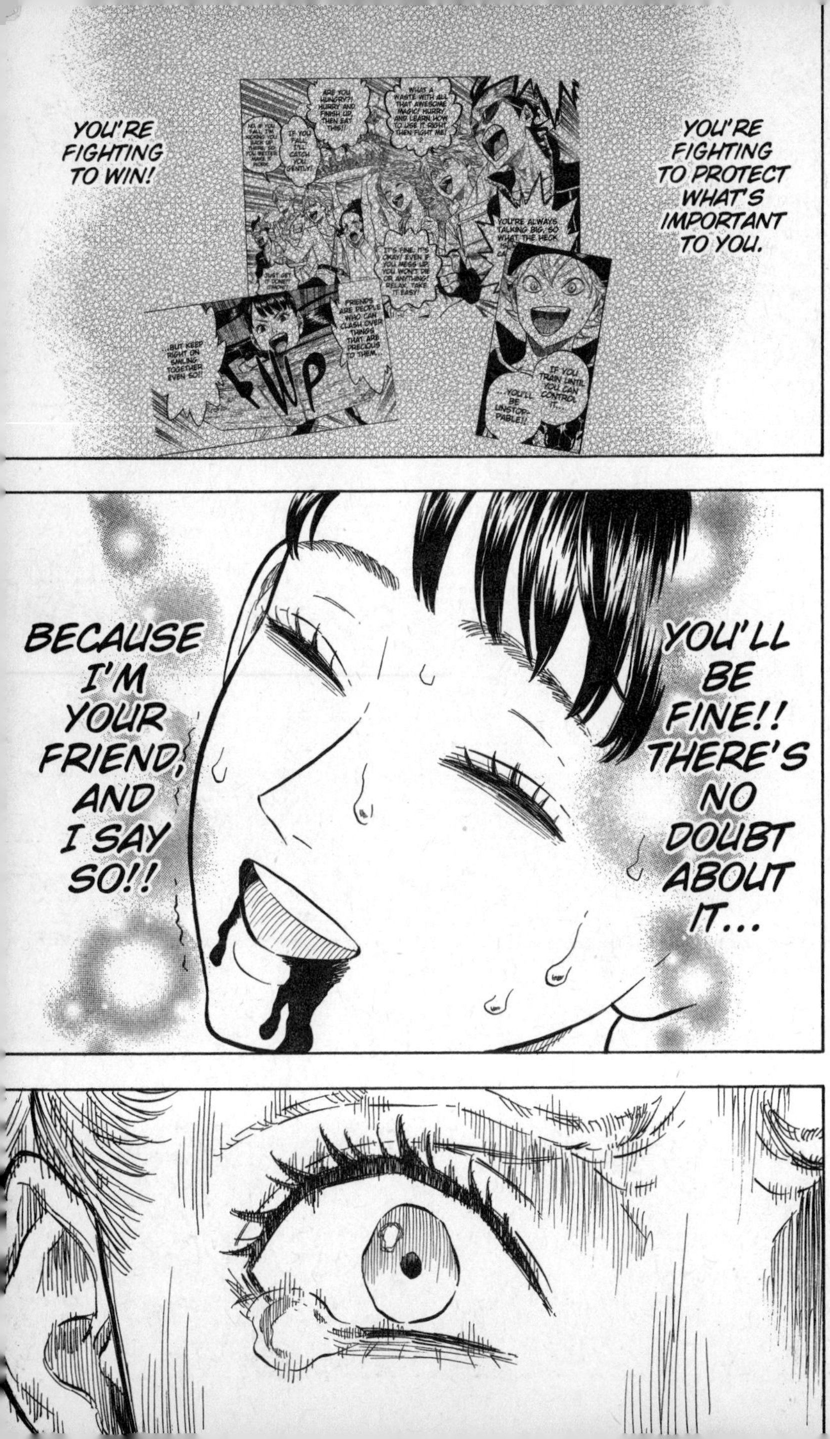
YOU'RE FIGHTING TO PROTECT WHAT'S IMPORTANT TO YOU.
YOU'RE FIGHTING TO WIN!
YOU'LL BE FINE!! THERE'S NO DOUBT ABOUT IT...
BECAUSE I'M YOUR FRIEND, AND I SAY SO!!

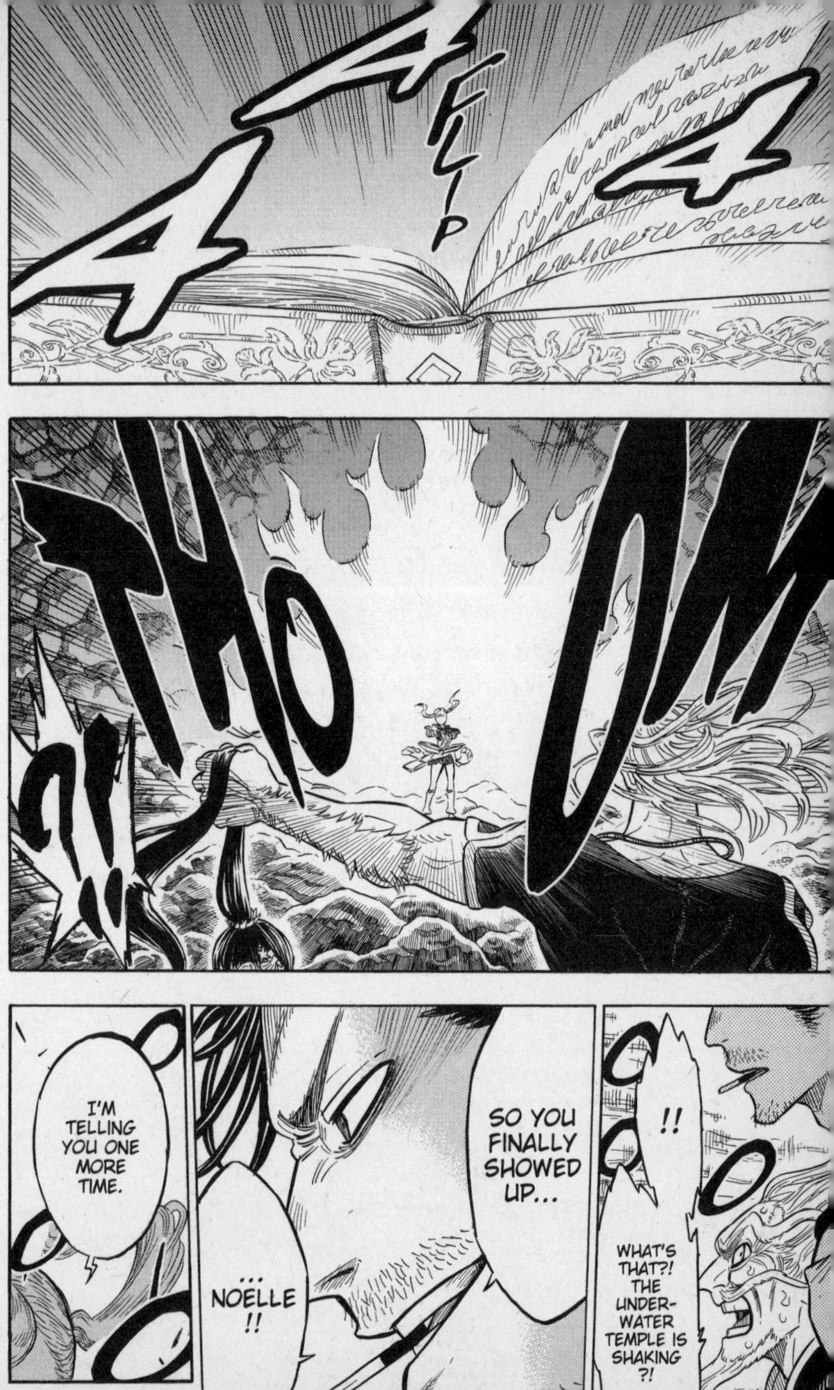
FLIP
THOOM
?!!
!!
WHAT'S THAT?! THE UNDER-WATER TEMPLE IS SHAKING?!
SO YOU FINALLY SHOWED UP...
...NOELLE!!
I'M TELLING YOU ONE MORE TIME.

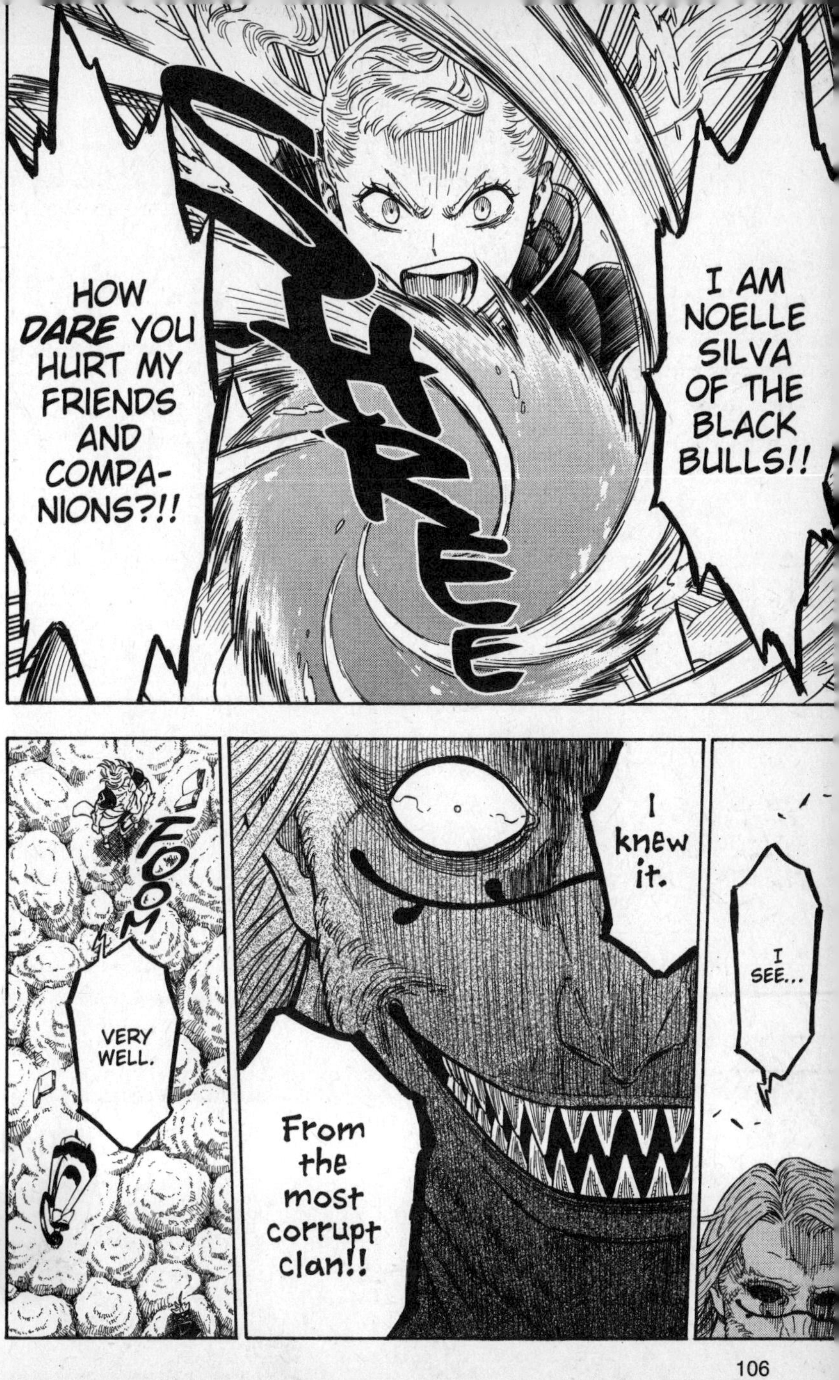
I AM NOELLE SILVA OF THE BLACK BULLS!!
HOW DARE YOU HURT MY FRIENDS AND COMPANIONS?!!
I SEE...
I knew it.
From the most corrupt clan!!
FOOOM
VERY WELL.

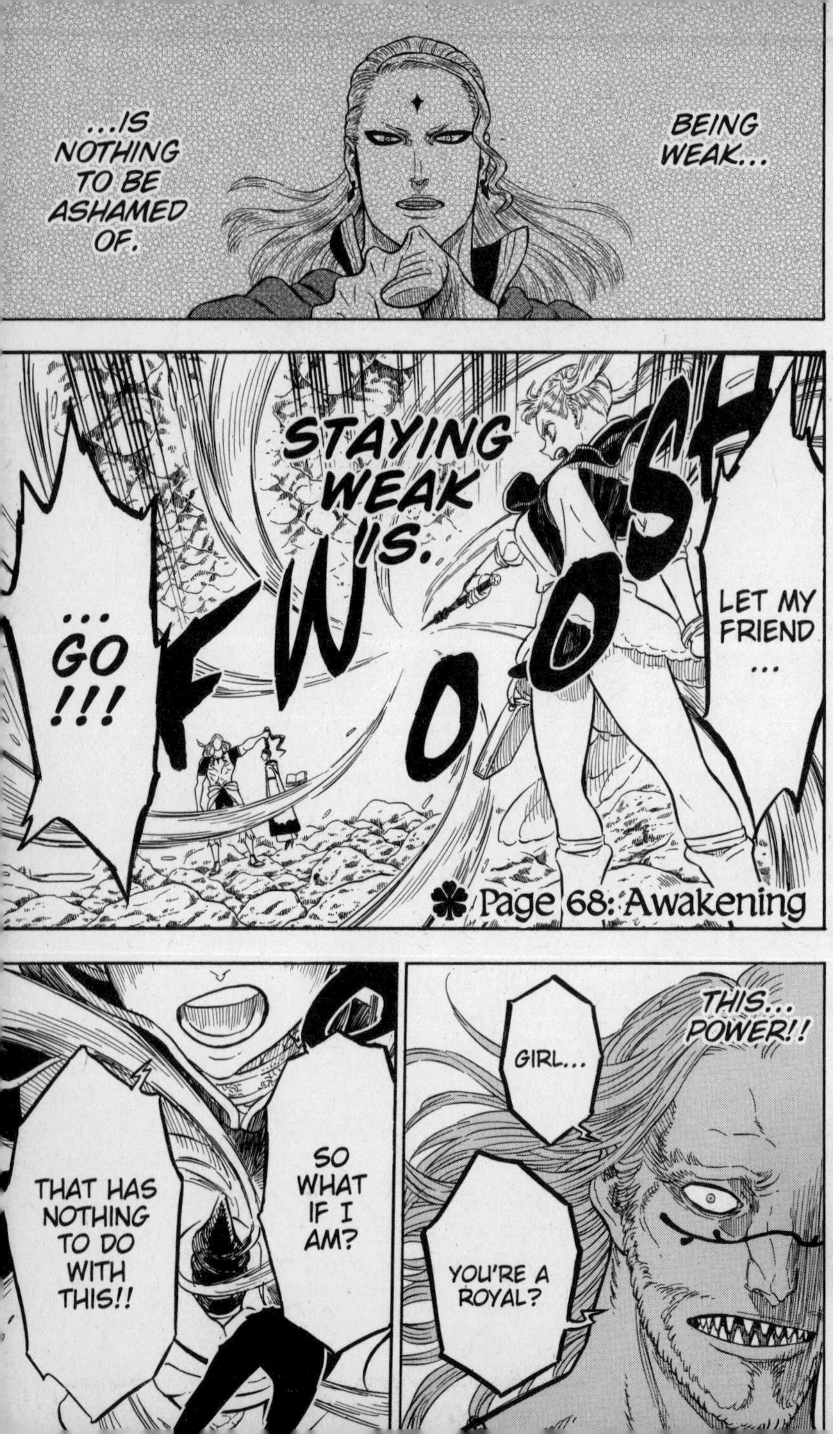
BEING WEAK...
...IS NOTHING TO BE ASHAMED OF.
STAYING WEAK IS.
LET MY FRIEND ...
FWOOSH
... GO !!!
Page 68: Awakening
THIS... POWER!!
GIRL...
YOU'RE A ROYAL?
SO WHAT IF I AM?
THAT HAS NOTHING TO DO WITH THIS!!

Kahono

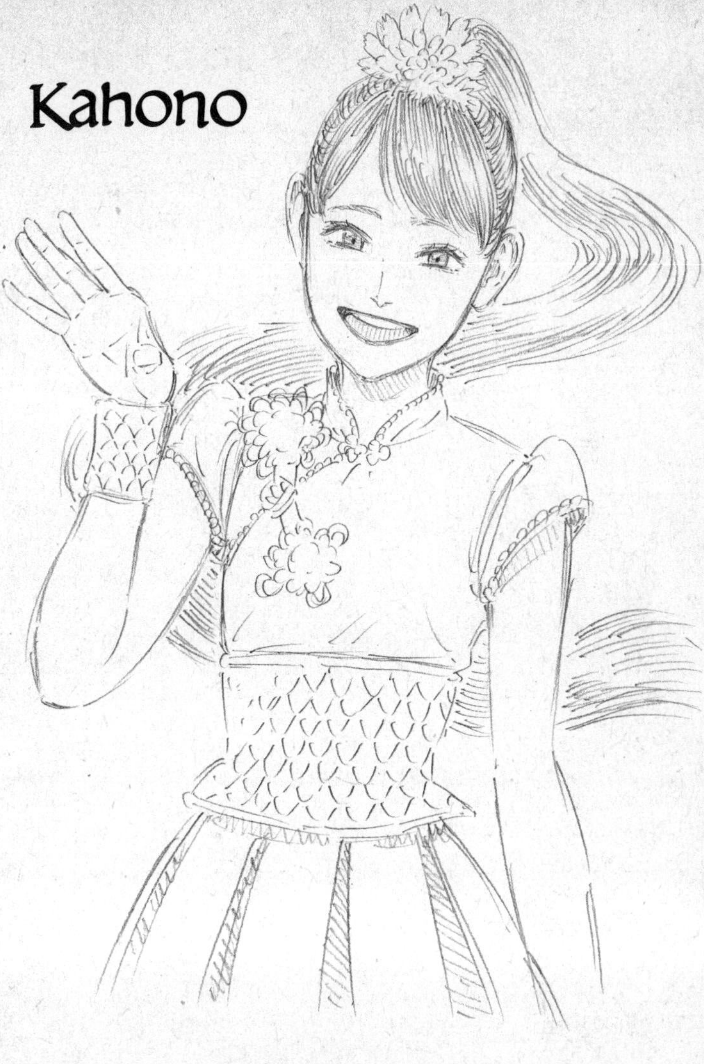

Age: 15 Height: 157 cm
Birthday: November 15 Sign: Scorpio Blood Type: A
Likes: Singing, money, ice cream

Character Profile

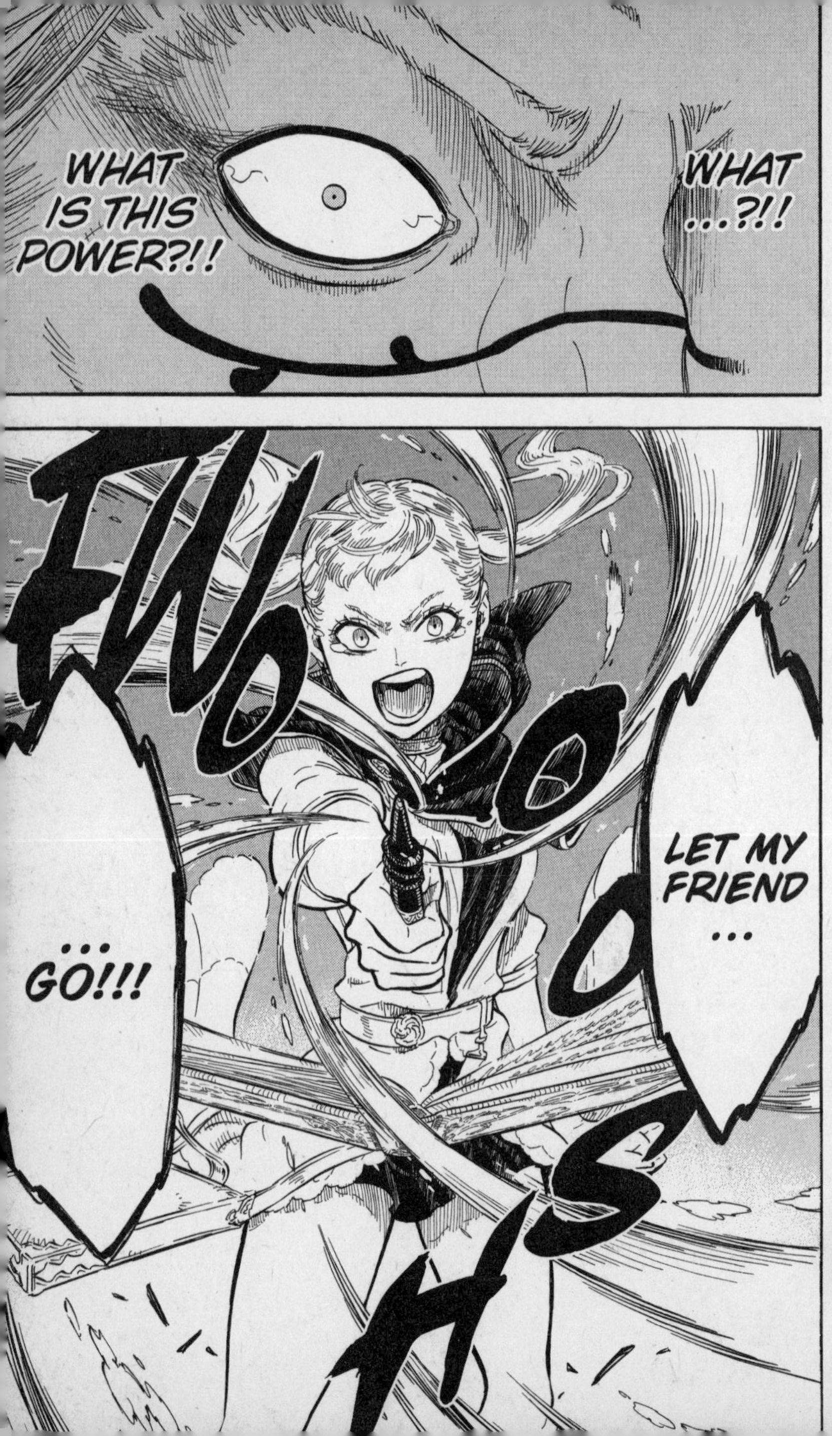
WHAT ...?!!
WHAT IS THIS POWER?!!
LET MY FRIEND ...
... GO!!!
FWOOOSH

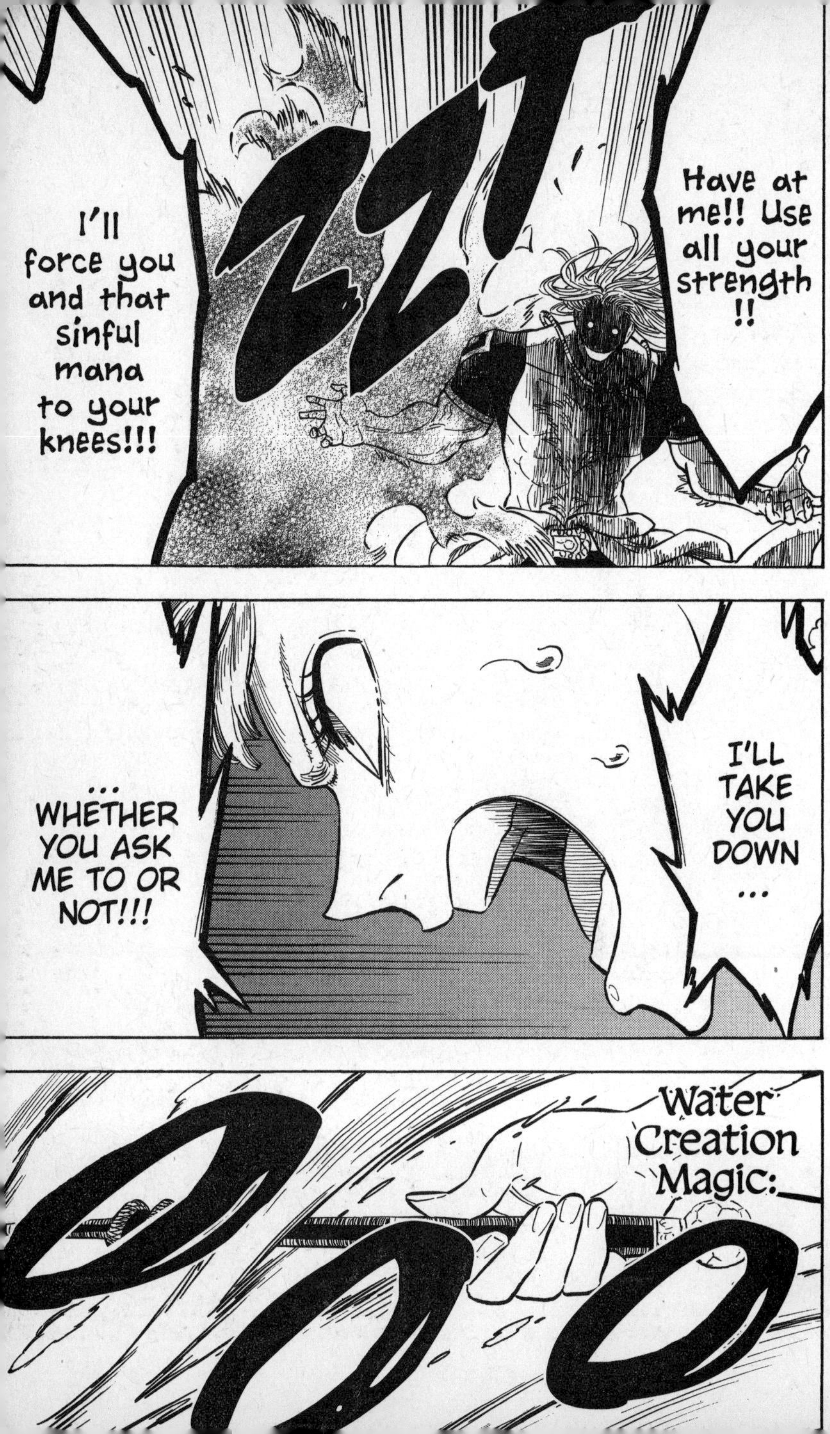

Have at me!! Use all your strength!!
I'll force you and that sinful mana to your knees!!!
I'LL TAKE YOU DOWN...
...WHETHER YOU ASK ME TO OR NOT!!!
Water Creation Magic:

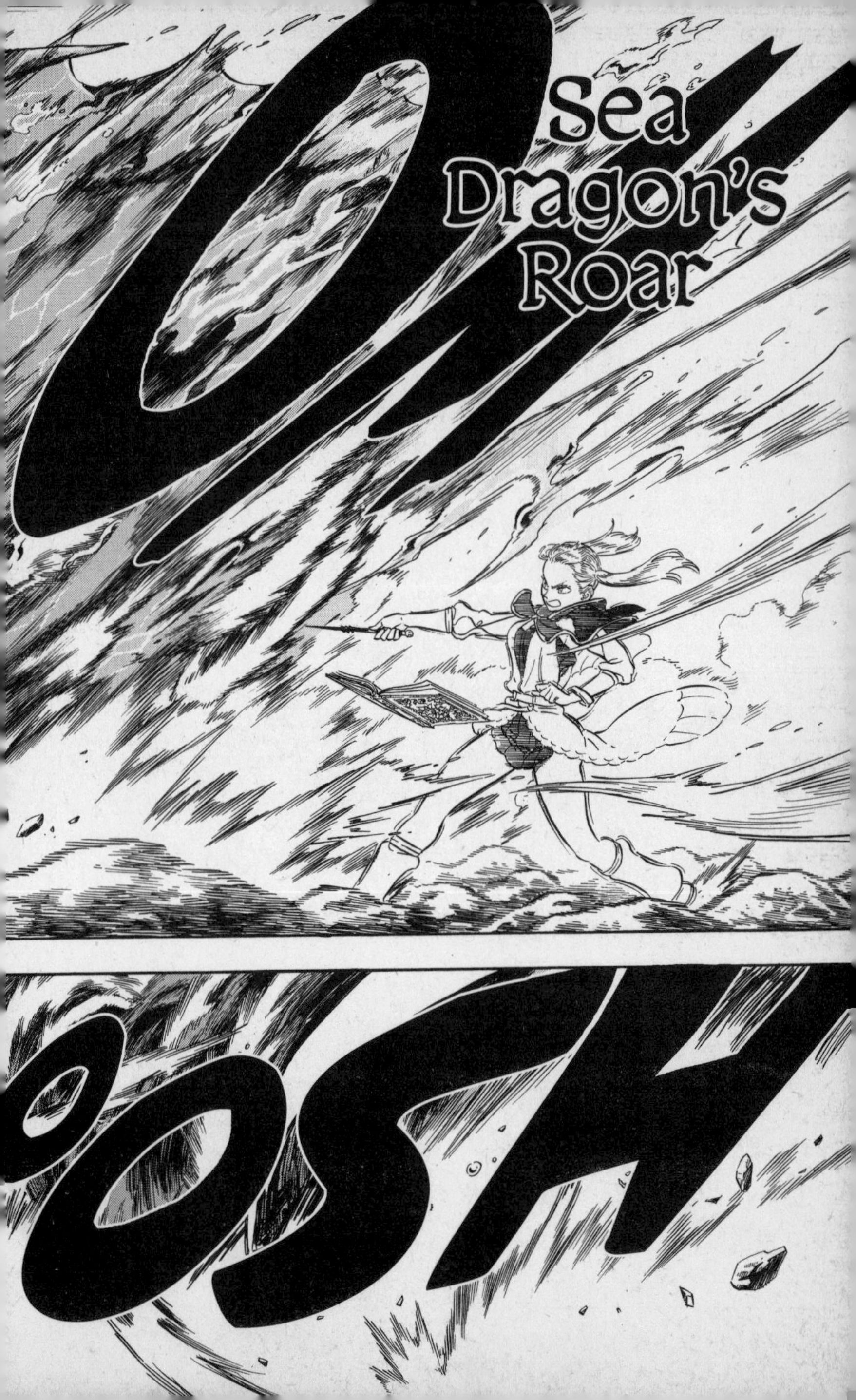
Sea Dragon's Roar

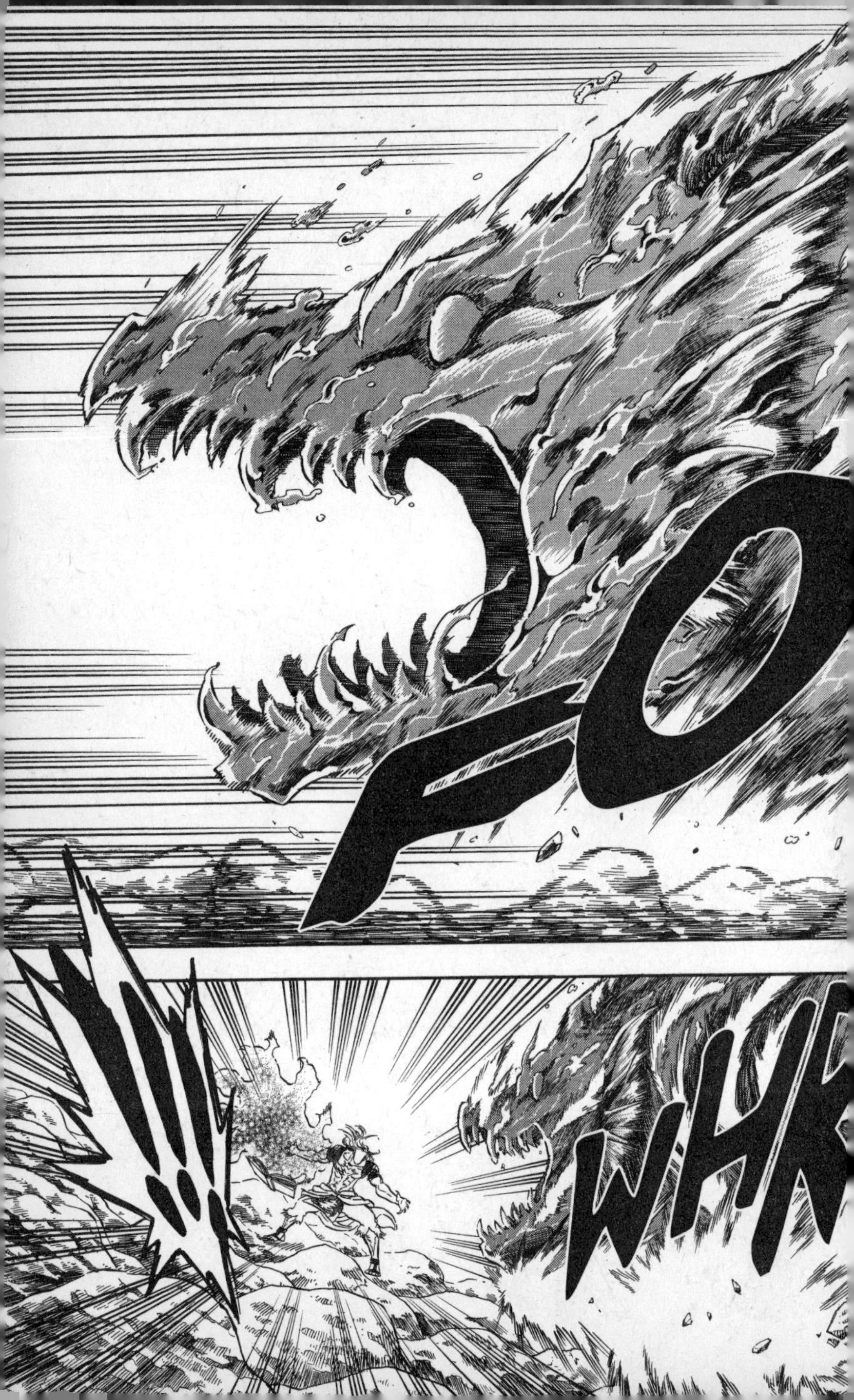
FO
WHR
!!!

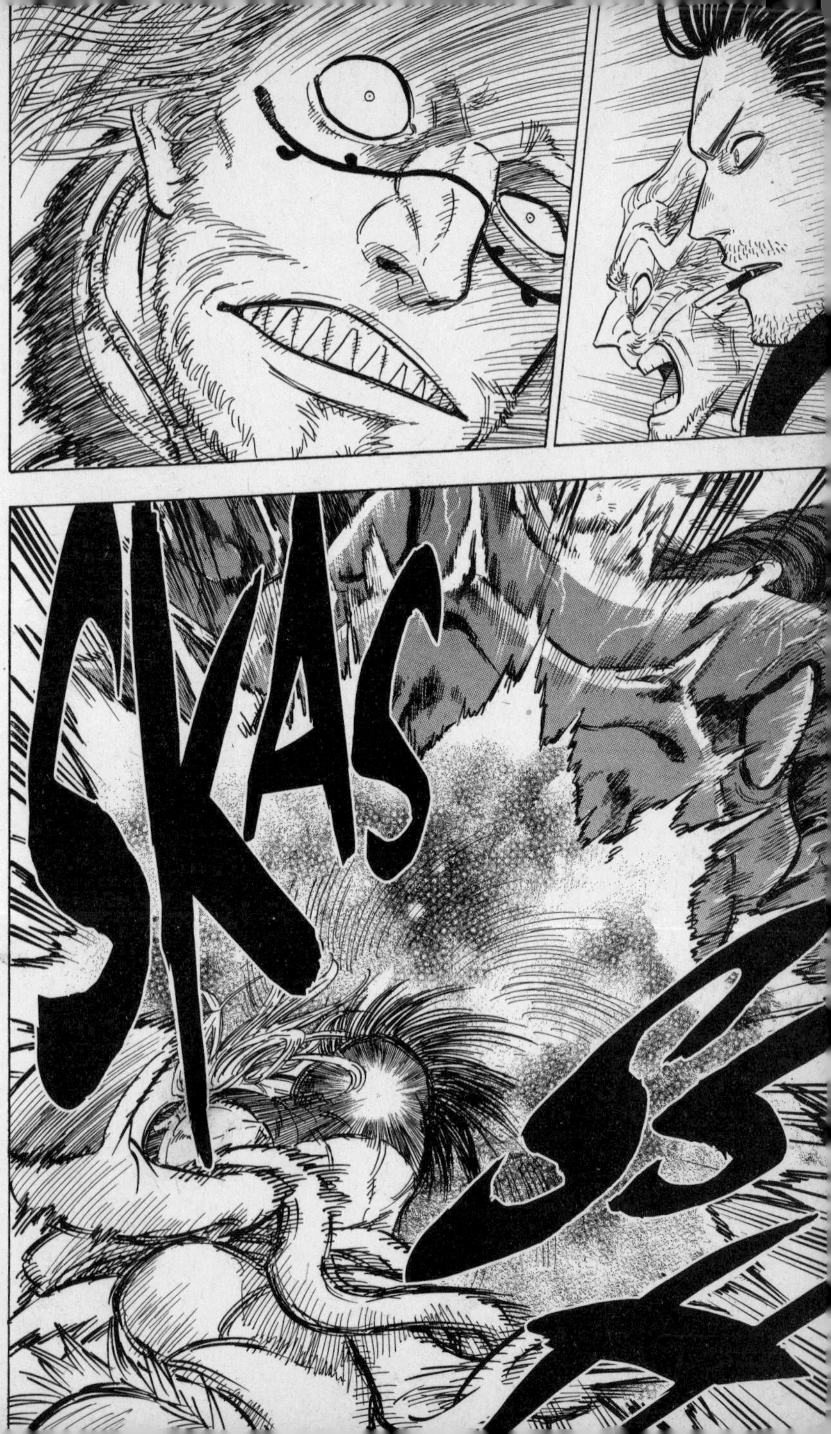
SKASSSH

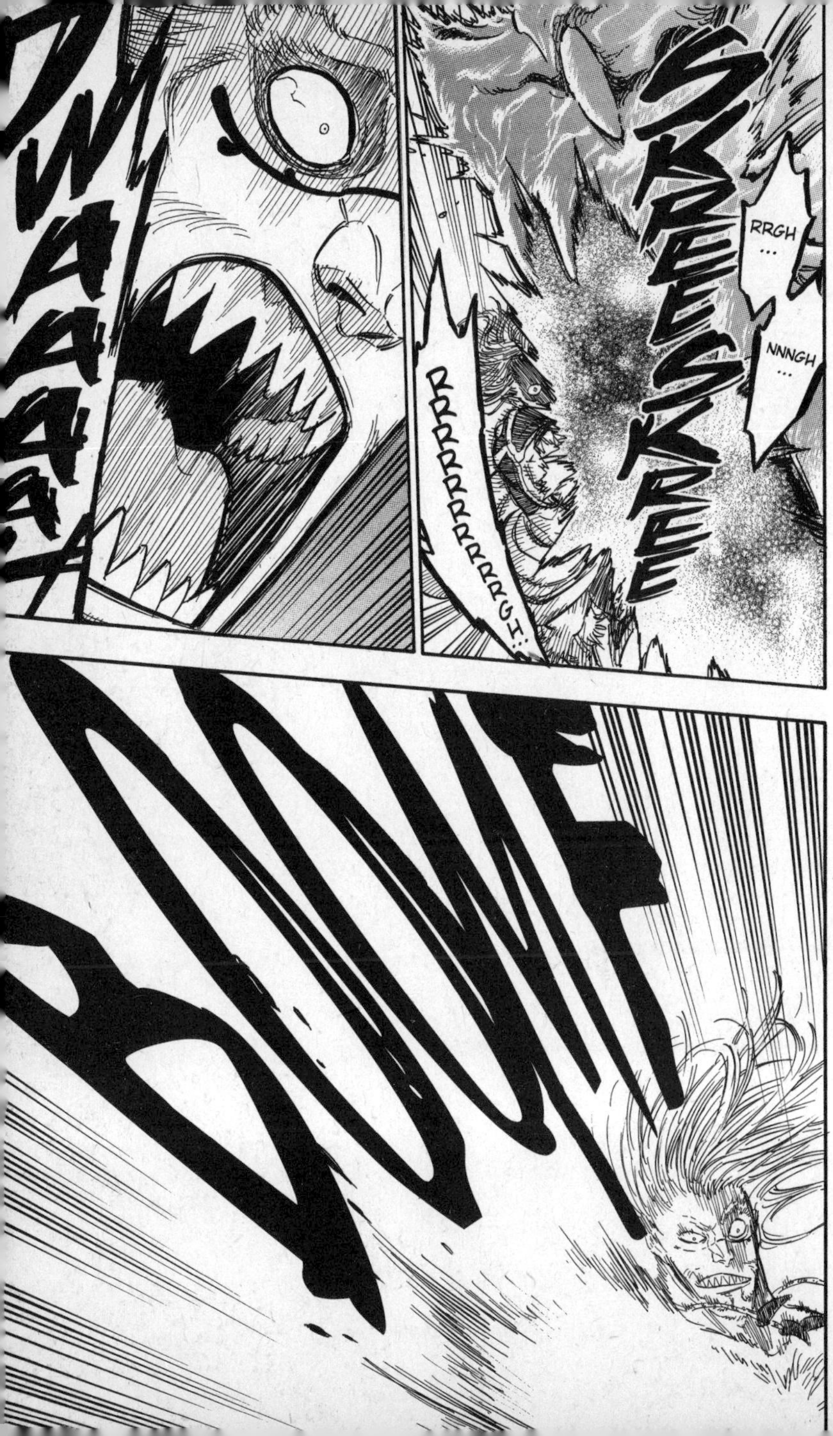
SKREESKREE
RRGH...
NNNGH...
RRRRRRRRRRGH!!

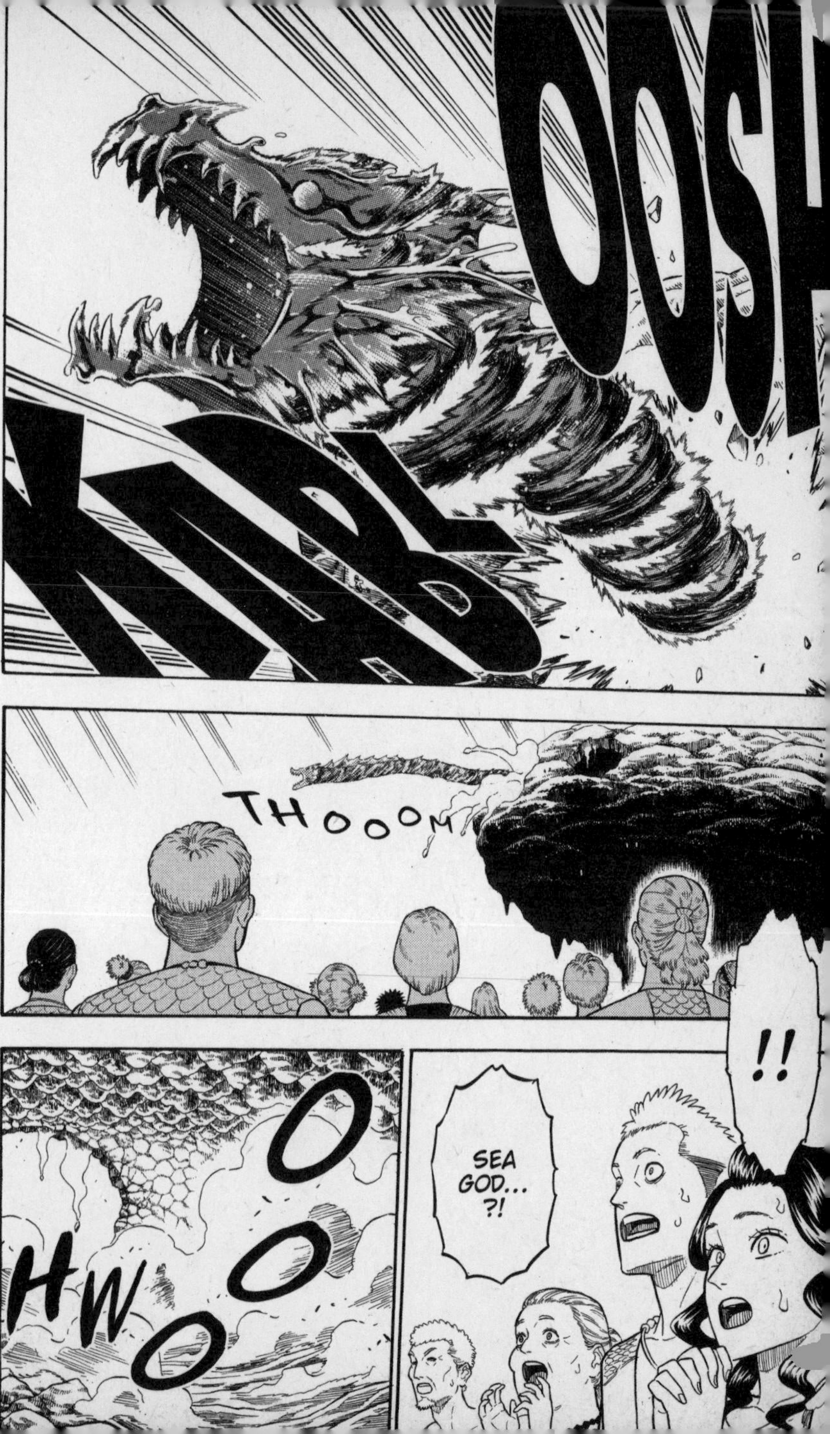
KABOOSH
THOOOM
!!
SEA GOD...?!
HWOOOO

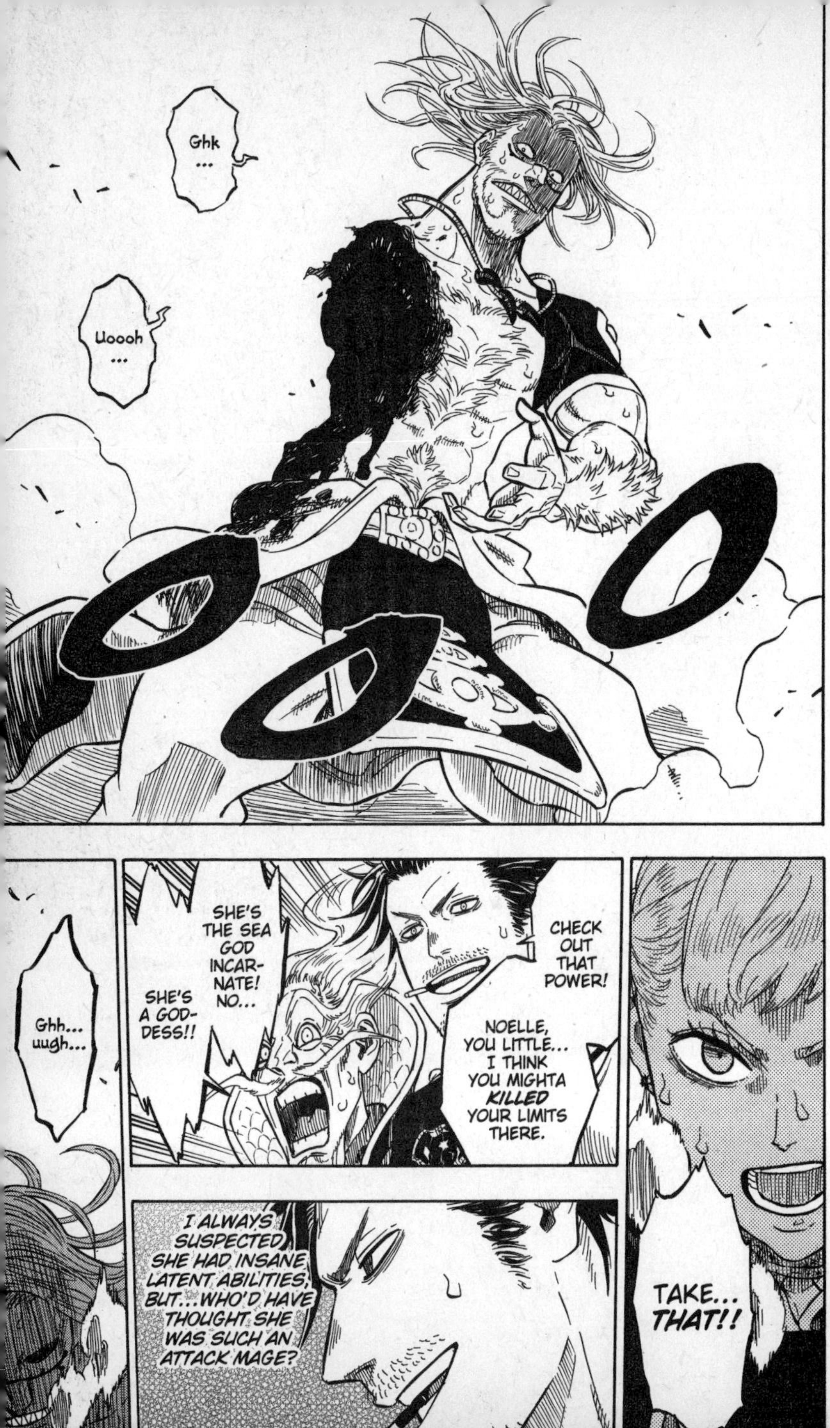
Ghk ...
Uoooh ...
TAKE... THAT!!
CHECK OUT THAT POWER!
SHE'S THE SEA GOD INCAR-NATE! NO...
SHE'S A GOD-DESS!!
NOELLE, YOU LITTLE... I THINK YOU MIGHTA KILLED YOUR LIMITS THERE.
I ALWAYS SUSPECTED SHE HAD INSANE LATENT ABILITIES, BUT... WHO'D HAVE THOUGHT SHE WAS SUCH AN ATTACK MAGE?
Ghh... uugh...

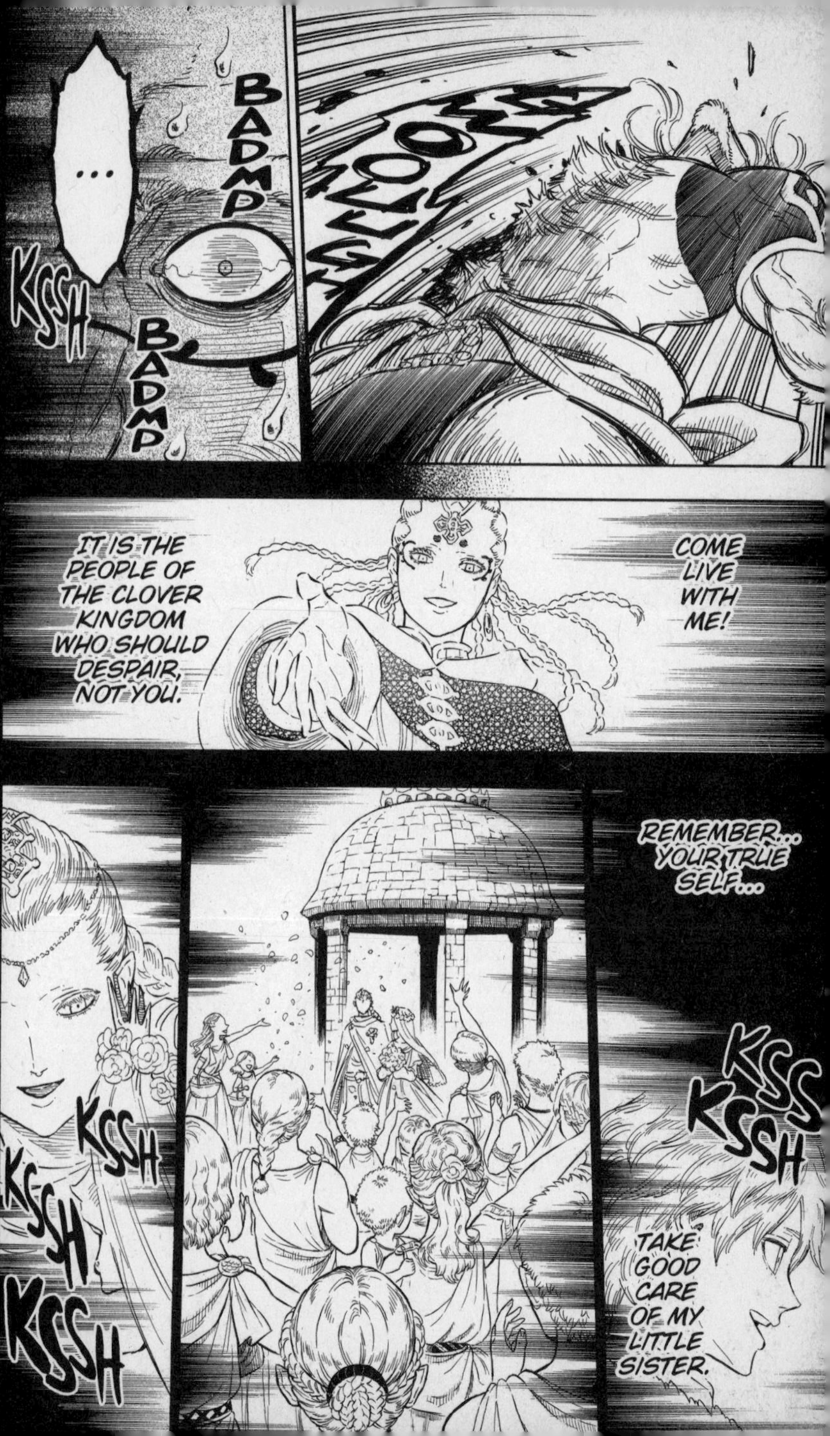
GWOOUGH
...
BADMP
BADMP
KSSH
IT IS THE PEOPLE OF THE CLOVER KINGDOM WHO SHOULD DESPAIR, NOT YOU.
COME LIVE WITH ME!
REMEMBER... YOUR TRUE SELF...
KSS
KSSH
TAKE GOOD CARE OF MY LITTLE SISTER.
KSSH
KSSH
KSSH

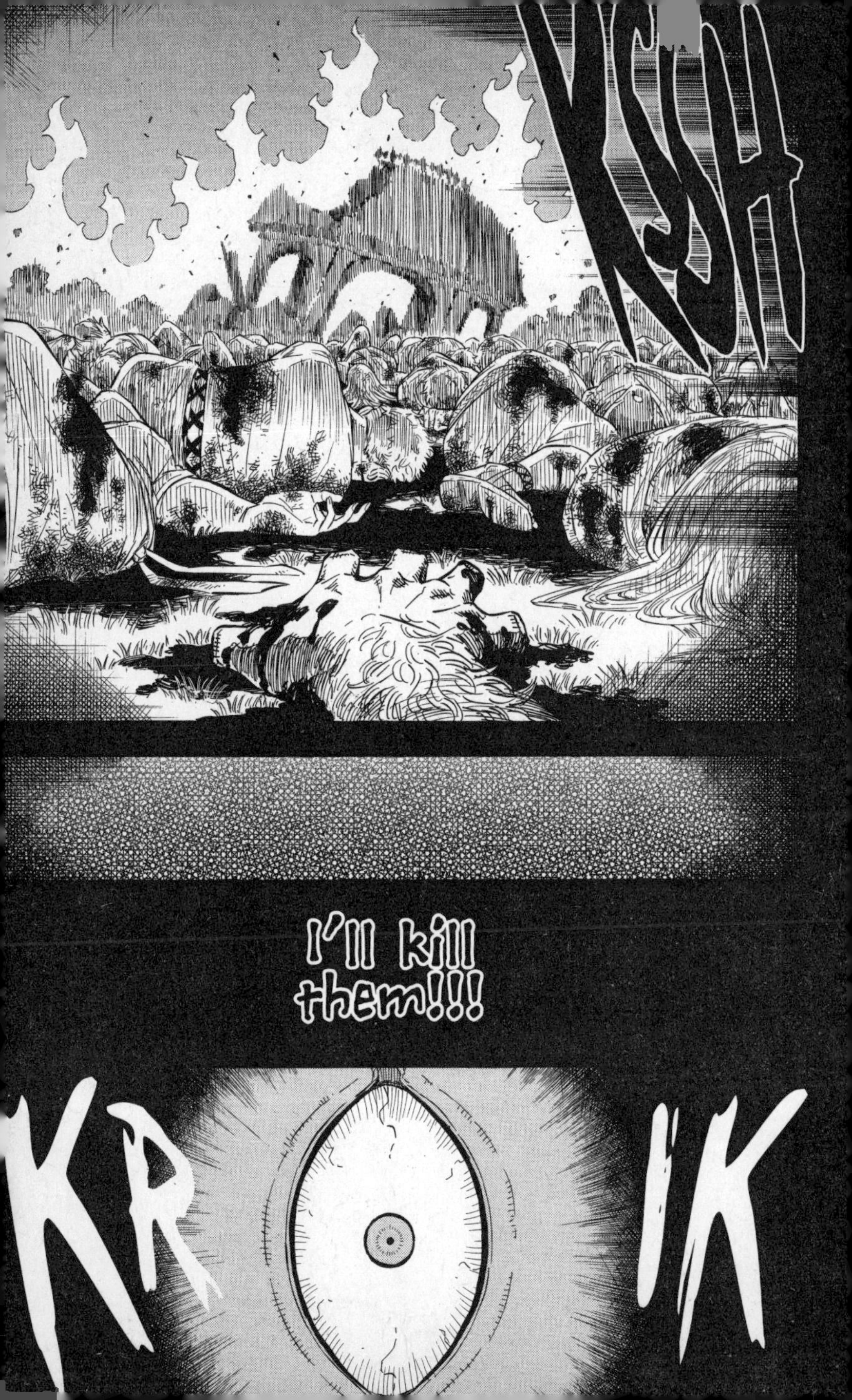
VSSH
I'll kill them!!!
KR
IK

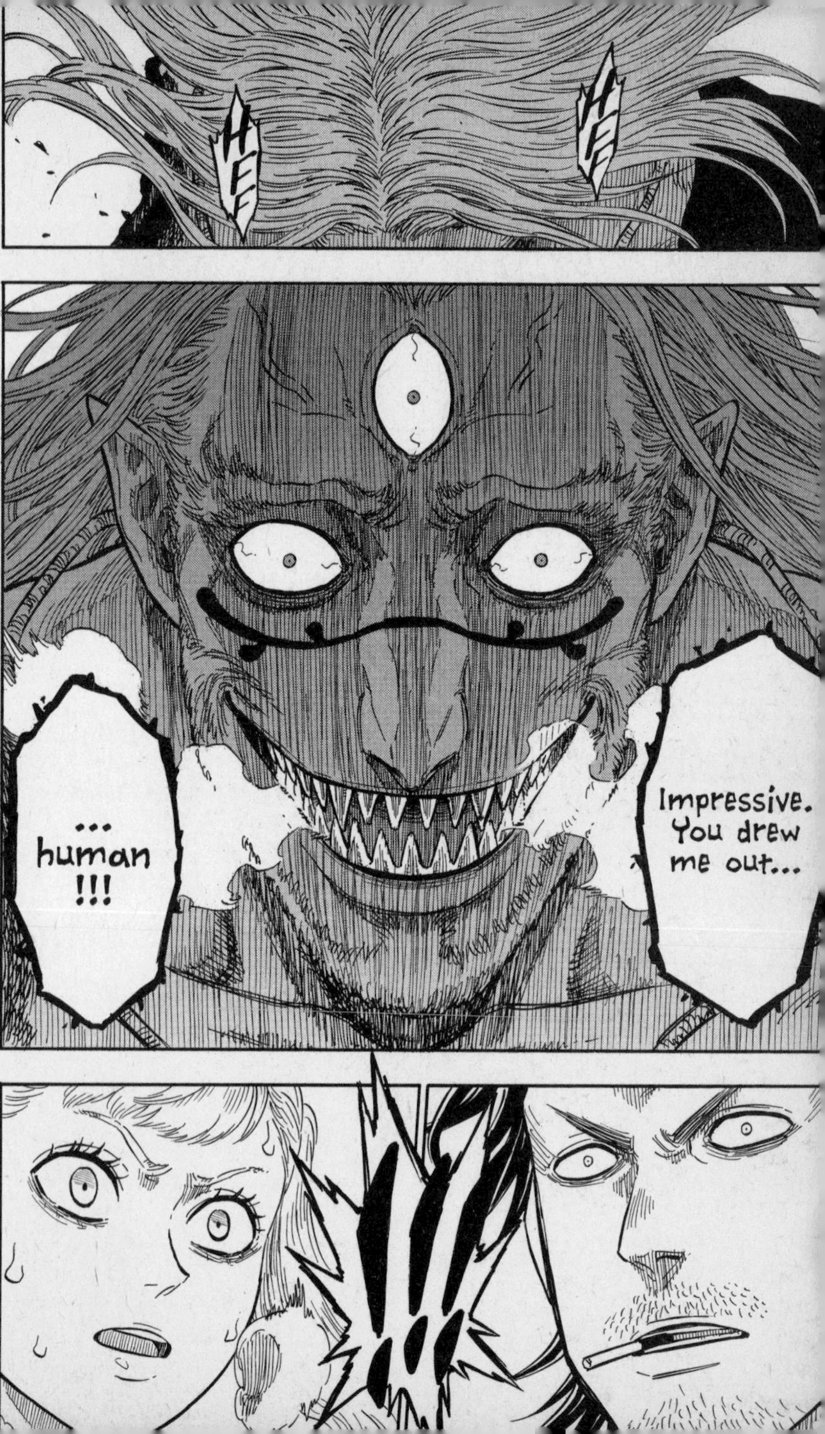
HEF
HEF
Impressive. You drew me out...
...human !!!

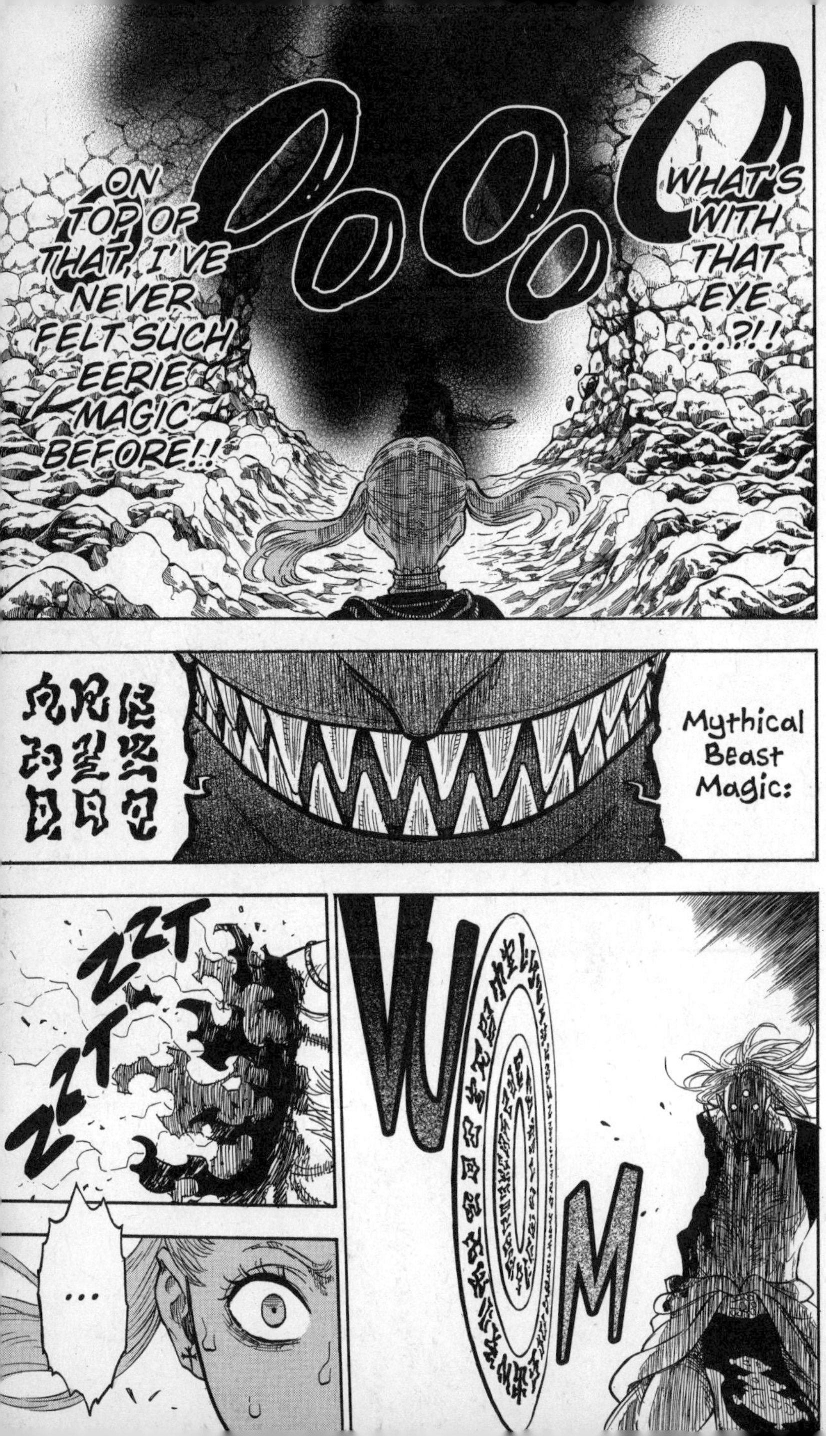
WHAT'S WITH THAT EYE...?!!
OOOOO
ON TOP OF THAT, I'VE NEVER FELT SUCH EERIE MAGIC BEFORE!!
Mythical Beast Magic:
ZZZT
ZZZT
...

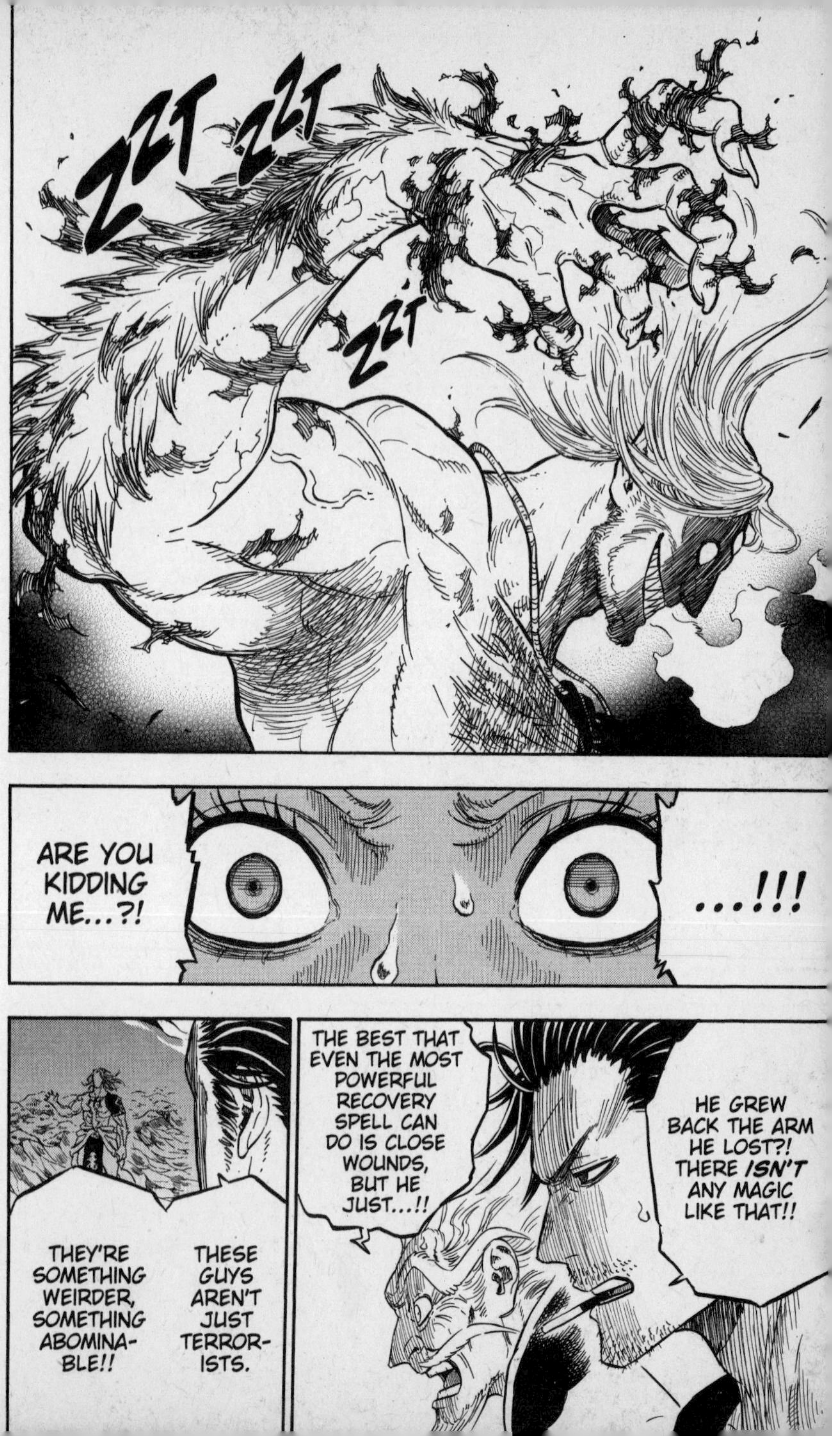
ZZZT
ZZZT
ZZZT
...!!!
ARE YOU KIDDING ME...?!
HE GREW BACK THE ARM HE LOST?! THERE *ISN'T* ANY MAGIC LIKE THAT!!
THE BEST THAT EVEN THE MOST POWERFUL RECOVERY SPELL CAN DO IS CLOSE WOUNDS, BUT HE JUST...!!
THESE GUYS AREN'T JUST TERROR-ISTS.
THEY'RE SOMETHING WEIRDER, SOMETHING ABOMINA-BLE!!

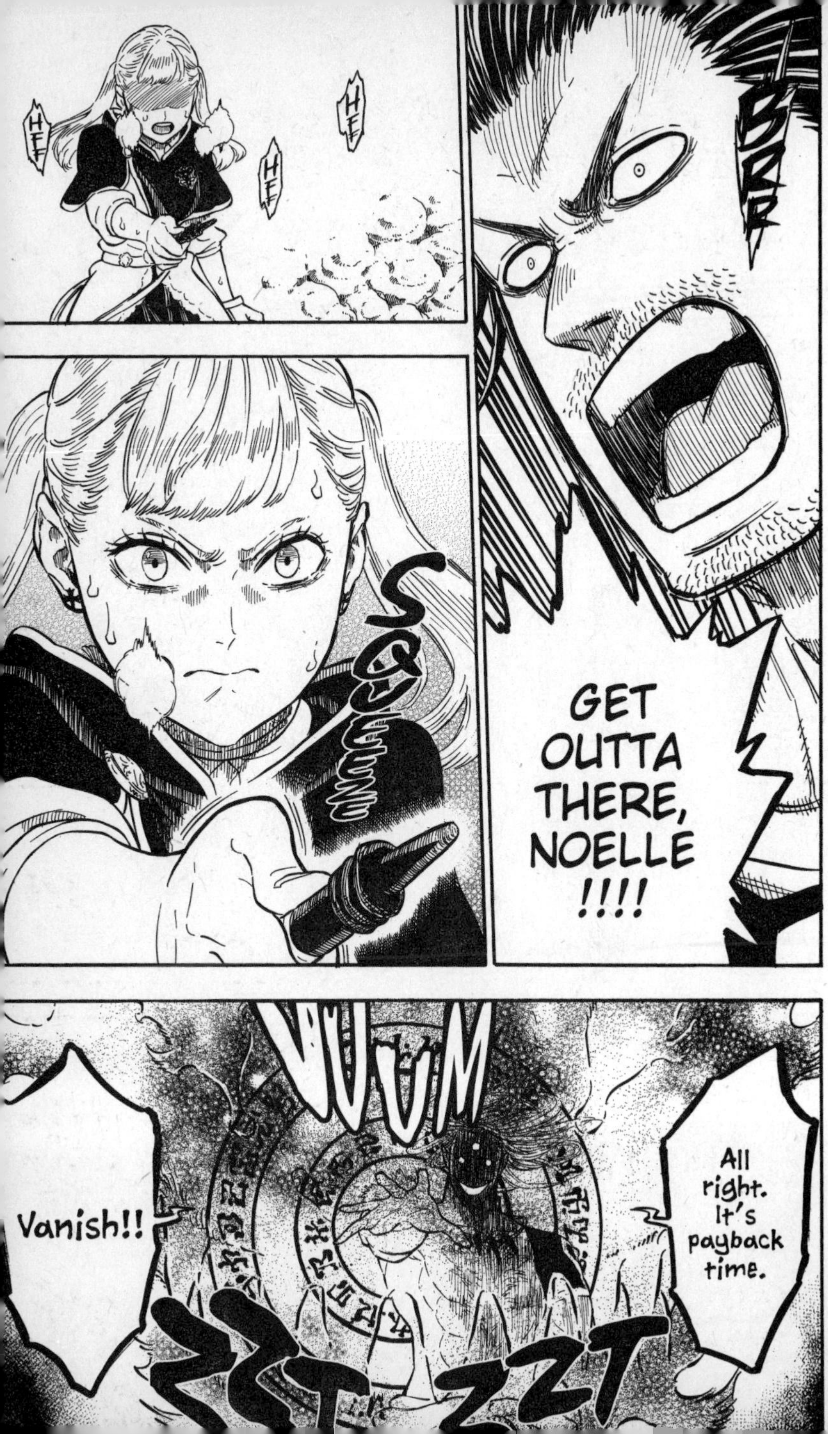
BRRR
GET OUTTA THERE, NOELLE !!!!
HEF
HEF
HEF
SQUEEEEZE
VOOM
All right. It's payback time.
Vanish!!
ZZZZT

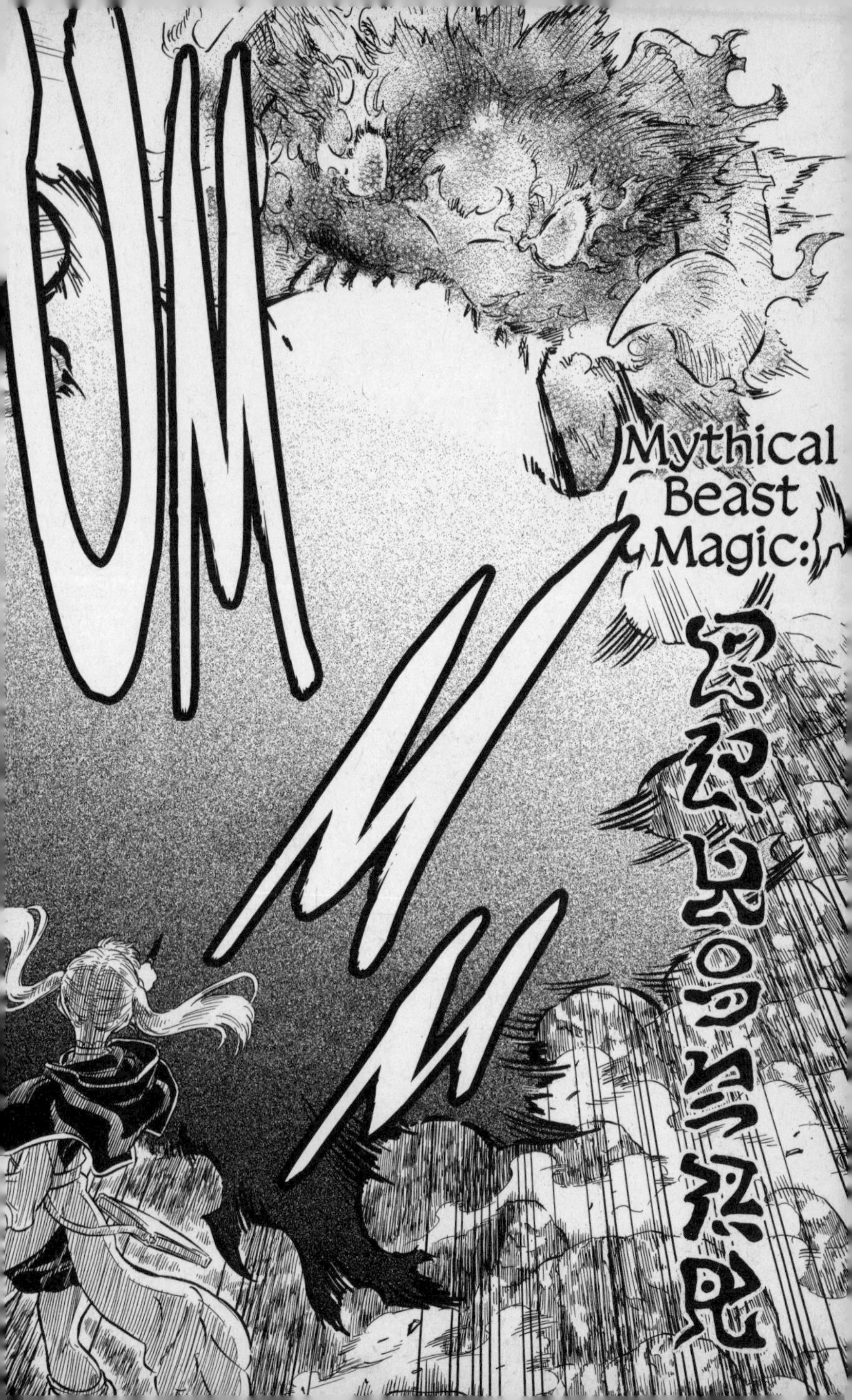
Mythical Beast Magic:

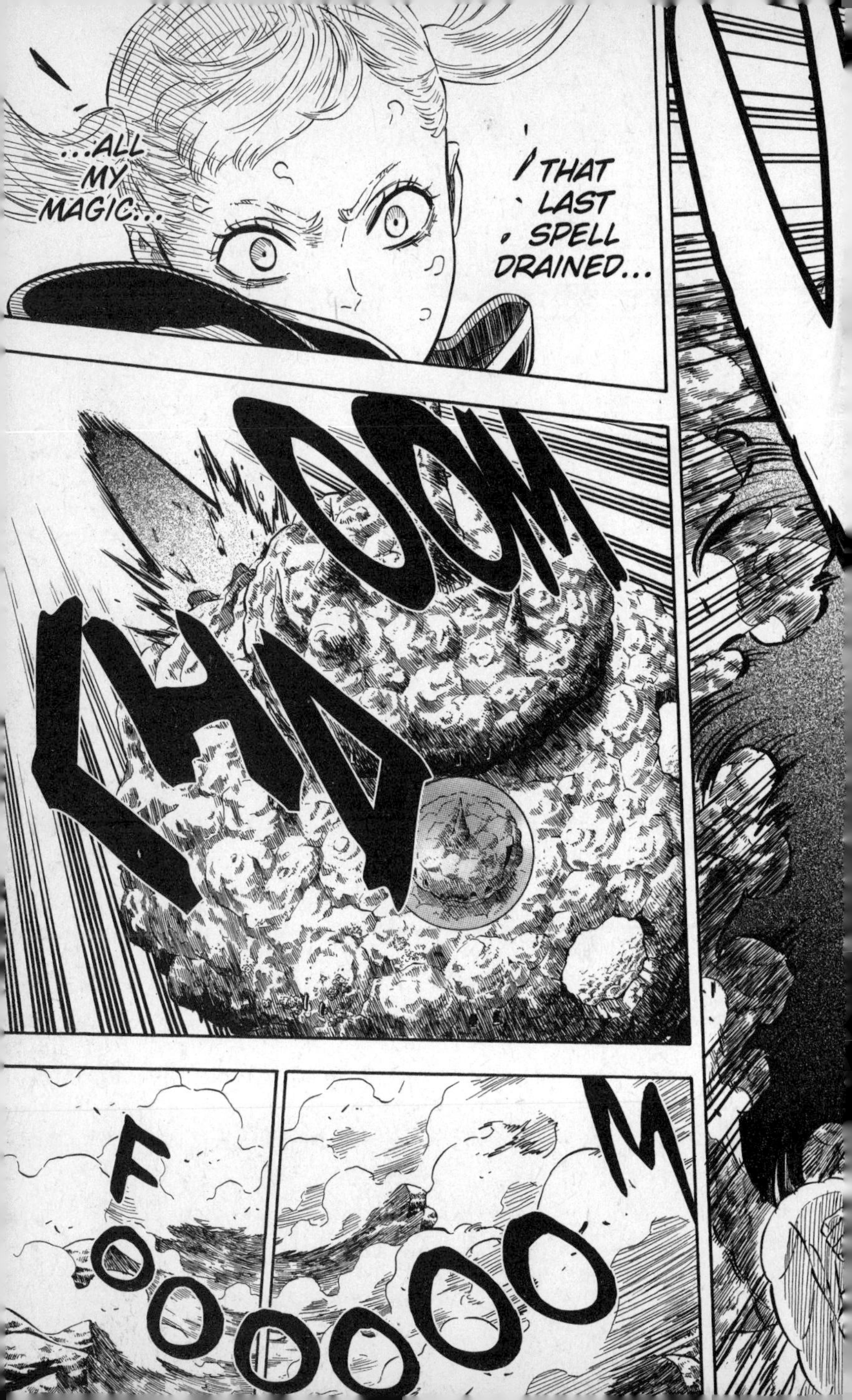
THAT LAST SPELL DRAINED...
...ALL MY MAGIC...

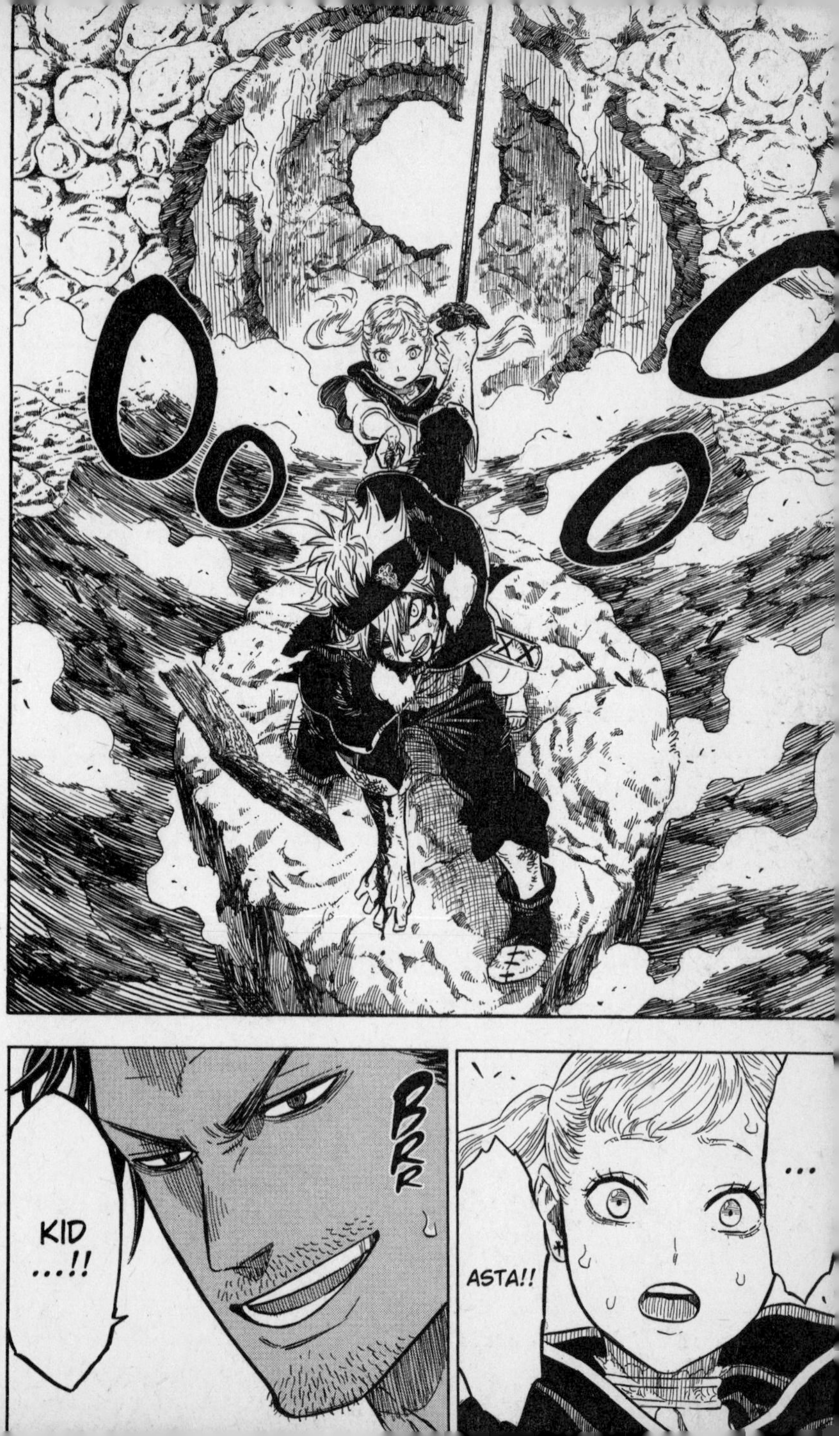
OOOO
...
ASTA!!
BRR
KID
...!!

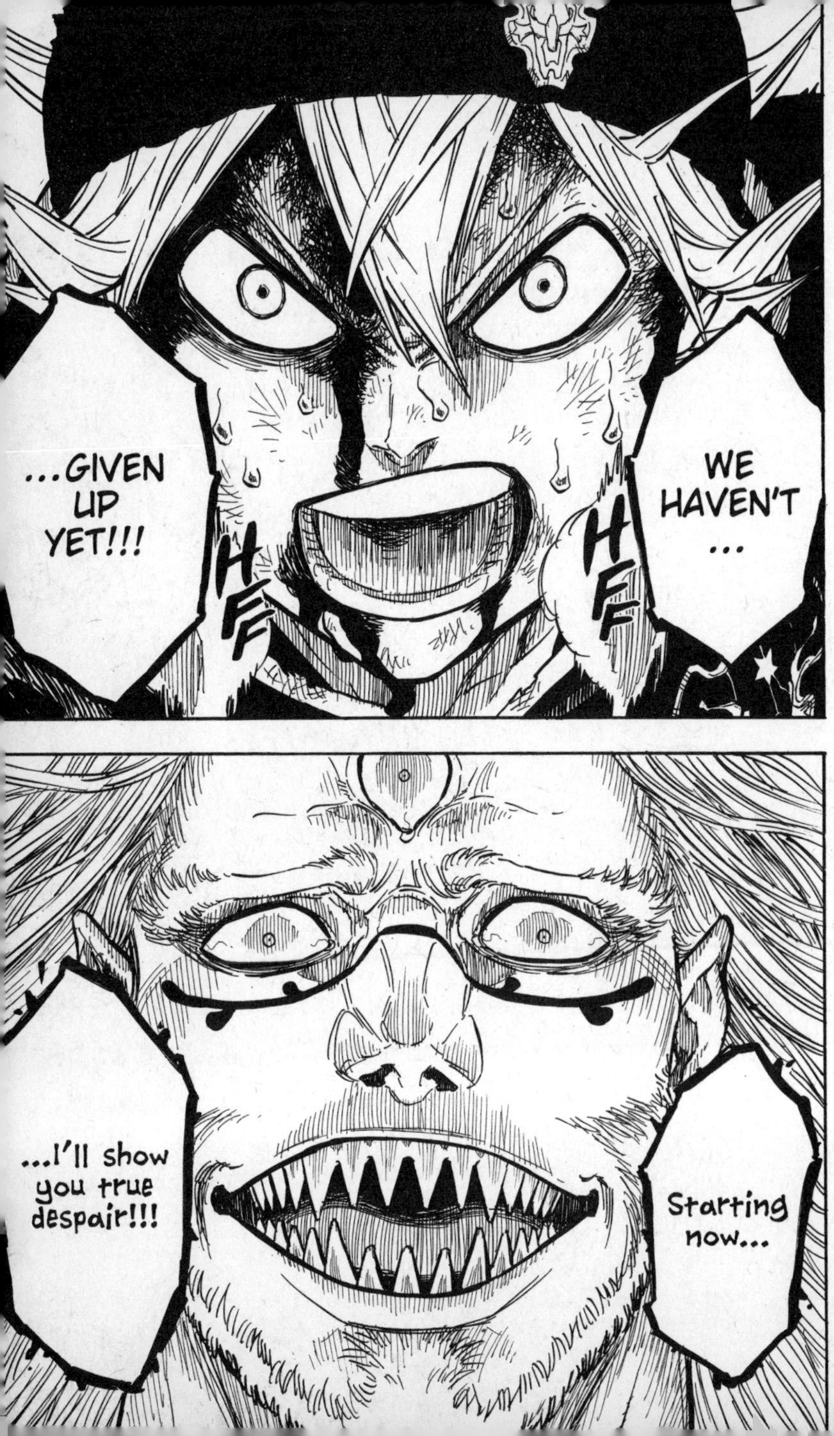
WE HAVEN'T ...
HFF
HFF
...GIVEN UP YET!!!
Starting now...
...I'll show you true despair!!!

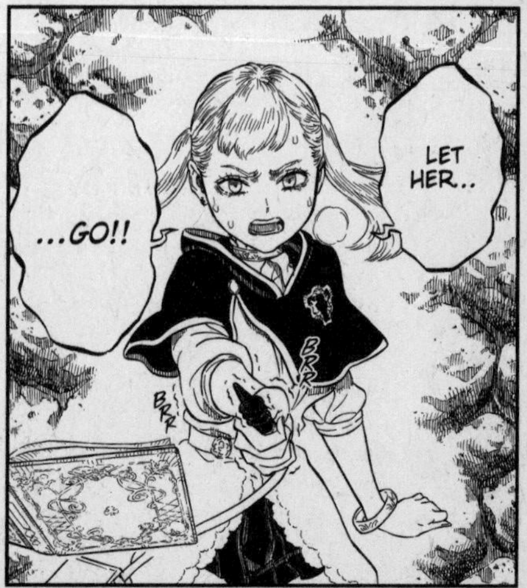
LET HER...
...GO!!
BRR
BRR

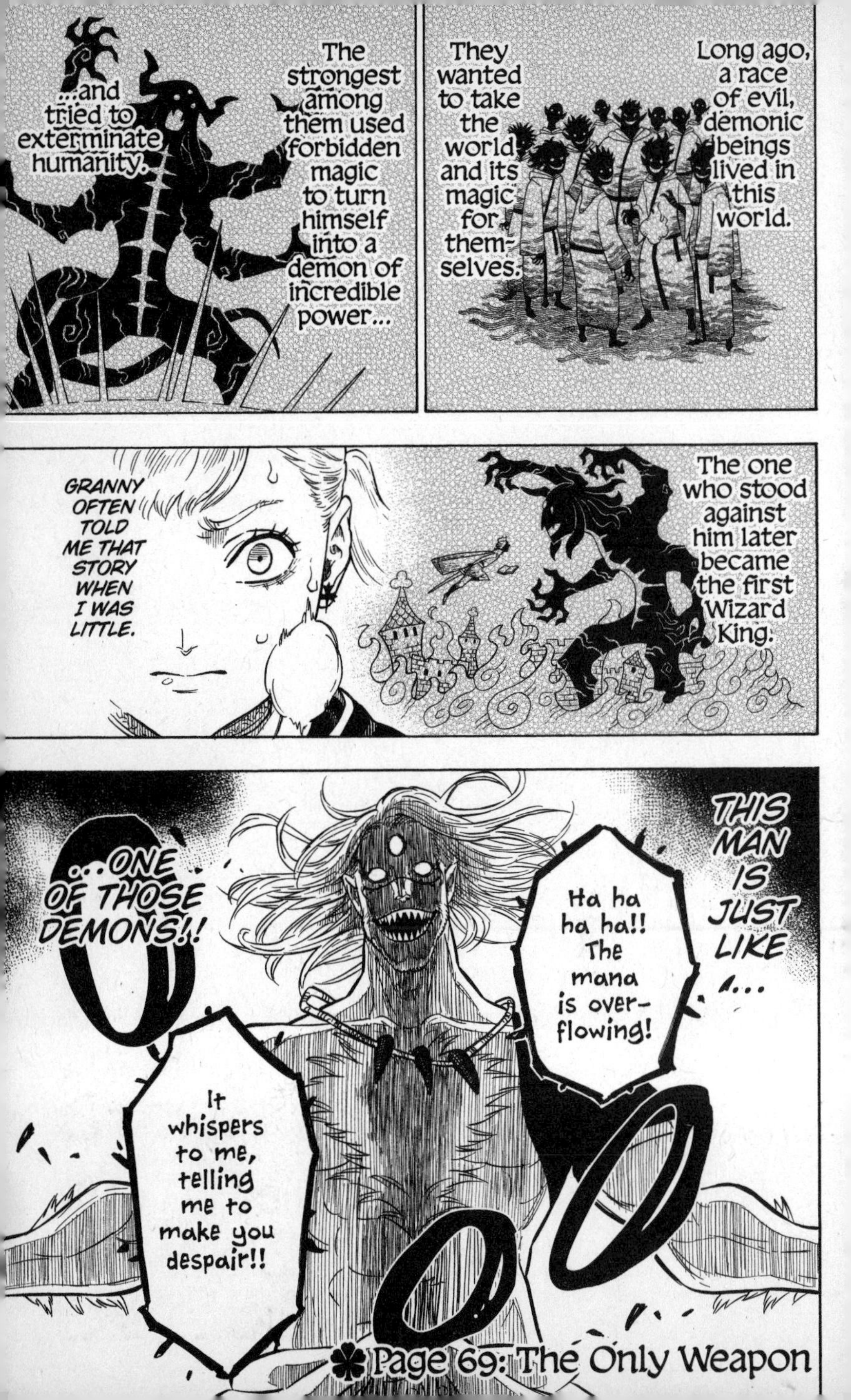
Long ago, a race of evil, demonic beings lived in this world.
They wanted to take the world and its magic for themselves.
The strongest among them used forbidden magic to turn himself into a demon of incredible power...
...and tried to exterminate humanity.
The one who stood against him later became the first Wizard King.
GRANNY OFTEN TOLD ME THAT STORY WHEN I WAS LITTLE.
THIS MAN IS JUST LIKE...
Ha ha ha ha!! The mana is overflowing!
...ONE OF THOSE DEMONS!!
It whispers to me, telling me to make you despair!!
Page 69: The Only Weapon

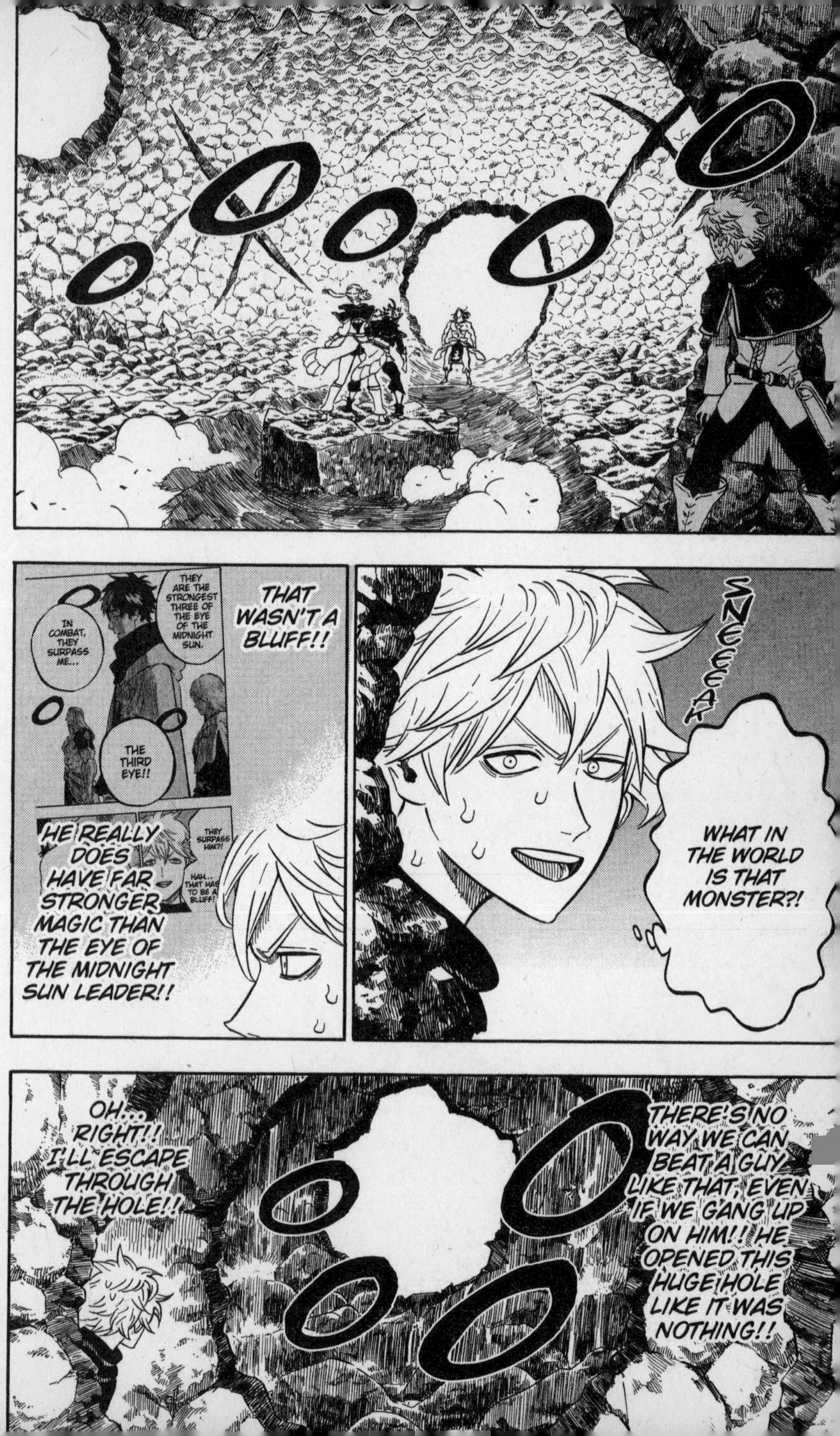
SNEEEAK
WHAT IN THE WORLD IS THAT MONSTER?!
THAT WASN'T A BLUFF!!
THEY ARE THE STRONGEST THREE OF THE EYE OF THE MIDNIGHT SUN.
IN COMBAT, THEY SURPASS ME...
THE THIRD EYE!!
HE REALLY DOES HAVE FAR STRONGER MAGIC THAN THE EYE OF THE MIDNIGHT SUN LEADER!!
THEY SURPASS HIM?
HAH... THAT HAS TO BE A BLUFF!
THERE'S NO WAY WE CAN BEAT A GUY LIKE THAT, EVEN IF WE GANG UP ON HIM!! HE OPENED THIS HUGE HOLE LIKE IT WAS NOTHING!!
OH... RIGHT!! I'LL ESCAPE THROUGH THE HOLE!!

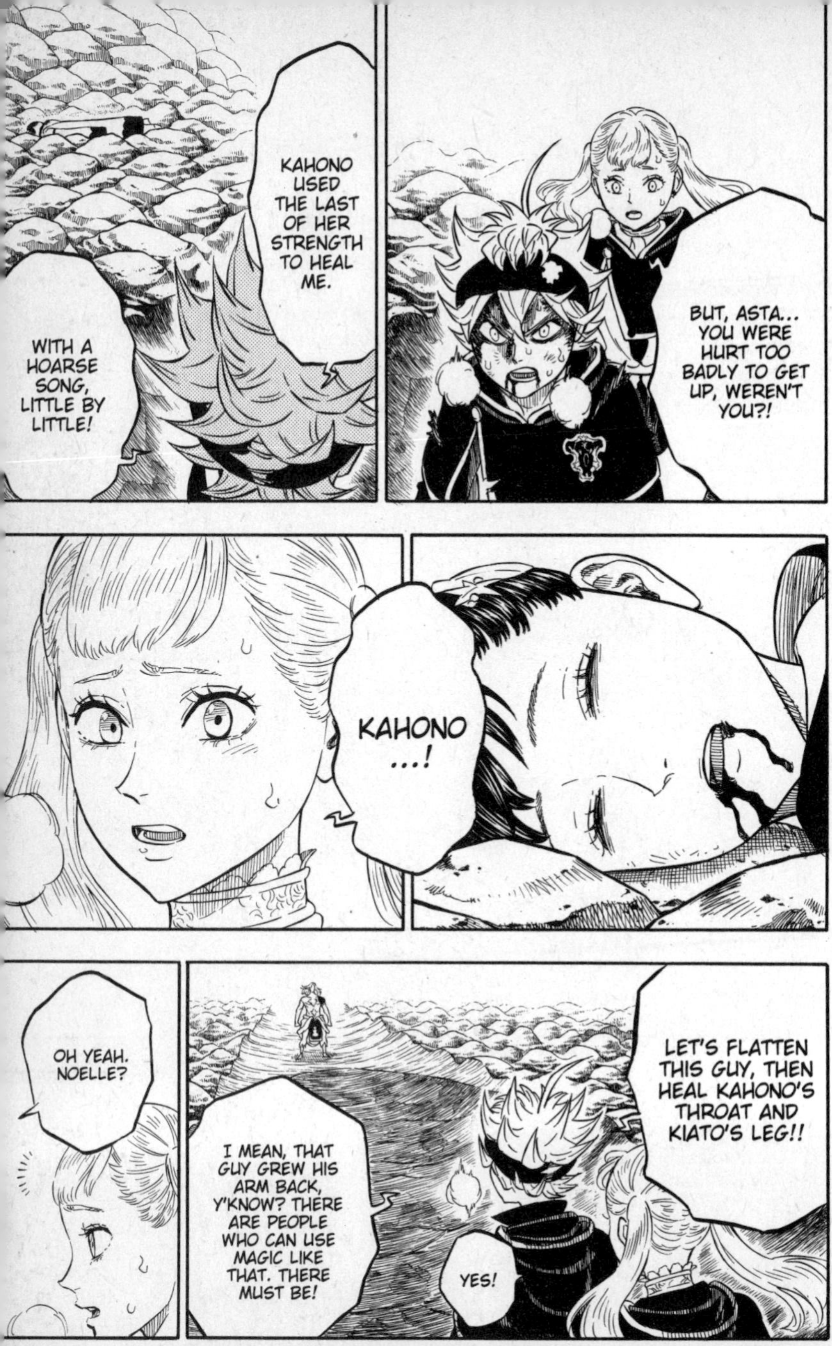
BUT, ASTA... YOU WERE HURT TOO BADLY TO GET UP, WEREN'T YOU?!
KAHONO USED THE LAST OF HER STRENGTH TO HEAL ME.
WITH A HOARSE SONG, LITTLE BY LITTLE!
KAHONO ...!
LET'S FLATTEN THIS GUY, THEN HEAL KAHONO'S THROAT AND KIATO'S LEG!!
I MEAN, THAT GUY GREW HIS ARM BACK, Y'KNOW? THERE ARE PEOPLE WHO CAN USE MAGIC LIKE THAT. THERE MUST BE!
YES!
OH YEAH. NOELLE?

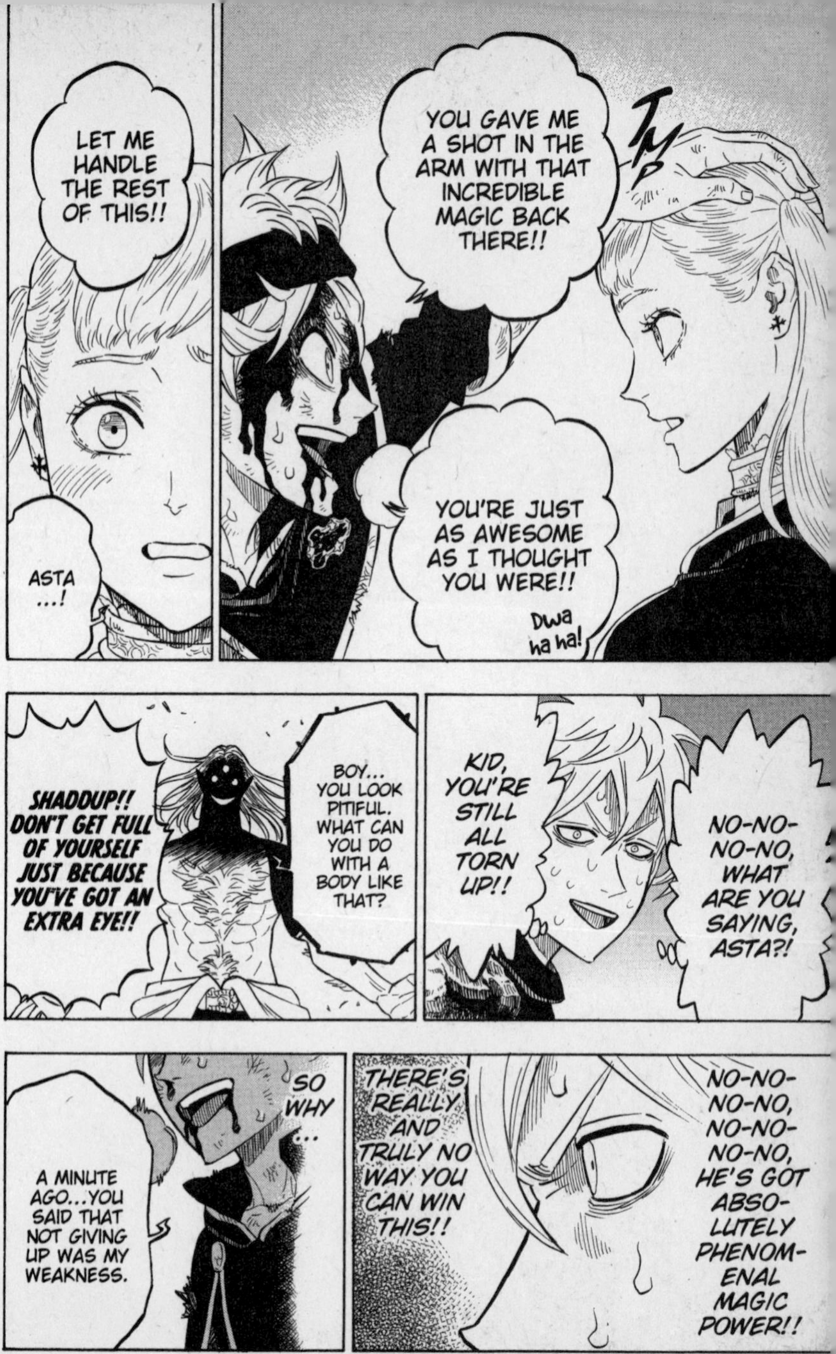
TMP
YOU GAVE ME A SHOT IN THE ARM WITH THAT INCREDIBLE MAGIC BACK THERE!!
YOU'RE JUST AS AWESOME AS I THOUGHT YOU WERE!!
Dwa ha ha!
LET ME HANDLE THE REST OF THIS!!
ASTA ...!
NO-NO-NO-NO, WHAT ARE YOU SAYING, ASTA?!
KID, YOU'RE STILL ALL TORN UP!!
BOY... YOU LOOK PITIFUL. WHAT CAN YOU DO WITH A BODY LIKE THAT?
SHADDUP!! DON'T GET FULL OF YOURSELF JUST BECAUSE YOU'VE GOT AN EXTRA EYE!!
NO-NO-NO-NO, NO-NO-NO-NO, HE'S GOT ABSOLUTELY PHENOMENAL MAGIC POWER!!
THERE'S REALLY AND TRULY NO WAY YOU CAN WIN THIS!!
SO WHY...
A MINUTE AGO...YOU SAID THAT NOT GIVING UP WAS MY WEAKNESS.

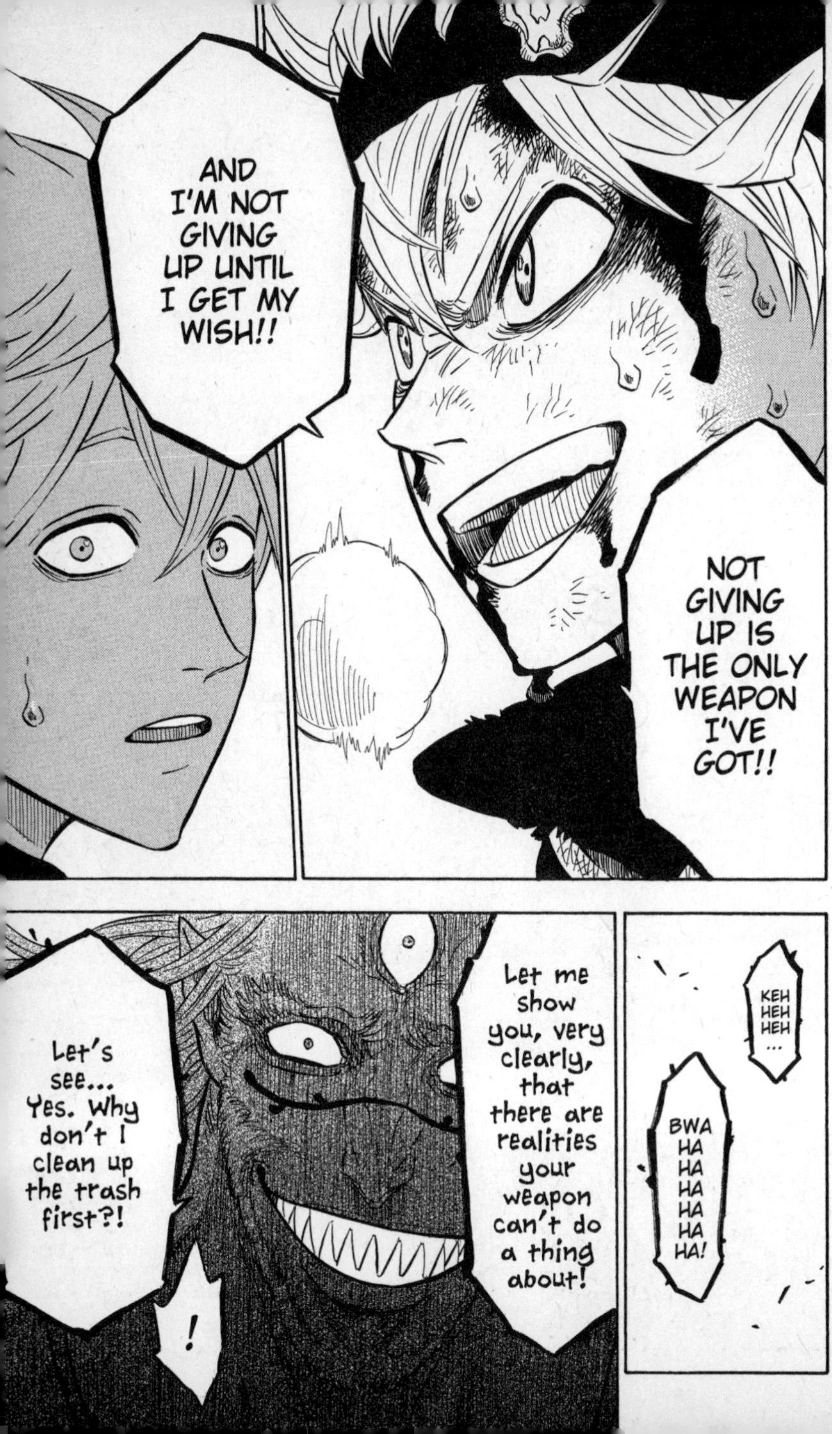
NOT GIVING UP IS THE ONLY WEAPON I'VE GOT!!
AND I'M NOT GIVING UP UNTIL I GET MY WISH!!
KEH HEH HEH...
BWA HA HA HA HA HA HA!
Let me show you, very clearly, that there are realities your weapon can't do a thing about!
Let's see... Yes. Why don't I clean up the trash first?!
!

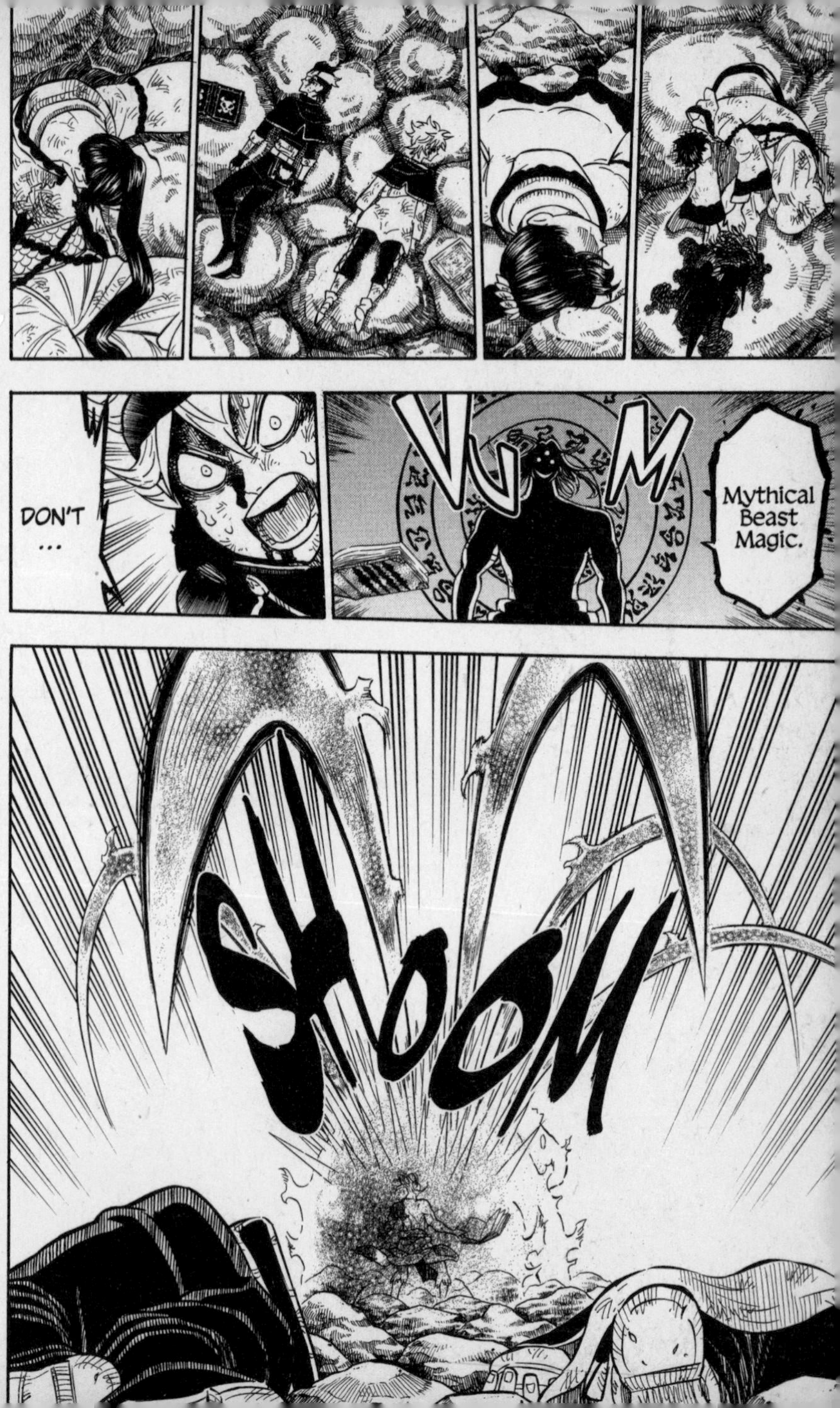
Mythical Beast Magic.
VMM
DON'T ...
SHOOM

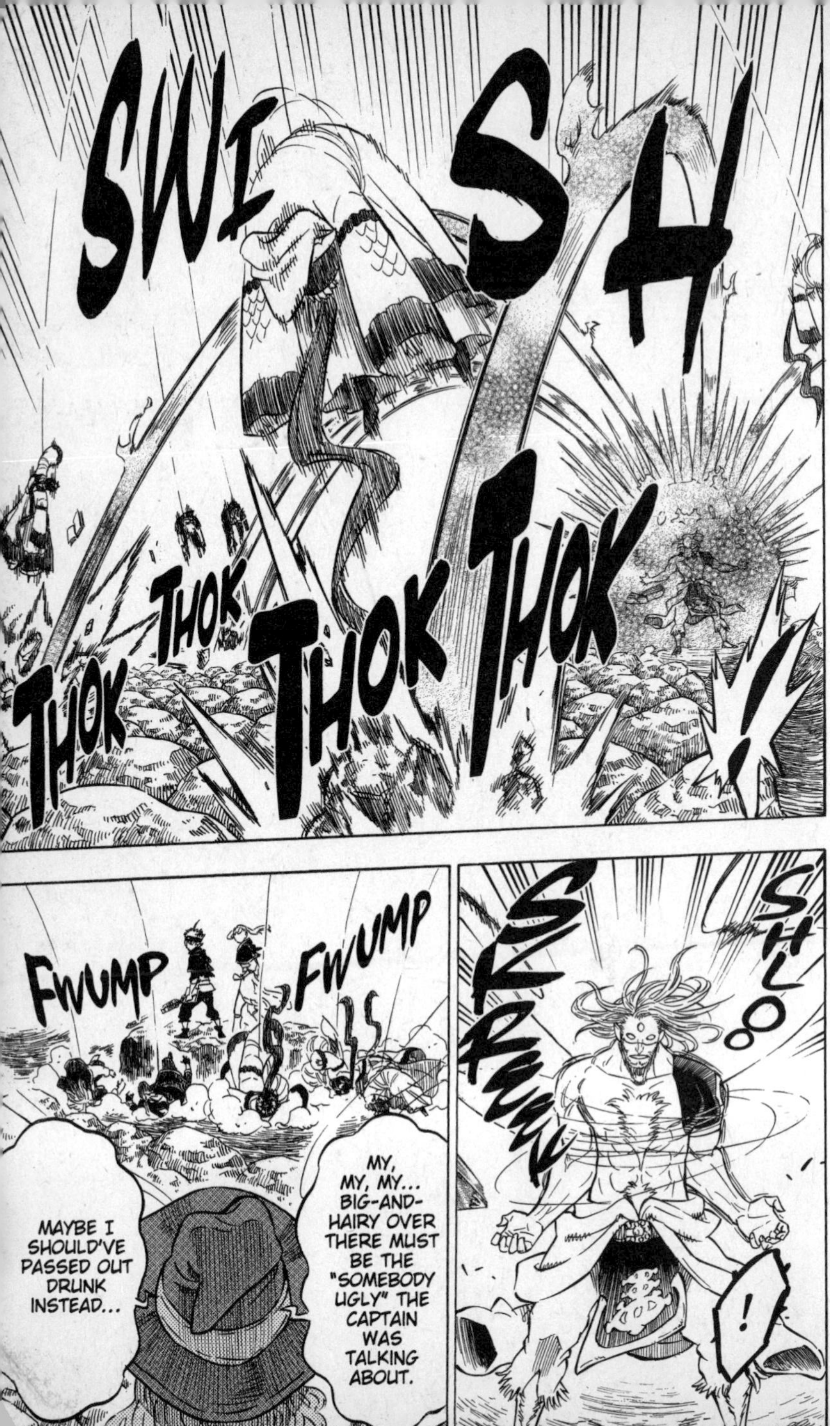
SWISH
THOK THOK THOK THOK
SHLOOO
SKRWWN
!
FWUMP FWUMP
MY, MY, MY... BIG-AND-HAIRY OVER THERE MUST BE THE "SOMEBODY UGLY" THE CAPTAIN WAS TALKING ABOUT.
MAYBE I SHOULD'VE PASSED OUT DRUNK INSTEAD...

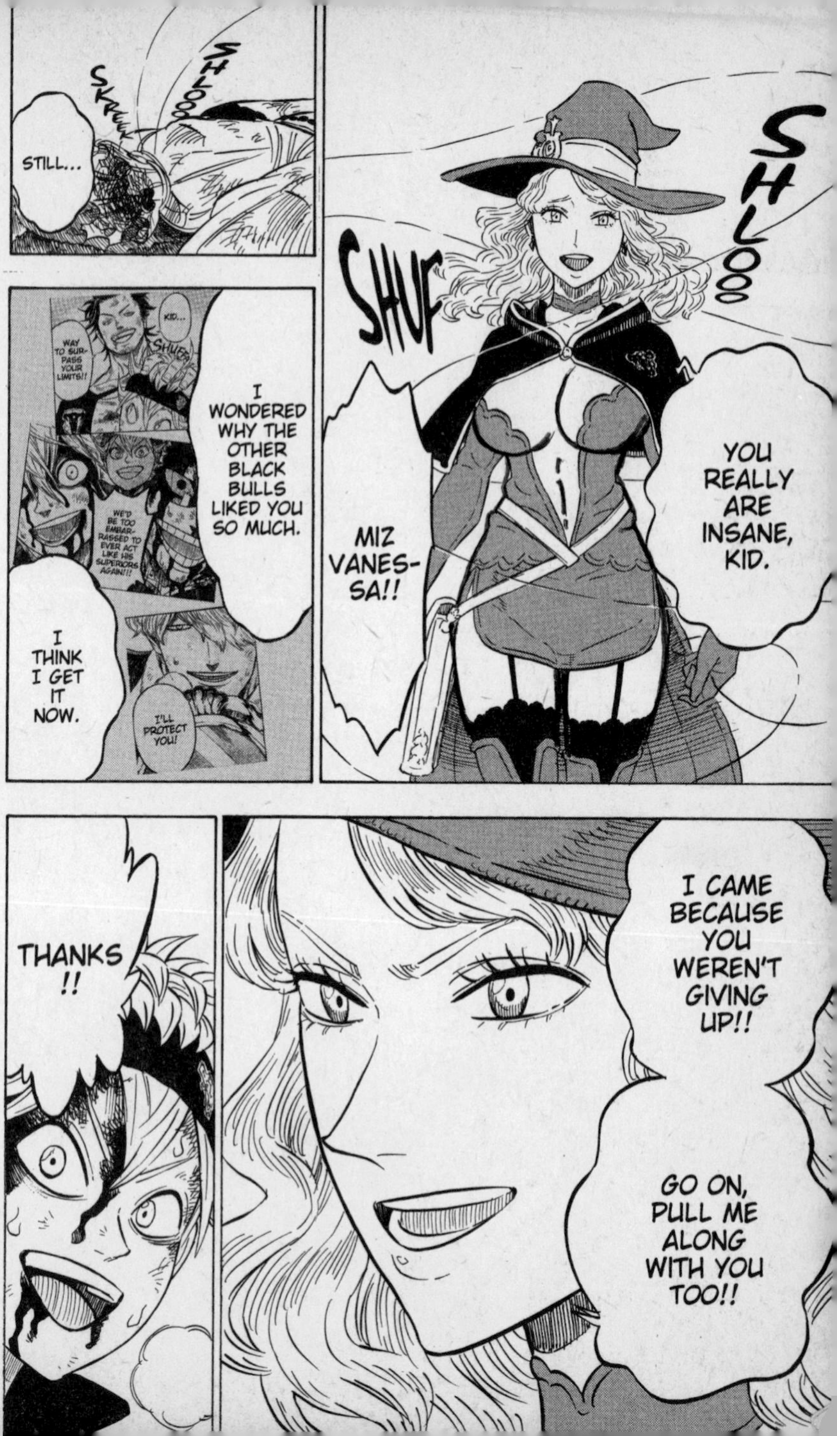
SHLOOO
SHUF
MIZ VANES-SA!!
YOU REALLY ARE INSANE, KID.
SHLOOO
SKREEK
STILL...
I WONDERED WHY THE OTHER BLACK BULLS LIKED YOU SO MUCH.
KID...
WAY TO SURPASS YOUR LIMITS!!
SHUFF
WE'D BE TOO EMBARRASSED TO EVER ACT LIKE HIS SUPERIORS AGAIN!!!
I THINK I GET IT NOW.
I'LL PROTECT YOU!
I CAME BECAUSE YOU WEREN'T GIVING UP!!
GO ON, PULL ME ALONG WITH YOU TOO!!
THANKS!!

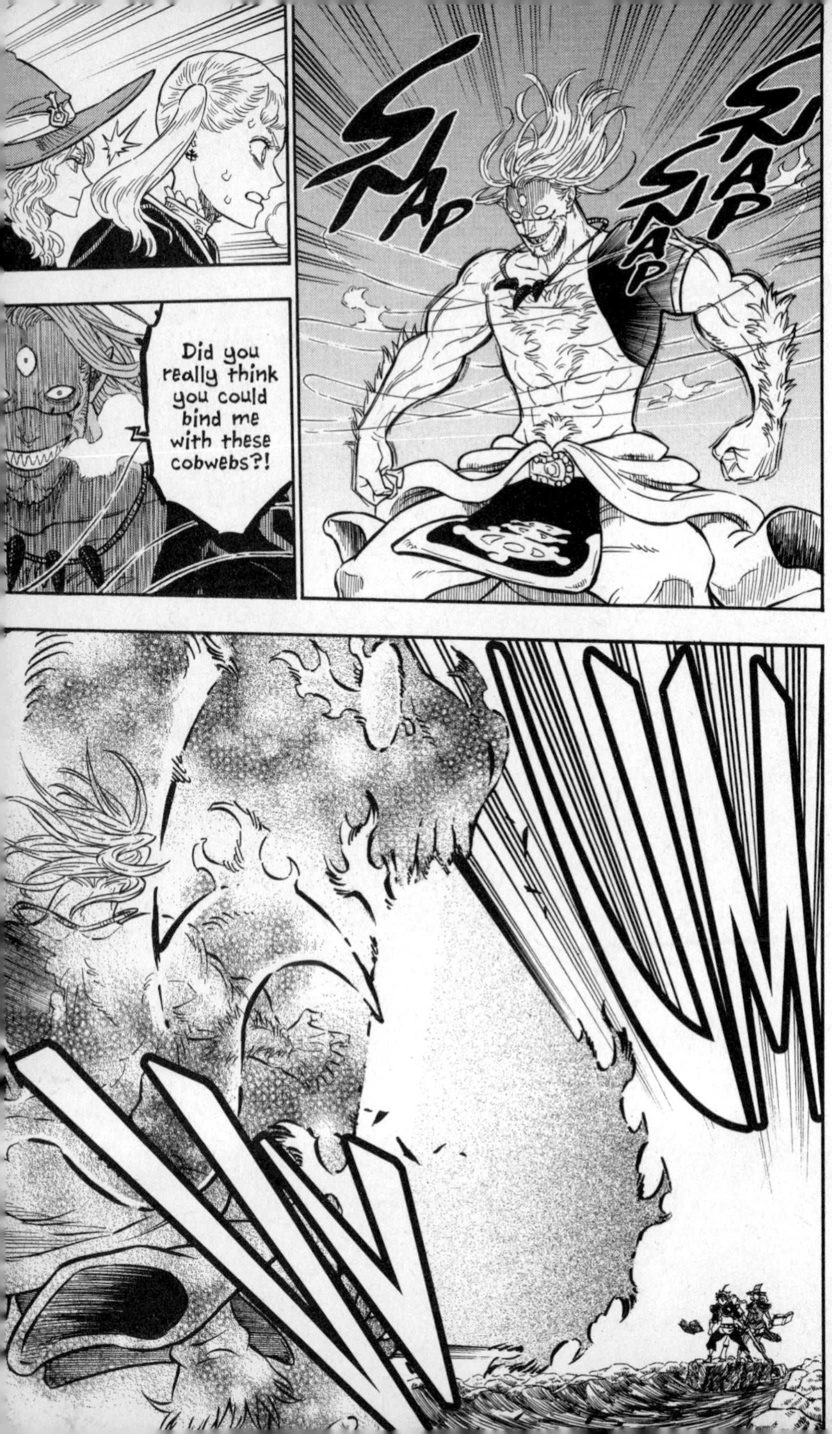
SNAP
SNAP
SNAP
Did you really think you could bind me with these cobwebs?!

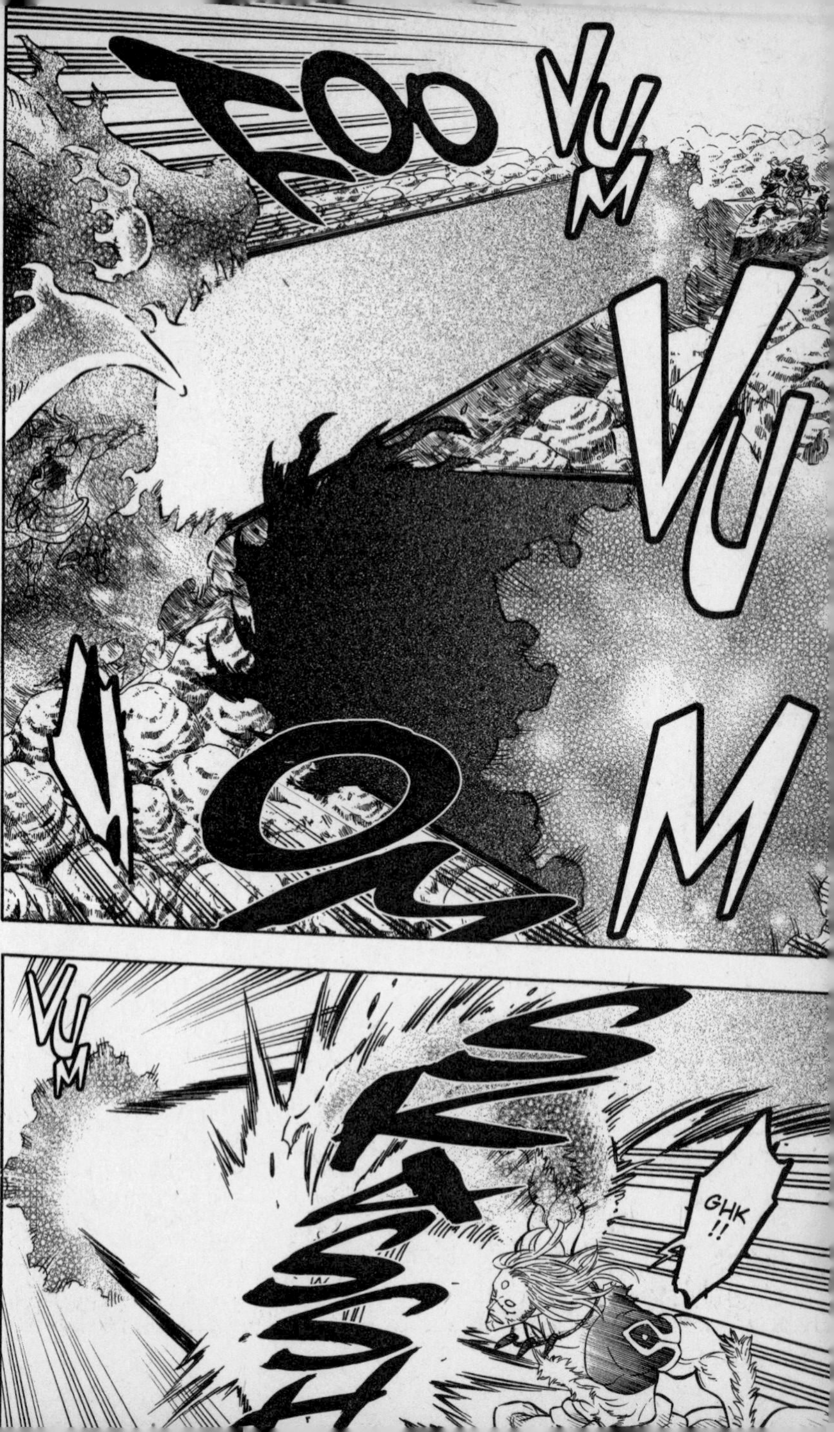
VUM
VUM
VUM
GHK !!

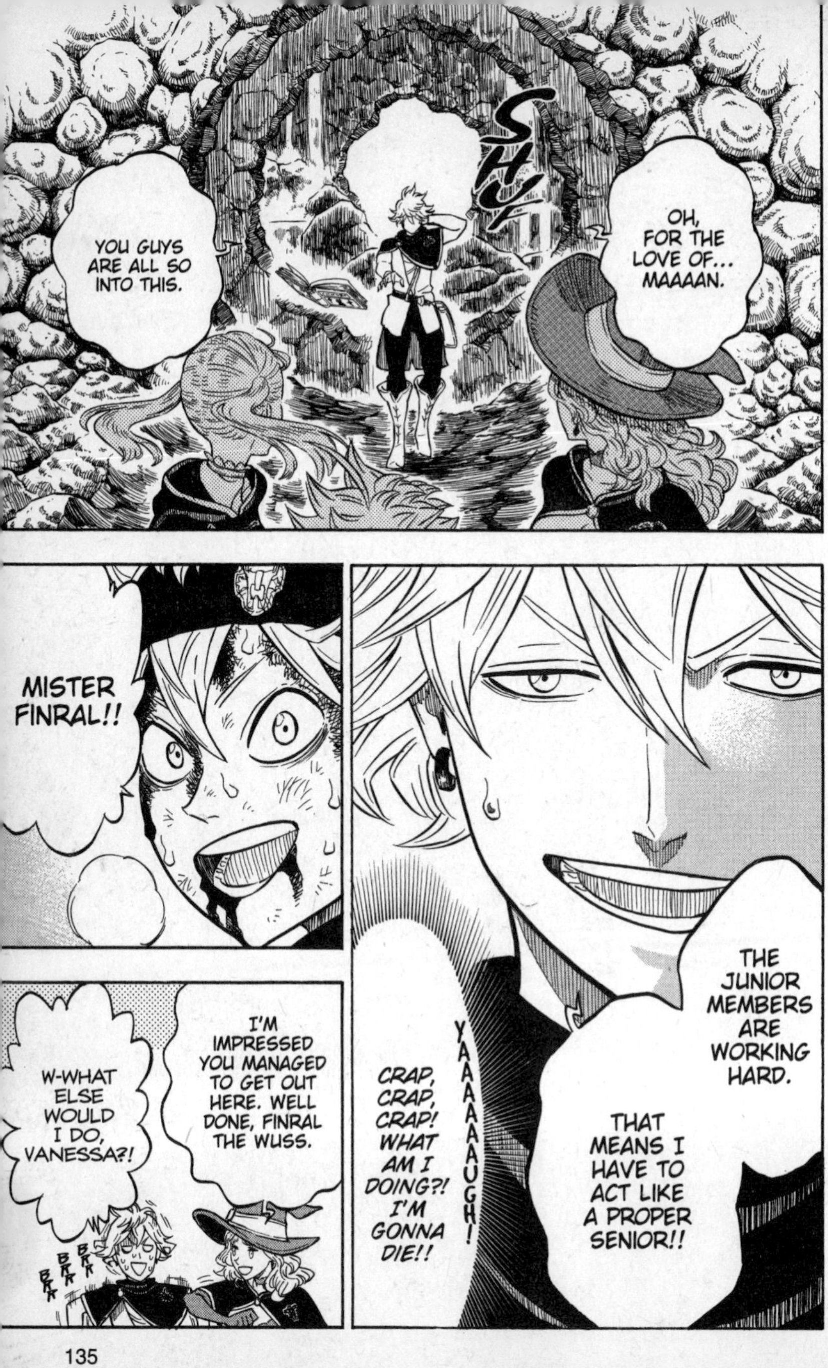
SHUF
OH, FOR THE LOVE OF... MAAAAN.
YOU GUYS ARE ALL SO INTO THIS.
THE JUNIOR MEMBERS ARE WORKING HARD.
THAT MEANS I HAVE TO ACT LIKE A PROPER SENIOR!!
YAAAAAAAUGH!
CRAP, CRAP, CRAP! WHAT AM I DOING?! I'M GONNA DIE!!
MISTER FINRAL!!
I'M IMPRESSED YOU MANAGED TO GET OUT HERE. WELL DONE, FINRAL THE WUSS.
W-WHAT ELSE WOULD I DO, VANESSA?!

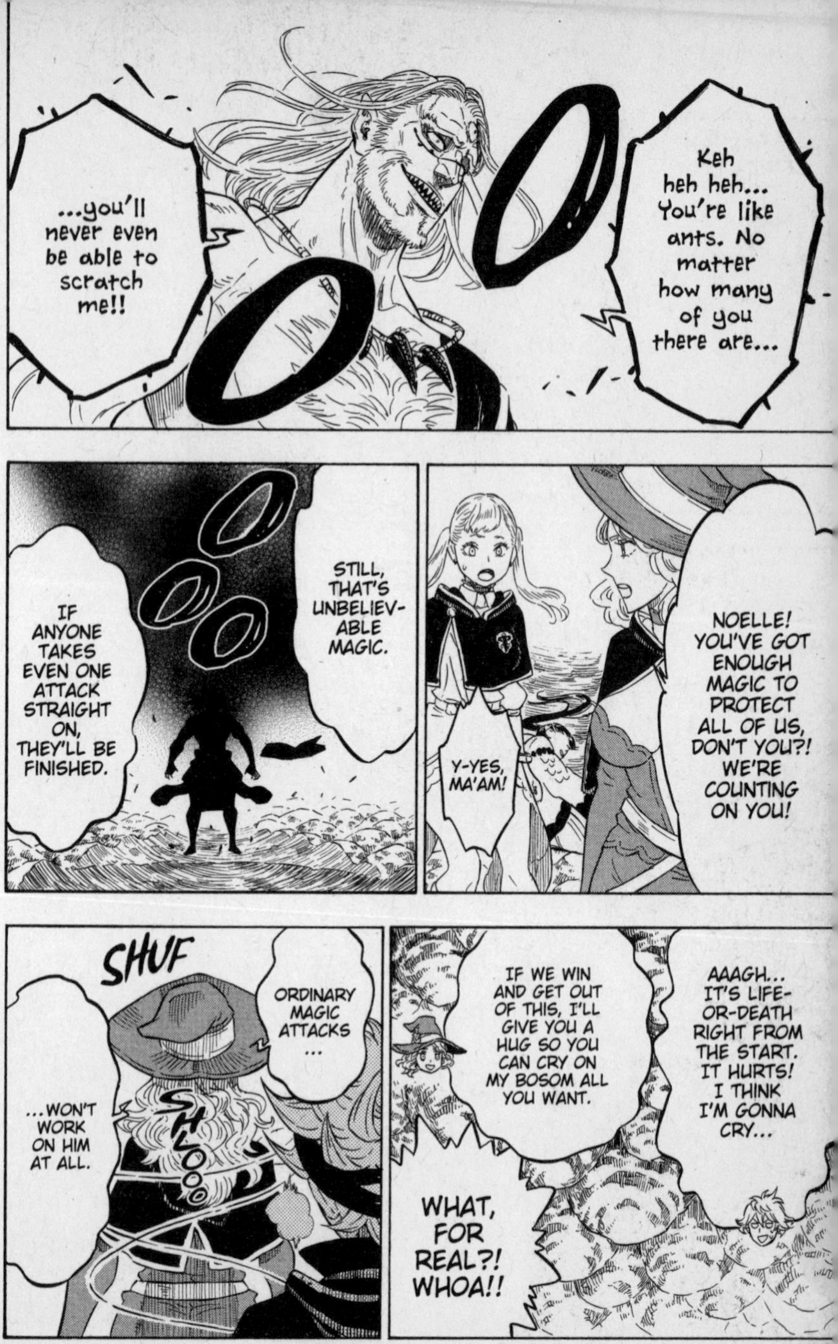
Keh heh heh... You're like ants. No matter how many of you there are...
...you'll never even be able to scratch me!!
NOELLE! YOU'VE GOT ENOUGH MAGIC TO PROTECT ALL OF US, DON'T YOU?! WE'RE COUNTING ON YOU!
Y-YES, MA'AM!
STILL, THAT'S UNBELIEVABLE MAGIC.
IF ANYONE TAKES EVEN ONE ATTACK STRAIGHT ON, THEY'LL BE FINISHED.
AAAGH... IT'S LIFE-OR-DEATH RIGHT FROM THE START. IT HURTS! I THINK I'M GONNA CRY...
IF WE WIN AND GET OUT OF THIS, I'LL GIVE YOU A HUG SO YOU CAN CRY ON MY BOSOM ALL YOU WANT.
WHAT, FOR REAL?! WHOA!!
SHUF
ORDINARY MAGIC ATTACKS...
...WON'T WORK ON HIM AT ALL.
SHLOOO

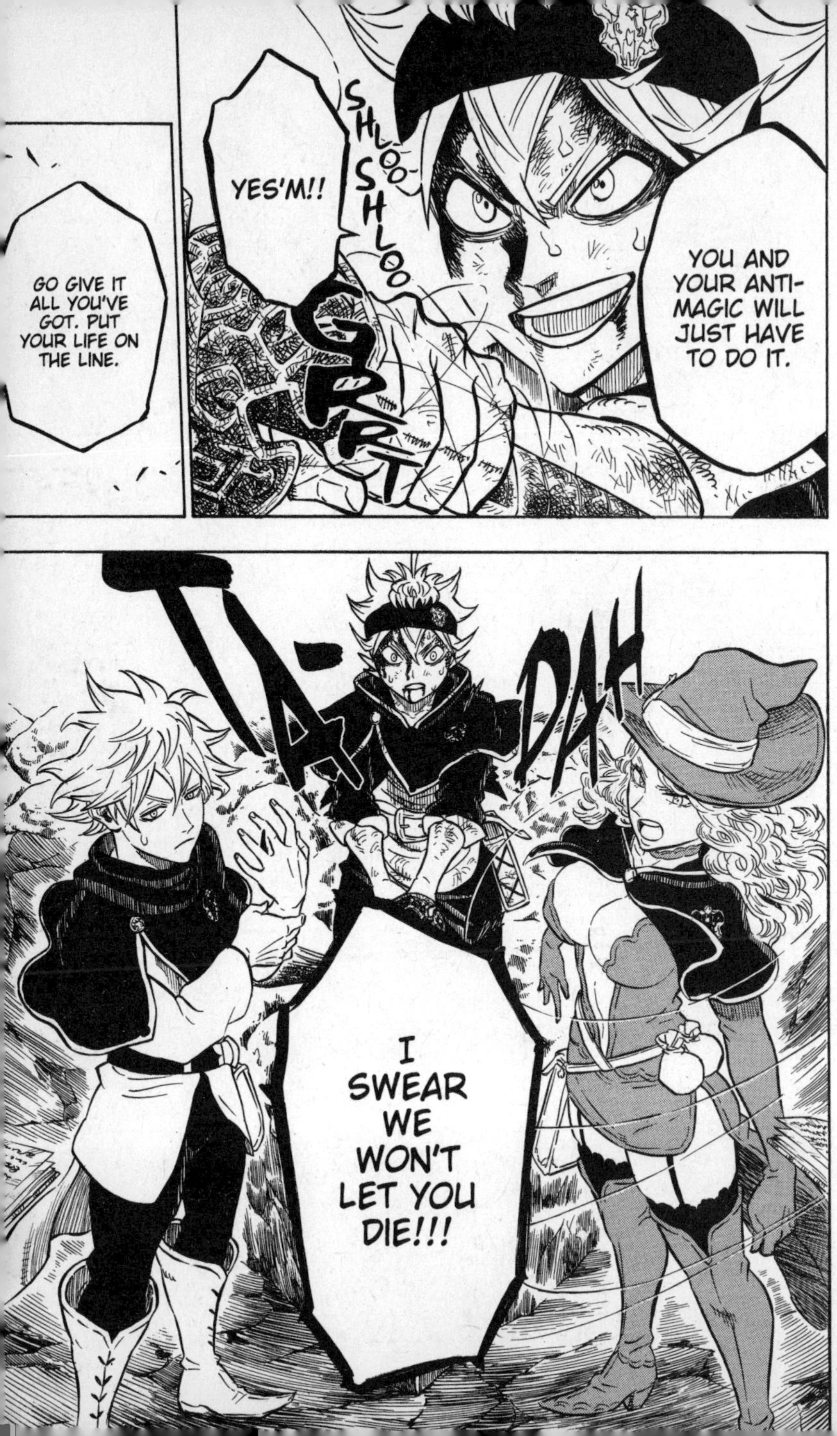
YOU AND YOUR ANTI-MAGIC WILL JUST HAVE TO DO IT.
YES'M!!
SHLOO SHLOO
GRRRT
GO GIVE IT ALL YOU'VE GOT. PUT YOUR LIFE ON THE LINE.
TA-DAH
I SWEAR WE WON'T LET YOU DIE!!!

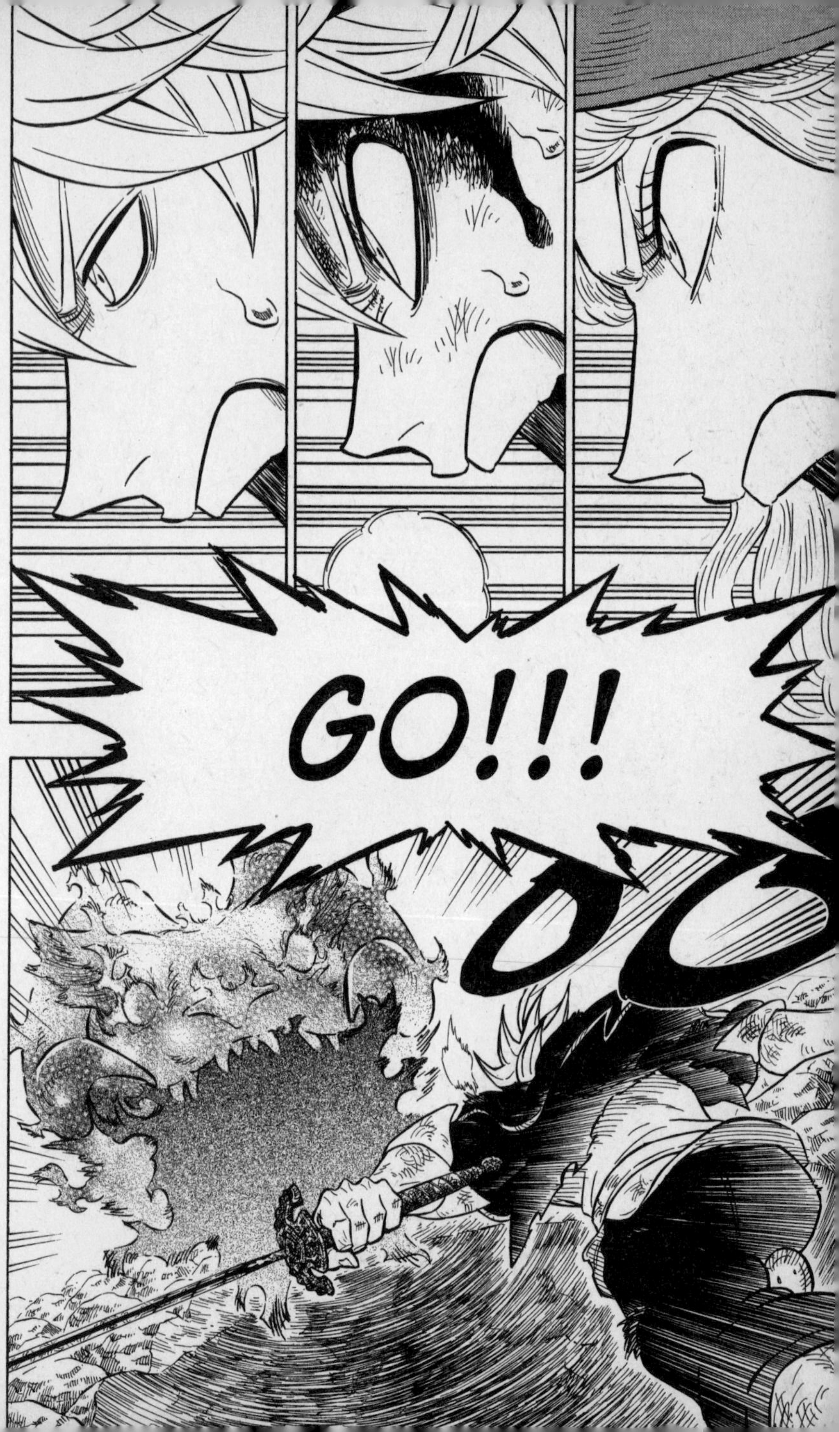
GO!!!
DO

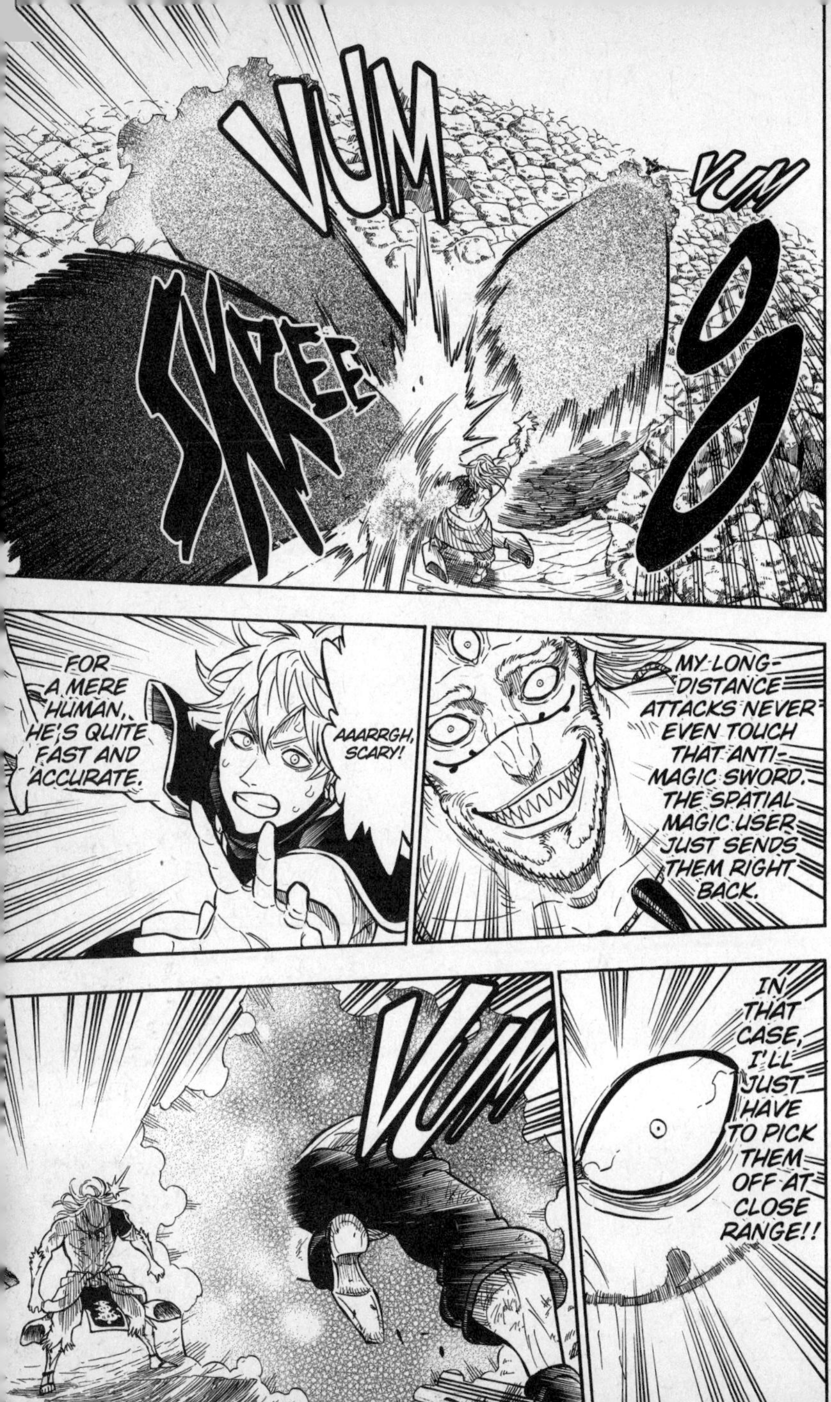
VUM
VUM
MY LONG-DISTANCE ATTACKS NEVER EVEN TOUCH THAT ANTI-MAGIC SWORD. THE SPATIAL MAGIC USER JUST SENDS THEM RIGHT BACK.
AAARRGH, SCARY!
FOR A MERE HUMAN, HE'S QUITE FAST AND ACCURATE.
IN THAT CASE, I'LL JUST HAVE TO PICK THEM OFF AT CLOSE RANGE!!
VUM

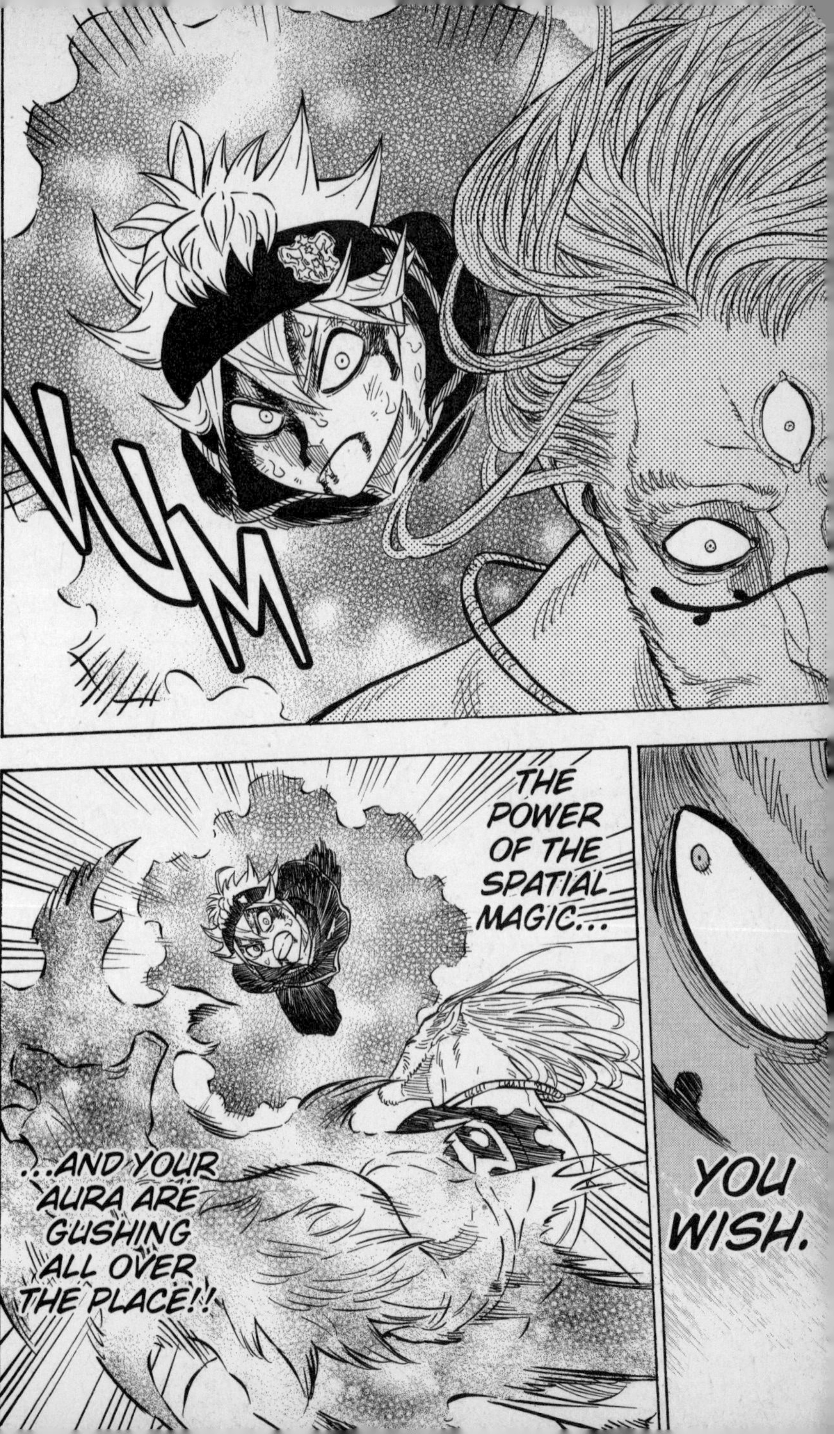
VWM
YOU WISH.
THE POWER OF THE SPATIAL MAGIC...
...AND YOUR AURA ARE GUSHING ALL OVER THE PLACE!!

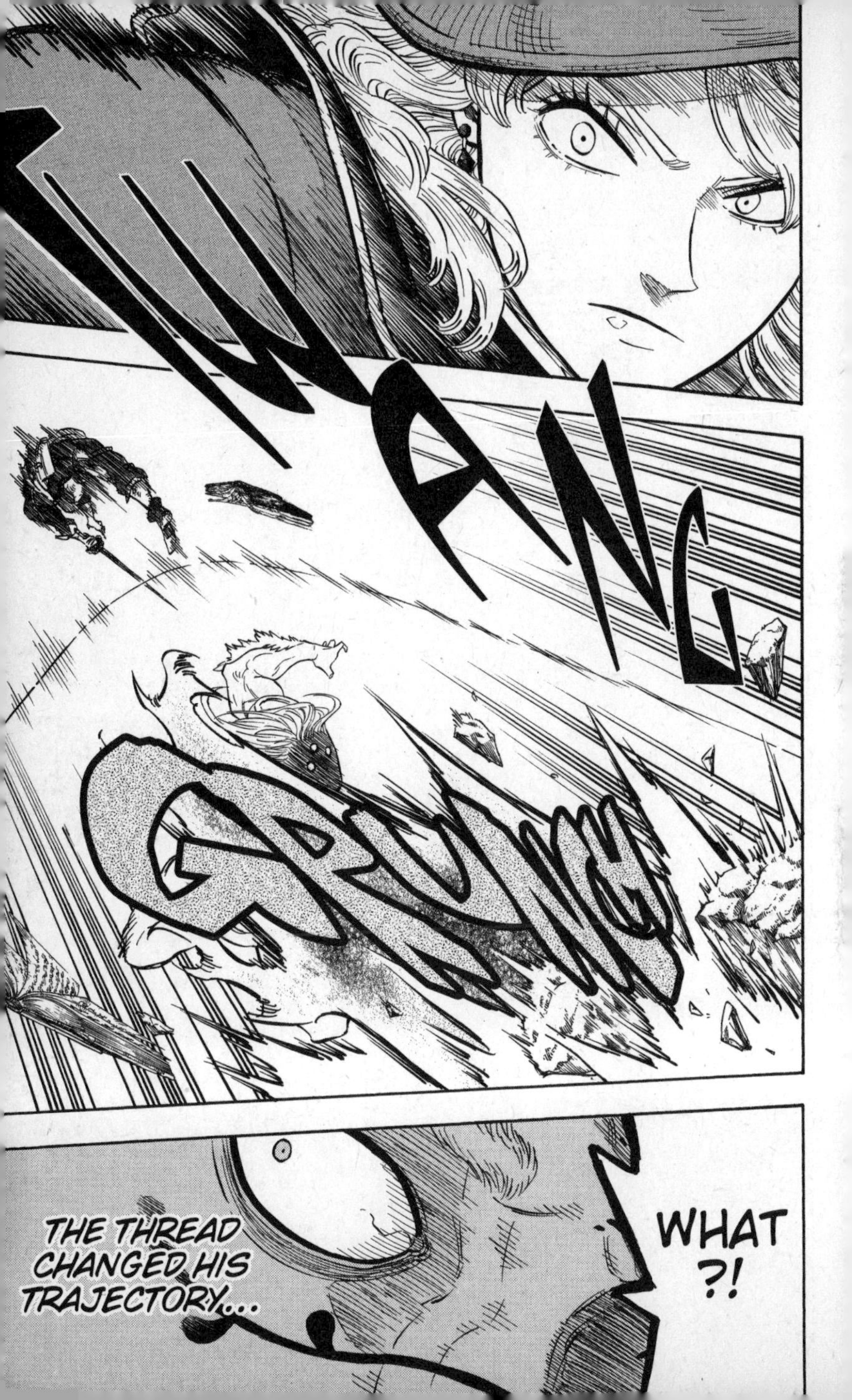
WHAT ?!
THE THREAD CHANGED HIS TRAJECTORY...

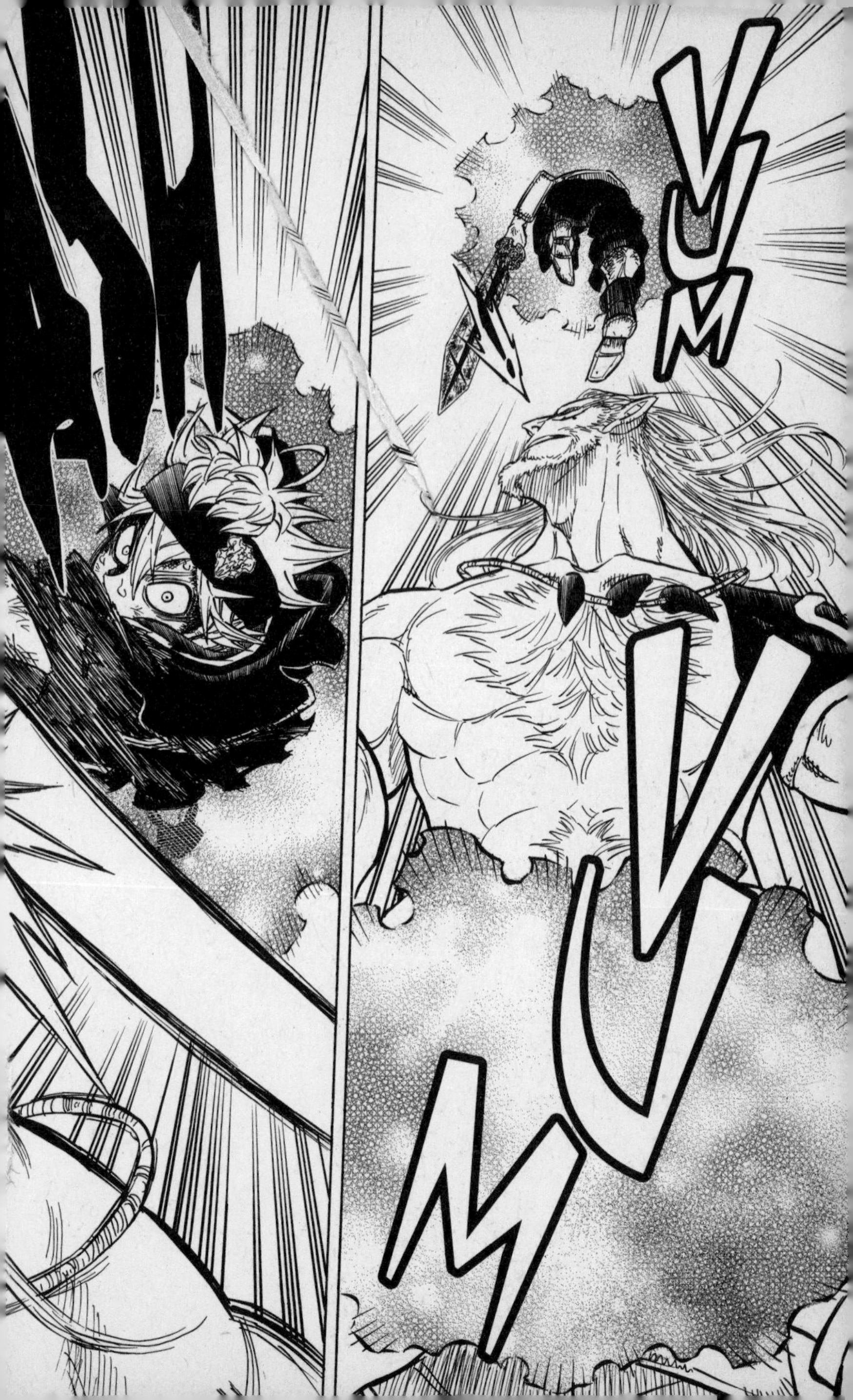
VUM
VUM

✤ Page 70: Despair vs. Hope

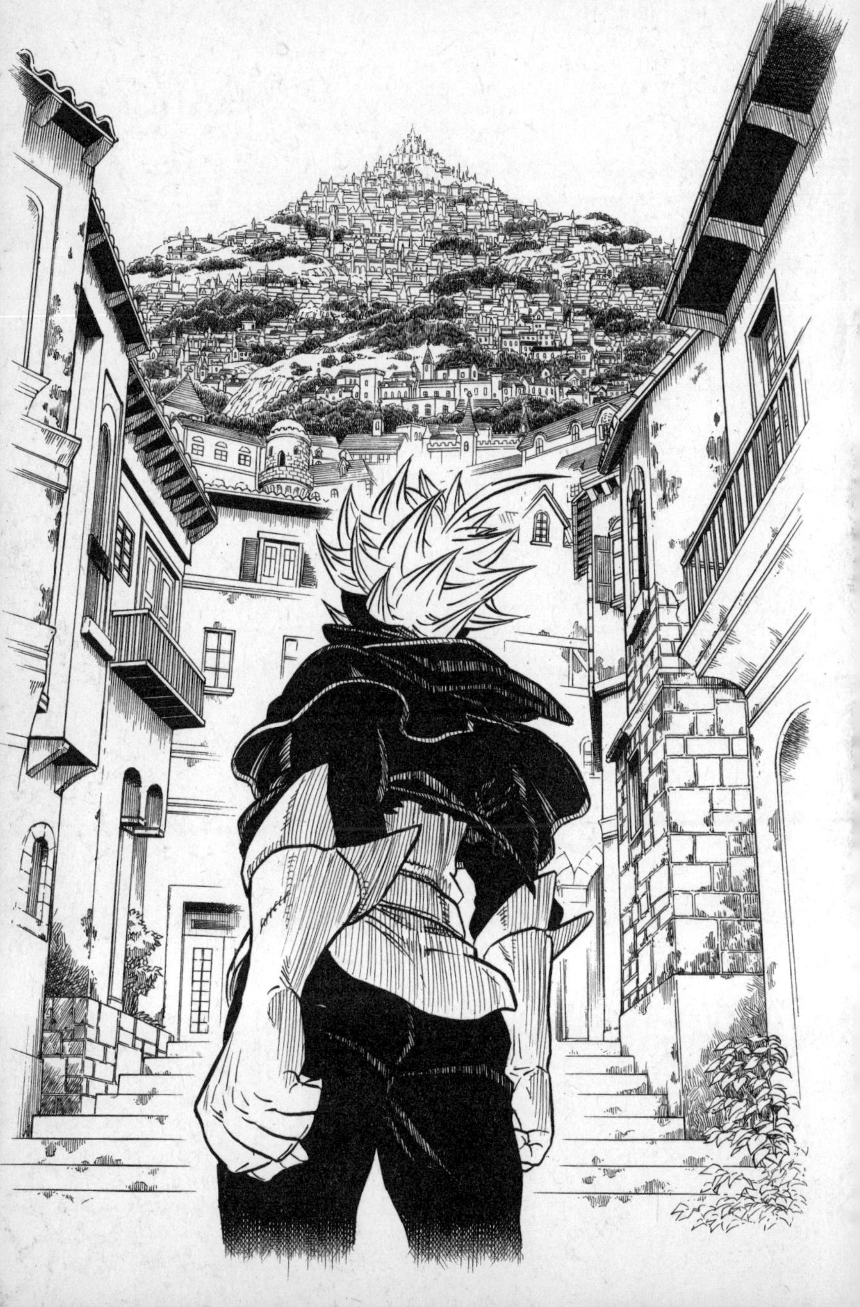

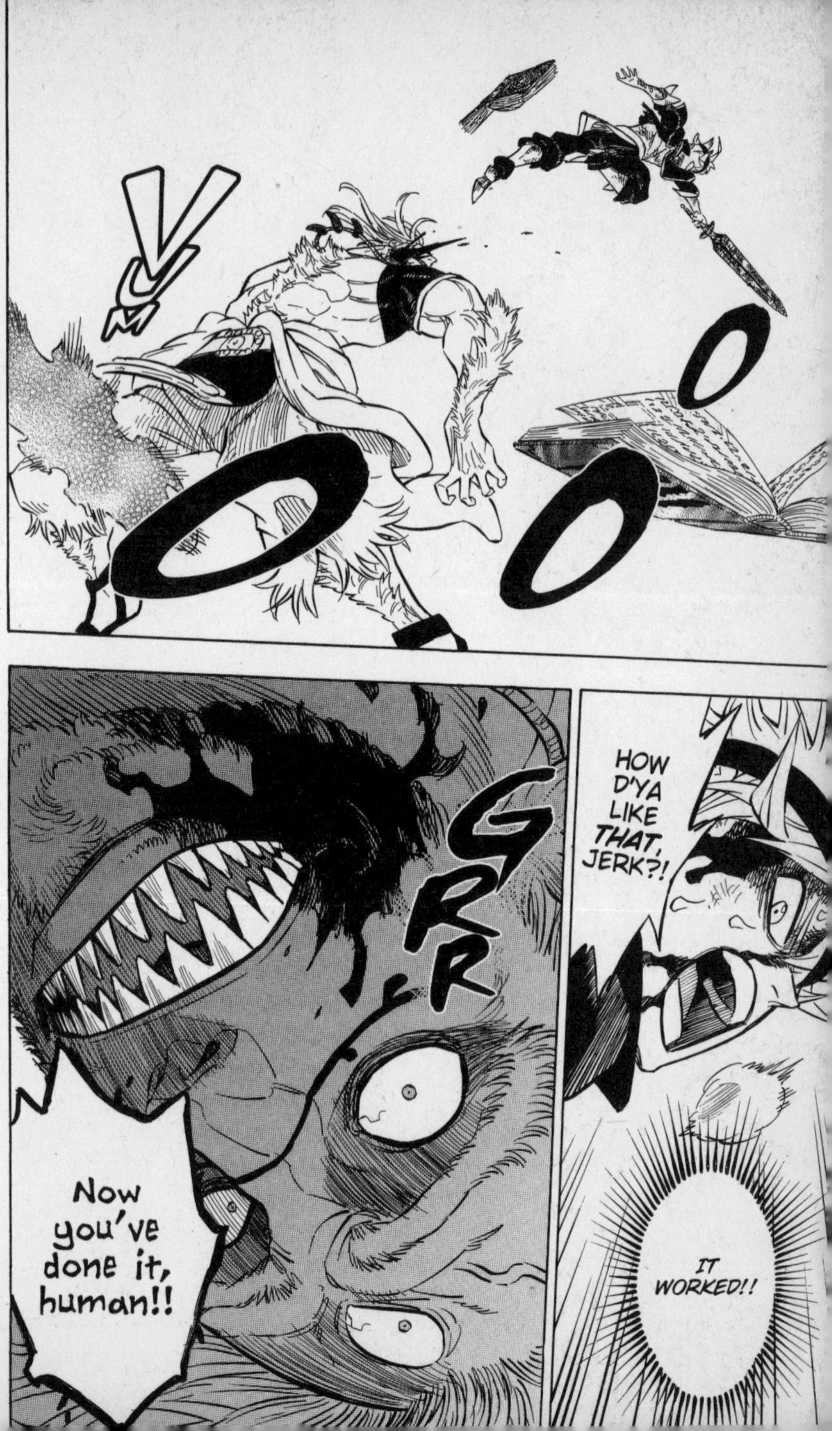
VOOO
HOW D'YA LIKE THAT, JERK?!
IT WORKED!!
GRR
Now you've done it, human!!

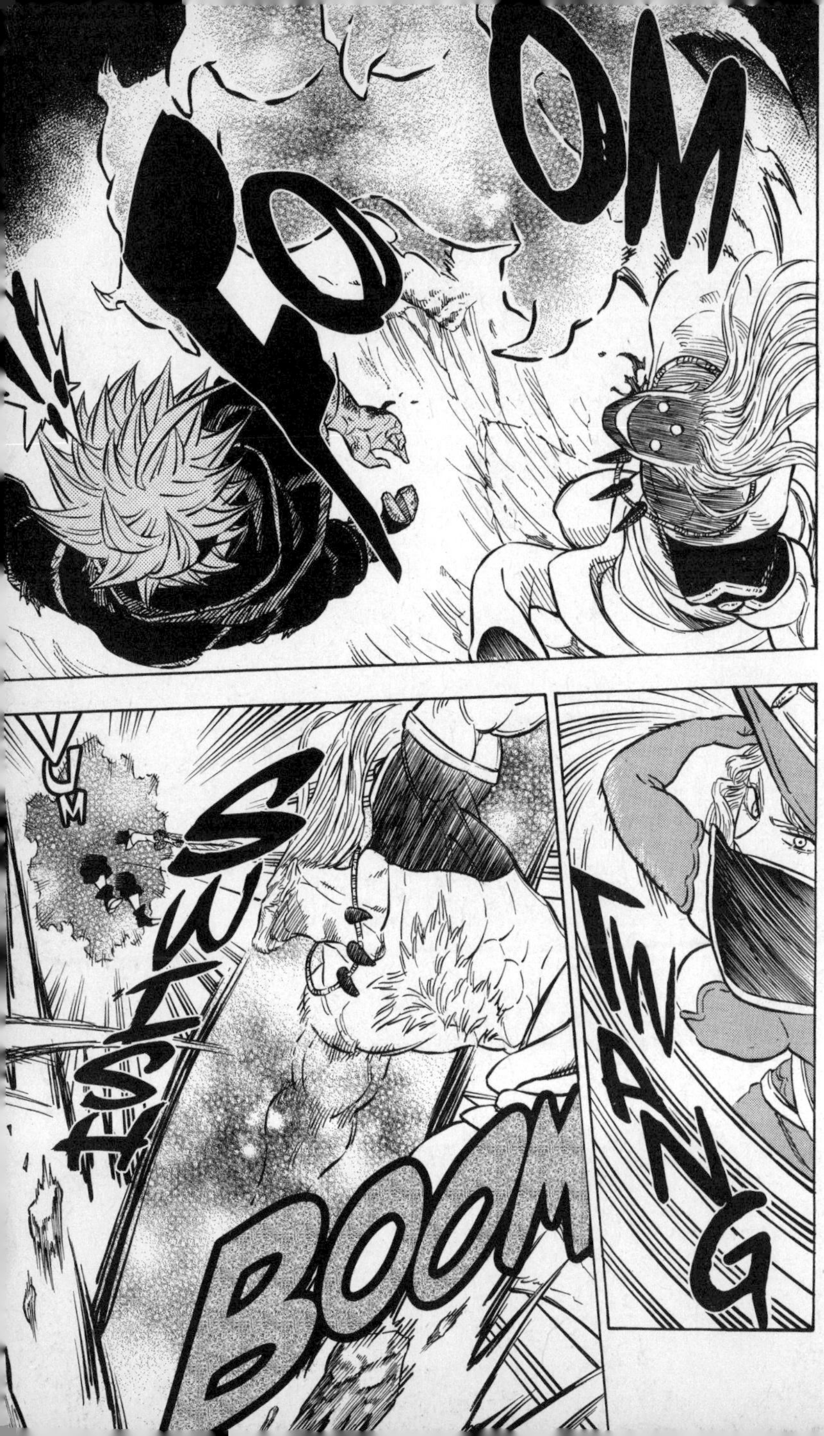
POOM
TWANG
BOOM
SWISH
VUM

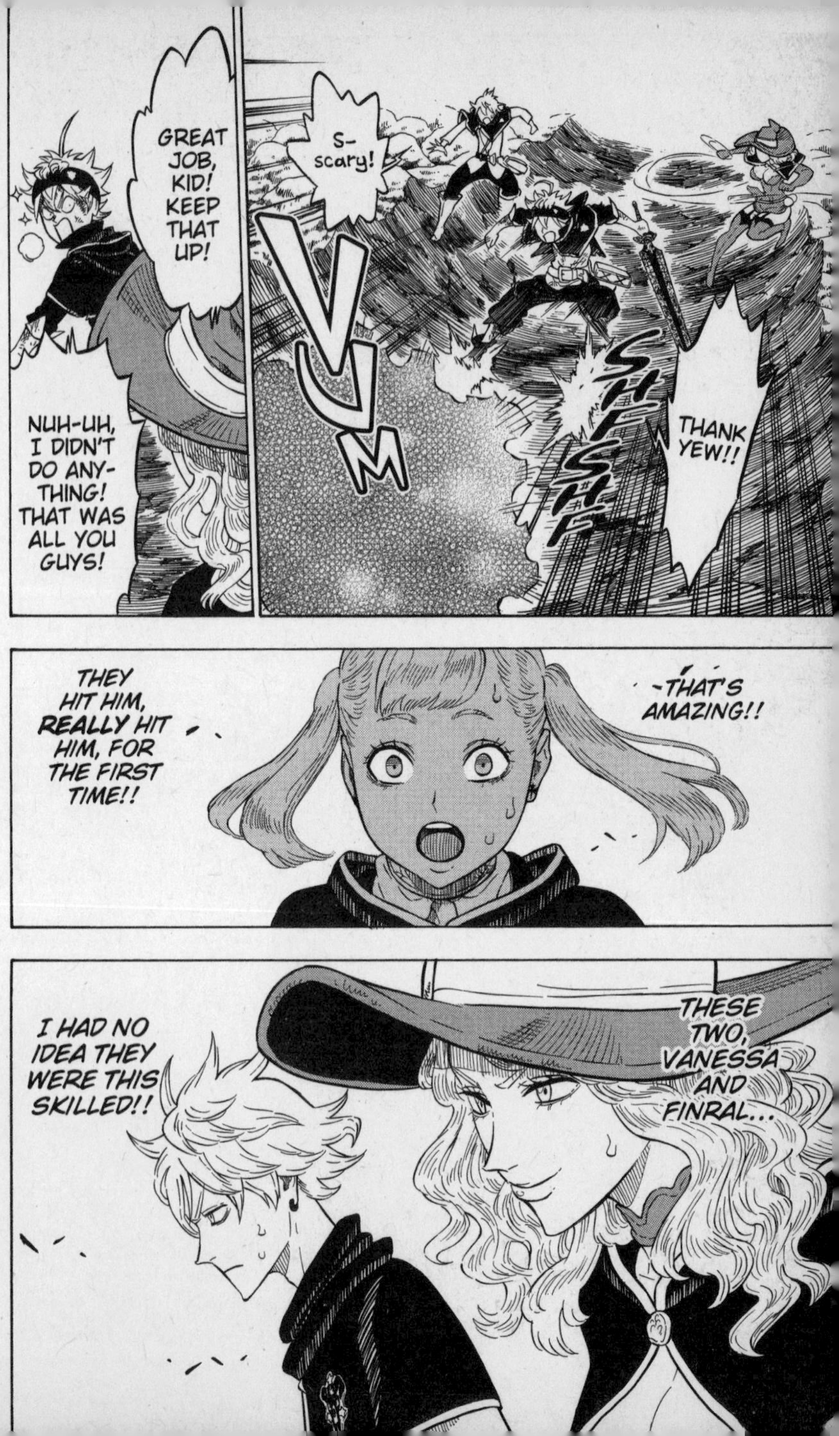
S-scary!
VUM
THANK YEW!!
GREAT JOB, KID! KEEP THAT UP!
NUH-UH, I DIDN'T DO ANYTHING! THAT WAS ALL YOU GUYS!
-THAT'S AMAZING!!
THEY HIT HIM, REALLY HIT HIM, FOR THE FIRST TIME!!
THESE TWO, VANESSA AND FINRAL...
I HAD NO IDEA THEY WERE THIS SKILLED!!

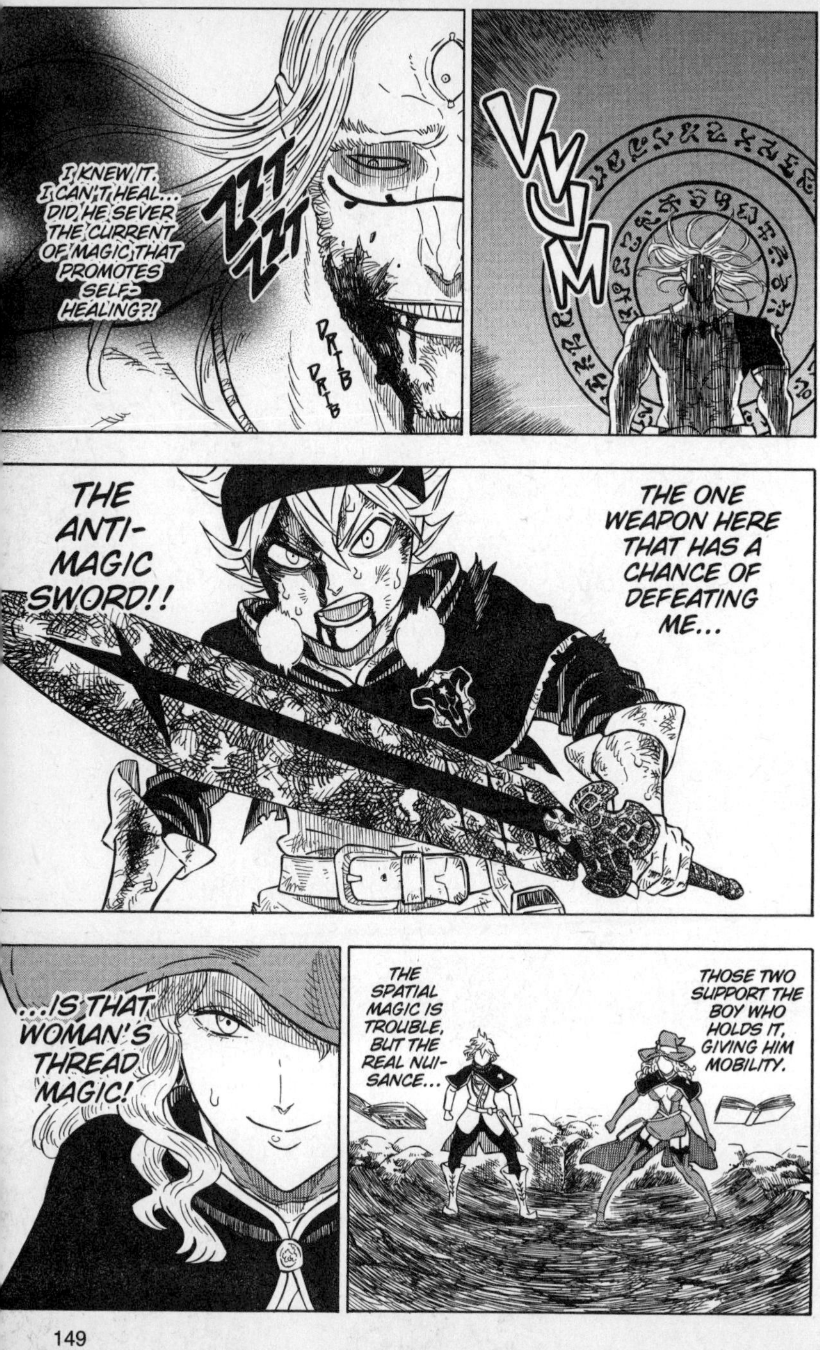
VVUM
ZZZT
ZZZT
I KNEW IT. I CAN'T HEAL... DID HE SEVER THE CURRENT OF MAGIC THAT PROMOTES SELF-HEALING?!
DRIB
DRIB
THE ONE WEAPON HERE THAT HAS A CHANCE OF DEFEATING ME...
THE ANTI-MAGIC SWORD!!
THOSE TWO SUPPORT THE BOY WHO HOLDS IT, GIVING HIM MOBILITY.
THE SPATIAL MAGIC IS TROUBLE, BUT THE REAL NUI-SANCE...
...IS THAT WOMAN'S THREAD MAGIC!

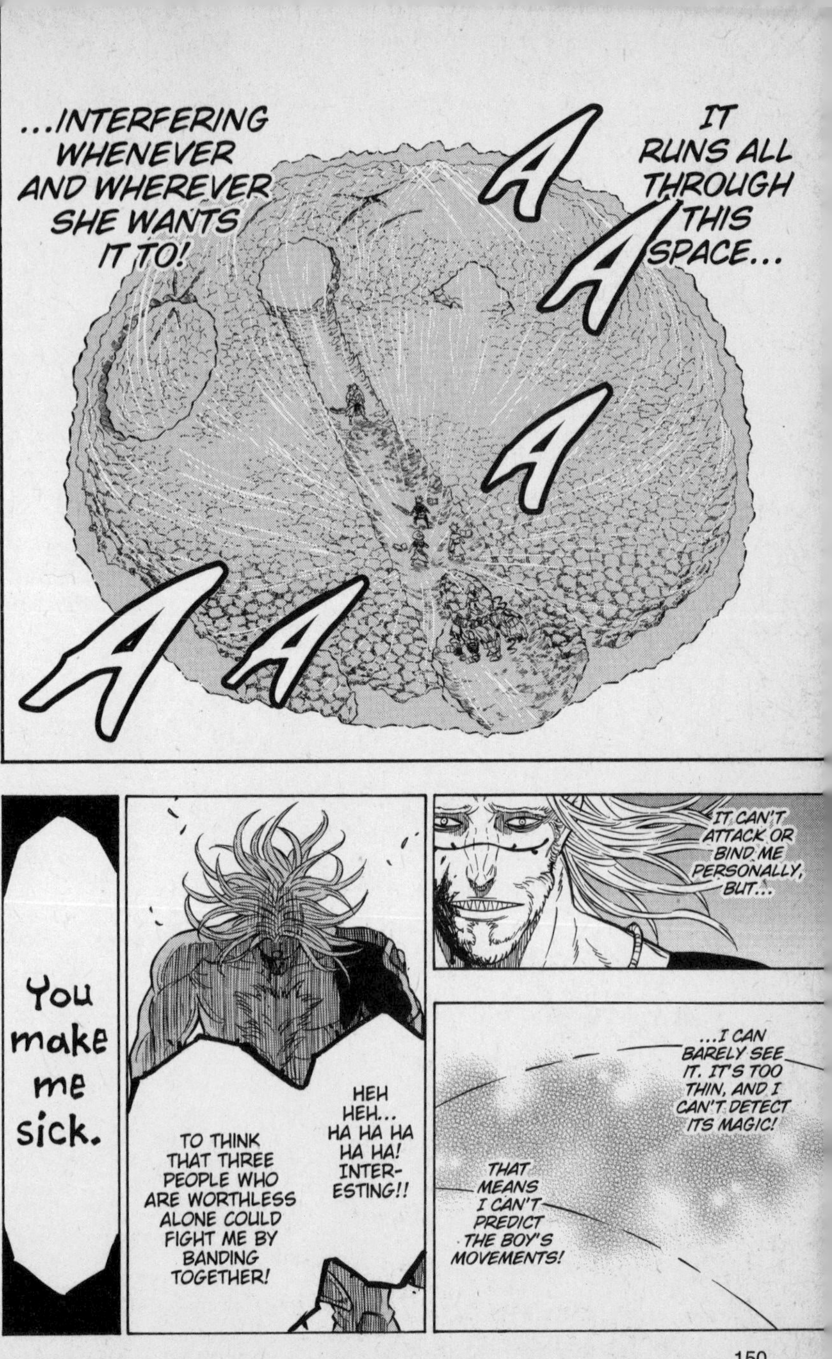
IT RUNS ALL THROUGH THIS SPACE...
AAAAA
...INTERFERING WHENEVER AND WHEREVER SHE WANTS IT TO!
IT CAN'T ATTACK OR BIND ME PERSONALLY, BUT...
...I CAN BARELY SEE IT. IT'S TOO THIN, AND I CAN'T DETECT ITS MAGIC!
THAT MEANS I CAN'T PREDICT THE BOY'S MOVEMENTS!
HEH HEH... HA HA HA HA HA! INTERESTING!!
TO THINK THAT THREE PEOPLE WHO ARE WORTHLESS ALONE COULD FIGHT ME BY BANDING TOGETHER!
You make me sick.

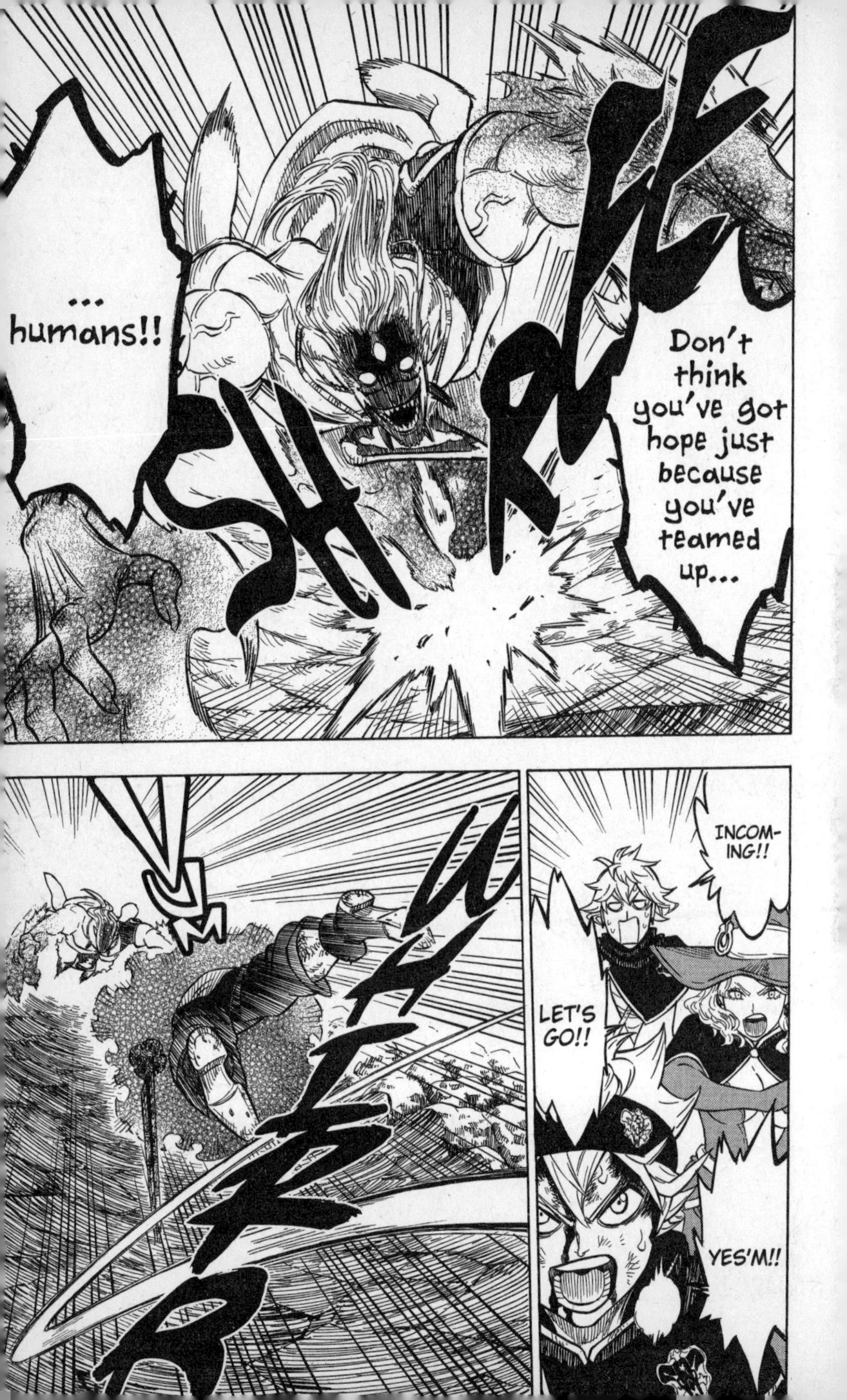
Don't think you've got hope just because you've teamed up...
...humans!!
INCOM-ING!!
LET'S GO!!
YES'M!!

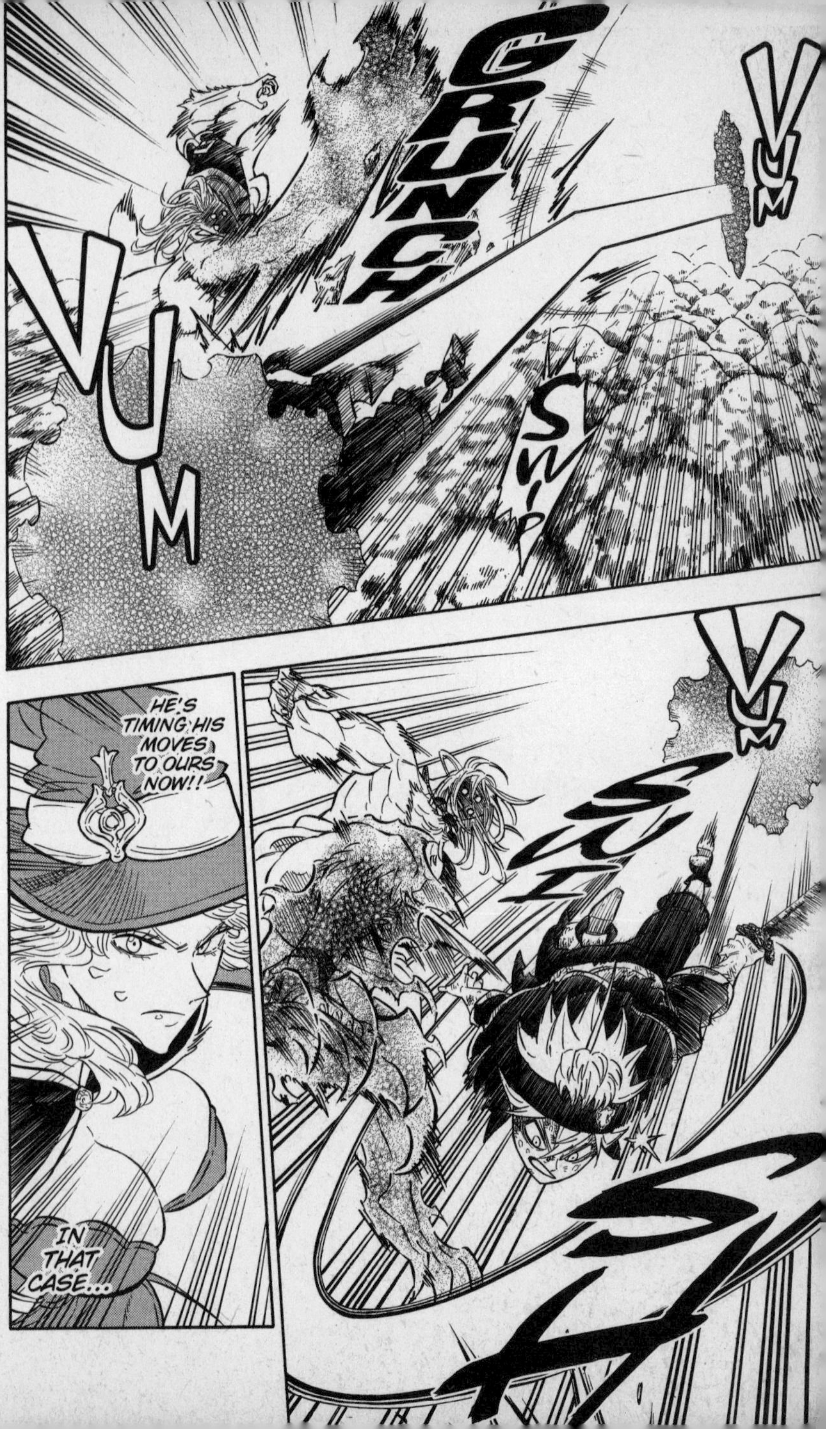
VUM
CRUNCH
SWIP
VUM
VUM
SWI
SH
HE'S TIMING HIS MOVES TO OURS NOW!!
IN THAT CASE...

RIGHT!!!

WE'RE SURPASSING OUR LIMITS AND SPEEDING UP!!!

KID... WHEN I SEE YOU FIGHTING, WITH YOUR LITTLE BODY AND NO MAGIC...

...IT GIVES ME COURAGE. THAT'S NOT LIKE ME, BUT IT DOES!!

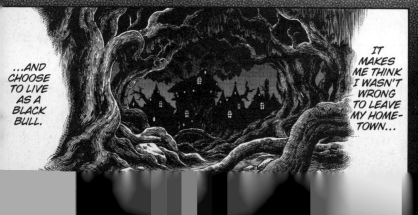

IT MAKES ME THINK I WASN'T WRONG TO LEAVE MY HOMETOWN...

...AND CHOOSE TO LIVE AS A BLACK BULL.

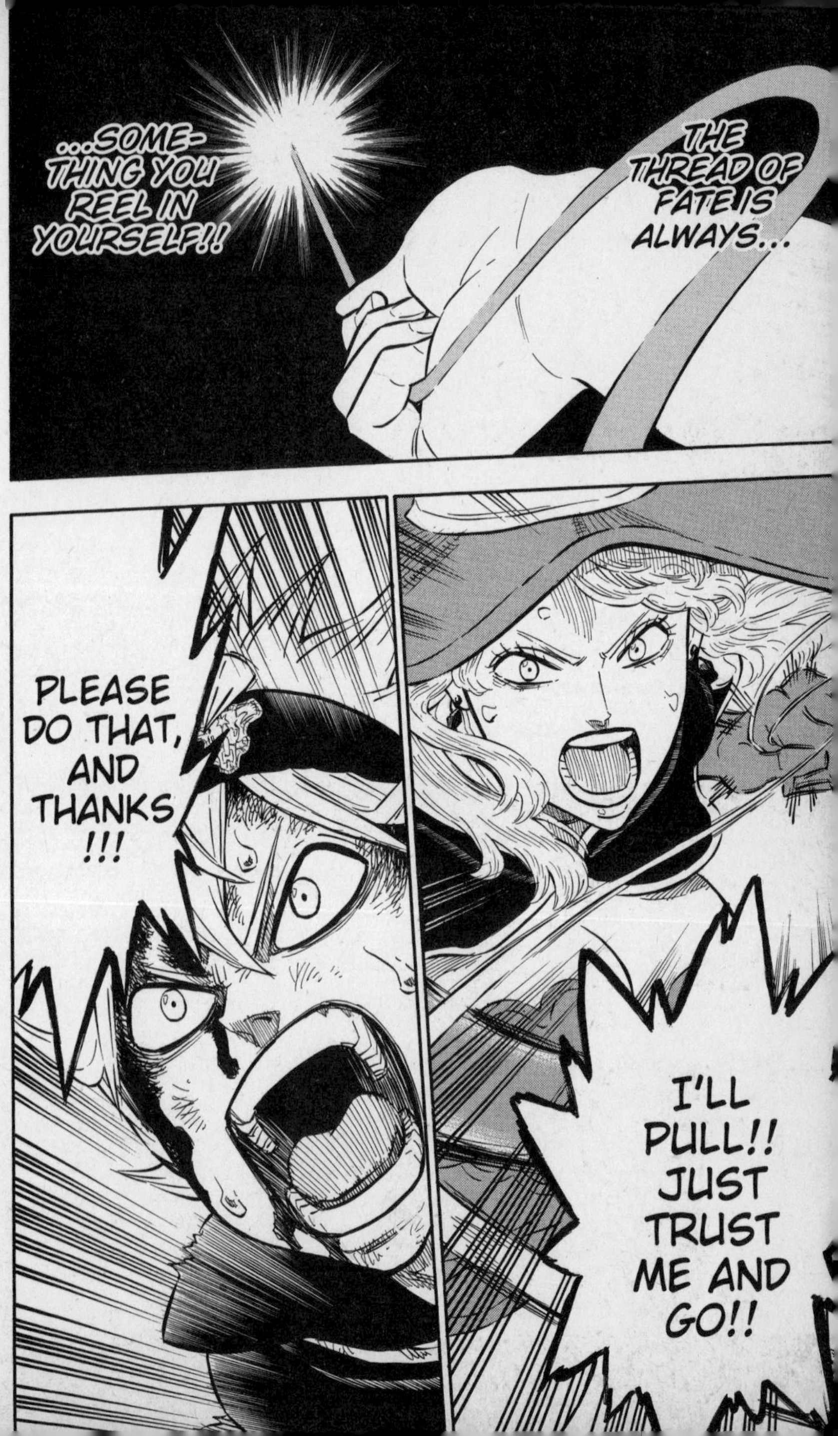
THE THREAD OF FATE IS ALWAYS...
...SOME-THING YOU REEL IN YOURSELF!!
I'LL PULL!! JUST TRUST ME AND GO!!
PLEASE DO THAT, AND THANKS!!!

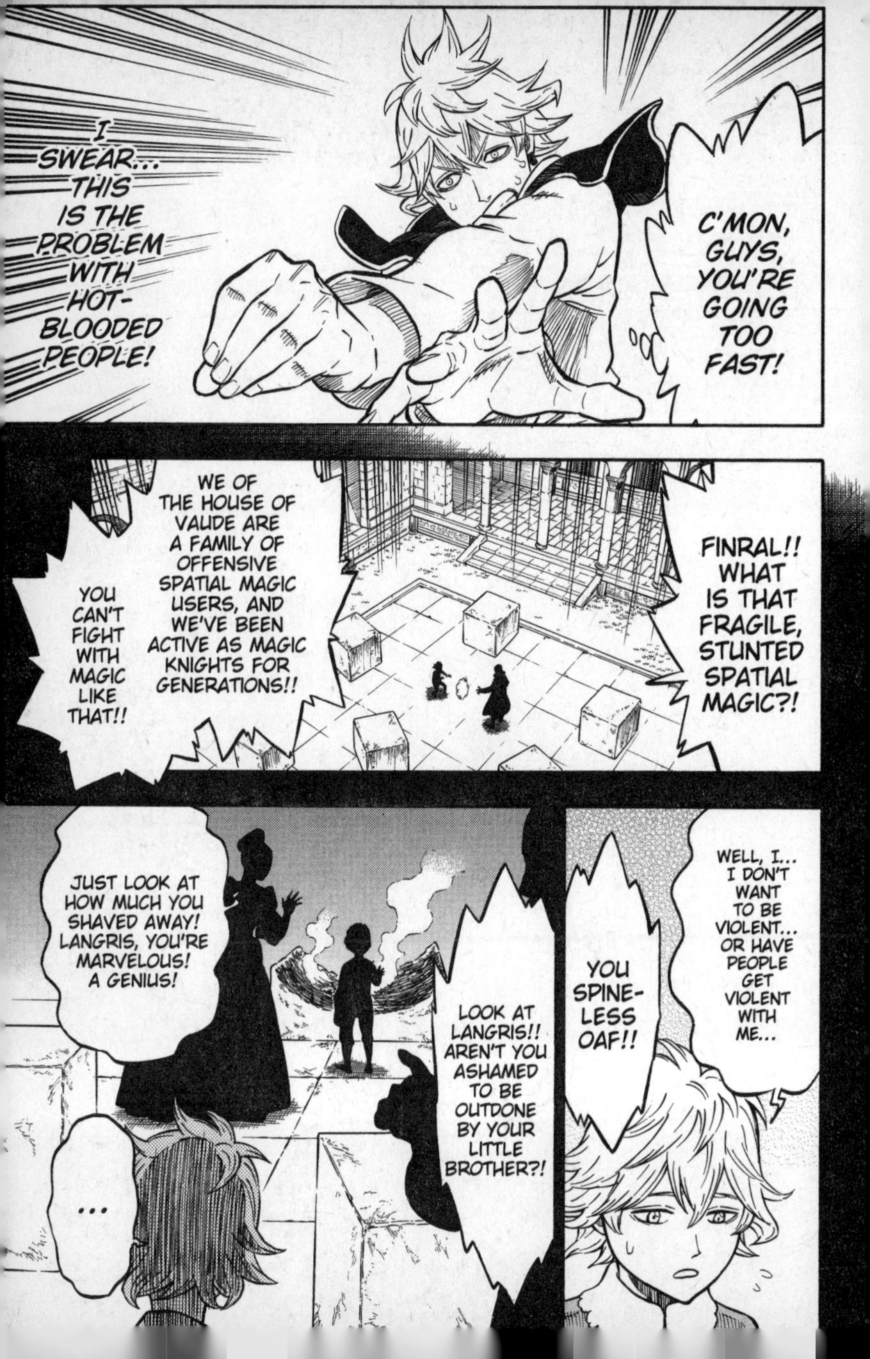
C'MON, GUYS, YOU'RE GOING TOO FAST!
I SWEAR... THIS IS THE PROBLEM WITH HOT-BLOODED PEOPLE!
FINRAL!! WHAT IS THAT FRAGILE, STUNTED SPATIAL MAGIC?!
WE OF THE HOUSE OF VAUDE ARE A FAMILY OF OFFENSIVE SPATIAL MAGIC USERS, AND WE'VE BEEN ACTIVE AS MAGIC KNIGHTS FOR GENERATIONS!!
YOU CAN'T FIGHT WITH MAGIC LIKE THAT!!
WELL, I... I DON'T WANT TO BE VIOLENT... OR HAVE PEOPLE GET VIOLENT WITH ME...
YOU SPINE-LESS OAF!!
LOOK AT LANGRIS!! AREN'T YOU ASHAMED TO BE OUTDONE BY YOUR LITTLE BROTHER?!
JUST LOOK AT HOW MUCH YOU SHAVED AWAY! LANGRIS, YOU'RE MARVELOUS! A GENIUS!
...

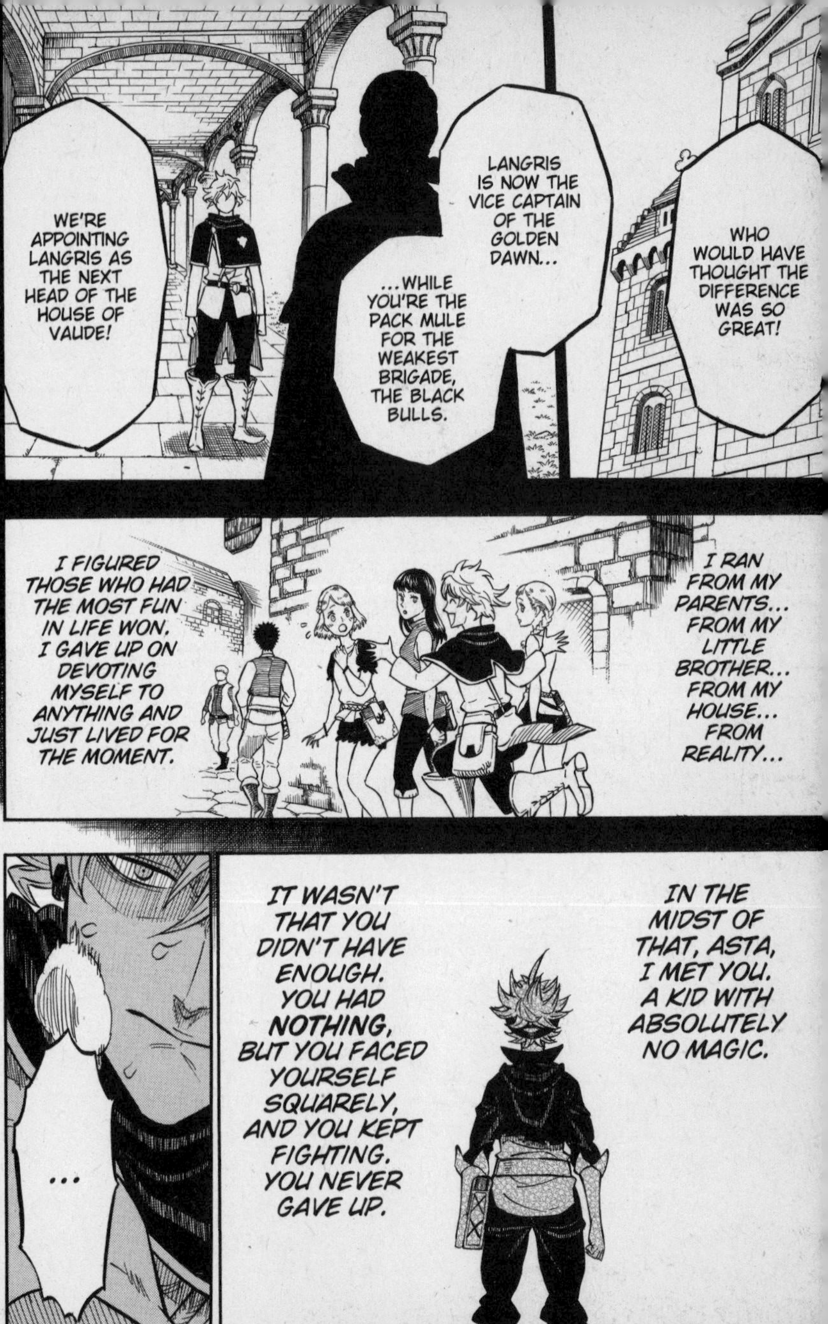
WHO WOULD HAVE THOUGHT THE DIFFERENCE WAS SO GREAT!
LANGRIS IS NOW THE VICE CAPTAIN OF THE GOLDEN DAWN...
...WHILE YOU'RE THE PACK MULE FOR THE WEAKEST BRIGADE, THE BLACK BULLS.
WE'RE APPOINTING LANGRIS AS THE NEXT HEAD OF THE HOUSE OF VAUDE!
I RAN FROM MY PARENTS... FROM MY LITTLE BROTHER... FROM MY HOUSE... FROM REALITY...
I FIGURED THOSE WHO HAD THE MOST FUN IN LIFE WON. I GAVE UP ON DEVOTING MYSELF TO ANYTHING AND JUST LIVED FOR THE MOMENT.
IN THE MIDST OF THAT, ASTA, I MET YOU. A KID WITH ABSOLUTELY NO MAGIC.
IT WASN'T THAT YOU DIDN'T HAVE ENOUGH. YOU HAD NOTHING, BUT YOU FACED YOURSELF SQUARELY, AND YOU KEPT FIGHTING. YOU NEVER GAVE UP.
...

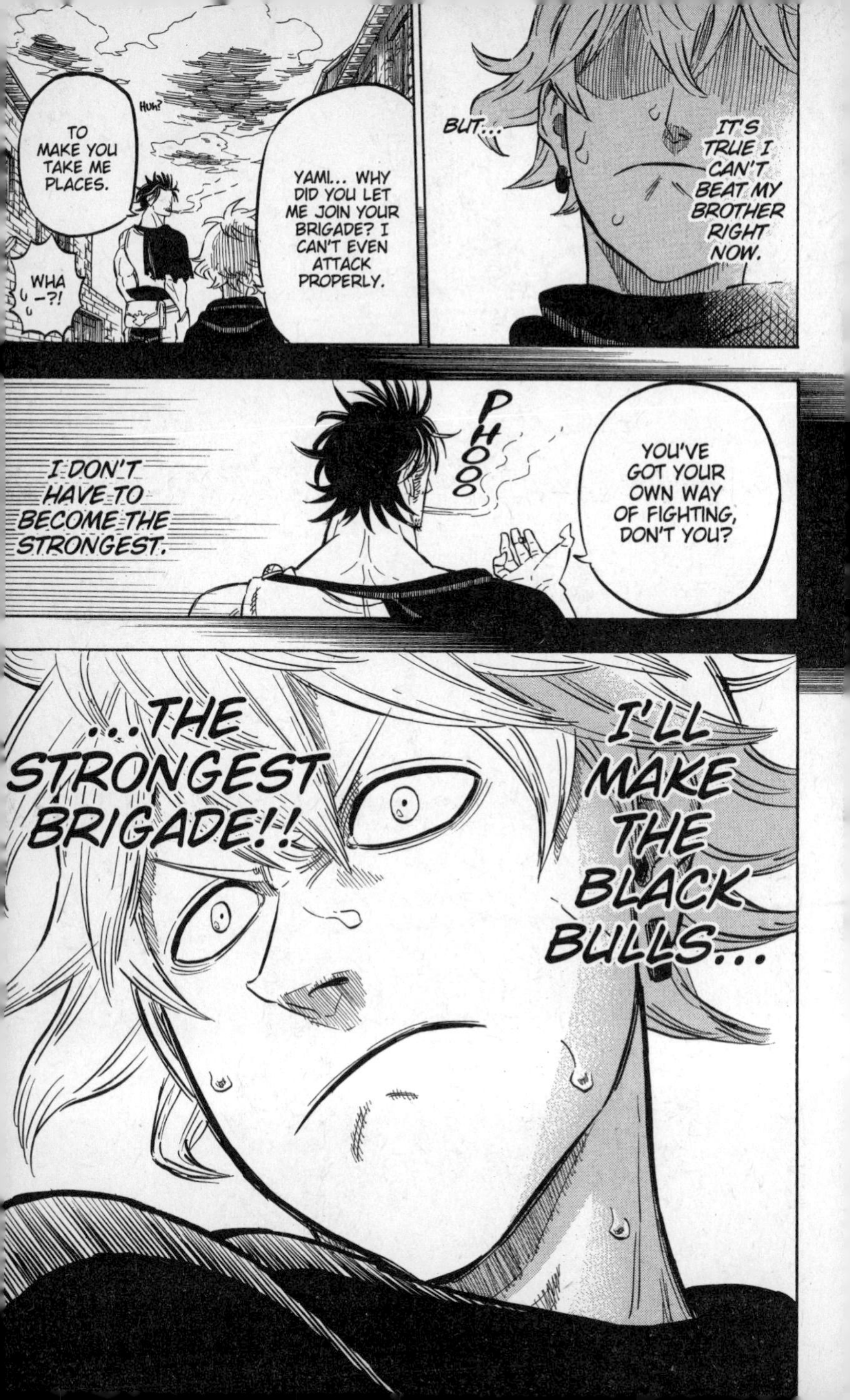
IT'S TRUE I CAN'T BEAT MY BROTHER RIGHT NOW.
BUT...
YAMI... WHY DID YOU LET ME JOIN YOUR BRIGADE? I CAN'T EVEN ATTACK PROPERLY.
Huh?
TO MAKE YOU TAKE ME PLACES.
WHA—?!
YOU'VE GOT YOUR OWN WAY OF FIGHTING, DON'T YOU?
PHOOO
I DON'T HAVE TO BECOME THE STRONGEST.
I'LL MAKE THE BLACK BULLS...
...THE STRONGEST BRIGADE!!

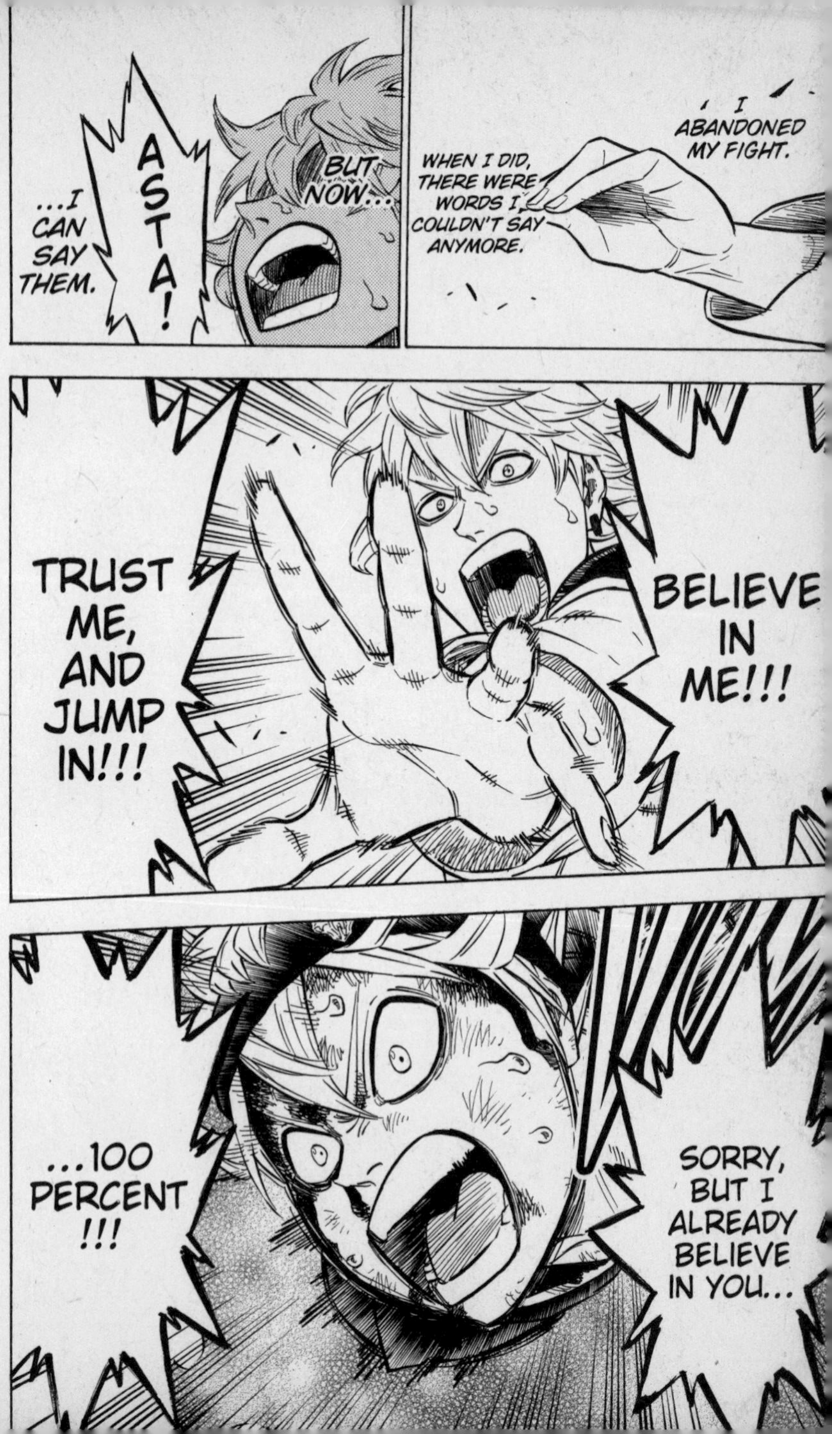
I ABANDONED MY FIGHT.
WHEN I DID, THERE WERE WORDS I COULDN'T SAY ANYMORE.
BUT NOW...
ASTA!
...I CAN SAY THEM.
BELIEVE IN ME!!!
TRUST ME, AND JUMP IN!!!
SORRY, BUT I ALREADY BELIEVE IN YOU...
...100 PERCENT !!!

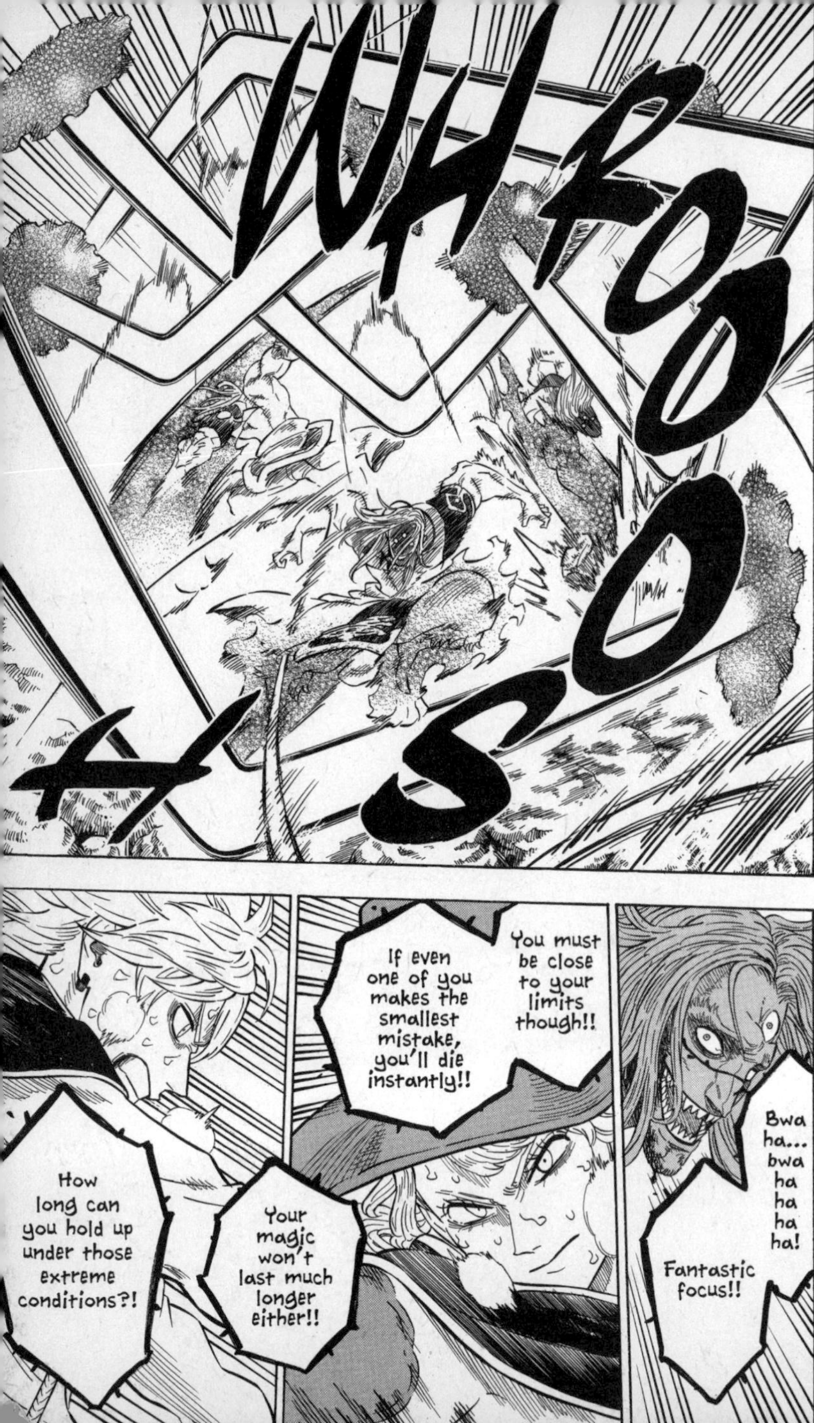
WHROOOSH
Bwa ha... bwa ha ha ha ha!
Fantastic focus!!
You must be close to your limits though!!
If even one of you makes the smallest mistake, you'll die instantly!!
Your magic won't last much longer either!!
How long can you hold up under those extreme conditions?!

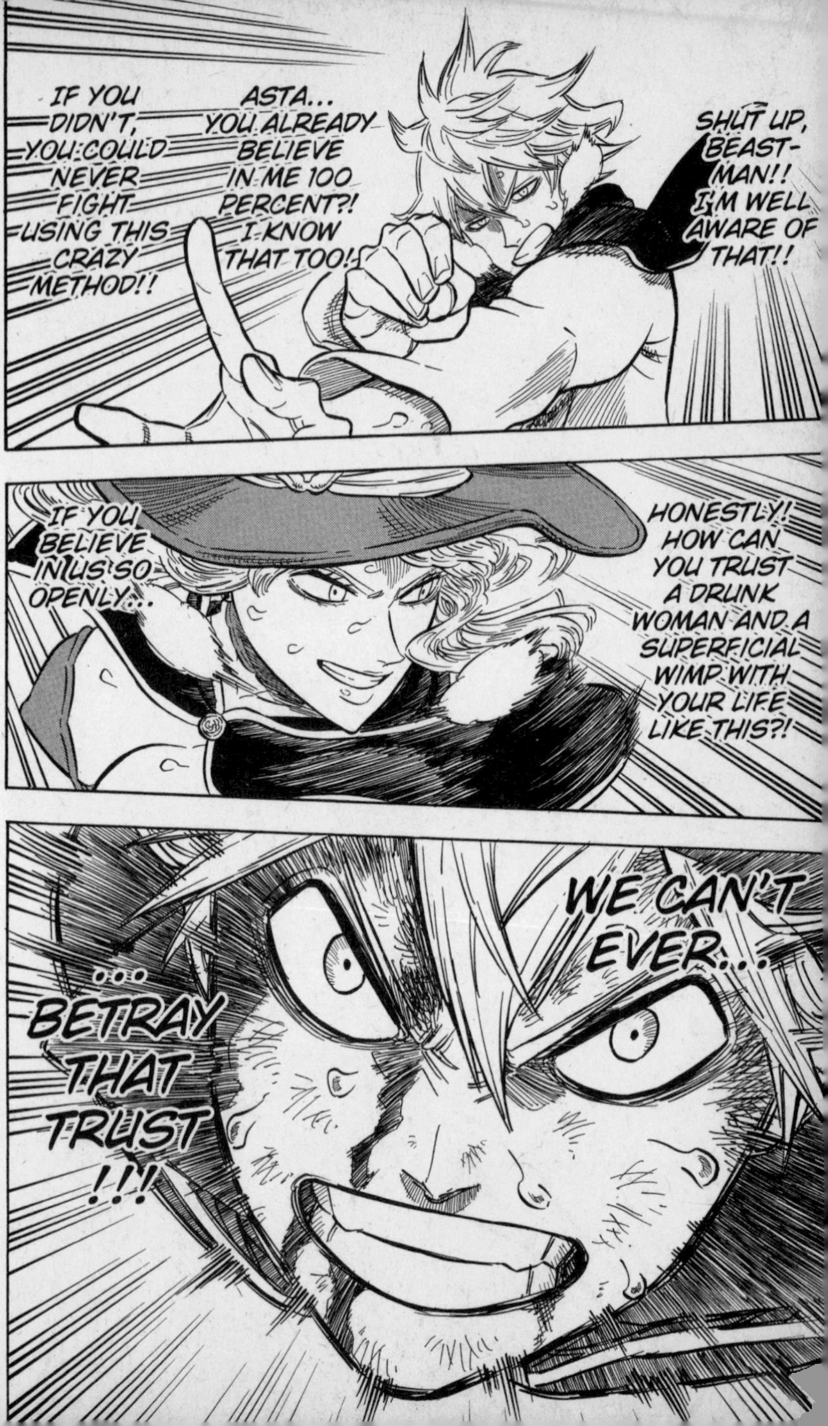
SHUT UP, BEAST-MAN!! I'M WELL AWARE OF THAT!!
ASTA... YOU ALREADY BELIEVE IN ME 100 PERCENT?! I KNOW THAT TOO!
IF YOU DIDN'T, YOU COULD NEVER FIGHT USING THIS CRAZY METHOD!!
HONESTLY! HOW CAN YOU TRUST A DRUNK WOMAN AND A SUPERFICIAL WIMP WITH YOUR LIFE LIKE THIS?!
IF YOU BELIEVE IN US SO OPENLY...
WE CAN'T EVER...
...BETRAY THAT TRUST!!!

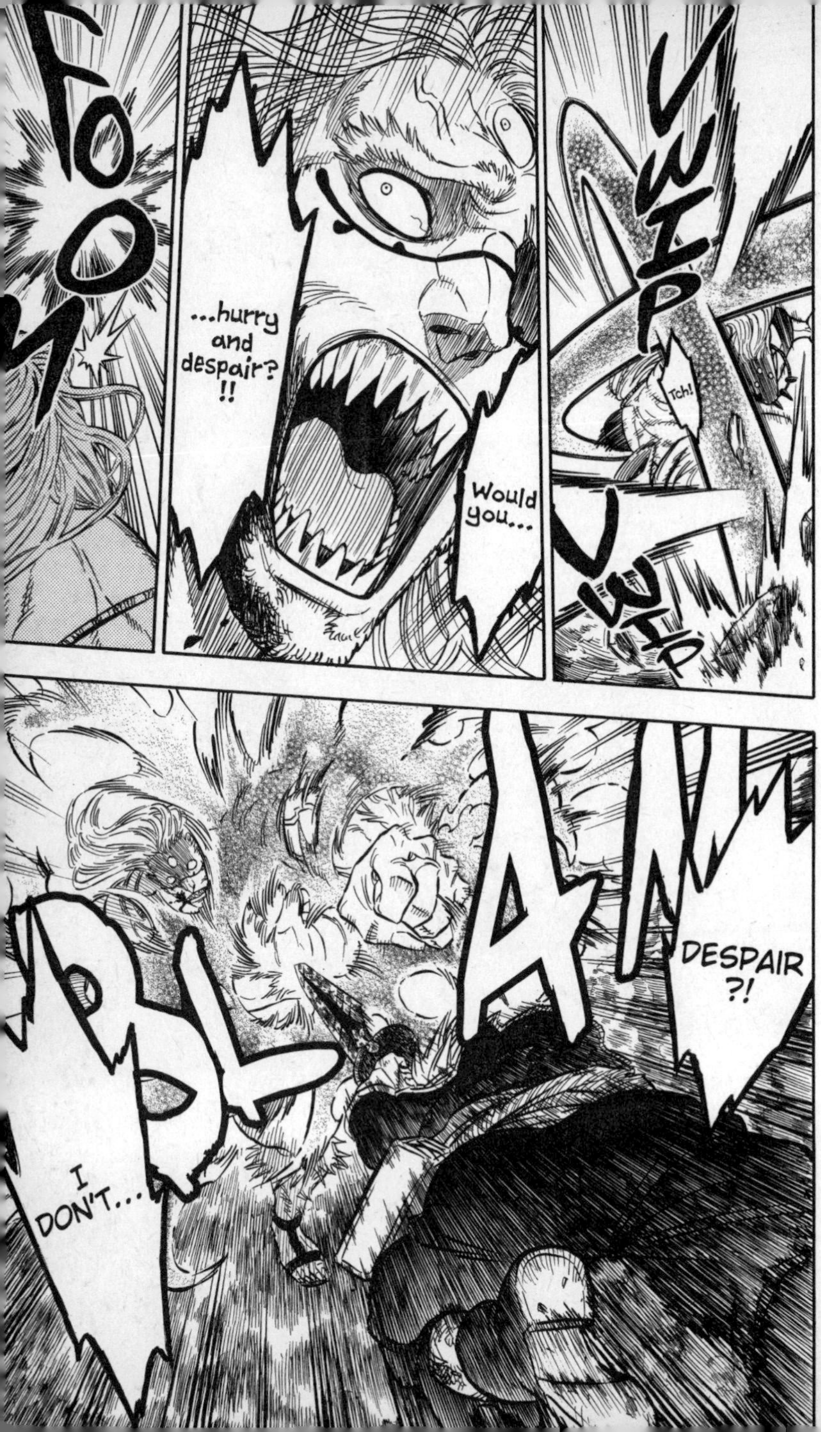
WHIP
Tch!
WHIP
Would you...
...hurry and despair?!!
FOOM
DESPAIR?!
I DON'T...

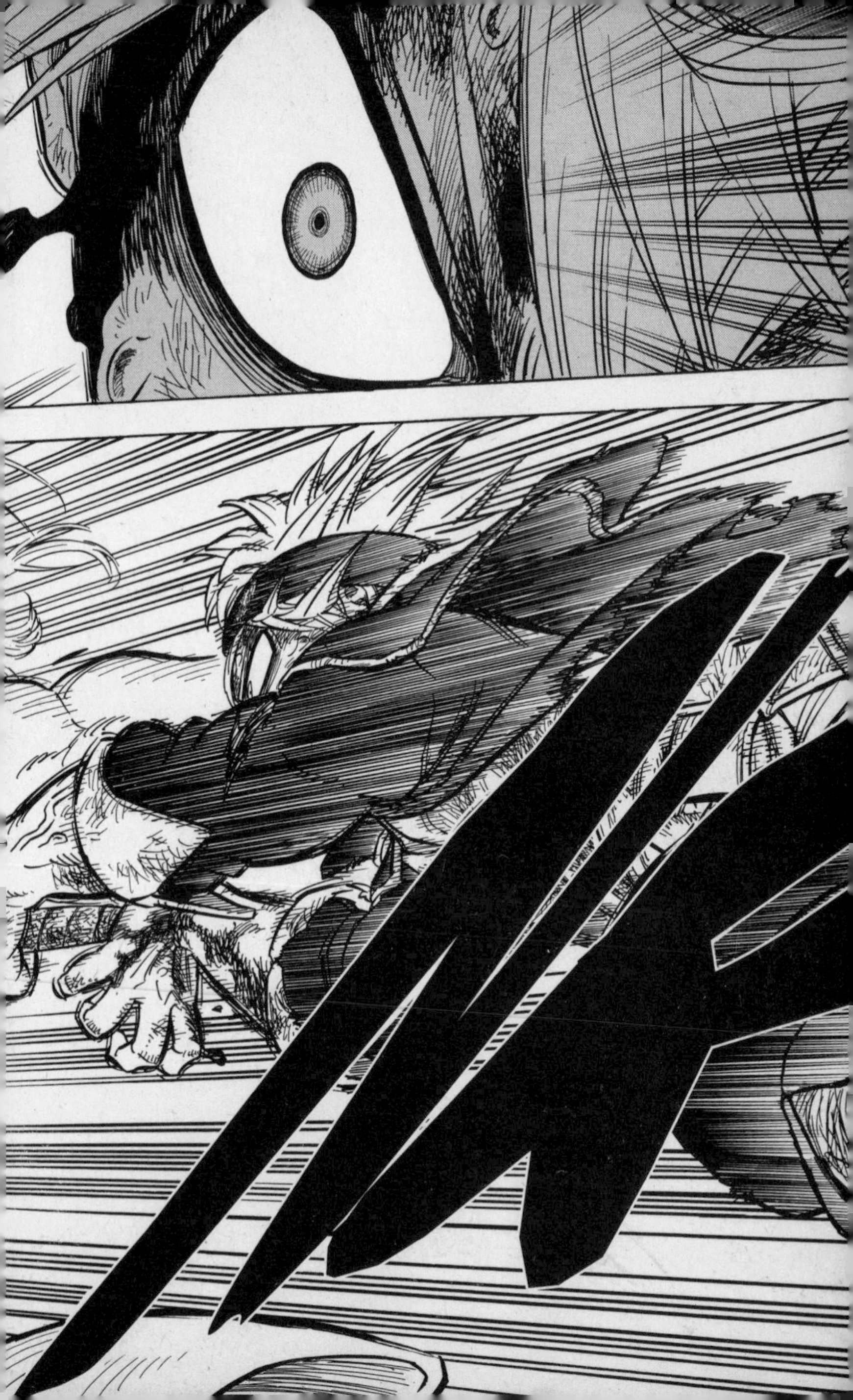

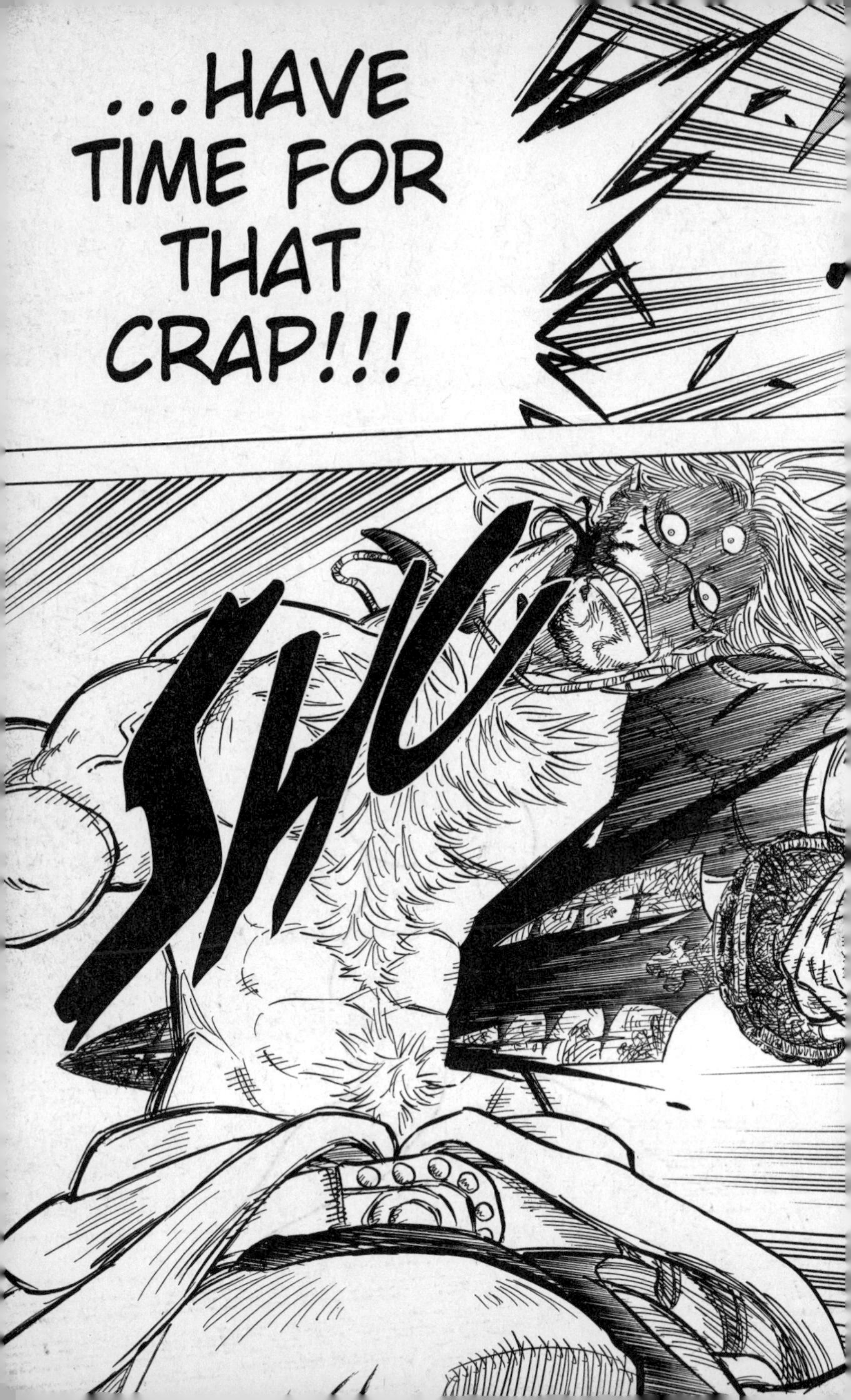
...HAVE TIME FOR THAT CRAP!!!

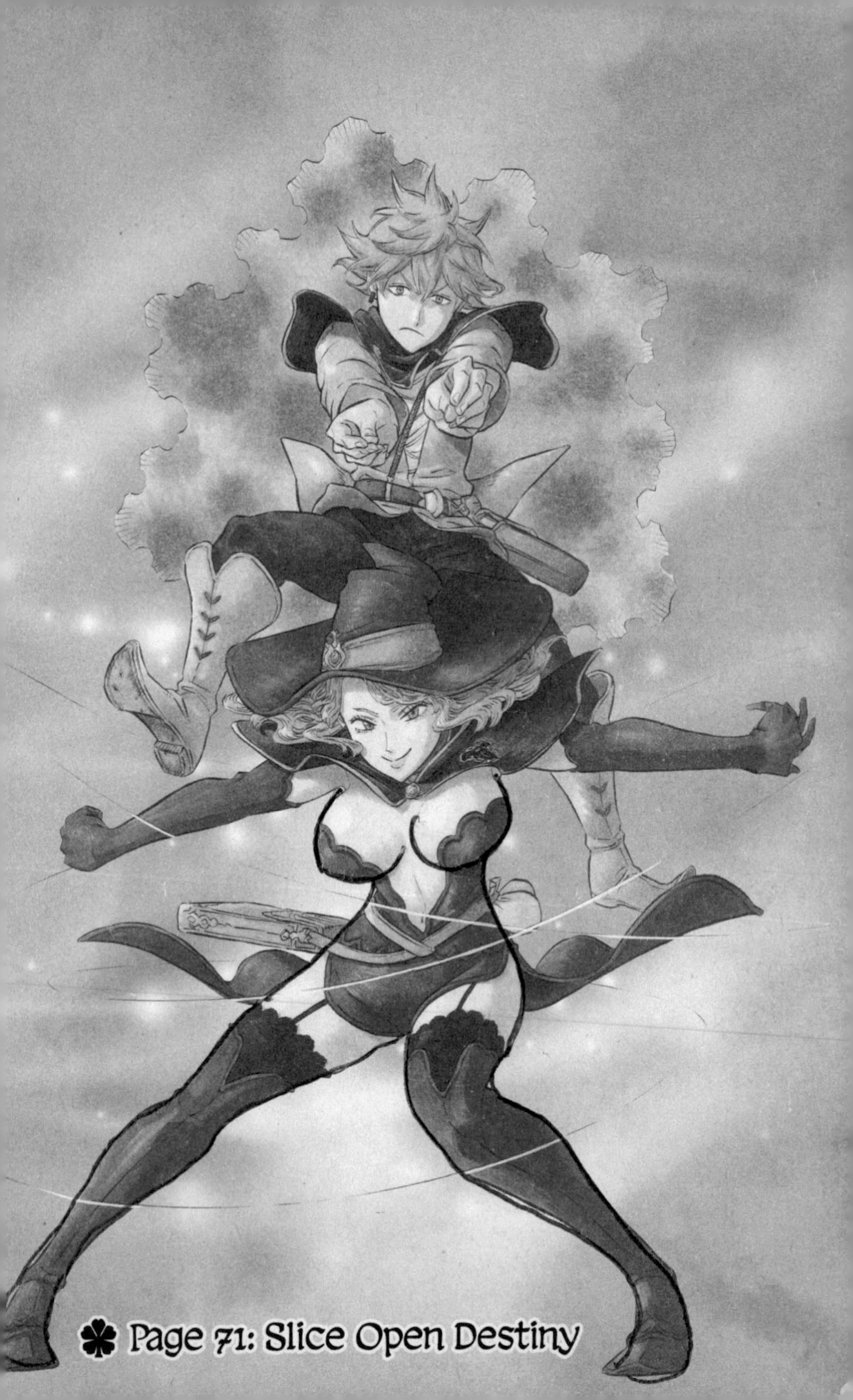

Page 71: Slice Open Destiny

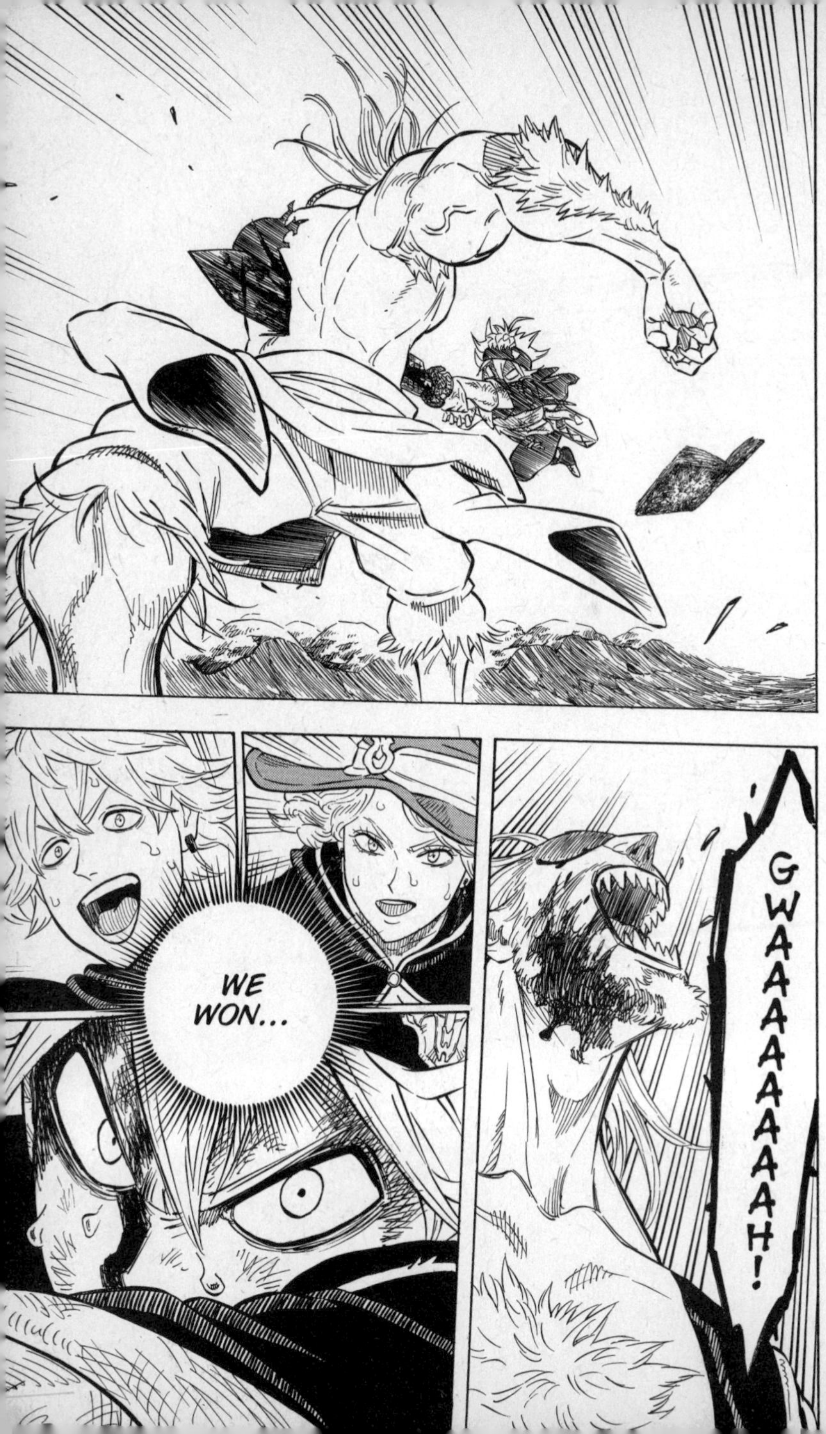
GWAAAAAAAAAH!
WE WON...

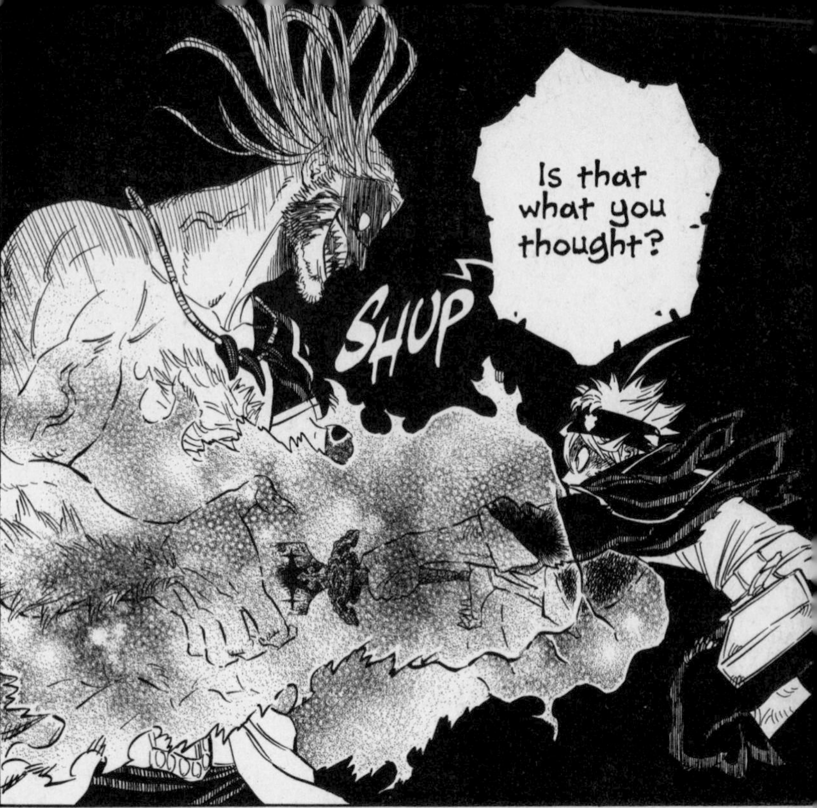
Is that what you thought?
SHUP
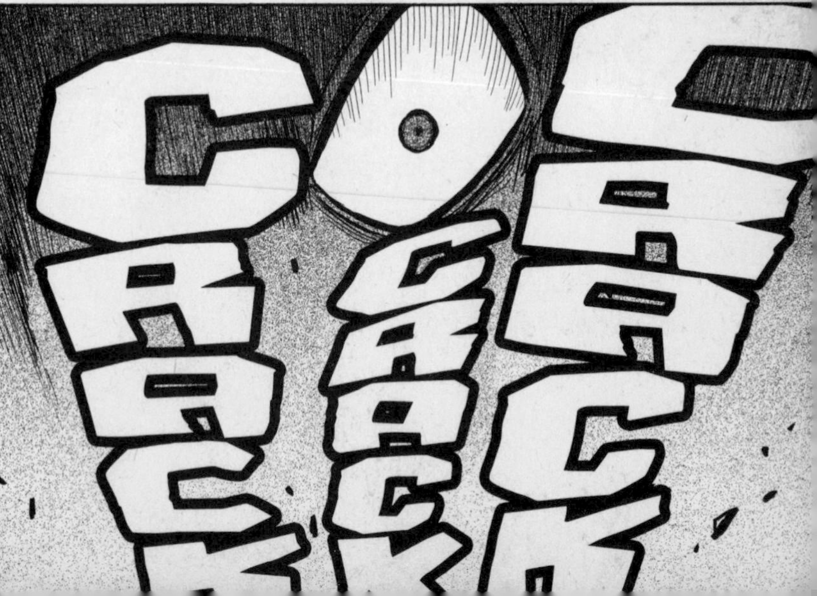
CRACK
CRACK
CRACK

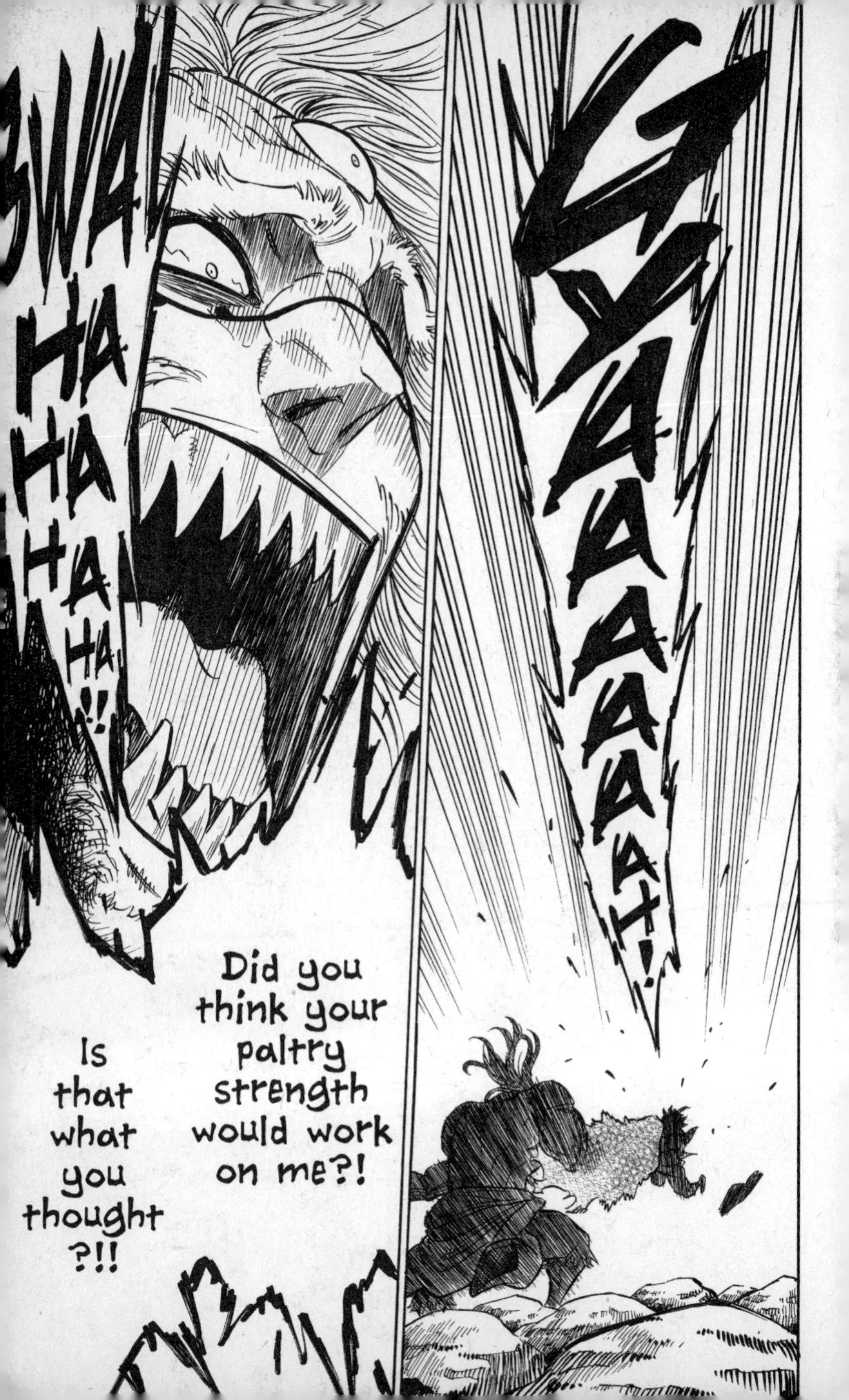
GYAAAAAAAAH!
SWAHAHAHAHAHA!!
Did you think your paltry strength would work on me?!
Is that what you thought?!!

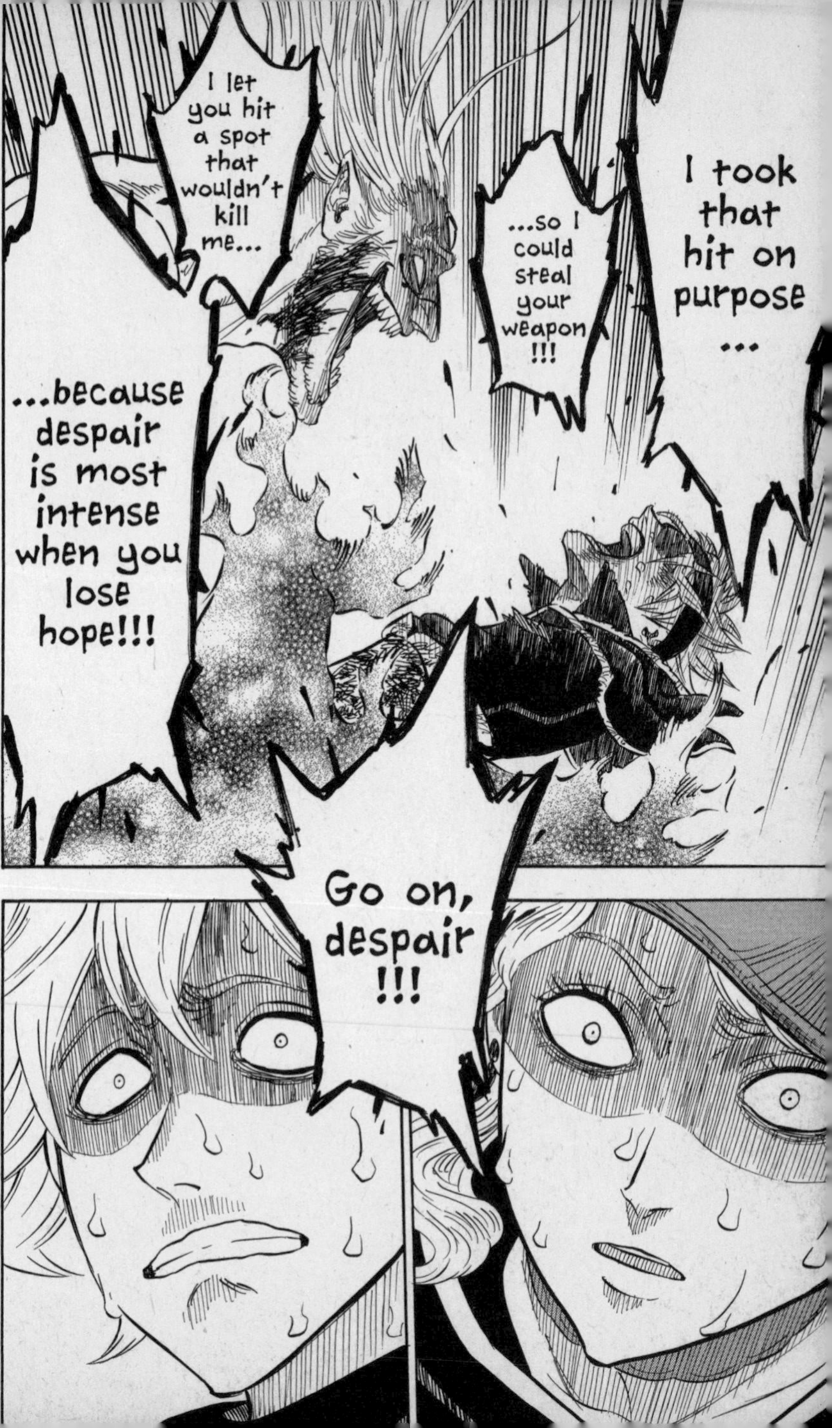
I took that hit on purpose...
I let you hit a spot that wouldn't kill me...
...so I could steal your weapon!!!
...because despair is most intense when you lose hope!!!
Go on, despair!!!

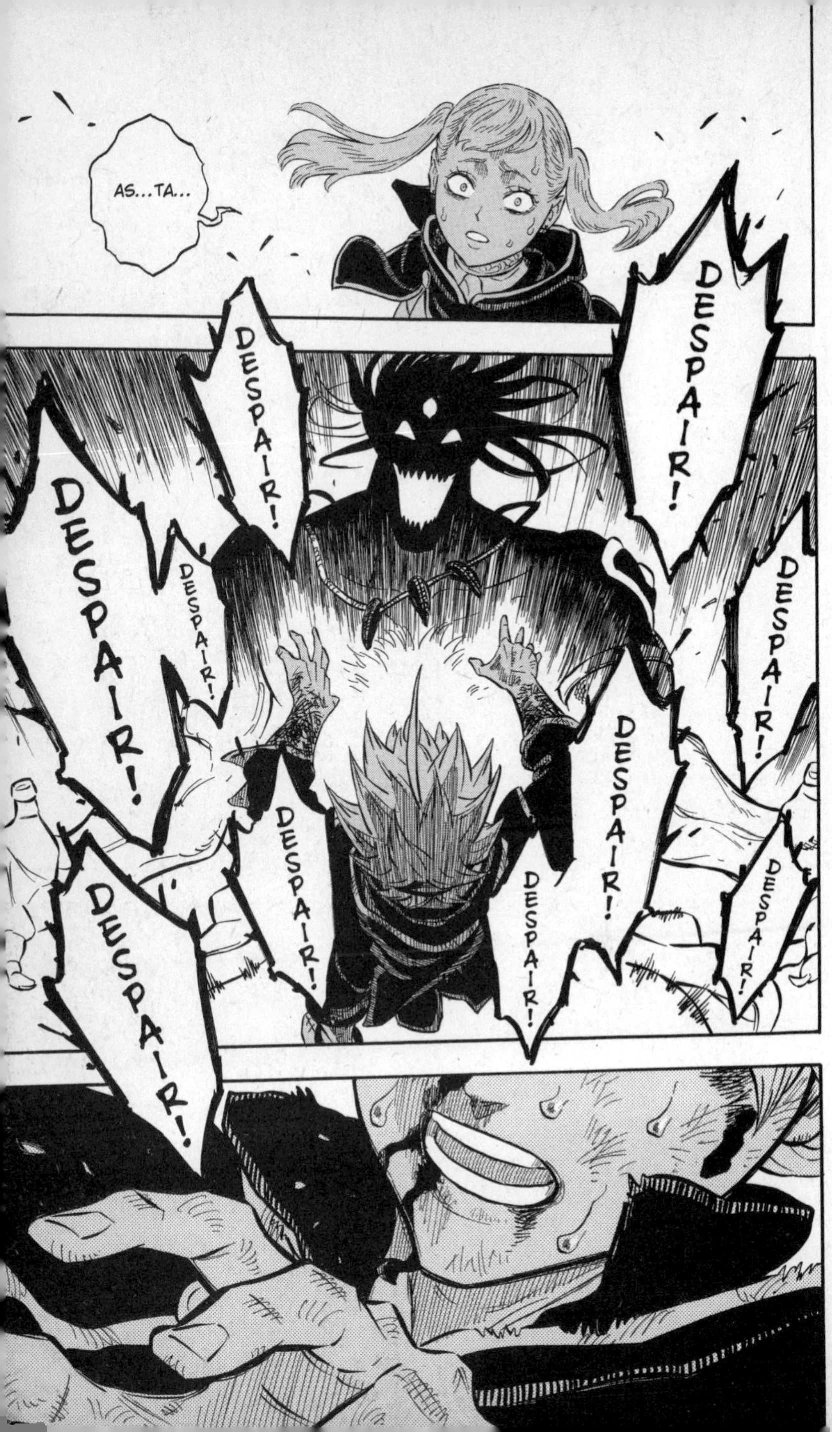
AS...TA...
DESPAIR!
DESPAIR!
DESPAIR!
DESPAIR!
DESPAIR!
DESPAIR!
DESPAIR!
DESPAIR!
DESPAIR!
DESPAIR!

NOT
YET
!!!

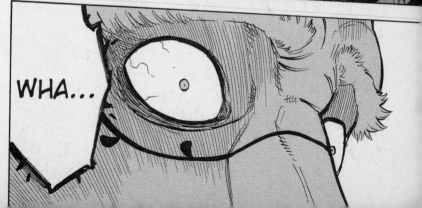

WHA...

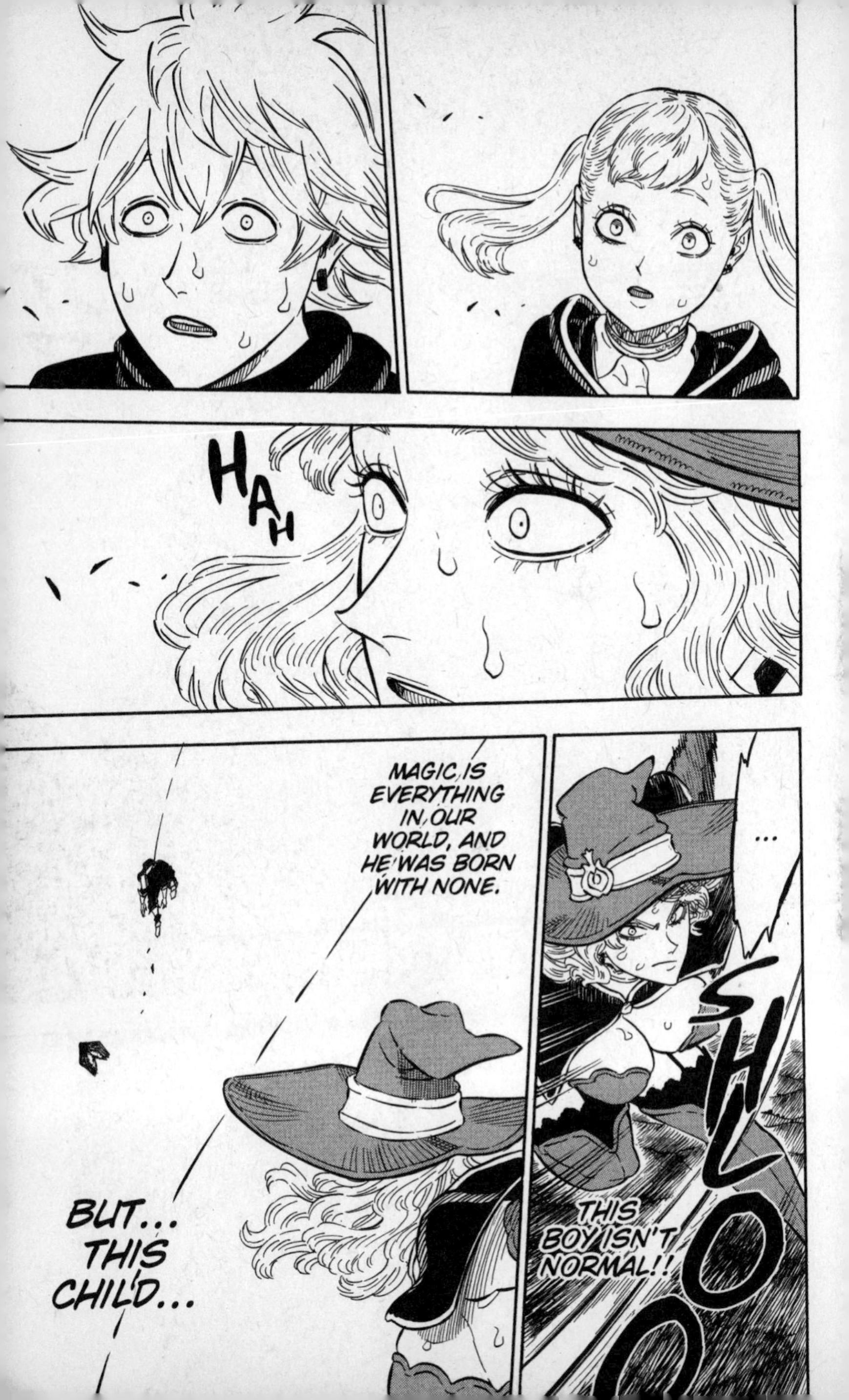
HAH
...
SHOOO
THIS BOY ISN'T NORMAL!!
MAGIC IS EVERYTHING IN OUR WORLD, AND HE WAS BORN WITH NONE.
BUT... THIS CHILD...

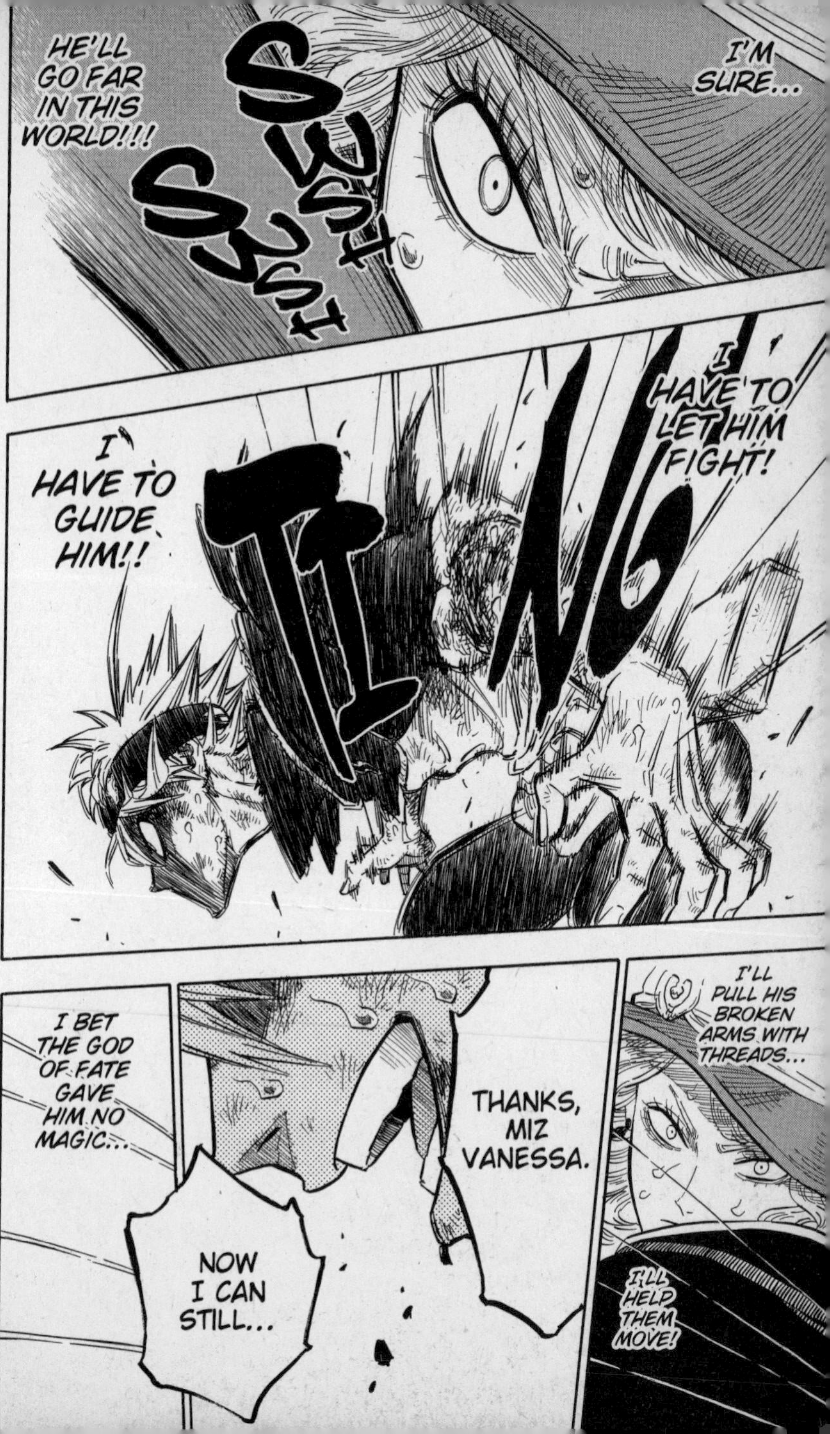
I'M SURE...
HE'LL GO FAR IN THIS WORLD!!!
I HAVE TO LET HIM FIGHT!
I HAVE TO GUIDE HIM!!
I'LL PULL HIS BROKEN ARMS WITH THREADS...
I'LL HELP THEM MOVE!
THANKS, MIZ VANESSA.
NOW I CAN STILL...
I BET THE GOD OF FATE GAVE HIM NO MAGIC...

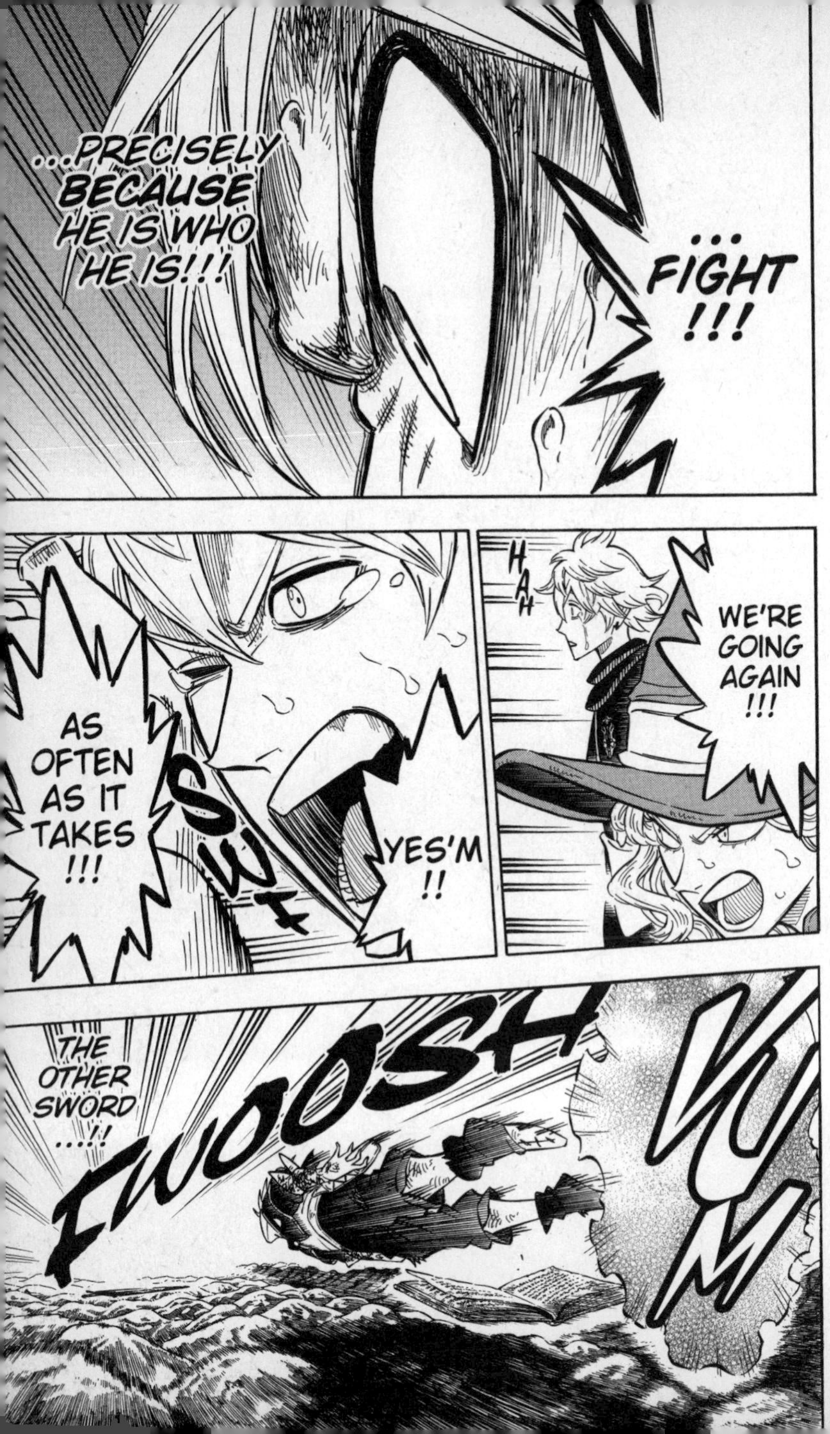
...FIGHT!!!
...PRECISELY BECAUSE HE IS WHO HE IS!!!
HAH
WE'RE GOING AGAIN!!!
YES'M!!
SWF
AS OFTEN AS IT TAKES!!!
VUM
FWOOSH
THE OTHER SWORD...!!

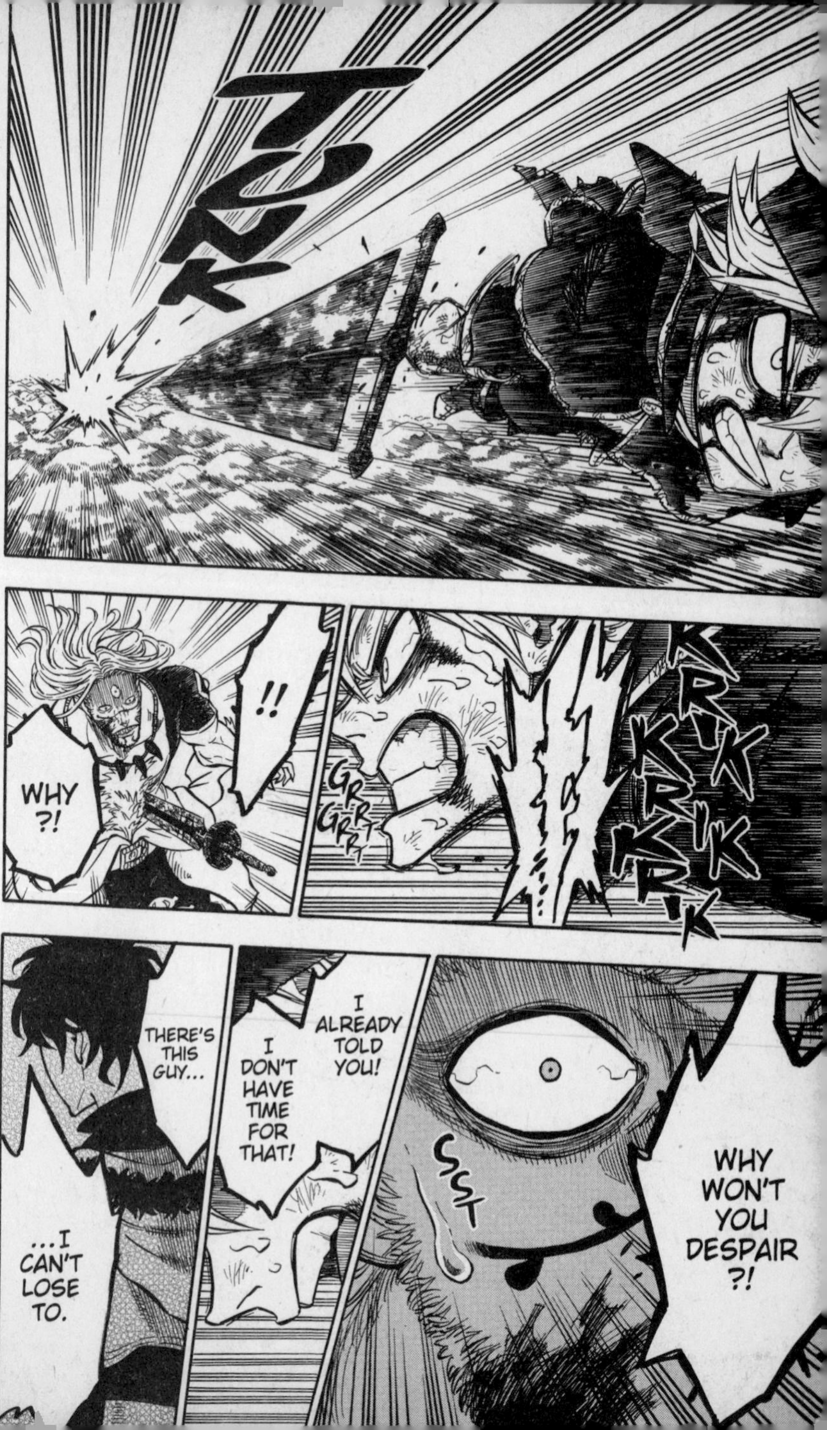
TUNK
KRIK KRIK KRIK KRIK
GRR GRR
!!
WHY?!
SST
WHY WON'T YOU DESPAIR?!
I ALREADY TOLD YOU!
I DON'T HAVE TIME FOR THAT!
THERE'S THIS GUY...
...I CAN'T LOSE TO.

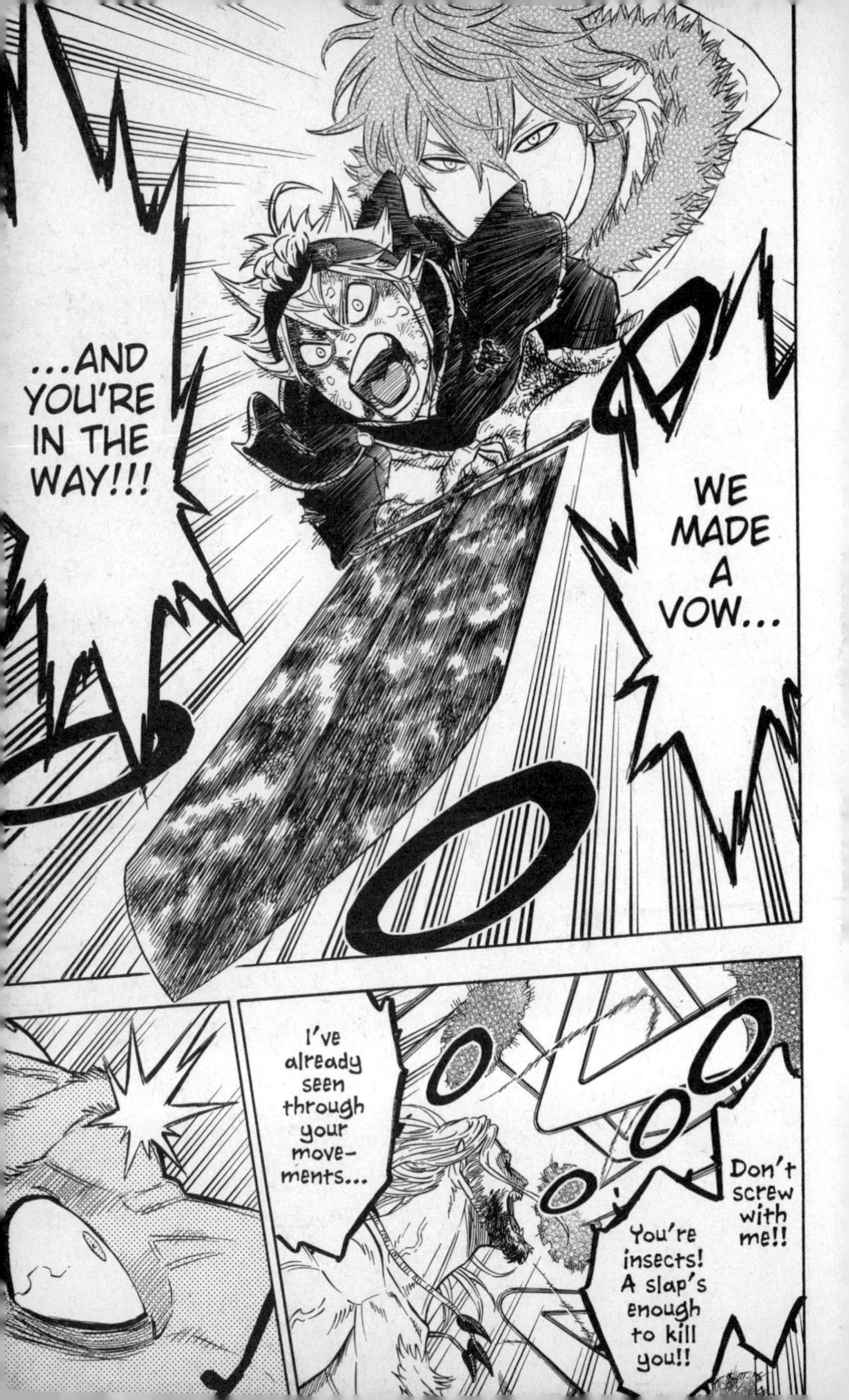
WE MADE A VOW...
...AND YOU'RE IN THE WAY!!!
Don't screw with me!!
You're insects! A slap's enough to kill you!!
I've already seen through your move-ments...

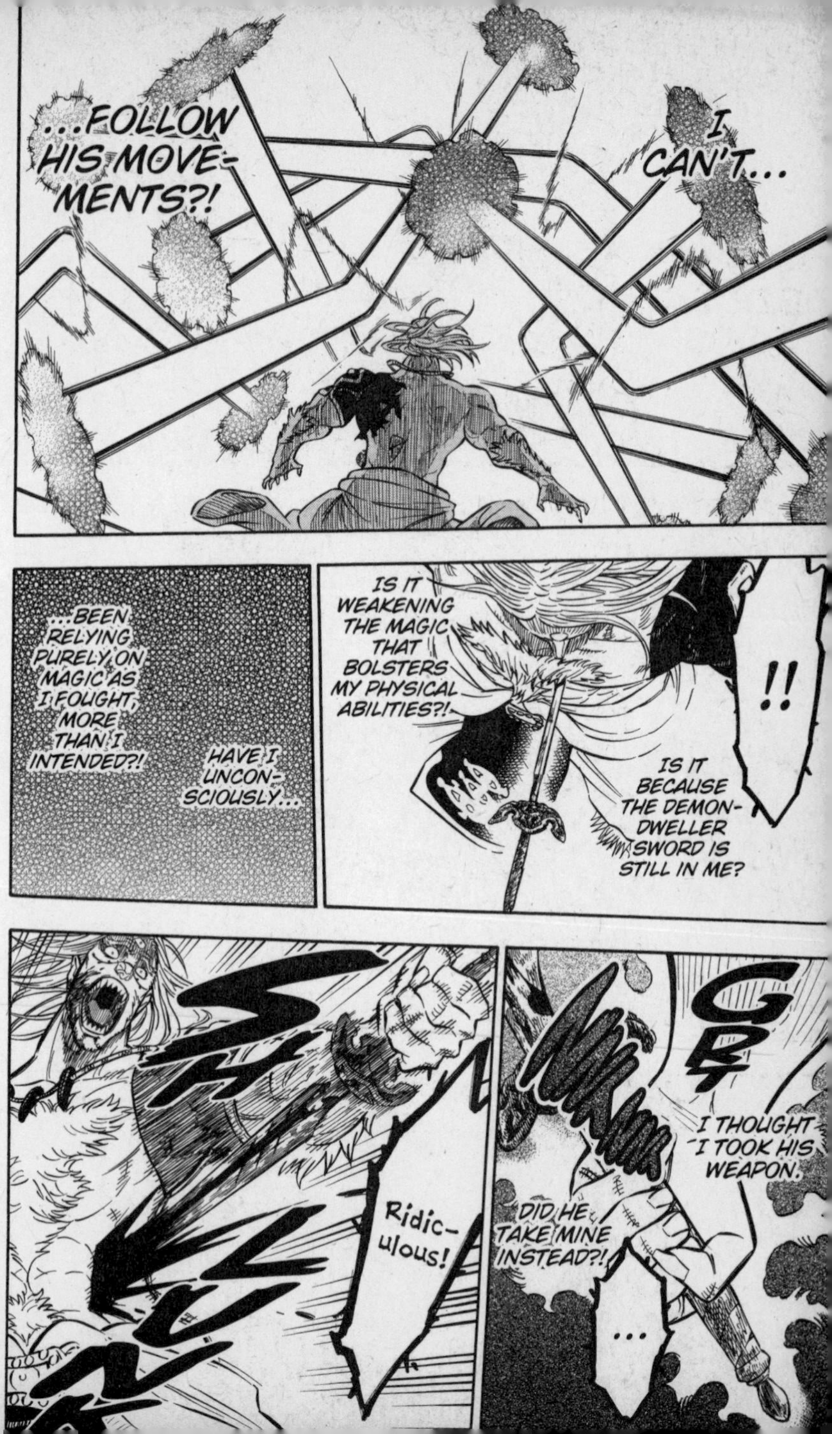
I CAN'T...
...FOLLOW HIS MOVE-MENTS?!
IS IT WEAKENING THE MAGIC THAT BOLSTERS MY PHYSICAL ABILITIES?!
!!
IS IT BECAUSE THE DEMON-DWELLER SWORD IS STILL IN ME?
HAVE I UNCON-SCIOUSLY...
...BEEN RELYING PURELY ON MAGIC AS I FOUGHT, MORE THAN I INTENDED?!
GRT
I THOUGHT I TOOK HIS WEAPON.
DID HE TAKE MINE INSTEAD?!
...
Ridic-ulous!

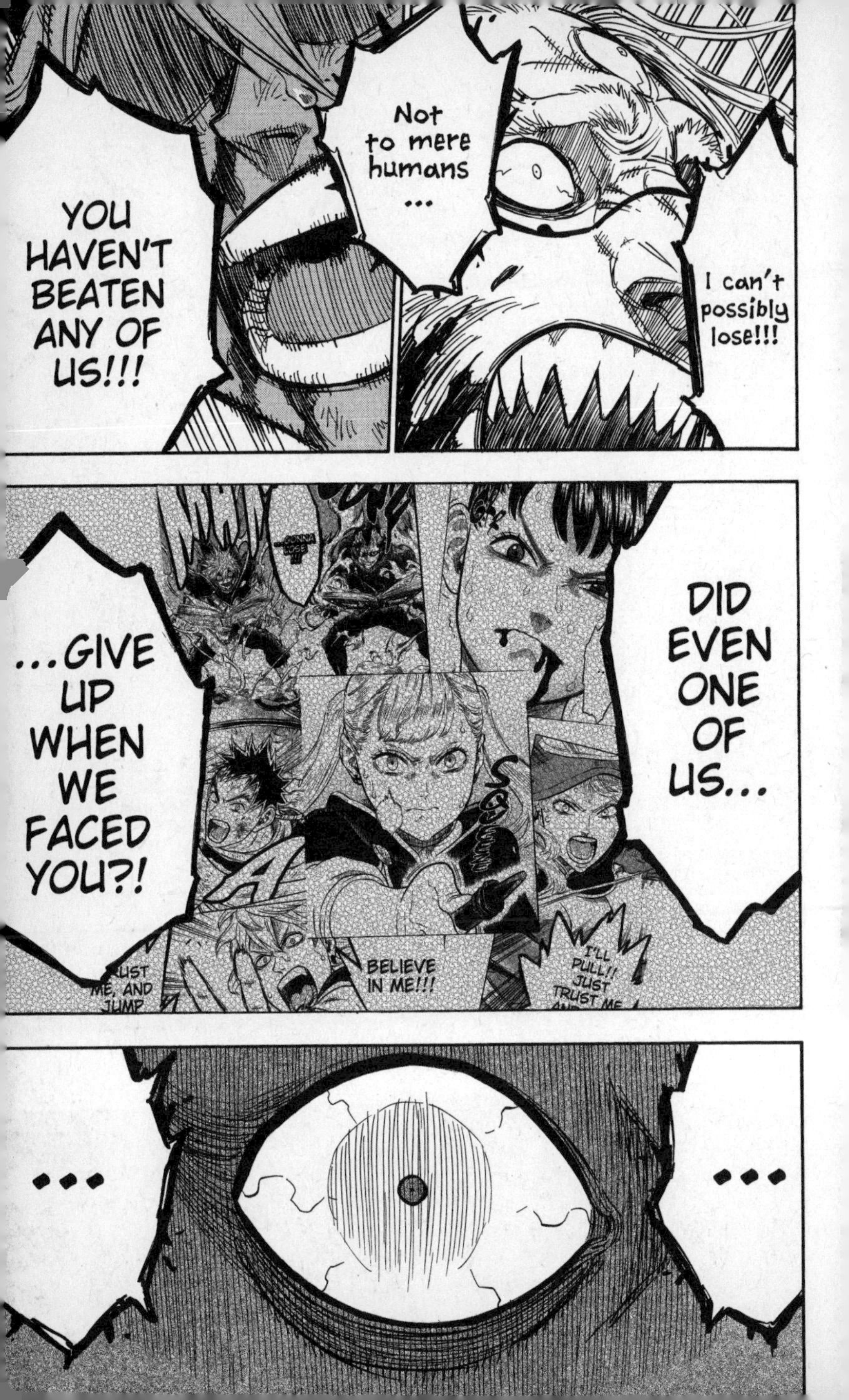
I can't possibly lose!!!
Not to mere humans...
YOU HAVEN'T BEATEN ANY OF US!!!
DID EVEN ONE OF US...
...GIVE UP WHEN WE FACED YOU?!
BELIEVE IN ME!!!
...
...

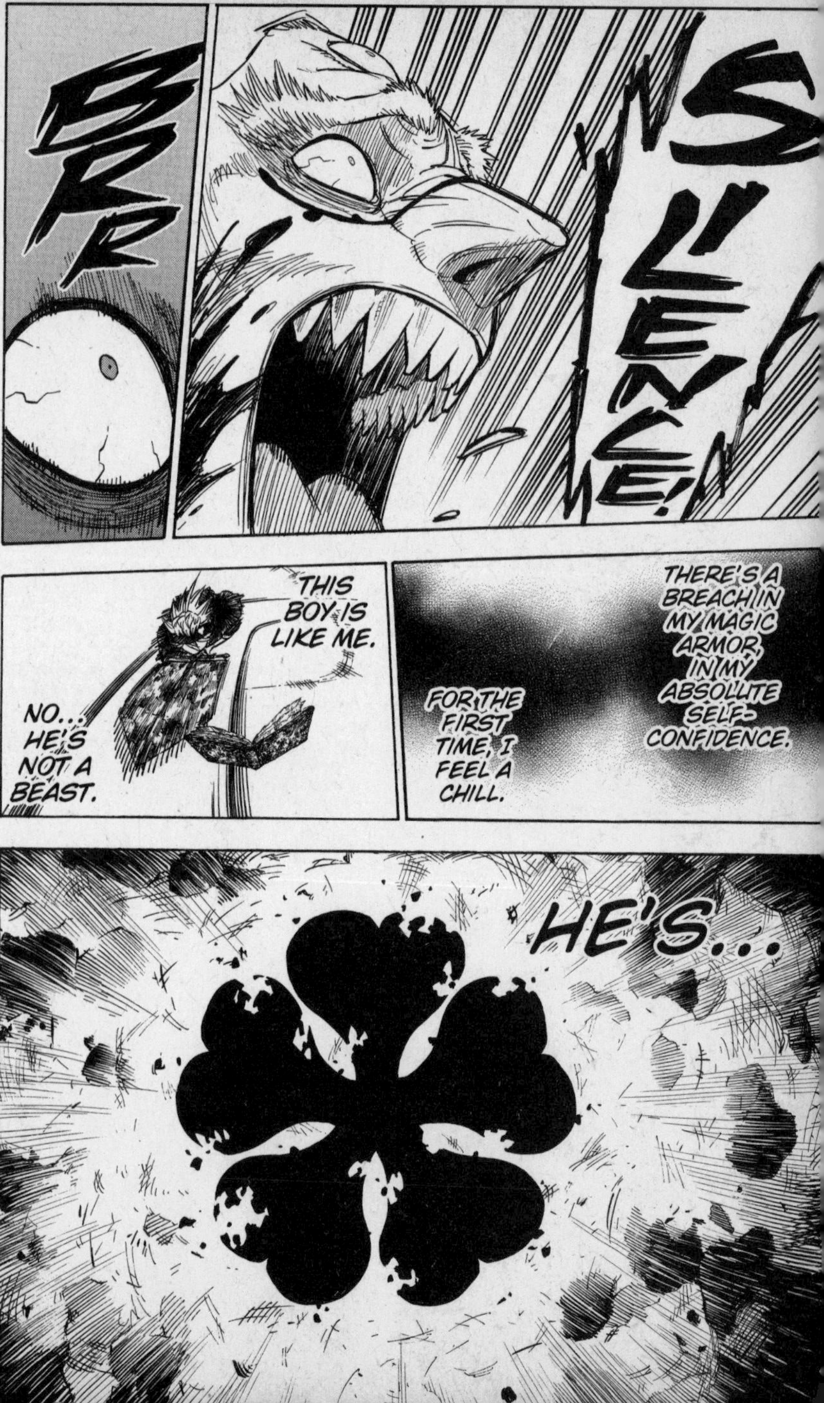
SILENCE!
BRR
THERE'S A BREACH IN MY MAGIC ARMOR, IN MY ABSOLUTE SELF-CONFIDENCE.
FOR THE FIRST TIME, I FEEL A CHILL.
THIS BOY IS LIKE ME.
NO... HE'S NOT A BEAST.
HE'S...

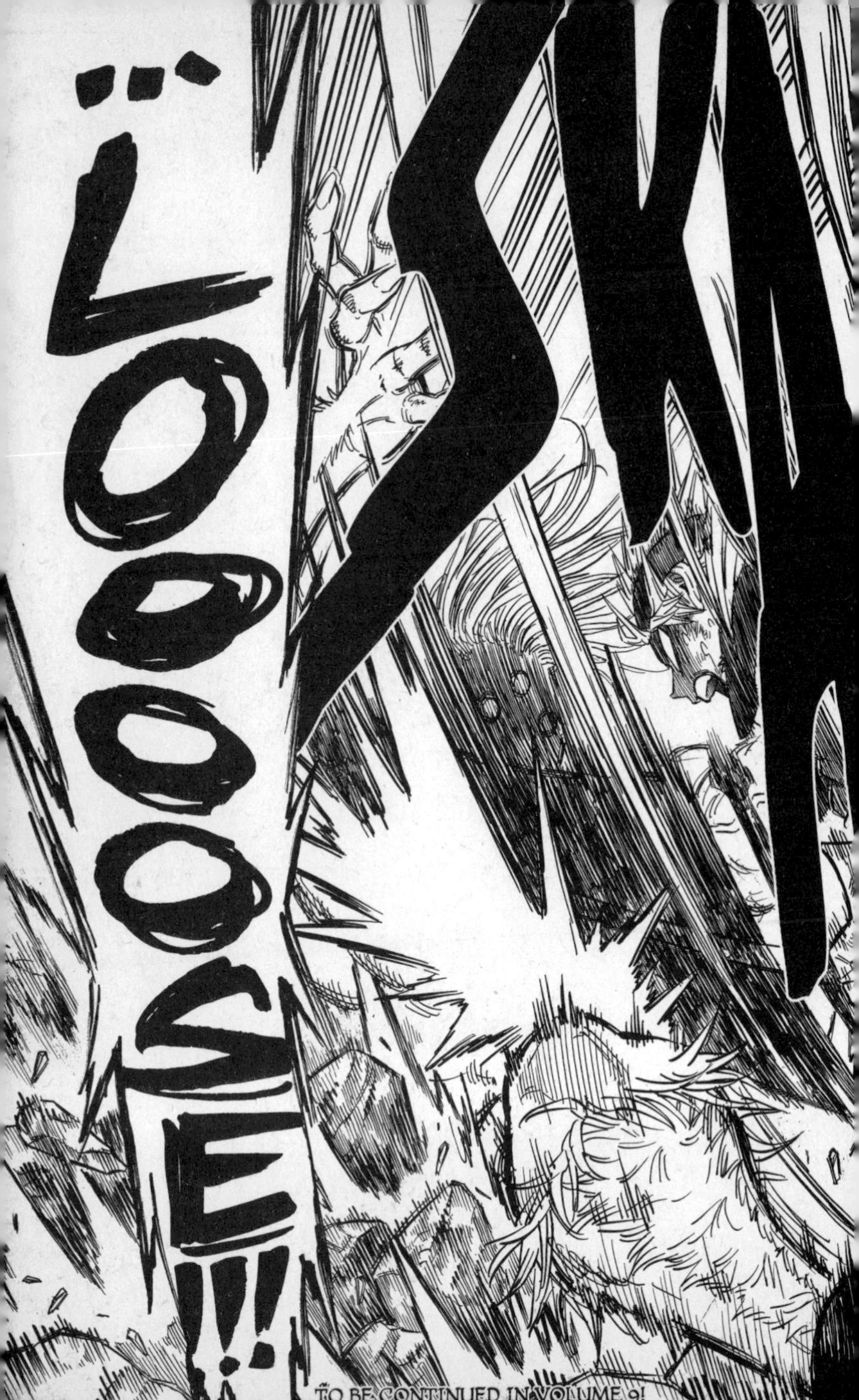
ZOOOOSH!!

TO BE CONTINUED IN VOLUME 9!

The Blank Page Brigade

This volume's topic:
What spell would you want to use?

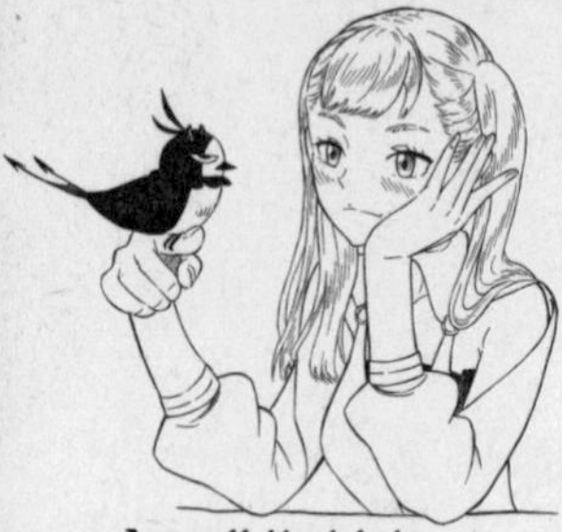

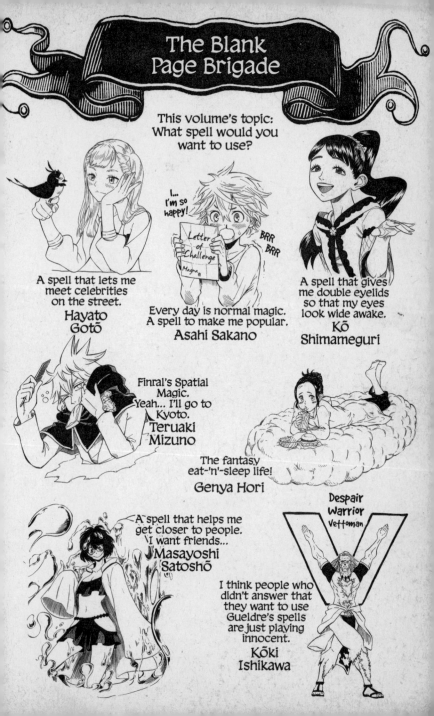

A spell that lets me meet celebrities on the street.

Hayato Gotō

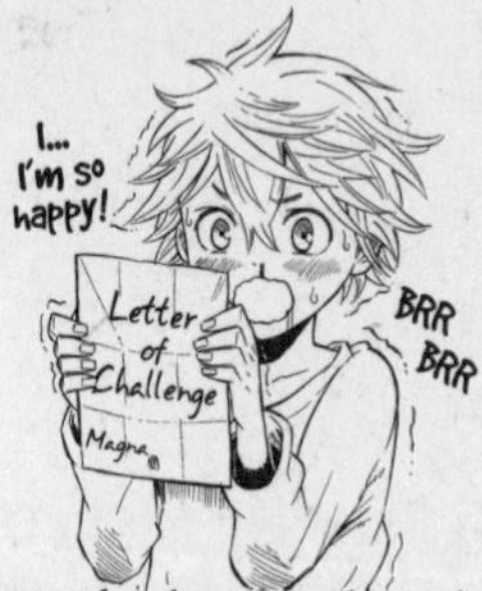
I... I'm so happy!
Letter of Challenge
Magna
BRR BRR

Every day is normal magic. A spell to make me popular.

Asahi Sakano

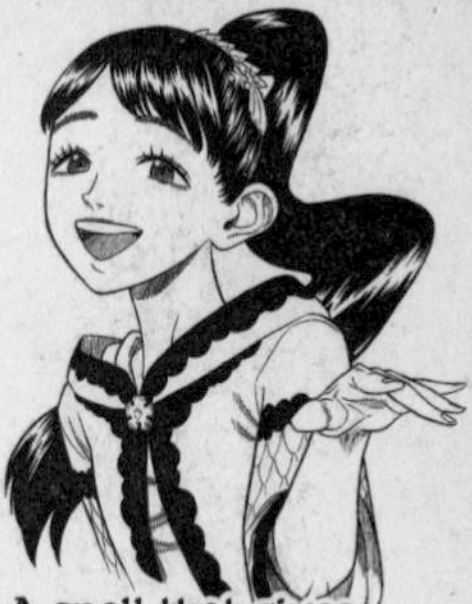

A spell that gives me double eyelids so that my eyes look wide awake.

Kō Shimameguri

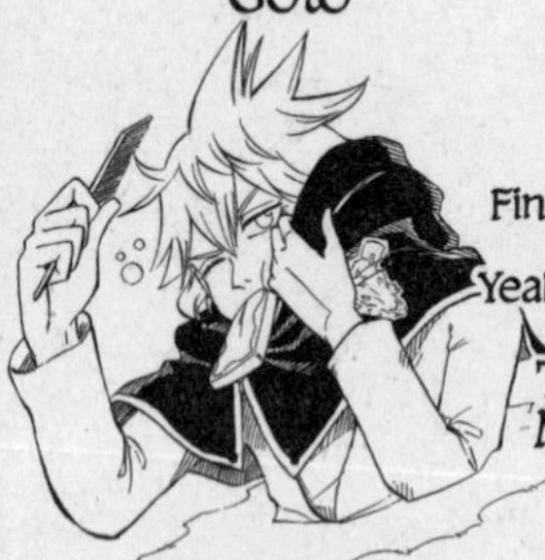

Finral's Spatial Magic. Yeah... I'll go to Kyoto.

Teruaki Mizuno

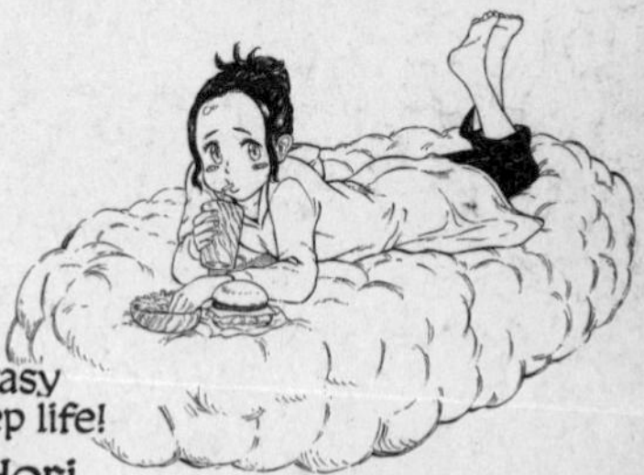

The fantasy eat-'n'-sleep life!

Genya Hori

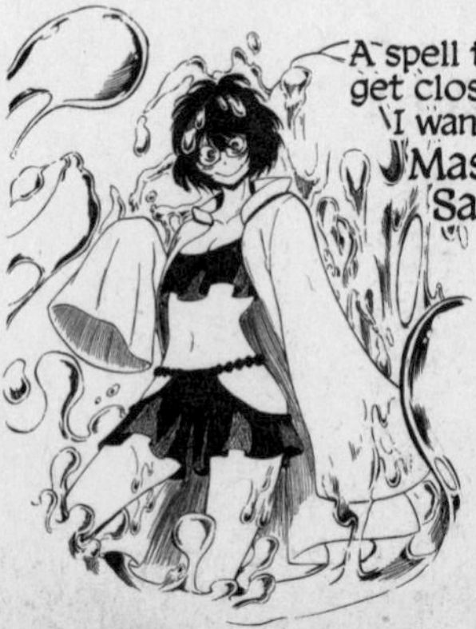

A spell that helps me get closer to people. I want friends...

Masayoshi Satoshō

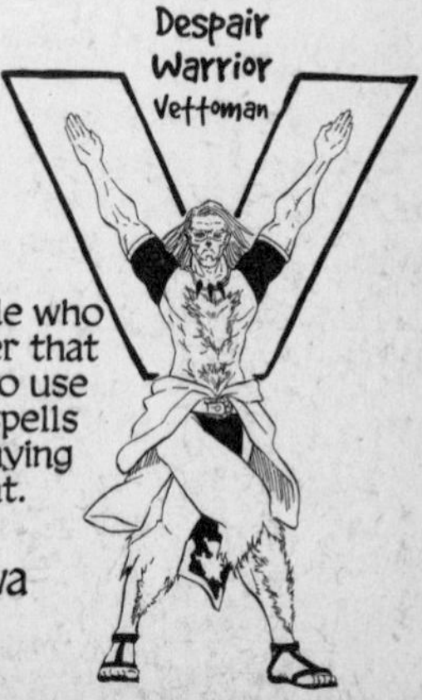
Despair Warrior
Vettoman

I think people who didn't answer that they want to use Gueldre's spells are just playing innocent.

Kōki Ishikawa

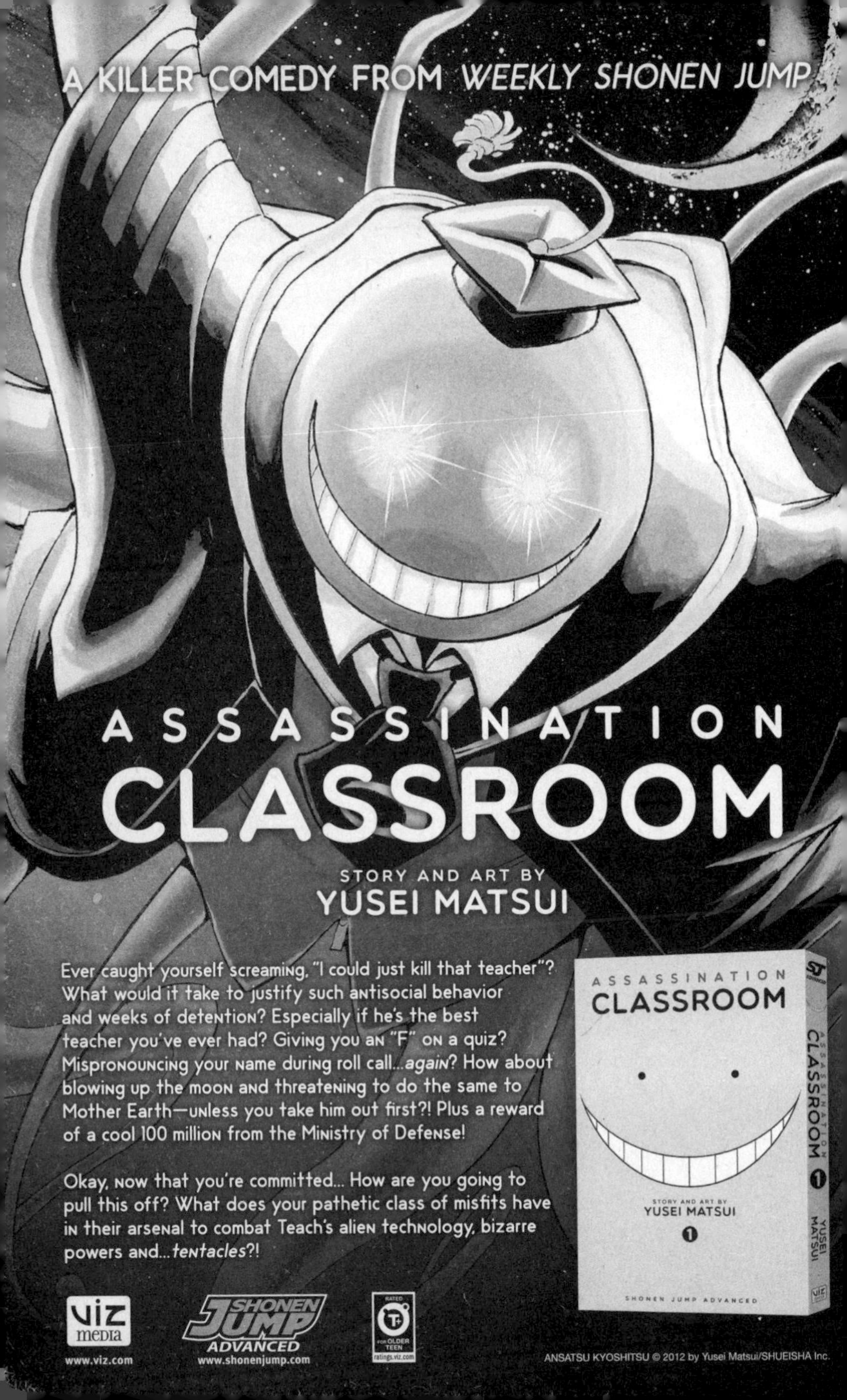
A KILLER COMEDY FROM WEEKLY SHONEN JUMP
ASSASSINATION CLASSROOM
STORY AND ART BY YUSEI MATSUI
Ever caught yourself screaming, "I could just kill that teacher"? What would it take to justify such antisocial behavior and weeks of detention? Especially if he's the best teacher you've ever had? Giving you an "F" on a quiz? Mispronouncing your name during roll call...again? How about blowing up the moon and threatening to do the same to Mother Earth—unless you take him out first?! Plus a reward of a cool 100 million from the Ministry of Defense!
Okay, now that you're committed... How are you going to pull this off? What does your pathetic class of misfits have in their arsenal to combat Teach's alien technology, bizarre powers and...tentacles?!
ASSASSINATION CLASSROOM
STORY AND ART BY YUSEI MATSUI
1
SHONEN JUMP ADVANCED
viz media
www.viz.com
SHONEN JUMP ADVANCED
www.shonenjump.com
RATED T+ FOR OLDER TEEN
ratings.viz.com
ANSATSU KYOSHITSU © 2012 by Yusei Matsui/SHUEISHA Inc.

Seraph of the End

VAMPIRE REIGN

STORY BY **Takaya Kagami** ART BY **Yamato Yamamoto**

STORYBOARDS BY **Daisuke Furuya**

Vampires reign— humans revolt!

Yuichiro's dream of killing every vampire is near-impossible, given that vampires are seven times stronger than humans, and the only way to kill them is by mastering Cursed Gear, advanced demon-possessed weaponry. Not to mention that humanity's most elite Vampire Extermination Unit, the Moon Demon Company, wants nothing to do with Yuichiro unless he can prove he's willing to work in a team—which is the last thing he wants!

THE LATEST CHAPTERS SERIALIZED IN WEEKLY SHONEN JUMP

The latest manga from the creator of *Dragon Ball*

THE GALACTIC PATROLMAN

Includes a **special chapter** revealing the secret of Goku's origins!

STORY AND ART BY
Akira Toriyama

Retired scientist Omori lives alone on a deserted island while continuing his research into time-travel. His quiet life is interrupted when galactic patrolman Jaco crash-lands and decides to move in with him. This agent from space claims to be elite, but sometimes it can be a little hard to believe. Can Jaco get along with the old man long enough to save the earth from a dangerous threat?

www.viz.com

www.shonenjump.com

RATED
A
ALL AGES
ratings.viz.com

JACO THE GALACTIC PATROLMAN © 2013 by BIRD STUDIO/SHUEISHA Inc.

NARUTO

**Story and Art by
Masashi Kishimoto**

Naruto is determined to become the greatest ninja ever!

Twelve years ago the Village Hidden in the Leaves was attacked by a fearsome threat. A nine-tailed fox spirit claimed the life of the village leader, the Hokage, and many others. Today, the village is at peace and a troublemaking kid named Naruto is struggling to graduate from Ninja Academy. His goal may be to become the next Hokage, but his true destiny will be much more complicated. The adventure begins now!

WORLD'S BEST SELLING MANGA!

NARUTO © 1999 by Masashi Kishimoto/SHUEISHA Inc.

www.shonenjump.com   www.viz.com

BLUE EXORCIST

STORY AND ART BY KAZUE KATO

❁ THE ORIGINAL MANGA BEHIND THE HIT ANIME! ❁

Raised by Father Fujimoto, a famous exorcist, Rin Okumura never knew his real father. One day a fateful argument with Father Fujimoto forces Rin to face a terrible truth — the blood of the demon lord Satan runs in Rin's veins! Rin swears to defeat Satan, but doing that means entering the mysterious True Cross Academy and becoming an exorcist himself.

Available wherever manga is sold.

AO NO EXORCIST © 2009 by Kazue Kato/SHUEISHA Inc.

Stop

YOU'RE READING
THE WRONG WAY!

BLACK CLOVER
reads from right to left, starting
in the upper-right corner. Japanese
is read from right to left, meaning
that action, sound effects, and
word-balloon order are completely
reversed from English order.